Exploring the Language of Poems, Plays and Prose

Mick Short

Longman

An imprint of Pearson Education

Harlow, England · London · New York · Reading, Massachusetts · San Francisco
Toronto · Don Mills, Ontario · Sydney · Tokyo · Singapore · Hong Kong · Seoul
Taipei · Cape Town · Madrid · Mexico City · Amsterdam · Munich · Paris · Milan

Pearson Education Limited
Edinburgh Gate, Harlow,
Essex CM20 2JE
United Kingdom

and Associated Companies throughout the world

Visit us on the World Wide Web at:
www.pearsoned.co.uk

© Addison Wesley Longman Limited 1996

First published 1996

ISBN 0 582 291305 Ppr

British Library Cataloguing-in-Publication Data

A catalogue record for this book is
available from the British Library

Library of Congress Cataloging-in-Publication Data

A catalog record for this book has been applied for

12 11
05 04

Set by
Printed in Malaysia, PPSB

For
Hilary, Hiroko and Ben,
both my Mums and Dads,
and Tom and Floozie

Contents

Preface: how to use this book

Aims

We all read literary texts because they are interesting, enjoyable and/or moving. This enjoyment, however, is only the first step (though obviously a very important one) in the *study* of such texts. An important aspect of the *study* of literature is that we must struggle to explain a very difficult thing, namely how it is that we come to understand literary works.

It is fashionable at the present time to stress the idea that different readers all have different understandings of the texts they read. To some extent, this must be true. We all have different experiences which may prompt us to have slightly different associations for particular words, for example. But if *all* we do is to understand things differently, there is little left to *study* (as opposed to enjoy) because we will not be able to argue rationally with one another about different interpretations of the work.

For me, the fascinating thing which needs to be explained is that we often agree over our understanding of poems, plays and novels *in spite* of the fact that we are all different. This book explores how it is that writers communicate with us and affect us. It examines the way in which the language of literary texts acts as the basis for our understanding and responses when we read. I assume that understanding involves an important contribution from the reader, who brings along background knowledge and processes for inferring meaning. But I also assume that the text plays an essential part in prompting and guiding our interpretative efforts.

The approach which I take is generally known in the English-speaking world as 'stylistics' or 'stylistic analysis'. But although the term 'stylistics' appears to suggest an overall concern with the study of *style* (and indeed, much early work did concentrate on trying to illuminate concepts like authorial style), the main effort in stylistic analysis over the last 15 years has been to try to understand the relationship between the literary text, on the one hand, and how we understand it, and are affected by it, on the other.

Level and approach

What I have written is intended to be accessible to people new to the field. I assume no previous knowledge of stylistic analysis or the various forms of language analysis on which stylistics is based. When new ways of analysing texts are described, brief explanatory descriptions of the linguistic approaches used are given, and these are intended to be sufficient for the beginner. Students always manage to fall into holes that writers do not foresee, however, and despite my best endeavours I am sure that I will not have managed to take into account everything the unwary may trip over. Consequently, I give references to other works for those who want to follow up particular areas in more detail.

Although this book is intended to be accessible to new readers, I hope it will also provide interest for more advanced students, and for colleagues researching and teaching stylistics. I analyse a considerable number of texts in detail, and hope that these new analyses will be stimulating. I also hope to suggest some new slants on areas well known to fellow stylisticians.

Structure

I examine the three main literary genres one at a time: poems (Chapters 1–5), plays (Chapters 6–8) and fictional prose (Chapters 9–11). In looking at each of these genres in turn, I introduce techniques for analysis from what I like to call my 'stylistician's tool-kit' which work particularly well on the relevant genre. However, one of my main general contentions is that techniques which have become associated with one particular genre also have relevance for the others (and indeed for the study of how we understand non-literary texts too). To this end, the final chapter (Chapter 12) is devoted to using analytical techniques associated with one genre on texts from another. As you go through the book I will point out the relevance of particular methods of description and analysis to other genres. This will be most obvious in Chapter 3, 'Style variation in texts', which by no means restricts itself to examples from poetry, in spite of the fact that it is in the middle of the 'poetry section' of the book.

Each chapter contains exercises which I hope you will attempt as you go along. Trying out approaches for yourself is the best way to understand and come to terms with them. I provide discussions of these exercises, at the end of the relevant chapter or point you to what other stylisticians have written about the relevant text. This should help you to gain an understanding of stylistics which is not entirely through my eyes, and introduce you to a number of interesting and accessible discussions of literary works. At the end of each chapter you will also find notes related to the main text.

At the end of most chapters there is a **checksheet** which you can use to apply the techniques described in that chapter to other texts. I hope that you will find these helpful. Their aim is to enable you to be more systematic in your approach to analysing texts. It is all too easy to miss important things because your attention is caught by one feature, making you forget to look for other relevant aspects which may be just as important. Note, however, that there are also some incipient dangers in being drawn along by checksheets. Don't become the linguistic-feature equivalent of a butterfly spotter. It is essential that, after spotting a feature, you go on to relate it to textual meaning and effect. And you shouldn't assume that the checksheets are exhaustive. For me, one of the most useful things about checksheets is that they help me to become aware of intuitions they don't capture, leading me on to new things to try to explain.

Finally, I hope you enjoy the analyses of the literary texts I examine as well as the texts themselves. There is considerable pleasure to be gained from analysing literature as well as from reading it in the first place.

Author's acknowledgements

This book has been rather a long time in the making, not least because of a couple of major illnesses and a rather faster descent down a steep Lake District hillside that I had originally intended. I owe the British National Health Service and the Penrith branch of the Lake District Mountain Rescue Service more thanks than I could ever muster.

Innumerable friends, colleagues and students have given me helpful comments, in particular Geoff Leech, Elena Semino, Jonathan Culpeper, Willie van Peer, Gerry Knowles, Richard Dutton, Tom Barney, Judith Poole, Anna Jordanidou, Les Killick, Joan Waller and John Heywood. Their excellent advice has made this work much better than it would otherwise have been. I apologise to them, and to those students on whom I have tried out various parts of the book, for the remaining inadequacies.

Jane Jellicoe provided the illustrations in Chapter 1 and Chapter 9, and Graeme Hughes and Zack Evans have given me excellent technical help. A number of people at Longman have also been very supportive. They will be unhappy for me to mention their names, but they know who they are, and I thank them.

Finally, my family has also played a large part in this book. Ben produced the camera-ready copy and helped to dig me out of various technical holes, Hiroko sorted out my references, and they both copy-read like mad. My wife, Hilary, who has always been the fiercest friendly critic of my work, has helped me to be much clearer than I would otherwise have been. And the cats have been supportive in the way that only cats understand.

Lancaster 1995

Publisher's acknowledgements

We are grateful to the following for permission to reproduce copyright material:

Jonathan Clowes Ltd on behalf of the poet, for part poem 'The Voice of Authority: A Language Game' by Kingsley Amis from *A Case of Samples* Copyright 1956 Kingsley Amis; Faber & Faber Ltd for part poems 'Esther's Tomcat', 'Thrushes' by Ted Hughes from *Lupercal*, 'October Dawn' by Ted Hughes from *Hawk in the Rain*, part poem 'Sunday Morning' by Louis Mac-Neice from *The Collected Poems of Louis MacNeice* edited by E.R. Dodds; Faber & Faber Ltd/Harcourt Brace Inc for part poems 'The Hollow Men', 'Prelude 1' by T.S. Eliot in *Collected Poems 1909–1962*. Copyright 1936 by Harcourt Brace & Co. Copyright © 1964, 1963 by T.S. Eliot, 'Little Gidding' by T.S. Eliot in *Collected Poems 1909–1962/Four Quartets*. Copyright 1943 by T.S. Eliot & renewed 1971 by Esme Valerie Eliot; Faber & Faber Ltd/Farrar, Straus & Giroux Inc. for part poems 'Send no Money', 'Take One Home for the Kiddies' by Philip Larkin in *The Whitsun Weddings/Collected Poems*. Copyright © 1988, 1989 by the Estate of Philip Larkin, 'High Windows' by Philip Larkin in *High Windows/Collected Poems*. Copyright © 1988, 1989 by the Estate of Philip Larkin; the poet, Michael Horovitz for his 'Man to Man Blues' from *Growing Up: Selected Poems & Pictures 1951–79*, Allison & Busby 1979, p 77; The Marvell Press, England & Australia for poem 'Wants' & part poem 'No Road' by Philip Larkin in *The Less Deceived*; authors' agents on behalf of The Royal Literary Fund for an extract from 'The Force of Circumstance' by W. Somerset Maugham from *The Complete Short Stories of W. Somerset Maugham*; W.W. Norton & Co Ltd for poem 'ygUDuh', part poems 'pity this busy monster, manunkind', 'i like my body when it is with your' by E.E. Cummings from *Complete Poems 1904–1962*, edited by George J. Firmage. Copyright © 1925, 1976, 1991 by the Trustees for the E.E. Cummings Trust and George James Firmage; Oxford University Press for part poem 'A Martian Sends a Postcard Home' by Craig Raine from *A Martian Sends a Postcard Home* (OUP 1979), poem 'Naming of Parts' by Henry Reed from *Collected Poems* edited by Jon Stallworthy (OUP 1991); authors' agents for part poem 'Light Breaks Where no Sun Shines' by Dylan Thomas from *The Poems*, published by J.M. Dent; authors' agents for the poem 'Long-Legged Fly', extracts from the poem 'Leda the Swan' by W.B. Yeats from *Selected Poetry*, edited by A. Norman Jeffares (Macmillan, 1962).

We have been unable to trace the copyright holder of the poem 'January' by R.S. Thomas and would appreciate any information which would enable us to do so.

CHAPTER 1

Who is stylistics?

1.1 Introduction

The short answer to the question 'Who is stylistics?' is that she is a friend of mine, and that I hope by the end of this book she might also become a friend of yours. You will find out who she is in the course of your reading; but another question you might like to ponder while you read this introductory chapter is *why* I have chosen that title for this chapter. I will tell you at the end of the chapter. The beginning of an answer to the question is that stylistics is an approach to the analysis of (literary) texts[1] using *linguistic description*. Thus, in a book such as this, which is devoted exclusively to the analysis of literary texts, stylistics spans the borders of the two subjects, literature and linguistics. As a result, stylistics can sometimes look like either linguistics or literary criticism, depending upon where you are standing when you are looking at it. So, some of my literary critical colleagues sometimes accuse me of being an unfeeling linguist, saying that my analyses of poems, say, are too analytical, being too full of linguistic jargon and leaving insufficient room for personal preference on the part of the reader. My linguist colleagues, on the other hand, sometimes say that I am no linguist at all, but a critic in disguise, who cannot make his descriptions of language precise enough to count as real linguistics. They think that I leave too much to intuition and that I am not analytical enough. I think I've got the mix just right, of course!

If you already have some basic familiarity with linguistics you should have no difficulty with the various linguistic concepts I use in this book. However, in case you have no knowledge of linguistics, in the further reading at the end of this chapter I will suggest a couple of books for you to refer to if you come across a term or concept which is new to you and not explained in the text. I will also mention more specific linguistic readings, where relevant, in the suggestions for further reading at the ends of subsequent chapters. Where possible, I will explain new terms as I introduce them, but as an ex–English student who himself had to struggle with introductory linguistics books in the past, I know too well that what a particular writer assumes is well known is not necessarily 'old hat' for the reader.

When modern linguists began to take an interest in the analysis of literature, there was quite a lot of discussion as to whether linguists could really be of help to the literary critic. Because the debate was a border dispute over territory, it was often rather acrimonious. It probably reached its height of silliness when, in a published debate one linguist asked the critic he was debating with if he would allow his sister to marry a linguist.[2] The critic replied that, knowing his sister, he would probably have little choice, but that he would much prefer *not* to have a linguist in the family.

I regard myself as someone who is both a linguist and a critic, and so I would prefer to leave the general debate about whether criticism needs linguistic description to one side and get on with the practicalities of using linguistic analysis in order to describe and analyse literary texts. In case you want to follow up the debate, I provide references at the end of this chapter.[3] The best way of seeing whether or not you find stylistic analysis helpful and enlightening will be to see it in action; but it will probably be useful if at first I make explicit some of *my* preconceptions. First of all, I regard literary criticism as having a 'core', its central, most important activity, and a less important 'periphery'. The *core* task for the critic is the job of *interpreting* (explicating) literary texts and *judging* them. Literary criticism can contain many other things; for example some specialists concern themselves almost entirely with the socio–cultural background against which particular works were written, and others look at the lives of authors and how their experiences led them to write in the way that they did. But these activities would not be of interest unless the culture to which the particular work belongs had decided that the writing concerned was valuable. Secondly, it seems to me that the essential core of criticism has three major parts:

Description ⟶ Interpretation ⟶ Evaluation

(where description is mainly but not entirely linguistic)

Most people will agree that, at the end of the day, critics are interested in *evaluating* works of literature, that is, saying that work X is as good as, or better than, work Y, and so on. But it should be obvious that in order to decide that work X is good, or bad, we must first be able to interpret it. It makes no sense to say that a poem is good (or bad) but that you don't really understand it; still less to say that it is good (or bad) *because* you don't understand it. It follows, then, that *interpretation* must be logically prior to *evaluation*. This is what the arrow represents between those two words in the diagram above. I suspect that it is because understanding logically precedes evaluation that twentieth–century criticism has concerned itself for the most part with *interpretations* of poems, novels and plays while merely *assuming* literary merit (few, if any, critics discuss works which they consider to have little value). We know much less about the processes and criteria involved in the act of evaluation than many people would be prepared to admit.

The concepts of interpretation and evaluation referred to in the last paragraph, and the logical relations between them, are essentially *post–processing* concepts. By this I mean that the kind of interpretative and evaluative activities which critics publicly involve themselves in (when giving lectures, or writing books or articles) are activities which take place *after reading the whole text*. Indeed, a critic will probably have read the text involved carefully more than once. The student equivalent of this critical post–processing is the writing of essays or the reading out of seminar papers.

Note, however, that although interpretation is logically prior to evaluation in the post–processing critical situation we do not necessarily wait in our *normal reading process* until we get to the end of a text before making judgements. We almost certainly make them as we go along, depending on how we understand the text at that point, but we will alter our judgements as we alter our interpretation of (parts of) the text. Indeed, making hypotheses and guesses of this sort appears to be an essential part of the process of understanding as well as evaluation. But when we get to the end of our reading, our final, critical, judgement will be dependent upon our final understanding.

If interpretation is logically prior to evaluation it is also the case that what I have called *description* (which in turn involves *analysis*) is logically prior to understanding. Consider the following mundane sentence:

Example 1
Mary pushed John over

In order to know that this sentence means something like:

rather than:

we must already know that *Mary* is the subject of the sentence and that *John* is the object. Normally, we do not *explicitly* do a grammatical analysis of the sentence to arrive at this knowledge; rather, we just know implicitly or intuitively what the grammatical relations in the sentence are.

Now let us take a more literary example, a metaphor:

Example 2
Come, we burn daylight, ho!

(William Shakespeare, *Romeo and Juliet*, I, iv, 43)

Besides the basic kind of linguistic information of the sort seen above, this time we also have to know that *daylight* cannot normally be the object of *burn*. The verb *burn* usually takes as its object a word or phrase which refers to something which can be burnt, but daylight does not fall into this category. It is only after deducing that what the line says cannot literally be true that we can go on to construct a non–literal interpretation for it (*e.g.* 'we are wasting time'). Stylistics is thus concerned with relating linguistic facts (linguistic description) to meaning (interpretation) in as *explicit* a way as possible. And what is true for sentences here is also true for texts. When we read, we must intuitively analyse linguistic structure at various levels (*e.g.* grammar, sounds, words, textual structure) in order (again intuitively) to understand the sentences of a text and the relations between them. We usually perform this complex set of tasks so fast that we do not even notice that we are doing it, let alone *how* we do it. Our understanding of the linguistic form and meaning is thus *implicit*. But when we discuss literature, as critics do, we need to discuss meaning in an *explicit* fashion. Stylisticians suggest that linguistic description and its relationship with inter–pretation should also be discussed as explicitly, as systematically, and in as detailed a way as possible. One advantage of this is that when we disagree over the meaning to ascribe to a text or part of a text, we can use stylistic analysis as a means to help to decide which of the various suggestions are most likely. There may, of course, be more than one valid interpretation, but, again, it is difficult to decide on such matters without detailed and explicit analysis. I want to suggest, then, that stylistic analysis, which attempts to relate linguistic description to interpretation, is part of the essential core of good criticism, as it constitutes a large part of what is involved, say, in supporting a particular view of a poem or arguing for one interpretation as against another. Of course it is not *all* that is involved. For example, in the understanding of a novel or a play we might well be involved in comparing one character with another or noticing a parallel between the main plot and the sub–plot. What we know about the characters must come from the text, the words which the author has written; but the ability which we possess to abstract notions like character and plot from the sentences of a text is linguistic only in a more indirect sense than our ability to make sense of grammatical or sound structure. Very little is known of how we infer plot and character from the sentences of a text, and it would be a very brave linguist indeed who would try to include such things in his or her description in the current state of knowledge. Note, then, that stylisticians do not by any means claim to have all the answers.

By now you may be wondering how the stylistic analysis of literature differs from traditional practical criticism. Literary critics do, after all, use textual evidence to support what they say. And indeed there is some considerable overlap between stylistic analysis and the more detailed forms of practical criticism. The difference is, in part, one of degree rather than kind. Practical critics use evidence from the text, and therefore sometimes the language of the text, to support what they say. But the evidence tends to be much more selective than that which a stylistician would want to bring to bear. In that sense, stylistics is the *logical extension* of practical criticism. In order to avoid as much as possible the dangers of partiality, stylisticians, as I have suggested above, try to make their descriptions and analyses as *detailed*, as *systematic* and as *thorough* as possible. This will sometimes involve stating what you might regard as obvious or going down to a level of analysis that literary critics would be unwilling to tackle.

There is also a difference of kind, however, which I would like to make clear as my third major preconception. For many critics, new interpretations and views on literary works are the major interest. If you write yet another book on *Hamlet*, for example, you are unlikely to get a good critical press if you do not come up with a new interpretation of the play or a new view on it. But stylistic analysis is just as interested, if not more so, in established interpretations as in new ones. This is because we are also profoundly interested in the *rules and procedures* which we, as readers, intuitively know and apply in order to understand what we read. Thus, stylisticians try to discover not just *what* a text means, but also *how* it comes to mean what it does. And in order to investigate the *how* it is usually best to start with established, agreed interpretations for a text. We are all different from one another: we have different experiences, have grown up in different places, and may well have some different associations or understandings for particular words. But the most interesting thing is that *in spite of these differences* there is a remarkable amount of agreement among readers over what particular texts mean. Of course there are disagreements too, and literary critics have often stressed them in the past in order to suggest that their enquiry is one involving considerable subjectivity. But these disagreements take place within a surprisingly wide range of agreement. Critics often debate the significance of a particular line in a poem, or scene in a play, while assuming large–scale agreement over their understanding of the rest of the text. And even a play with as many commentaries on it as *Hamlet* has relatively few interpretations compared with the infinitely large set of things that it cannot possibly mean. Because we are all different from one another and yet agree on meaning to the extent that we do, we must have something in common that does the trick. In large part, that thing is the language which we share (in this case English). But this means not just a shared knowledge of the *structure* of English (for example that 'seem' is a verb and 'television' is a noun; that 'table' is more closely connected with 'chair' than 'carrot', and so on), but also the common *procedures of inference* which we use in order to interpret utterances. As an example, let us return to the line from *Romeo and Juliet*, which we looked at earlier, *Come, we burn daylight, ho!* We noted before that *daylight* cannot normally be the object of *burn*. We can demonstrate this by constructing a **normal paradigm** (set of possible substitution instances) for the verb with which to compare the metaphorical construction:

Normal paradigm	Abnormal paradigm
we burn paper	we burn daylight
we burn wood	
we burn coal	
we burn oil	
we burn fuel	
etc.	

By comparing the normal with the **abnormal paradigm** we can begin to see how the line gets its meaning. The object of *burn* has to denote a concrete, combustible material or be a more general term for such materials. When it is burnt it is destroyed or used up. A likely possible meaning for the phrase could be 'we are using up daylight'. This is still a metaphor, although one which is fairly dead in English.[4] We cannot physically use up daylight; but of course daylight is a medium which we use to do lots of things in, and if we do not use it properly then we may run out of time to do what needs to be done. In this sense, as in my original suggested interpretation, we can waste time. This may not be the only possible interpretation, of course, but note that there are many more meanings that are *not* valid for the line than ones that are. For example, it cannot possibly mean 'it is raining' or even 'we keep ourselves warm'.

Now let us take stock of what we have done with this line. We have compared an unusual clause with a set of constructed normal equivalents and we have used a combination of our knowledge about English and about the world in order to arrive at an interpretation. To understand the sentence completely we also have to see it in its context. In fact it is a joke in which the burning is literal and the daylight is metaphorical. It is dark at the time, and Mercutio, when he utters the sentence, is referring to the burning torches that the Montagues are holding as they go to gatecrash the Capulet ball where Romeo and Juliet will meet for the first time. Thus we combine linguistic, contextual and general world knowledge, as the basis for **inferring** an appropriate interpretation. The meaning, then, comes from the text, but notice that we cannot get at that meaning just by doing linguistic analysis (although that is an essential and important part of the process). The linguistic features in the text do not constitute the meaning in themselves; rather they *constrain* readers from inferring unreasonable meanings and *prompt* them towards reasonable ones. We can see this more obviously by changing the various kinds of information at our disposal. If we change the linguistic structure, by replacing *daylight* with 'torches', the line becomes literally true in this context. If we change the situational context, having the conversation take place in the day–time, the 'joke' interpretation is ruled out. If we change our general world knowledge (by assuming that in our world important things are always done in the dark, for example), the line might indicate that the characters are at leisure. And changing the linguistic context will also change the meaning. If we pretend that the sentence comes from a twentieth-century article on fuel conservation, the meaning which we rejected earlier, 'we keep ourselves warm' might be more plausible – the utterance could be understood as an injunction to use solar heating as a source of heat and light, instead of coal or oil.

Exercise 1

Examine the metaphor *the crimson seeds/Of blood* in the following
extract from the beginning of 'January' by R. S. Thomas:

The fox drags its wounded belly
Over the snow, the crimson seeds
Of blood burst with a mild explosion,
Soft as excrement, bold as roses.

Why is the phrase metaphorical? What do you understand by the
phrase? Try to work out the inferential steps which you would need to
use to get from the structure of the phrase to the meaning you have
assigned to it.

The reason that I have spent a comparatively long time on a
very small example is to make clear what is involved in the
process of understanding. When authors write, they use
various kinds of knowledge which they share with the reader
(linguistic, contextual, general world knowledge) to constrain
the reader into interpreting what he or she reads in a particular
way. The author may not constrain the reader absolutely —
hence the possibility of varying interpretations. But the range
of possible meaning is still relatively narrow. Stylistic analysis,
besides helping you to acquire an explicit and rational basis for
deciding between interpretations, should also help you to
become more consciously aware of the processes of interpretation which you use in order to get to grips with the texts
you read.

This long explication is in fact an explanation of my fourth
major assumption, namely that the meaning which we ascribe
to sentences and texts is at the same time heavily constrained
and yet variable to some limited degree because of the
interaction between readers and what they read. Readers are
different and so bring along the possibility of fresh ways of
interpreting a particular text; but the linguistic configurations
in a text are stable and common to us all, as are the multitude
of rules and procedures which we use in order to interpret
utterances. It is on these *shared* phenomena that we must
concentrate in order to understand *how* we interpret texts as
well as *what* we understand them to mean.

This concentration on *how* we understand texts means that

stylistic analysis can often be of help when you find it difficult to come to grips with, say, a particular poem. For example, you can use the methodology I have used for the line from *Romeo and Juliet* in example 2 above to help unravel other metaphorical constructions. Various useful aids in the task of understanding will become clear as the book unfolds. It should also be remembered that the techniques discussed in this book will often throw light on our understanding of non–literary texts. Stylistic analysis can be applied to non–literary works, and you may well wish to try out what you learn from this volume on other sorts of texts. But the focus of this book happens to be on the three major literary genres poetry, drama and prose.

1.2 Foregrounding

1.2.1 Deviation and foregrounding

In fact, without giving it its technical term, I have, through the *Romeo and Juliet* example, introduced one of the most fundamental concepts in stylistic analysis, namely that of **linguistic deviation**. Because *daylight* cannot normally turn up in English as object to the verb *burn* we can say that the line deviates from the rules of English. Poetry in particular uses much deviation, and so we will examine deviation as a key to our understanding of poems. But you should always remember that deviation turns up in other modes of literary writing, and indeed in non–literary writing as well.

In fact this last point is a general one to bear in mind as you read this book. I will discuss particular kinds of analysis in relation to the literary genre that they give us most analytical purchase on. So, I will discuss sound patterning in relation to poetry, for example, and patterns of conversational turn–taking when we examine drama. But all of the forms of analysis we will look at in the book can be used on any genre and any text. Novels and plays can have effects gained through sound patterning for example, and most novels and some poems make meaningful use of patterns of conversational turn–taking. So it is important to remember that, as you go through the book, you will build up a repertoire of methods for examination and explanation that apply to *all* texts, not just those from the genre that I happen to be discussing when I introduce the methods to you.

Deviation, which is a *linguistic* phenomenon, has an important *psychological* effect on readers (and hearers). If a part of a poem is deviant, it becomes especially noticeable, or perceptually prominent. We call this psychological effect **foregrounding**.[5] There are many ways in which poets can produce deviation and hence foregrounding, and we will shortly go on to look at some of those ways. But we will first consider the general nature of foregrounding and its textual purpose. The term 'foregrounding' is borrowed from art criticism. Let us examine it in terms of the illustrations below:

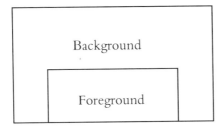

Art critics usually distinguish the foreground of a painting from its background. The foreground is that part of a painting which is in the centre and towards the bottom of the canvas. Note that the items which occur in the foreground of a painting will usually appear large in relation to the rest of the objects in the picture because of conventional perceptual 'rules' of perspective and so on, and will normally be thought of as constituting the subject matter of the painting. Hence, the picture below is one of two people in front of some houses rather than a picture of some houses with two people in front of them. This is in spite of the fact that the houses take up a larger area of the painting than the people:

Of course the background of the picture also contributes to the whole. Nothing in a work of art is insignificant. But the matter in the foreground is more important than the rest. It is often said of poetry that even if you change something as small as a comma you can change the meaning of the poem as a whole. But even so, some elements remain more important than others, and the foregrounded parts can be regarded as the most important of all. Indeed, if we produced an interpretation of a poem which ignored or did not explain properly its most foregrounded parts, others would be bound to criticise us for not giving a reasonable or adequate analysis of the text. In language, the background is what is linguistically normal – the rules, norms and expectations which we associate with a particular kind of speaking or writing; the foreground is, in large part (but see the discussion of parallelism in 1.2.2 and 2.3), the portions of text or talk which do not conform to these expectations. Foregrounding is thus produced as a result of deviation from linguistic (and non–linguistic)[6] **norms** of various kinds. In Chapter 2 we will examine the relation between deviation and foregrounding in more detail. But to help you become more familiar with the concepts I will illustrate them here with one or two examples from part of a description of a tomcat, who:

Example 3
1 Like a bundle of old rope and iron
2 Sleeps till blue dusk. Then reappear
3 His eyes, green as ringstones: he yawns wide red,
4 Fangs fine as a lady's needle and bright.
                              (Ted Hughes, 'Esther's Tomcat')

The first thing to notice is the deviation, via **inversion**, in lines 2–3, of the normal sequence *his eyes reappear*. In this poem the cat has fearsome and quasi–magical properties. Here the inversion, linked with the splitting of verb and subject over the line division, helps us to see the cat's eyes appearing apparently from nowhere, an effect particularly appropriate to the meaning of the verb and also helpful for the poem's overall textual strategy. Another example of deviation in this extract is *he yawns wide red*, where, again, Hughes produces a description of the yawn appropriate to his overall characterisation of the cat. The adjective phrase *wide red* would normally come after a linking, or copular, verb like 'be' (*e.g.* 'that flower is red') but here it follows and modifies an intransitive verb, *yawns*. Hence the phrase seems to be a description of the cat's mouth and a characterisation of how he yawns at the same time – a meaning blend of the normal function of the phrase and the grammatical function it appears to have in the deviant structure. The phrase itself, which has the adjective *red* at its head (the headword of a phrase is the most important word, around which the others 'revolve') is also deviant (this time in terms of semantic structure, not grammar) because we do not normally conceive of colours as having physical dimensions. A road can be wide because it is a physical object, and we all have some notion of what the normal width of a road is; but the 'extent' of a colour is inherently variable, depending upon the object of which it is predicated. By this deviation Hughes helps us to see the cat as almost all red, and all mouth, when he yawns. Given that *red* is easily associated with blood, particularly in the context of the next word in the poem, *fangs*, it is easy to see how *he yawns wide red* helps to build up the image of the cat as a predatory, fearsome animal.

Exercise 2

The following two lines are from the beginning of a poem (one is stanza–initial and one stanza–final). In what ways are the lines foregrounded? In what ways do the foregrounded features help you to begin to frame an interpretation for the poem?

pity this busy monster, manunkind,

not. Progress is a comfortable disease;

(e. e. cummings, 'pity this busy monster manunkind')

1.2.2 Foregrounding and parallelism

So far I have given the impression that poets can only foreground parts of their poems by breaking the rules of language. But this is not so. Another obvious method of foregrounding is **repetition,** as we can see in example 4:

Example 4

Blow, blow, thou winter wind

(William Shakespeare, *As You Like It*, II, vii, 174)

It should be obvious that the repetition of *blow* makes it stand out, and that by inference we are likely to conclude that the wind has a greater, more prolonged force than usual, or that the speaker (Amiens) who is addressing the wind has stronger feelings about it than usual. In this case only one word is repeated, but of course whole structures might be:

Example 5

Come hither, come hither, come hither.

(William Shakespeare, *As You Like It*, II, v, 5)

Simple repetition is, however, a relatively restricted method of producing foregrounding. A much more interesting method is that of **parallelism**, where some features are held constant (usually structural features) while others (usually lexical items, *e.g.* words, idioms) are varied:

Example 6

But he was wounded for our transgressions, he was bruised for our iniquities.

(*Isaiah*, 53, v)

Here, the structure and some of the words in the first clause are repeated in the second, giving us a parallel structure which is a 'repetition' of 'He was Xed for our Ys'. What is interesting about parallel structures, in addition to their perceptual prominence, is that they invite the reader to search for meaning connections between the parallel structures, in particular in terms of the parts which are varied. I like to call this the **'parallelism rule'** for interpretation (see also 2.3). In this example it is obvious that *wounded* and *bruised* are intended to be viewed as equivalent in some way, as are *transgressions* and *iniquities*. This leads us on to a more general interpretation of the two clauses, where wounding and bruising, and transgressions and iniquities, are linked. In this example the parallel meaning, promoted by the parallel structure, is obvious be—

cause of the similarity in meaning of the two pairs of words involved. Notice, however, that if you happen *not* to know the meaning of one of the words the parallel structure will help you to infer roughly the meaning of the word concerned. This can be seen easily in example 7, which I have constructed:

Example 7
He was kicked, beaten and lupped.

I have invented the last word in the sequence, and so you could not possibly have known what it might mean in advance. However, given the fact that it is paralleled with *kicked* and *beaten*, we are forced into deducing that it is an unpleasant, violent physical action which the person involved is subjected to. It is very unlikely to be a rough synonym of 'kissed'!

In the example from *Isaiah*, the words which are varied in the parallel structures are in any case closely related in meaning. But many examples can be found where the varied elements are not so close together. Example 4, *Blow, blow, thou winter wind*, which I quoted above, is paralleled a few lines later in the same speech:

Example 8
Freeze, freeze, thou bitter sky
                    (William Shakespeare, *As You Like It,* II, vii, 184)

Again, the invitation to the sky and the wind would appear to be equivalent, and meaning connections can be made between the words which are paralleled. The sky and the wind are both elements of nature; freezing and blowing can be construed as cold and unpleasant actions towards man on the part of nature, and *winter* and *bitter* can also be linked in terms of cold. Thus parallelism has the power not just to foreground parts of a text for us, but also to make us look for parallel or contrastive meaning links between those parallel parts. This may well involve us in construing new aspects of meaning for the words concerned, or in searching among the possible connotations that a word might have for the one that is most appropriate in the particular structure. For example, *blow* and *freeze* are not

normally thought of as parallel in meaning in English, and
wind and *sky* have many connotations and associations which
are ignored by readers when they read these particular lines.
Parallelism is thus one of the devices that a writer can use to
control our understanding of, and reactions to, what is
written. Repetition of whole phrases or clauses is the limiting
case of parallelism, where everything is paralleled and nothing
is varied.

Exercise 3

What kind of semantic links are you invited to infer from the following
examples of parallelism extracted from T. S. Eliot's 'The Hollow Men'?
Do your friends come to the same conclusions? Try to work out the
chain of inference which you have to go through to get to the
meaning at which you intuitively arrive:

> We are the hollow men
> We are the stuffed men
> [8 lines omitted]
> Shape without form, shade without colour,
> Paralysed force, gesture without motion;
> [26 lines omitted]
> This is the dead land
> This is the cactus land . . .
> (T. S. Eliot, 'The Hollow Men')

1.3   An example of stylistic analysis

So far I have only introduced you very briefly to the idea of
stylistic analysis and in particular to the analytical notions of
deviation, parallelism and foregrounding. I will say more
about these concepts in Chapter 2. But we probably have
enough common ground now for me to attempt a
demonstration analysis of a short poem by Philip Larkin.
Larkin is a poet who is noted for his preoccupation with death
and growing old, and also for his acute observations on
English social life. In this poem all of these concerns are
displayed:

Example 9

Beyond all this, the wish to be alone: (1)
However the sky grows dark with invitation–cards
However we follow the printed directions of sex
However the family is photographed under the flagstaff –
Beyond all this, the wish to be alone. (5)

Beneath it all, desire of oblivion runs:
Despite the artful tensions of the calendar,
The life insurance, the tabled fertility rites,
The costly aversion of the eyes from death –
Beneath it all, desire of oblivion runs. (10)
(Philip Larkin, 'Wants')

I will begin my analysis of the poem by giving a general interpretation for it. I will then go on to point out what seem to me to be the significant stylistic features in the text, making extensive, but not exclusive, use of the concepts I have introduced so far. Finally, I will try to show how the formal stylistic features are used as the basis for inferring the poem's meaning and effect. In other words, I will be using *linguistic description* in order to *interpret* the poem and thus suggest why it is interesting (*i.e. evaluate* it).

1.3.1 General interpretation

In the first stanza of the poem Larkin sets us in the middle of mundane, middle–class English social life. He notes that we involve ourselves in all sorts of socialising; but even though we fill up our time with such social activities, Larkin suggests that such a life is empty, and that although we disguise it from ourselves, underneath we really want to be alone. In the second stanza he extends the wish to be alone to its logical terminus, death. He suggests, then, that in spite of our existence as social beings, we all have a death–wish within us, and that immersing ourselves in the social round is harmful in that it is a mechanism we use to prevent ourselves from coming to terms with death and our subconscious desire for it. Unlike many modern poems, this one is not a crossword puzzle; it is fairly easy to understand. What I hope to do with my analysis is to explain how that meaning comes about, and give some indication of why the poem is critically interesting:

it satisfies Larkin's meaning requirements while at the same time obeying the dictates of the poetic form he chooses.

1.3.2 Linguistic stylistic features

In this analysis I will restrict myself to linguistic features which, for some reason or other (*e.g.* deviation, parallelism, repetition), attract some degree of foregrounding. In other words, they are linguistic features which are stylistically relevant, or **stylistic features**. Where appropriate, I will also begin to include interpretative comments.

Lexis

(i) Lexical repetition
The last line of each stanza is a repetition of its first line. As a result of this, the following content words are repeated: *wish, alone, desire, oblivion, run.* So also are the prepositions *beyond* and *beneath,* which also happen to be fuller lexically than most prepositions (*e.g.* 'of', 'to'). *longer?*

(ii) Lexical groupings
The foregrounding through repetition helps us to notice that almost all of the repeated words (*run* is the exception) belong to a series of conceptual groups in the poem:

1 *wish, desire, wants. Wish* and *desire* are synonyms indicating a felt lack (in this case a lack of being alone, or nothingness). 'Want' is also a near–synonym of *wish,* and hence *desire* (*cf.* 'I want to be alone'; 'I wish to be alone'*). Wants, wish* and *desire* are all nouns in this poem, nouns derived from verbs.
2 *alone, oblivion, death.* These three words all have to do with solitude, though death and oblivion (which can sometimes be used as synonyms in English) are rather extreme forms of it.
3 *beyond, beneath.* The two prepositions, which are also in equivalent syntactic and metrical positions (see below), both express remoteness, either horizontally or vertically from the locus of the speaker.
4 *invitation–cards, printed directions of sex, photographed, calendar, life insurance, tabled fertility rites.* All of these lexical items are

capable of interpretation as having to do with printed matter. If the object of *photographed* (the only verb in the list), *family*, is added to the list it also becomes apparent that the words and phrases all have to do with social life on a scale from the most general (large social groups) to the most personal (relations between individuals, in this case couples) *via* an intermediate unit, the family:

LARGE SOCIAL GROUPS
invitation–cards, calendar (here *calendar* refers to the social calendar – *i.e.* dates for engagements, social events, etc.).

FAMILY
family is photographed, life insurance (a method of providing material welfare for your family after death).

COUPLES
(*i.e.* sexual relations): *printed directions of sex, tabled fertility rites* (see next section for interpretative remarks).

Semantico–syntactic deviations

I deal here with metaphors and the like, areas of language which are in some ways on the borderline between grammar and meaning:

the sky grows dark with invitation–cards (2)

I ignore the notion of the sky *growing* dark, as that is a dead metaphor in English. Note, however, that the structural linking with *invitation–cards* is odd. The normal expression would be something like 'the sky grows dark with (rain) clouds'. Here the deviation (along with the generic plural *cards*) helps us to suppose an overwhelming number of social invitations (obligations?).

the printed directions of sex (3)

Sex cannot literally have printed directions as it is an abstract noun. The easiest way to normalise the phrase would appear to be to interpret it as elliptical for a phrase like 'the printed directions of sex manuals' or 'the printed directions of leaflets about sex'. The ellipsis allows a number of possible interpretations. The phrase could refer to books on sexual positions, etc., or instructions on contraceptive packets, or how to calculate ovulation periods in order to ensure, or avoid, conception. The first possibility, which seems to me to be the most likely, as it fits in best with the tone of the rest of the poem, helps us to view love–making as a mere matter of mechanics. The other possibilities I mention also do this, but to a lesser extent.

the tabled fertility rites (8)

I take this phrase out of order as it helps to explain why I list the possible interpretations that I do for *the printed directions of sex* (3). Fertility rites, which obviously have to do with sex, are usually associated with primitive, non–literate tribes. Here, however, they are modified by *tabled*, which indicates that whatever is referred to is written down in a tabular fashion (hence mechanical). The fact that what is referred to here is described as a ritual reinforces the mechanical associations for *sex* seen in line 3. The tabled fertility rites can either be seen as a reference to the calculation of natural ovulation cycles in order for couples to work out when to make love in order to conceive, or prevent conception, or a reference to sets of instructions on packets of contraceptive pills. Given the tone of the poem as a whole, one of the two interpretations involving the *prevention* of conception looks most likely. Note that these possible interpretations parallel those for line 3 in that they make sexual love–making appear unspontaneous and hence unappealing. If the phrase is interpreted by the reader as referring to periods when one should make love in order to *encourage* conception, *fertility rites* is semi–literal. However, if it is interpreted as having to do with avoidance of conception the phrase is obviously ironic. There are some important general principles for interpretation at work here. First of all, we try to interpret similar or connected items in a text in a related or similar way if we can (unless, of course, there is some specific, over–riding reason to go against this reading 'rule'). Hence, we need an interpretation which connects together in some way *printed* and *tabled* and *sex* and *fertility rites*. Secondly, the two phrases *the printed directions of sex* and *the tabled fertility rites* are parallel to one another as a result of a series of features paralleling the two stanzas together (see the section on grammatical parallelism below), and parallelism also promotes an attempt on our part to connect the parallel items together, with 'parallel meaning' being a likely interpretative possibility.

> *desire of oblivion runs* (6, 10)

As *desire of oblivion* is abstract it cannot literally run. However, *run* turns up in many dead, or near–dead, metaphorical constructions in English and so many readers will not perceive this as a particularly marked deviation. Presumably *desire of oblivion* is being likened to a river or some such, and as it appears both as subject and actor to *runs* it appears that the individual's desire is one which is unconsciously motivated. Compare 'I desire oblivion', where having 'I' in the subject/actor position makes the act of desire appear to be much more consciously intended.

> *the artful tensions of the calendar* (7)

Calendars do not literally have tensions. The easiest way to interpret this oddity is to note that social engagements may conflict with one another. However, there is another oddity to explain in that tensions are not usually artful. *Artful* has to do with *intended* actions. So here it appears that the events on the calendar are *designed* purposefully to conflict with one another (note that people sometimes excuse themselves from a social engagement they do not want to attend by pleading a prior commitment).

> *the costly aversion of the eyes from death* (9)

The first thing to notice here is that Larkin has foregrounded the line by blending two different expressions together. To have an *aversion* to something means that you have a strong dislike for it. And there is also an idiomatic expression in English, 'to *avert* your eyes', which means to turn your eyes away from something you feel you should not see for some reason or other. *Aversion of the eyes*, then, which at first sight looks like a nominalisation of 'avert the eyes' expresses neatly the idea of turning away from something which is viewed as distasteful – in this case death. In addition, *aversion* is here modified by *costly*. This creates another metaphor. Aversions cannot literally *cost* money; but 'cost' turns up in many expressions in English (*e.g.* 'his mistakes cost him dearly') where it is indicated that whatever is referred to turns out to be disadvantageous to the individual concerned. This metaphor is thus easily interpretable and not markedly foregrounded compared with *aversion of the eyes*, because of its similarity to other dead or quasi–dead metaphorical constructions.

Grammar

For convenience of presentation I include information on punctuation and lineation in this section. If I were being completely consistent I should really have a separate section devoted to graphological information.

(i) Grammatical parallelism

1 The middle three lines of each stanza consist of a set of parallels:

> In stanza 1, lines 2–4 each consist of a subordinate clause beginning with the linking word *however*. In spite of the colon at the end of line 1 and the dash at the end of line 4, which separate the repeated lines (1 and 5) from the middle three lines, it appears that syntactically the three 'middle line' clauses are all subordinated to the elliptical, verbless clause of line 1.

> In stanza 2, the middle three lines consist of the preposition *despite* plus a list of noun phrases which are all complements to that preposition. The head nouns of the noun phrases involved are all abstract.

2 The repeated lines in the two stanzas show similarities. They all begin with fronted three–word prepositional phrases including the word *all*. The prepositional phrases are all separated off from the rest of their lines by a comma. All four lines end with a major punctuation boundary (lines 1 and 6 end with a colon and lines 5 and 10 with a full stop). The obvious parallel in the repeated lines helps us to notice that the two stanzas of the poem are parallel to one another more generally. They both consist of five unrhyming lines. They both consist of one sentence. They both have colons at the end of their first lines and a dash at the end of their fourth lines. They both repeat exactly their first and last

lines. This observation of structural parallelism of a more pervasive type than we normally find between stanzas in the same poem (the traditional 'rule' is that they should have the same number of lines and the same metre and rhyme scheme, and even these 'rules' are relaxed in much modern poetry) helps us to notice that the two stanzas have a similar syntactic, and thus semantic, structure:

Lines 1 and 6 (Stanza–initial lines):
    Outside (*beneath, beyond*) X, Y

Lines 2–4 and 7–9 ('Middle' lines):
    No matter how (*however, despite*) X, Y

Lines 5 and 10 (Stanza–final lines):
    Outside (*beneath, beyond*) X, Y

(ii) Definiteness and generics
There are no indefinite noun phrases (*e.g.* 'a chair') whatsoever in the poem. Every lexicalised noun phrase either begins with the definite article (*e.g. the sky*) or has a generic noun (one which, as a consequence of having no article or other kind of determiner before it, has general rather than specific reference: compare 'man' with 'the man' and 'her man') at its head (*e.g. invitation–cards, desire of oblivion*). This suggests a tension between *specificity* (the speaker in the poem is referring to the specific situation around him, his life) and *generality*. The generic nouns (note that the title is also a generic noun) force us into seeing the speaker's comments as being not just about his own situation but also about modern life in general. As a result just about all of the definite noun phrases are capable of both specific and general interpretations at the same time (*e.g.* the speaker's wish, the wish of people in general).

(iii) Tense
The whole poem is in the present tense. This aids the 'specific but at the same time general' aspect of the interpretation, as the present tense can be used to refer to the specific situation for a particular speaker and also to timeless, universal matters (*cf.* 'Those daffodils are dying' and 'Daffodils are yellow'). These two aspects of the English present tense are what Quirk and Greenbaum (1973: 41) refer to as the 'instantaneous' and

'timeless' present.

(iv) Pronouns

There are four pronouns in this poem, which in effect are two pairs of repetitions in the first and last line of each stanza. *All this* in line 1 appears to be demonstrative, referring out **exophorically** to the situation around the speaker (**exophora** is the name given to linguistic items which refer to items in the immediate situational context of the speaker, as in 'this chair', 'that table'). As line 5 is a repeat of line 1, we might expect the same referring function to hold. But in fact *all this* in line 5 can also be seen as functioning **anaphorically** – that is, it refers back to the clauses in lines 2–4 (**anaphora** is the name given to linguistic items which refer back to some previous linguistic item already mentioned in a text, like 'It' in 'We climbed the mountain. It was high.'). As a result, *all this* in line 5 reflects the specific/general tension which we have seen above. The same can be said of *it all* in lines 6 and 10, with the added point that the first *it all* is also capable of anaphoric reference back to the first stanza. Thus the poem can be seen as becoming more generalising in the second stanza. This observation is supported by the incidence of syntactically generic nouns:

Title	1	
Stanza 1	1	
Stanza 2	5	(including two repetitions, as line 6, the repeated line, contains two generics)

Sound (phonetic) patterns

Phonetic transcriptions of words are placed inside slash brackets and follow Knowles (1987: 221–2), whose notation is reproduced in the appendix at the end of this book (see also Chapter 4 below):

beyond all this, beneath it all (1, 5, 6, 10)

From the point of view of interpretation the most important phonetic fact in the poem is the similarity in the two repeated prepositional phrases at the beginnings of lines 1, 5, 6 and 10. They all consist of three words, with a 2–1–1 syllable pattern.

The first syllable of the first word of the two lines is phonetically and graphologically identical – _beyond_ /bijond/; _beneath_ /biniːθ/. _All_ is repeated, and the two other words share the same vowel and similar consonants (voiceless fricatives, see 4.2.1). This phonetic parallelism helps reinforce the structural parallels pointed out earlier and hence the system of parallel meanings (see below). Apart from these examples, there are a number of alliterative and assonantal patterns within these lines, which help link important words together:

this /ðis/; _wish_ /wiʃ/ (1)
(present _vs_ hypothetical state);

dark /daːk/; _cards_ /kaːdz/ (2)
(_dark_ has connotations of threat, and sometimes death; _card_ here has an obvious social connotation);

directions /dərekʃnz/; _sex_ /seks/ (3)
(here the assonance and alliteration help bring out the ritual and mechanical aspects of the personal relations described in the poem: note how useful for Larkin it is that the word _sex_ (instead of, say, 'love') has unromantic connotations as well as phonetic parallels with _directions_);

family /familiː/; _photographed_ /foutəgraːft/;
flagstaff /flagstaːf/ (4)
(given the comments on line 3, the alliteration here may be interpreted by some readers as having a similar effect).

1.3.3 The link between stylistic features and interpretation

In a sense my comments above contain my detailed interpretation for the poem. Here I will draw the various observations together so that the link between form and meaning (which we, as readers, deduce from form by intuitively applying a set of unconscious procedures for inferring meaning) can be seen more clearly. You have probably noticed from my comments on stylistic features that the main unifying feature of 'Wants' is parallelism. In stanza 1, lines 2–4 are parallel and Larkin thus invites us to see them as being in some sense the same, in spite of the different things to which they refer. This condition can be satisfied by noticing that all three lines describe aspects of social life, which is then contrasted with *the wish to be alone*, a contrast pointed up by a further parallelism, the assonance (and quasi–alliteration) between *this* and *wish*.

When we come to stanza 2 we can first notice that because lines 6 and 10 are parallel in various ways (phonetics, grammar, punctuation) to lines 1 and 5, the two sets of repeated lines can be interpreted in terms of parallel meaning. Hence the wish to be alone is equivalent to the wish for oblivion or death (note, incidentally, that *wish* and the title word *wants* alliterate as well as being synonyms in English). Once the similarities between the first and last lines of the two stanzas have been noticed it is easier for us to see that the middle three lines in stanza 2, like those in stanza 1, consist of a series of parallel structures, which, again like those in stanza 1, have to do with social life. In turn we can see that the three parallel items in each of the three middle lines of each stanza can be related together to show in each stanza three finer aspects of that social life: the social gathering, the family and the sexually related couple.

The parallelisms all point, then, to a disjunction between the social reality, man as a social animal in various guises, and the wish for loneliness and death. The reason for the wish to be removed from one's companions comes in the deviant, mainly metaphorical, expressions in lines 2–4 and 7–9, which indicate the unreal, mechanical nature of social reality, especially, and paradoxically, at the most personal end of the scale.

What I have said so far counts as an indication of the way in which my observations about linguistic form substantiate my initial interpretative comments. One further point remains to be drawn out, however, namely the tension between the specific (the speaker's particular social life) and the general (the way in which we feel that his remarks apply to us all). It is a commonplace in discussions of literature to say that it often demonstrates universal truths from descriptions of the particular. But here it is important to note, there is also a *structural* motivation for making the move from the particular to the general, namely:

1 the fact that the Noun Phrases in the poem either have definite or generic reference or, on some occasions can hold both kinds of reference at the same time (see the

section on definiteness and generics in 1.3.2); and

2 the way in which the pronouns in the poem can bear both exophoric and anaphoric interpretations (see the section on pronouns above), and where, because of their link with the universalising quantifier *all* they appear to refer to the *groups* of clauses describing social life, not just to a single phrase or clause.

Perhaps the most interesting thing about this last general interpretative point is that it is one which did not strike me on my initial careful reading of the poem. Rather, it became apparent in the process of performing the detailed stylistic analysis. In this way, detailed and systematic stylistic analysis can be seen as an aid to our understanding and appreciation of the text under discussion as well as providing a rational language–based account to support interpretation and giving insights into the processes by which we interpret when we read. My interpretation of 'Wants' may well not be the only possible one. But the important thing to notice is that any reasonable interpretation of the poem will have to take into account the foregrounded features revealed and accounted for in my stylistic analysis.

1.4   Who   was   stylistics?

By now it should be apparent that stylistic analysis is a method of linking linguistic form, *via* reader inference, to interpretation in a detailed way and thereby providing as much explicit evidence as possible for and against particular interpretations of texts. My use of the term 'stylistics' may still seem a little odd to you, however, in that it suggests that the main interest of this area of enquiry should be on the study of *style*. Some stylisticians do use linguistic analysis to uncover authorial styles, text styles and other kinds of style, and, indeed, the history of stylistics began with an attempt to understand the various concepts invoked by the term 'style' and how, for example, we manage as readers to recognise a piece of writing as belonging to a particular author even when we have not been told who wrote it. But this work also led stylisticians to recognise that style and meaning are inextricably linked with one another (Chapters 3 and 11 discuss some of the issues involved in the study of style, and also how it is related to meaning), and this recognition has led to the modern concern with the relationship between linguistic form on the one hand and the meanings and effects which readers infer from it on the other.

During your reading of this chapter you should also have been able to work out my reason for choosing 'Who is stylistics?' as the title for the first chapter of this book. The sentence itself is, of course, syntactically deviant. The pronoun 'who' in English has to have human reference, but stylistics is an abstract concept, and hence foregrounded. As a result, even if you forget entirely the content of this chapter, you are unlikely to forget its title.

Discussion of exercises

Exercise 1

The crimson seeds of blood is metaphorical because seeds, being a part of the reproductive system of plants, are vegetable and so cannot be made of blood. We could normalise the phrase by substituting the name of a plant which has red seeds instead of *blood* (*e.g.* 'the crimson seeds of pomegranate'), or alternatively by replacing *seeds* with a noun which refers to something which can be composed of blood (*e.g.* 'the crimson drops of blood'). From the linguistic context we know that the fox is wounded, and hence it is highly probable that we will interpret *the crimson seeds of blood* as referring to drops of blood. The use of *seeds* relates to *roses* in line 4 as both words have to do with plants, and, as roses are usually thought of as being beautiful, we seem to be invited to see the sight described here as beautiful. Yet the seeds are also said to be *soft as excrement.* This contrast of comparisons forces an ironic clash: the physical *beauty* of an animal in *pain* and probably dying. This irony in turn will help to alert us to another ironic possibility, in that *seeds*, associated with reproduction, is specifically related in these lines to *blood*, which is associated with death. Obviously we would need to relate the above possibilities to the text as a whole in order to be sure of the best interpretative moves to make. However, these interpretative suggestions, which are based on an examination of the linguistic structure of the phrase concerned, do look like reasonable hypotheses to check against the rest of the text.

Exercise 2

The lines of this poem do not begin with capital letters. This graphological feature is foregrounded against the traditional set of norms which we have for the genre of poetry. It is unlikely to be significant in the interpretation of this particular poem, *internal* however, as lack of line–initial capitalisation is a consistent feature of e. e. cummings's poetry. It appears to be one of the ways in which he marks off his verse as 'Modern' (*i.e.* as breaking with the more traditional verse forms of the nineteenth century and before).

The word *manunkind* is foregrounded as a result of the fact that it has been invented by cummings in this text (*i.e.* it is a **neologism**). We can compare it with the nearest normal equivalent, 'mankind'. The disruption of the normal word by the prefix *un–* helps us to see the 'kind' in 'mankind' as related to the concept of kindness. Hence in cummings's poem, mankind appears to be intrinsically unkind.

The first line of this poem has an imperative structure, which is relatively unusual in written texts and so is most easily interpretable as a 'spoken' command. This suggests that the 'speaker' is directly addressing some other person, perhaps the reader. The use of the demonstrative pronoun *this,* which normally refers out exophorically (see the discussion of pronouns in 1.3.2) to the immediate situational context, supports this view.

The negative construction *pity . . . not* is unusual in modern English (though not in some earlier forms of the language). We notice this feature for the first time when we reach the word *not*. Hence the negation is foregrounded. Moreover, the first line looks grammatically complete at first sight, and so when we read on to the second line, and discover that *not* belongs to the clause contained in the first line, this enjambment (see 6.7) also makes *not* a point of foregrounding. Cummings's negative attitude to humanity in the poem is thus doubly stressed.

The noun *manunkind* is in apposition to *this busy monster,* and thus counts as a gloss on it. We normally distinguish between monsters and men, and so at first sight there is a tension between the grammatical dictates of the appositional relation and the semantic content involved. But as the appositional word is cummings's invented *manunkind* there is also a strand of semantic appropriateness, in that our understanding of *monster* involves connotations relatable to unkindness.

We need to be able to relate the second sentence to the first, and one obvious possibility is that *progress is a comfortable disease* counts as a reason for not pitying mankind. This clause is deviant semantically because (i) progress is not a disease (from this we can deduce that the speaker does not approve of progress), and (ii) diseases are not normally thought of as comfortable (from this we can deduce that progress is to be regarded as superficially good, though as it is a disease, it will be disadvantageous in the long run).

One important general point to note here is that this pair of lines contains a considerable number of foregrounded items, which all play an important part in the way in which we begin to build up an interpretation for the poem. If there is so much foregrounding, where are the background items? And if all the lines were foregrounded like this, wouldn't the foreground/background distinction disappear? Think about this. We will return to it in Chapter 2.

Exercise 3

The first pair of lines from 'The Hollow Men' are identical except for the replacement of *hollow* by *stuffed*. In spite of the fact that the two words normally have opposite meanings we are thus invited to construe a relation between them of parallel meaning. One way to begin to do this is to notice that being hollow is a precondition for being stuffed. Men, of course, are neither hollow nor stuffed in normal circumstances. This poem has an epigraph, *A penny for the Old Guy* just before these two lines, and so one obvious way to interpret the lines is to see them as relating to the effigies burnt on bonfire night in Britain. But bonfire guys are inanimate and so cannot talk. Hence these guys are still rather unusual. This allows the possibility that the guys stand for real human beings, which in turn forces another set of possible, metaphorical, meanings for *hollow* and *stuffed*, for example people that have no ideas of their own and who rely on others for what to say and do. You may be able to think up other possible explanations; but note that whatever account of the poem you produce will have to account for the parallelisms I have outlined.

The parallelism within the next line is a little less exact, the only repeated word being *without*. The syntactic structure is constant, however ('X without Y', where X and Y are abstract, generic nouns), and there is alliteration and assonance between *shape* and *shade*. Because of the abstract lexical items it is difficult to put your finger on an exact interpretation, but it is obvious that *shape* and *shade* can be related together as bodiless forms, and that the states of being without form and without colour can also be construed as somehow equivalent, and contributing to this general intangible meaning. In addition, inside each phrase there is a semantic opposition. The meaning of *shape* presupposes some outline, but its modifying material *without form* negates that assumption. A similar opposition can be seen in *shade without colour*. When we move on to the next line we can see that *gesture without motion* shares the same syntactic and lexical structure but not the phonetic parallels. It obviously contains the same kind of semantic opposition as the two phrases in the previous line, and so the insubstantial meaning which we are building up now includes the first, second and last of the noun phrases listed in the two lines. Because *paralysed force* is also a noun phrase in this list of noun phrases, it is, to a lesser extent, parallel with the other three, and indeed it also contains an opposed semantic relation between the headword and modifier in the phrase. The meaning at which we tentatively arrive, then (we would, of course, need eventually to integrate our hypotheses about meaning for this extract with the rest of the text in a detailed and consistent way), is one involving a yoking together of a series of four sets of abstract oppositions. We should also note that there are closer parallels in meaning between the pairs of phrases within each line than there are across the lines. The first two phrases relate to static perceptions of things without physical form, whereas the pair in the next line involve the negation of dynamic motion. This two–line example shows us that parallelism can involve more than just a pair of items, as here we have four items paralleled to one another, in two pairs of two. Parallel meaning of a rather complex kind is involved.

The final pair of parallel lines from 'The Hollow Men', like the first pair, involves parallelism with only one word being varied – *dead* for *cactus*. At first sight these two words appear to be opposed to one another in that cacti are living, not dead. But again we have parallel structures with parallel meaning, as the sort of land where cacti grow is desert land, *i.e.* land where almost nothing else grows. All of the parallelisms we have picked out from this poem exhibit internal paradoxes or semantic oppositions. This pattern looks as if it must be a salient one, and we are thus apparently being invited to search for similar relations in other parts of the poem and to relate them together as an interpretative key for the text.

Notes

1. There are also linguists who examine non–literary texts. For example Leech (1966a), Crystal and Davy (1969), O'Donnell and Todd (1980), Myers (1990, 1994) and Cook (1992).
2. Fowler (1971a: 67).
3. The first six papers in Fowler (1971a) address this matter and the whole debate between Fowler and Bateson is included.
4. Dead metaphors are metaphors which are used so habitually that their metaphorical force becomes almost invisible to us. Lakoff and Johnson (1980: 117–18) note that it is typical of a number of the dead metaphors we 'live by' to take abstract notions like time and life, and represent them in more experientially basic terms, including physical objects, as in 'time is money' or 'life is a precious gift'.
5. For a clear discussion see Leech (1969: Ch. 4). For a more advanced discussion of the validity of foregrounding as a psychological phenomenon see van Peer (1986).
6. Once you have any rule–system, linguistic or not, it is possible to deviate from the rules and so produce foregrounded behaviour. For example, when we go to a lecture we all obey the social rule of arriving clothed, even in hot weather. If I arrived with no clothes on to give a lecture on foregrounding, my behaviour would be deviant, and hence foregrounded. As a consequence it would also be highly *interpretable*. You would feel the need to infer an explanation for, or interpretation of, my aberrant be–haviour. That interpretation would be constructed on the basis of contextual knowledge as well as the information directly in front of you. If you had heard that I was a lecturer who gave striking lectures, you might decide that I was making a memorable point about my topic, foregrounding. If, on the other hand, you had seen me behaving strangely on a number of occasions beforehand, you might decide to ring the local mental hospital.

. Further reading

Introductory work on the stylistics of poetry
Short (1990) is an introductory article about stylistics which examines extracts from each of the three major literary genres. Short (1993) (in Verdonk 1993, which contains a number of stylistic essays analysing particular poems) gives advice on how to go about doing a stylistic analysis, using a poem by Ted Hughes. Verdonk (1988) discusses three poems. Cluysenaar (1976) and Fowler (1986) are reliable introductions to stylistics, and Leech (1969) is a very thorough linguistic account of English poetry.

Handy reference books
The best book to have by you is Wales (1989) which is a comprehensive and entertaining dictionary of stylistics and related linguistic and critical terminology. Crystal (1984a) is a dictionary of linguistic terms, Fowler (1973) is a dictionary of modern critical terms and Leech (1989), although written primarily for advanced learners of the English language, is a good dictionary of grammar. Another clear dictionary of grammar is Hurford (1994).

Linguistics textbooks
Traugott and Pratt (1980) is a Linguistics textbook designed for Literature students. Fromkin and Rodman (1988), Graddol, Cheshire and Swann (1987) and Simpson (1979) are accessible general introductions to Linguistics.
   There are a number of good introductory accounts of particular areas of Linguistics, some of which are in the same series as the present volume: Burton–Roberts (1986) and Jackson (1990) are both accessible introductions to English grammar, Knowles (1987) is an account of English phonetics designed particularly for students of English, and Thomas (1994) is a good introduction to pragmatics. The grammar books to which this volume most closely relates are Leech, Deuchar and Hoogenraad (1982) and Quirk and Greenbaum (1973), both of which are relatives of the compendious reference grammar, Quirk, Greenbaum, Leech and Svartvik (1985). Hurford and Heasley (1983) and Leech (1974) are clear introductions to semantics. Wardhaugh (1986) is a very accessible introduction to discourse analysis and pragmatics, and Brown and Yule (1983) is a more advanced and

comprehensive, yet also accessible introduction.

CHECKSHEET 1: DEVIATION, PARALLELISM AND FOREGROUNDING

This is the first of a series of checksheets which you will find at the end of chapters, and which you can use when doing your own stylistic analysis of texts to make sure that you are systematic in your analysis and do not miss important aspects of the text. As you go through the book you will be able to make use of more and more checksheets to arrive at ever more comprehensive textual analyses. The position of the other checksheets in the book can be found by using the index or by looking at the contents list at the front of the book. This particular checksheet relates both to the present chapter and also to Chapter 2, which looks in more detail at matters to do with deviation and parallelism raised in this chapter. So, if you are unsure about any of the terms below, you can find out by reading Chapter 2.

A. **Note down each deviation and parallelism you can find in the text:**

Deviation

(a)   Is the deviation *internal* (deviates from some established pattern internal to the text) or *external* (deviates from some norm external to the text)?

(b)   If the deviation is external, what external norm does it deviate from (*e.g.* the norms for English, the norms for the genre, the norms of the particular author)?

(c)   At what linguistic level does the deviation occur:

Phonetic	Lexical
Graphological	Discoursal
Metrical	Semantic
Morphological	Pragmatic
Syntactic	Other

(d)   Are there any other deviations occurring at the same place in the text (if so, re-apply (a)–(c)). Note the extra foregrounding.

(e)   Do the deviations lead to new, non–literal meanings for the text–parts concerned? If so, what are they in each case?

Parallelism

(f)   Are there any parallelisms? If so, note the linguistic levels at which they occur by using the list of levels in (c) above (note that parallelism may occur at more than one linguistic level at the same time).

(g)   Does the 'parallelism rule' (look for same or opposite meaning) apply? If so, what is the meaning–result?

B. Examine cohesion and function of foregrounding

(h)   How do the foregrounded portions of the text relate together and contribute to the interpretation of the poem as a whole? Does looking at the whole pattern help you in any way (i) to interpret particular deviations or parallelisms that you could not satisfactorily explain before, or (ii) to reinterpret others?

(i)   Note down any other points which occur to you.

CHAPTER 2

More on foregrounding, deviation and parallelism

2.1 Introduction

In Chapter 1 we noticed that in exploring poetry it is sensible to begin by examining the foregrounded aspects of texts, as these almost invariably turn out to be important in interpretation. Indeed a good starting point for the analysis of any poem is to examine the foregrounded parts and provide an interpretation which links those parts together. This is what I did in the analysis of 'Wants' by Philip Larkin. Foregrounded features are the parts of the text which the author, consciously or unconsciously, is signalling as crucial to our understanding of what he has written. A well known stylistician, Leech (1970), has called this strategy of linking together foregrounded features **cohesion of foregrounding**.

Before we can properly account for textual interpretation *via* cohesion of foregrounding we need to be able to describe and categorise the various kinds of deviation and parallelism which give rise to foregrounding. Native speakers of a language, and indeed many second language learners, often intuitively know that a stretch of text is odd; but in order to make sure that our intuitions are reasonable, and not based on personal whim, we will need to be able to show the nature of the deviation. Another reason for needing a systematic account of different kinds of deviation and parallelism is that it is all too easy to miss some aspects of deviation at the conscious level. We can often react subconsciously to deviance, perceive the deviant parts of a text as foregrounded and interpret it accordingly without even realising that we have done it. This certainly happened to me when I first read *Come, we burn daylight, ho!*, the line from *Romeo and Juliet* which we examined in 1.1 above. It was only when I came to analyse the line in order to provide for this book a clear example of semantic deviation giving rise to metaphorical, or non–literal interpretation that I properly understood how I understood it.

2.2 Kinds of deviation

As a result of this need to analyse and categorise explicitly, much of this chapter will be a description of different kinds of deviation which can produce foregrounding. The account which I give will certainly not be exhaustive (though it may be exhausting!). It should, however, give you some idea of the different sorts of things you react to when you read, whether or not you are conscious of doing so. And you can use what I say in this chapter as a more detailed spelling out of what to look for in the checksheet at the end of Chapter 1 (Checksheet 1: Deviation, Parallelism and Foregrounding) when you analyse poems, novels or plays.

2.2.1 Discoursal deviation

Most linguistic discussion has concerned itself with linguistic structure below the level of the sentence. But it should be apparent that for the user of a language there is a higher level, that of **discourse**. In discourses, sentences are related together to form higher units of linguistic organisation. This book, which is a *written* discourse, or *text*, organises groups of sentences into paragraphs, groups of paragraphs into sections, and groups of sections into chapters. People take part in different *kinds* of discourses: we have conversations, listen to speeches, read poems, notices, articles, novels, and so on. Although it is often more difficult to describe in an explicit and systematic way, linguistic behaviour at the discoursal level has norms just as much as linguistic behaviour at the grammatical level, for example.

There is a general assumption in language that one should begin at the beginning. Texts should therefore begin at the beginning of a sentence. The most notorious example of a text which deviates from this rule is James Joyce's novel, *Finnegans Wake*, which both begins and ends in mid–sentence. Indeed, the end can be joined to the beginning so that the novel goes round and round in a circle. *Finnegans Wake* is an extra–ordinarily complex and difficult read; but from noticing just this one deviant, and hence foregrounded feature, we can begin to understand that Joyce is creating a work which in a sense has no beginning and no end. This observation is an important clue to the understanding of a novel where Finnegan observes his own funeral wake and tries to take part in it, thus blurring our commonplace distinction between life and death.

Discourses should also begin at the beginning of discourses as well as at the beginning of sentences. A political speech which began 'And, in conclusion . . .' would seem very strange, as would one which ended with the sentence 'First let me deal with Anglo–Soviet relations'. But some texts do not begin at the beginning:

Example 1

[1] For God's sake hold your tongue, and let me love,

(John Donne, 'The Canonization')

[2] Yes. I remember Adlestrop –

(Edward Thomas, 'Adlestrop')

At the start of both of these poems we are apparently projected into the middle of a conversation. In the example from Donne, beginning in the middle (a technique which critics often refer to by its Latin name, **in medias res**) helps to increase the sense of energy in the argument, seen also in the imperatives and the swear word. In Thomas's poem the first line, with its initial answering *Yes* helps to create a conversational tone in the first half of the poem, which is then contrasted with a second half much more 'poetic' in type (for a fuller analysis of this poem see 3.5). Many novels and plays also begin 'in the middle' (see 9.3.3).

Literary texts are also often deviant with respect to the interactants in the discourse. In 'To a Grecian Urn' Keats directly addresses a piece of pottery, and Marianne Moore talks to a machine in 'To a Steam Roller'. In Dylan Thomas's 'The Force that Through the Green Fuse Drives the Flower', the speaker is someone who not only is dead, but whose corpse has been spread, *via* the process of decomposition and the workings of the nitrogen cycle, to become part of the natural surroundings, the flowers, trees and streams.

The prototypical **discourse situation** which springs to most people's minds is that of a conversation between two people. We might represent such a discourse situation as follows:

In this model, there is one addresser who talks, or gives messages, to one addressee. When the other person in the conversation talks, the roles become reversed. The model also accounts for letters written from one person to another (except that the context of situation would not normally be the same for the two participants). Although this one–to–one pattern is common, there are many other permutations. In a lecture there is usually one addresser and many addressees (the same is true of published written work). If you have ever been on the receiving end of a diatribe from your parents on staying out too late or not doing your share of the housework, you have probably been in a discourse situation with only one addressee but more than one addresser, and if you talk to yourself you are both addresser and addressee.

Much poetry is adequately accounted for in discourse terms by the diagram above, except that there is one addresser and many addressees (the readers) and that (unlike spoken conversation) in written communication there is no context of situation which is shared by both participants. The writer writes in one place and time and the reader reads in another. Wordsworth's 'The Daffodils' is a poem where the poet directly addresses the reader, each reader in turn, whoever he or she might be. The same is true of the beginning of Gray's 'Elegy':

Example 2
The curfew tolls the knell of parting day,
The lowing herd wind slowly o'er the lea,
The ploughman homeward plods his weary way,
And leaves the world to darkness and to me.
(Thomas Gray, 'Elegy Written in a Country Churchyard')

Although much poetry can be handled via this 'direct address' mode, it cannot all be. In T. S. Eliot's 'The Love Song of J. Alfred Prufrock', for example, Eliot writes the poem, but the words appear to come out of the mouth of another person, Prufrock. Where the speaker in a poem is obviously not the poet, critics usually reserve the term **persona** for the speaker. They do not usually have a special term to cover the situation where, instead of, or in addition to more than one addresser, there is also more than one addressee. Consider 'Long–Legged Fly' by W. B. Yeats:

Example 3
That civilisation may not sink,
Its great battle lost,
Quiet the dog, tether the pony
To a distant post;
Our master Caesar is in the tent
Where the maps are spread,
His eyes fixed upon nothing,
A hand under his head.
Like a long–legged fly upon the stream
His mind moves upon silence.

That the topless towers be burnt
And men recall that face,
Move most gently if move you must
In this lonely place.
She thinks, part woman, three parts a child,
That nobody looks; her feet
Practise a tinker shuffle
Picked up on a street.
Like a long–legged fly upon the stream
Her mind moves upon silence.

That girls at puberty may find
The first Adam in their thought,
Shut the door of the Pope's chapel,
Keep those children out.
There on that scaffolding reclines
Michael Angelo.
With no more sound than the mice make
His hand moves to and fro.
Like a long–legged fly upon the stream
His mind moves upon silence.

(W. B. Yeats, 'Long–Legged Fly')

It should be obvious that in this poem it is not the poet who is talking, and indeed the reader is also not addressed directly. Rather, the reader apparently 'overhears' three separate pieces of talk. In the first stanza, someone, presumably a servant or a soldier in Caesar's army (*cf. our master Caesar*) tells another soldier or servant to keep things quiet for Caesar. In the second stanza an anonymous person tells someone else not to disturb Helen of Troy. In stanza three, yet another person tells someone else to prevent the children from disturbing Michael Angelo while he paints the ceiling of the Sistine chapel. Neither the poet nor the reader is directly involved in the discourses represented on the page. We might represent the discourse situation of this poem as follows:

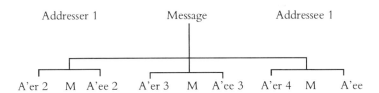

(A'er = Addresser, A'ee = Addressee, M = Message)

In order to be able to interpret the poem successfully we need first of all to be able to recognise the participants who are involved in the text's various sub-discourses. Then we need to work out a *reason* for Yeats's choosing to put these three discourses together as a poem.

So far we have assumed that each participant in the discourse, at whatever level, represents himself or herself uniquely. But this is not always the case, as we can see from the following extract:

Example 4
Do this. Don't move. O'Grady says do this,
You get a move on, see, do what I say.
Look lively when I say O'Grady says.

Say this. Shut up. O'Grady says say this,
You talk fast without thinking what to say.
What goes is what I say O'Grady says.
  (Kingsley Amis, 'The Voice of Authority: A Language Game')

In this poem, Amis uses the format of the children's game 'O'Grady Says' to explore the way in which we often use spurious authority to give weight to what we say. The *persona* who is the main addresser in the poem is apparently conveying the orders of another, the higher authority, O'Grady. But at various points in the speech it becomes clear that the *persona* is really using O'Grady's authority as an *excuse* to order others around in the way that he or she wants. Of course in the children's game, O'Grady does not exist either. He is the fictional excuse for the orders that a child gives to the others playing the game. In real life, we can (i) hand down the words of others directly, (ii) mediate what others say through our own words, possibly distorting the original intent or (iii) pretend that we are representing higher authority merely to get our own way. The possible complexities in this reporting relationship can be seen in the rather topsy–turvy example of the Queen at the beginning of a session of the British Parliament reading out *verbatim* a speech written for her by officials in the government which indicates what policies are to be carried out during that session of Parliament – the discourse is always presented as if she is saying what she has directed the government to do, but in fact it is she who is directed in what to say; in this case who counts as the higher authority becomes a rather difficult matter to decide.

This discussion of what we might call **mixed addressers** has some bearing on Yeats's 'Long–Legged Fly'. We have seen that each stanza has three different addressers (none of whom is the poet) and three different addressees (none of whom is the reader). But the refrain appearing at the end of each stanza adds another level of complexity. Is it really said by the *persona* to whoever he or she addresses; or is this a direct address from poet to reader? And some of what looks at first sight like the words of one or other of the *personae* are almost certainly not. It seems reasonable to assume, in stanza 2, for example, that the *persona* orders someone else *move most gently*. But to be able to give *that the topless towers be burnt/And men recall that face* as the reason for moving gently, the *persona* would require knowledge of what, for that person, are future events (*e.g.* the fall of Troy). So, perhaps we have a mixed addresser here too? Providing answers to these discoursal puzzles are an essential part of providing an overall interpretation for the poem.

2.2.2   Semantic deviation

It is sometimes difficult to keep examples neatly pigeon–holed, especially those at the borderline between semantics and syntax. But for the moment let us define semantic deviation as meaning relations which are logically inconsistent or para–doxical in some way. Metaphors fit into this characterisation (inconsistent semantic relations), as we noticed in 1.1. Here is an example containing obvious paradoxes:

Example 5
Light breaks where no sun shines;
Where no sea runs, the waters of the heart
Push in their tides;
And, broken ghosts with glow–worms in their heads,
The things of light
File through the flesh where no flesh decks the bones.
                    (Dylan Thomas, 'Light Breaks Where No Sun Shines')

In this poem Dylan Thomas confronts us with a series of paradoxes. There is light where there is no sun, flesh where no flesh exists and tides where there is no sea. A major part of the interpretation of the poem thus resides in our imagining a situation where these paradoxes can be resolved. In this sense, poems, especially modern poems, are often rather like cryptic crossword clues. The reader is invited to think up an 'answer' which makes sense of what at first sight looks like nonsense. Another example is the beginning of T. S. Eliot's 'Little Gidding', where we are told that *Midwinter spring is its own season,* and, a few lines later:

Example 6
The brief sun flames the ice, on pond and ditches,
In windless cold that is the heart's heat,
Reflecting in a watery mirror
A glare that is blindness in the early afternoon.

(T. S Eliot, 'Little Gidding')

Cold is defined in terms of heat and intense light in terms of blindness. Eliot also heightens our sense of paradox by exploiting the grammar and semantic relations of the English noun phrase. In noun phrases the material which modifies the head noun, coming either before it or after it, helps us to delimit the reference of the head noun. So, in a phrase like 'the old man wearing a green coat', the noun 'man' possibly refers to any one of a class of beings which we call men. The definite article 'the', the adjective 'old' (both pre–modifiers – *i.e.* coming before the head noun) and the relative clause 'wearing a green coat' (a post–modifier, *i.e.* coming after the head noun) all help to cut down the possible referents to which the head noun can refer. Assuming that the whole phrase is produced in a particular situation, the hearer will probably be able to identify uniquely the individual that the speaker is referring to. But all this rests on an assumption that the modifiers in the noun phrase will be semantically compatible with the head word. It is this assumption which Eliot undermines with *midwinter spring*, *windless cold that is the heart's heat* and *a glare that is blindness*. Eliot is describing a bright, sunny day which is in the middle of winter. The day itself, then, is in a sense paradoxical. It occurs in a period of the year which we associate with coldness and dark, and yet in spite of the wintry conditions (*cf. the ice*) it has features of warmth and light which we associate with Spring. On bright winter days we can often feel quite warm even though the ground is still frozen. These features, along with many others in the poem, help us to see that Eliot is setting up a description of a day which is in a sense outside time. It is both Winter and Spring; and this in turn enables him to use the Spring/Winter opposition to symbolise, a little later in the poem, the opposition between life and death.

Here we can begin to see what is involved in the notion of cohesion of foregrounding. By taking foregrounded items (in this case semantically odd ones) and providing an account which relates them together we begin to construct an interpretation for the poem concerned. If I continue my earlier analogy between poetry and crossword puzzles, cohesion of foregrounding is rather like the process of fitting the clues which we have solved together into the crossword frame. Except that for the interpretation of poems we have to make up the frame ourselves as well as provide solutions for the individual clues. We are constantly involved, then, in framing interpretations which make sense of apparent non-sense and providing pattern and consistency where at first none can be seen. It is this fact which makes much modern poetry difficult to understand; but it is also an integral part of what makes good poetry so valuable. It is precisely by facing us with paradoxes and forcing us to resolve them that poets make us look at the world in fresh and interesting ways.

2.2.3 Lexical deviation

The most obvious examples of lexical deviation are those where a poet makes up a word which did not previously exist. This is usually called **neologism**. One example of this is the word *manunkind* in exercise 2 from Chapter 1. Dylan Thomas is fond of making one word out of two:

Example 7
The boys are dreaming wicked or of the bucking ranches of the night and the jollyrodgered sea.
(Dylan Thomas, *Under Milk Wood*, p. 1)

The jolly ro(d)ger is, of course, the name for the pirates' skull and crossbones flag. Here Thomas runs the two words together to make a compound noun *jollyrodger*. This would already count as a new word, but by adding the −*ed* ending he then converts the whole into a participial adjective *jollyrodgered,* which in turn modifies *sea*. The result of this double invention is a sea which is imbued with piracy and the romantic associations attached to that notion.
The process of converting a word from one grammatical class to another (**functional conversion**) is common in English (*cf.* words like 'strike' and 'bank', which can be nouns or verbs), and so, not surprisingly, we often find new and sometimes rather outrageous functional conversions in English poetry:

Example 8
. . . My heart in hiding
Stirred for a bird, → the achieve of, the mastery of the thing!
(Gerard Manley Hopkins, 'The Windhover')

Here Hopkins takes the verb *achieve* and uses it as a noun, in spite of the fact that English already has a noun, 'achievement' derived from that verb. It is obvious that the word is a noun here because of (i) the preceding definite article, (ii) the *of* apparently beginning a post–modifying prepositional phrase, and (iii) the grammatical parallel with *mastery*. Why does Hopkins bother to make up a new noun when the language has already provided one for him? He is describing the flight of the windhover in all its miraculous splendour. By using the word *achieve* as a noun instead of a verb he foregrounds the extent of the achievement of the bird in flight and also increases the sense of physical energy which we associate with the windhover.

Another way in which writers can produce foregrounding through lexical deviation is by taking words associated with one variety of English and inserting them in a variety where they do not normally belong:

Example 9
Half life is over now,
And I meet full face on dark mornings
The bestial visor, bent in
By the blows of what happened to happen.
What does it prove? Sod all.
In this way I spent youth,
Tracing the trite untransferable
Truss–advertisement, truth.
(Philip Larkin, 'Send No Money')

Larkin is talking about love and sexual relations. In the first part of the poem, the *persona* has described his youth, where he avoided casual sexual relationships because of his quest for romantic love. In his middle age, that attitude now seems silly to him, and he crushes his earlier naive romanticism by the swear word answer *sod all* to his question and by the reference to the truss advertisement. The prototypical view of poetry tends to be a romantic one, whereby only certain subjects (*e.g.* love, nature) and a particular subset of related vocabulary (formal, often archaic) are deemed to be appropriate. This is not to say, of course, that poetry cannot ever be written about more mundane subjects or have informal vocabulary; but poems which break out of the prototypical mould are noticeably deviant. Here, the taboo vocabulary and the semi–taboo subject matter underline the more down to earth, if not cynical, attitude of the middle–aged view of love, as the alliteration connecting *truss, trite* and *truth*, and the odd apposition between *truss–advertisement* and *truth* show.

Exercise 1

Comment on the lexical oddities underlined below, indicating (i) what makes them deviant, (ii) the meanings which you feel result, and (iii) how you managed to arrive at those meanings:

(a)   The Forgettle

(an advertisement for a brand of electric kettle which switches itself off automatically when it boils)

(b)   A windpuff bonnet of fáwn–fróth
Turns and twindles over the broth
Of a pool so pitchblack, fell–frowning,
It rounds and rounds Despair to drowning.

                                          (G. M. Hopkins, 'Inversnaid')

2.2.4 Grammatical deviation

The number of grammatical rules in English is large, and therefore the foregrounding possibilities *via* grammatical deviation is also very large. However, some deviations of word–order have occurred so often in the history of English poetry that they are now associated with our prototypical assumptions about poetry – what we might call 'Poetic poetry' or 'poetry with a capital "P" '. This applies, for example, to the word order inside noun phrases where, in poetry, unlike the rest of modern English, the adjective can come after the noun.[1] In the following two examples, some of the 'Poetic' flavour is imparted by adjectives appearing after the nouns they modify:

Example 10

[1]   O goddess! hear these tuneless numbers, wrung
      By sweet enforcement and remembrance dear . . .
                              (John Keats, 'Ode to Psyche')

[2]   Little enough I sought:
      But a word compassionate . . .
                              (Ernest Dowson, 'Exchanges')

Part of the motivation for *remembrance dear* in [1] and *a word compassionate* in [2] is presumably to adhere to the rhyme scheme that the poet has chosen. But the imparting of a 'poetic' flavour is also appropriate.

The fact that in the twentieth–century the placing of adjectives after nouns is associated with traditional poetry and poetic subject matter means that by using these forms, modern poets can allude productively to the more poetic styles of previous eras. In 2.2.1, I pointed out that Edward Thomas's poem 'Adlestrop' began in a conversational style which contrasted with a more poetic style found later in the poem. This later style is created in part by noun–adjective ordering inside the noun phrase:

Example 11

And willows, willow herb, and grass
And meadowsweet, and haycocks dry . . .
                              (Edward Thomas, 'Adlestrop')

Besides the re–ordering of 'dry haycocks' we can also note the use of archaic lexis (*haycocks* instead of 'haystacks') and the occurrence of nouns to do with nature, a prototypical subject matter for poetry.

Re–orderings are by no means restricted to the noun phrase. Re–sequencing of phrases inside the clause away from the normal subject–verb–object–adverbial order is also prototypical for our notion of poetry:

Example 12

Then spake King Arthur to Sir Bedivere
      (Alfred Lord Tennyson, 'Morte d'Arthur', l. 15)

The subject–verb inversion (*spake King Arthur*) is allied to the archaic pronunciation *spake*.

There are many ways in which poems can deviate from grammatical norms besides the use of re–ordering. English literature abounds with examples, but we will have to make do with just a few. First of all, consider list constructions in English. The rule is that lists of coordinated nouns have the conjunction 'and' suppressed between each pair of nouns except the last. In writing, these deleted 'ands' are replaced by commas. Hence 'cats, dogs and birds' is a normal English phrase but 'cats and dogs and birds' is not, and would be corrected if it appeared in the writing of a student learning English. But we assume that poets have already learnt the rules of their language, and so if they produce such 'errors' we construe them as purposeful. This in turn means that we must work out some appropriate interpretative reason for their breaking the rule. Such is the case with the following description of the flight of a butterfly:

Example 13
He lurches here and here by guess
And God and hope and hopelessness.

(Robert Graves, 'Flying Crooked')

If we compare what Graves wrote with the more normal construction, 'by guess, God, hope and hopelessness', we can see that some of his effect would be lost. Interpolating the *and*s between each noun helps us to notice the nouns individually, like individual beads spaced out on a string. This gives them roughly equal prominence and enables us to perceive more easily the two pairs of oppositions between the nouns, which is also marked by the pairs of alliteration. *Hope* and *hopelessness* are opposites, and this helps us to see that *guess* and *God* can also be construed as opposites, *guess* being connected with uncertainty and *God* with certainty. In more striking, and much more appropriate words, Graves is saying that the butterfly gets where he is going sometimes by luck and sometimes by judgement.

Moreover, this interpretation accounts for the deviant phrase *here and here* (instead of 'here and there'), suggesting that the butterfly keeps turning up in unexpected places, and also for the awkward construction of the poem's last noun phrase:

Example 14
Even the aerobatic swift
Has not his flying crooked gift
>   (Robert Graves, 'Flying Crooked')

where we would normally expect the more balanced
construction 'his gift of flying crooked'. In the manner of our
best poets, Graves manages to have his cake *and* eat it. By
rearranging the word order within the last noun phrase he
adheres to the poem's couplet rhyme scheme and also manages
to enact syntactically the butterfly's awkward flight.

The above example is one where Graves has created a list
construction which has too many *and*s. Here is one which has
none (my emboldening):

Example 15
And there are so many stories to tell, too many, such an excess of
intertwined **lives events miracles places rumours**, so dense a
commingling of the improbable and the mundane!
>   (Salman Rushdie, *Midnight's Children*, p. 9)

In this case the list is just a sequence of nouns with no
intervening 'ands' or commas. The effect of this deviation is
the opposite of the previous one. Instead of being separated
out, the items in the list can be read as 'pushed together' in a
somewhat undifferentiated way. The effect of this list is also
appropriate in the context, as we are told that the items in the
list are densely intertwined.[2]

Exercise 2

(a) Write a couple of stanzas of 'poetic' poetry, getting in as many
     'poetic' features as you can. Then examine what you have written
     to see what makes it 'poetic', concentrating particularly on the
     grammatical features.

(b) Describe the grammatical deviations which you find in the
     following stanzas from Blake's 'The Tyger'. In what way do the
     grammatical oddities contribute to the fearsome qualities of the
     Tyger?

In what distant deeps or skies
Burnt the fire of thine eyes!
On what wings dare he aspire?
What the hand, dare seize the fire?

And what shoulder, & what art,
Could twist the sinews of thy heart?
And when thy heart began to beat,
What dread hand? & what dread feet?

What the hammer? what the chain?
In what furnace was thy brain?
What the anvil? what dread grasp,
Dare its deadly terrors clasp?

2.2.5 Morphological deviation

The lowest unit of syntactic organisation is the word. Phrases consist of words. **Morphemes** are the building blocks for words. 'Bookshelf', for example, consists of two morphemes, 'book' and 'shelf'. These two morphemes can also stand freely on their own as words, and so are usually called **free** morphemes. But not all morphemes are free: for example, the word 'unclean' has two units of meaning, 'clean' and the negation marker 'un–'. Here 'un–' is a **bound** morpheme. 'Un/fortun/ate/ly' has four morphemes (one free and three bound). Incidentally, I have just used a *graphological deviation* in order to indicate where the boundaries between the morphemes are. One way of producing deviation at a morphological level is by adding an ending to a word it would not normally be added to:

Example 16
perhapsless mystery of paradise
(e. e. cummings, 'from spiralling ecstatically this')

Here e. e. cummings is playing on our knowledge that there is an easily extendible morphological series by which we can produce a list of words by adding the suffix '–less' to a noun (*e.g.* 'hopeless', 'hatless', 'sunless'). 'But perhaps' is not normally a noun but an adverb. By comparing *perhapsless* with the normal paradigm we can see that cummings is pointing to an apparently contradictory quality of heaven, namely that it is a mystery with no uncertainty. A similar example, but using an invented 'morpheme' is *museyroom* from James Joyce's *Finnegans Wake*. There is no such thing as a *musey*, but on an analogy with 'bathroom', 'bedroom' etc. it is presumably a room where one museys or puts museys. Given that there is a verb 'to muse' in English and also that the '–y' suffix is often used to give a diminutive flavour to a word (*cf.* 'potty', 'doggy'), one obvious interpretation is that a *museyroom* is a room where one muses a little. It is clear from the context in which the word occurs that *museyroom* is in fact substituting for *museum*, and so we can see that the connotations which we have noted are particularly appropriate.

Another way in which poets can make us contemplate the otherwise unremarked morphological structure of words is by playing around with word boundaries:

Example 17
I caught this morning morning's minion, king–
dom of daylight's dauphin, dapple–dawn–drawn Falcon . . .
(Gerard Manley Hopkins, 'The Windhover')

Here the word *kingdom* is broken over a line boundary (a graphological deviation). As a result we are invited to think harder than usual about the meaning of the two morphemes which constitute the word 'kingdom'. 'King' is obvious enough, but most twentieth–century speakers of English will not be aware that '–dom' is historically the same morpheme as 'doom', meaning 'judgement' (*cf. The Doomsday Book*). Foregrounding both the 'king' and 'judgement' parts of the word has special significance in a poem where Hopkins, through his description of the windhover, is writing a paean of praise to Christ. Educated readers at the time Hopkins was writing were much more aware of word–derivations than most readers are now, and so he could assume that the significance of his foregrounding would not go unnoticed.

The opposite process to separating morphemes off as quasi–separate words is to run more than one word together as if they were one. Although in spoken language words are not normally separated by silences, in English we conventionally write as if there were gaps between the words. This convention is not *necessary*, but merely makes it a bit easier to read what is written. You can test this by writing out a few sentences without gaps between the words and then asking a friend to read out what you have written. An obviously appropriate use of such a deviation can be seen in the poem 'she being Brand' by e. e. cummings, in which he playfully likens making love to driving a car. The manner in which he slams on the brakes, which he parallels with the moment of orgasm, is *Bothatonce*. Removing the gaps between the words makes us feel that the words on the page enact what they mean. Here is another example:

Example 18
'Oh', said Sheila, 'of course you two haven't met. Strange, isn't it, really? Nigeledwin Edwinigel.'
(Anthony Burgess, *The Doctor is Sick*, p.63)

Sheila is introducing her husband to her lover. Running their names together in this way enables Burgess to suggest that Sheila is speaking very fast and as a result we can infer that she is either trying to appear unconcerned or is trying to get the confrontation over as soon as possible. We may even go on to infer that from Sheila's viewpoint there is little to choose between the two men. If we compare the inferential strategies at work in the last two examples we can see how different contextual factors lead us to different, textually appropriate, interpretations of the same linguistic phenomenon.

Exercise 3
_____

Describe the morphological deviations in the underlined parts of the following examples, and try to work out what you can infer based on the deviations:

(a)   – electrons deify one razorblade
      into a <u>mountainrange</u>; lenses extend

      unwish through curving <u>wherewhen</u> till <u>unwish</u>
      returns on its <u>unself</u>.
           (e. e. cummings, 'pity this busy monster, manunkind')

(b)   Corrigan's pulse and <u>varicoarse veins</u>
                (James Joyce, *Finnegans Wake*, p. 214)

(c) Beside the rivering waters of, <u>hitherandthithering</u>
     <u>waters of. Night!</u>

(James Joyce, *Finnegans Wake*, p. 216)

2.2.6 Phonological and graphological deviation

Because the sound dimension of language belongs to speech
and most of our literature is written, there is relatively little
scope for phonological deviation apart from that already
covered under parallelism in Chapter 1 (*e.g.* alliteration,
assonance, rhyme). We can think of examples where words
are pronounced or stressed oddly, *e.g. wind* pronounced as
/waind/ to conform to a rhyme scheme, but in terms of poetic
meaning and effect, these are cases of marginal interest.

On the other hand, because literature is written, the written
equivalent of the phonological level can be much more
liberally and usefully exploited. Indeed, poetry itself is marked
off from other forms of writing by *graphological*[3] means in that
it has lines which do not run out to the right hand edge of
the page and begins all lines with capital letters. In fact some of
the examples we discussed under the heading of
'morphological deviation' (see 2.2.5 above) depend themselves
on deviation at the graphological level. As with deviation at
other linguistic levels, we are led to make inferences about the
meaning and significance of the deviation. Often, because of
the relations between writing and speech, these inferences
have to do with how we might read the text out loud, and
this in turn leads to deductions about meaning.

In 'Crow's First Lesson' by Ted Hughes, God is trying to
teach Crow to speak by getting him to pronounce the word
'love'. The absurd Crow tries harder and harder but only
succeeds in being sick, and in the process creates the world in a
manner which is the antithesis of the account given in the
book of Genesis in the Bible. God tries time and again to get
Crow to say 'love', and even though he does not lose his
temper, we do sense his exasperation:

Example 19
[1] 'Love,' said God. 'Say, Love.' (stanza 1)
[2] 'No, no,' said God, 'Say Love. Now try it. LOVE.'

(stanza 2)

[3]   'A final try,' said God. 'Now, LOVE.' (stanza 3)
             (Ted Hughes, 'Crow's First Lesson')

The capital letter in the first three instances of the word *Love*
indicate that it has to have some kind of special
pronunciation. Given the teaching situation God is in, if we
read the poem out loud we are likely to make the
pronunciation very clear and deliberate. Then, when we
come to the version of the word written in capitals we must
give it an even more marked phonetic form, perhaps by saying
it louder, more slowly and with a very wide pitch span. The
repetition and the increasingly deviant *graphological* forms lead
us to an interpretation with an increasingly marked *phonetic*
form. This in turn leads us to infer a reason for the change:
God is becoming more and more exasperated at his unGodlike
failure to cope with Crow's education.

Example 20
. . . now sing each and all fortissimo A–
mer
i

ca, I
love,
You...
             (e. e. cummings, 'Poem, or Beauty Hurts Mr Vinal')

In this example, the splitting up of *America I love you* forces us
into a phonetic interpretation where the syllables are somehow
'pronounced separately'. This might be realised either by
having small pauses at the end of each line, or alternatively by
lengthening the vowels in the relevant syllables. Another very
likely result will be the equalisation of stresses among the
various syllables. And all this will lead many readers to
recognise that the words are a quotation from a famous
patriotic American song where these sorts of pronunciation
features occur. Given that these lines occur in a poem which
is critical of the American life style we are led to realise that
cummings is making an ironic comment on the naive
simplicity of the song and those who sing it without thinking.
    Not all graphological deviation is relatable to some phonetic
reality, however. In the first of T. S. Eliot's group of poems
called 'Preludes' the last line of the 13–line text is set apart

graphologically from the rest in order to help the reader notice that the tone of that line contrasts with the rest of the poem. Michael Horovitz uses graphological deviation to represent the descent to hell visually on the page:

Example 21
– Think you're in
Heaven?
Well – you'll soon be
in H
   E
   L
   L –
     (Michael Horovitz, 'Man–to–Man Blues')

Another kind of example can be seen in the following poem by Ted Hughes:

Example 22
Looking close in the evil mirror Crow saw
Mistings of civilisations   towers   gardens
Battles he wiped the glass . . .
     (Ted Hughes, 'Crow's Vanity')

Here, the oddities have to do not with sound, but with an absence of punctuation and larger than normal spacing between some words as Hughes enacts a point of view – the manner in which Crow *perceived* what he saw (for an extensive discussion of point of view see Chapter 8). The large gaps between the noun phrases in the second line of the extract suggest that when Crow looked in the mirror he did not notice at once all of the things reflected there. Rather, he first noticed the mistings of civilisations, and then, after a time, he became aware of the towers, and so on. In retrospect the reader may well interpret the 'space' between the end of the first line and the beginning of the second in the same way.

By way of contrast, a new syntactic sentence begins at the second word of the third line, but there is no large gap, full stop or capital letter. Given the perceptual interpretation I have suggested so far, a natural characterisation of the fact that there is no orthographic 'space' to indicate the new sentence beginning with *he wiped the glass* is that when Crow sees the battles he wipes the glass *immediately*, presumably because he does not like what he sees and hopes to remove the 'visual distortion' by his action.

Most of the examples of deviation that I have discussed have been from poetry because deviations form an important part of what is involved in reading and understanding poetry. But such features are by no means the exclusive province of poetry, or of literature for that matter. Similarly, most of my examples have been from relatively modern texts, but what I have said applies in general terms to literature of all ages. This is true even for graphological deviation, which many might believe to be a phenomenon associated with modern concrete poetry. George Herbert exploited graphological deviation interestingly in the seventeenth–century, and examples of it can even be found in ancient Greek poetry. Graphological deviation also occurs in abundance in Sterne's novel *Tristram Shandy*, the first two books of which were published in 1759. When parson Yorick dies Sterne includes two totally black pages in mourning. Later, we are enjoined to:

Example 23
Read, read, read, my unlearned reader! Read – or by the knowledge of the great saint *Paraleipomenon* – I tell you beforehand, you had better throw down the book at once; for without *much reading*, by which your reverence knows I mean *much knowledge*, you will no more be able to penetrate the moral of the next marbled page (motley emblem of my work!) than the world with all its sagacity has been able to unravel the many opinions, transactions, and truths which still lie mystically hid under the dark veil of the black one.
                (Lawrence Sterne, *Tristram Shandy*, Book III, Ch. 36)

As we read we are almost certain to treat *marbled page* as a metaphorical construction meaning something like 'a page of writing in a grand and stylish manner'. But when we come to the next page, it really does turn out to be a printed marbled page, with no words at all. In the next example, Dr Slop is discussing possible difficulties in delivering babies while he is attending the birth of the narrator, Tristram:

Example 24
. . . Sir, if the hip is mistaken for the head – there is a possibility (if it is a boy) that the forceps ★★★★★★★★★★★★★★★★★★★★★★★★★★★★★★

** — What the possibility was, Dr *Slop* whispered very low to my father, and then to my uncle *Toby*. — There is no such danger, continued he, with the head. — No, in truth, quoth my father — but when your possibility has taken place at the hip — you may as well take off the head too.

(Lawrence Sterne, *Tristram Shandy*, Book III, Ch. 17)

The asterisks indicate graphologically the doctor's whispering and its inordinate length. Choosing asterisks, which are conventionally used to mark important points in a text, also helps to suggest the socially delicate nature of the information which Tristram is overhearing at this rather inopportune moment. It is easy to infer from the context what awful calamity might happen to the male baby, but Sterne's representation of it in this way helps to make it amusing.

Exercise 4

Analyse the graphological and phonological deviations in the following poem, relating what you discover to meaning and effect:

ygUDuh
      ydoan
      yunnuhstan

      ydoan o
      yunnuhstan dem
      yguduh ged

      yunnuhstan dem doidee
      yguduh ged riduh
      ydoan o nudn

LISN bud LISN
            dem
            gud
            am

lidl yelluh bas
tuds weer goin

duhSIVILEYEzum

(e. e. cummings, 'ygUDuh')

2.2.7 Internal and external deviation

It will be useful at this point to introduce a distinction made
by Levin (1965) between **internal** and **external deviation**.
So far we have been dealing with *external* deviation, that is
deviation from some norm which is external to the text.
Indeed, our examples have been almost exclusively related to
one particular system of norms, namely the rule–system which
constitutes the English language. It should take no more than
a moment's thought, however, to see that deviation from
other kinds of norms are also possible. When e. e. cummings
begins his poems with lower case letters at the beginning of
each line, he is not breaking a rule of English. Rather, he is
deviating from a *genre norm*, that for poetry. If, after years of
writing poems with lines beginning in lower case letters, he
suddenly wrote a poem which conformed to our genre norm,
in this respect he would still surprise knowledgeable readers of
his poetry, as he would now have deviated from his personal
authorial norm which he had established over a long period of
writing. The examples of archaism which I have sometimes
referred to deviate from *period* norms: for example words no
longer in use in modern English can be introduced .for
particular effects. I mention these other kinds of deviation
from external norms merely in order that you should be aware
of them. There is not enough space in this book to examine
deviations from all these external norms in any detail. Instead,
we will turn to the important phenomenon of *internal*
deviation.

Internal deviation is deviation against a norm set up by *the
text itself*. Very often, internal deviation is the reverse side of
the coin from parallelism. This is because a predictable pattern
has to be established before it can be deviated from. Suppose
that a poem is written in rhyming couplets, but then the fifth
couplet does not rhyme. The rhyme is a pattern of parallelism
at the phonetic level, which is then broken at stanza five. This

stanza will thus be foregrounded as a result of the internal
deviation. Now let us look at an example:

Example 25
The stranger lighted from his steed,
And ere he spake a word,
He seiz'd my lady's lily hand,
And kiss'd it all unheard.

The stranger walk'd into the hall,   (5)
And ere he spake a word,
He kiss'd my lady's cherry lips,
And kiss'd 'em all unheard.

The stranger walk'd into the bower –
But my lady first did go, –   (10)
Aye hand in hand into the bower,
Where my lord's roses blow.

My lady's maid had a silken scarf,
And a golden ring had she,
And a kiss from the stranger, as off he went   (15)
Again on his fair palfrey.

(John Keats, 'Song')

If we look at stanzas one and two we can see that there are
extensive parallels between them in terms of grammar and
partial lexical repetition:

[S=subject; V=verb; O=object; A=adverbial; Cj=conjunction]

Lines 1 & 5:	The stranger		lighted	from his steed
	The stranger		walk'd	into the hall
	S		V	A

Lines 2 & 6:	And	ere	he	spake	a word
	Cj	A	S	V	O

Lines 3 & 7:	He	seiz'd	my lady's lily hand
	He	kiss'd	my lady's cherry lips
	S	V	O

Lines 4 & 8:	And	kiss'd	it	all unheard
	And	kiss'd	'em	all unheard
	Cj	V	O	A

The first line of stanza three conforms to the pattern established in the previous two stanzas, and so we expect the next line to be *And ere he spake a word*, as before. But instead we get *But my lady first did go*. This is a very obvious point of internal deviation and hence foregrounding. What explanation can we give for Keats deviating at this point from the pattern he has set up? If we look carefully at the first two stanzas we can also see that the stranger is consistently portrayed as the *active participant* by being indicated as the subject to dynamic transitive or intransitive verbs[4] (transitive: *spake, seiz'd, kiss'd* [repeated three times]; intransitive: *lighted, walk'd*). On the other hand, phrases referring to the lady, or parts of her, consistently occur in object position and so she is portrayed as being *acted upon* rather than as an actor in her own right. Hence at first sight it appears that the stranger is making all the running in what is presumably an illicit love affair with the lady, a relationship which is consistent with the medieval convention of Courtly Love, to which the poem alludes. Line 10 begins with the contrastive *But*, a word which prepares us to look for an opposition with what has gone before, and when we examine the structure of the clause in that line we see that for the first time the lady is subject to a verb of action and that she leads the stranger into the bower. She is portrayed explicitly as an active participant in the love—making at the very point where they retire into the lady's private room. This helps to explain the *persona's* sense of shock seen in the exclamatory structure of line 10. The coincidence of two kinds of internal deviation thus mark the most important narrative moment in the poem, a moment when our assumptions about the relationship between the characters are dramatically altered.

It will be clear by now that we expect foregrounded stretches of text to carry special interpretative weight, particularly when, as in the above example, the foregrounding is very marked. But what happens if no good interpretative reason for the foregrounding can be found?

Consider 'October Dawn' by Ted Hughes. In this poem Hughes portrays the month of October as the beginning of winter. The movement towards winter is itself seen as the beginning of a movement which will take us back to the ice–age. The ice–age, in turn, represents forces antagonistic to humanity and human emotions. The pleasant autumn image which begins the poem, 'October is marigold' thus becomes an insidious beginning of a terrible end. The poem is written in half–rhyming couplets (*e.g.* *yet/out; if/heave; ice/place*). But there is internal deviation in the last stanza, which has the text's only full rhyme:

Example 26
. . . while a fist of cold
Squeezes the fire at the core of the world,

Squeezes the fire at the core of the heart,
And now it is about to start.
                              (Ted Hughes, 'October Dawn')

The last stanza is also foregrounded for a number of other reasons. Its first line is the second part of a vary marked two–part parallelism, its second line is the last of the poem (and therefore inevitably attracts some degree of foregrounding), and this line is also the climactic end of a series of lines related together by adverbial linkers (*First . . . Soon . . . Then . . . And now . . .*). But the content of the poem's last line hardly seems to deserve all this foregrounding, as it says nothing that we cannot already have deduced from the rest of the poem. As a consequence I feel somewhat let down at the end of the poem, experiencing an effect often called **bathos**. Perhaps you can find a sensible justification for the foregrounding. In that case you will have done better than I have interpretatively, and at the same time will have helped to make 'October Dawn' an even better poem than it already appears to be.

Exercise 5

Examine the following anonymous English ballad for internal deviation, explaining how this deviation contributes to the meaning and effect of the whole. The refrain which is printed at the beginning and end of the ballad is also repeated after each two–line verse; it is omitted in this version to save space. Note that *Make* = 'mate', or 'love' and *may* = 'maid', 'maiden']

Lully, lulley! Lully, lulley!
The falcon hath borne my make away!

He bare him up, he bare him down,
He bare him into an orchard brown.

In that orchard there was an halle,
That was hanged with purple and pall.

And in that hall there was a bed,
And it was hanged with gold so red.

And in that bed there li'th a knight
His woundes bleeding day and night.

At that bed's foot there li'eth a hound,
Licking the blood as it runs down.

By that bed-side kneeleth a may,
And she weepeth both night and day.

And at that bed's head standeth a stone,
Corpus Christi written thereon.

Lully, lulley! Lully, lulley!
The falcon hath borne my make away!

(Anonymous, 'The Falcon')

2.3 More about parallelism

In Chapter 1 we noticed that parallel structures can prompt
readers to infer parallel meanings between those structures.
Now we need to take the study of parallelism further. First of
all, consider the following extract from a poem describing a
town in winter:

Example 27
And now a gusty shower wraps
The grimy scraps
Of withered leaves about your feet
And newspapers from vacant lots;

(T. S. Eliot, 'Preludes: 1')

I have often asked my students what associations spring to their minds when they read *a gusty shower* in line 1. After noting the connotations of wet and wind which are obvious from the words of the phrase itself, they usually go on to suggest that the rain has a dirty quality, unlike, for example, the cleansing rain we associate with Spring. This association is not automatically a part of the meaning of the phrase and yet many readers will agree that *in this poem* the association is there. Where does it come from? One conceivable answer is that it comes from general world knowledge – the scene described is that of a town in winter, and so the grime in the air would become mixed with the rain. But this *situational* explanation, although attractive at first sight, has its drawbacks. My students do not normally associate cold with the phrase, for example, and yet winter rain in England is almost always cold. A better explanation is afforded by the parallelism of *a gusty shower* with *the grimy scraps* of the next line. These two phrases have exactly the same overall grammatical structure (determiner–adjective–noun) with the adjective in each case being two syllables long and having the –*y* adjective ending. They are also parallel phonetically because of the alliteration between *gusty* and *grimy* and the partial alliteration between *shower* and *scraps*. Moreover, it is interesting to note that the two lines rhyme in a poem which has a very irregular rhyme scheme, and that Eliot seems to have made a point of ending line 2 with *scraps*. Besides enabling the rhyme, this lineation takes the first part of what is actually a longer noun phrase, *the grimy scraps of withered leaves* and, by giving it a line of its own, makes it look at first sight as if it is a completed phrase. Eliot has thus gone to considerable trouble to make the parallelism between the two phrases obvious, and if we apply the 'parallelism rule' (see 1.2.2) of trying to make the two phrases 'equivalent' in some way, we can do it by taking the meaning of *grimy* over to *gusty shower* as an added association. In other words, parallelism often gives us a motivation for deciding which associations are appropriate for a given word or phrase. This is an important matter, as the area of word–association is one of the most vexed in literary criticism. Different readers can have different associations for the same word in the same context and it is often difficult to decide which associations are reasonable and which are not. Similarly, the same word or phrase appears to be able to have different, even opposing associations in different texts, and this fact needs to be explained. Parallelism is one of the mechanisms which writers have at their disposal for controlling the associative connections which readers make.

We can see parallelism at work in another example from 'Preludes: I'. In other contexts, the word *newspapers* may have associations which do not seem relevant here, for example a newspaper can be seen as an organ of communication or propaganda, a thick folded object on the news–stand or what comes through the letter–box in the morning. For me *newspapers* brings with it personal associations of tea in bed, as my wife and I always start the day by reading the newspaper in bed while drinking tea. I would suggest that neither my personal association nor the more general ones I have mentioned here are relevant in 'Preludes: 1'. Rather, if you ask people to give you associations for the word *in this particular context* you will find a broad measure of agreement that the newspapers are old, dirty, yellowing or even brown with age, and tattered and torn into fragments. How is it that the 'standard' associations for *newspapers* are suppressed and these others are enlivened in their place? Again parallelism plays an important role. Note that *the grimy scraps / Of withered leaves* and *newspapers from vacant lots* are parallel to one another in that they are both objects to the verb *wraps* (in a rather odd grammatical structure, with the adverbial phrase *about your feet* intervening between the two object phrases). Once we have noticed this, we can see that the associations for *newspapers* mentioned above are all more obviously present in *the grimy scraps / Of withered leaves*. These aspects (*grimy* = dirty; *scraps* = tattered and torn; *withered* = old and yellow or brown) are then carried over onto the newspaper phrase as the 'parallelism rule' is applied. It is often said of poetry that it opens up associations for words that they do not have in other contexts. Parallelism is one of the devices which are used by writers to *open up* associations; but it is important to note that, at the same time, it also *suppresses* other, non–relevant aspects of meaning. It is thus an essential device of *poetic control*.

So far we have only looked at parallelism between pairs of items, and parallelism of form resulting in parallel meaning. But the role which parallelism plays is wider than this. The 'parallelism rule' might be better characterised as follows: 'if two structures are obviously parallel in linguistic form look for a semantic relation as well'. Consider Pope's description of the lady Narcissa:

Example 28

A fool to Pleasure, and a slave to Fame:
Now deep in Taylor and the Book of Martyrs,
Now drinking citron with his Grace and Chartres.
Now Conscience chills her, and now Passion burns;
And Atheism and Religion take their turns;
A very Heathen in the carnal part,
Yet still a sad, good Christian at her heart.

(Alexander Pope, 'Epistle II: "To a Lady"', 62–8)

The first line of this quotation contains two parallel noun phrases which are opposed to one another. This is the first of a series of pairs of parallels, all of which enter into a relationship of opposition. Taylor's works were devotional, and Foxe's *Book of Martyrs* was a rather extreme anti–papist description of the deaths of a series of Protestant martyrs. Hence this line has to do with things religious. The next line, which is parallel to it, describes opposing, worldly activities. Citron was brandy flavoured with lemon peel, and Chartres was a usurer and libertine. The next line contains two more structures paralleled and contrasted (*cf. chills* vs *burns* and *Conscience* vs *Passion*). In the last two lines the *sad, good Christian* is opposed to the *very Heathen* in terms of parts of the body. The relationships throughout this extract, then, are of quasi–antonymy. As we noticed with the quasi–synonymic relations in the parallelisms discussed in Chapter 1, the items that enter into the relationship do not have to be formally related in the semantic structure of English. Their mere presence in the parallel structures is enough for us to want to construe them in that way. Thus, *Conscience* and *Passion* are not opposites in English, but they *are* opposites in the above quotation.

In the next extract, each line has a parallel structure within it, and each parallel pair contains an opposition:

Example 29

I can love both fair and brown;
Her whom abundance melts, and her whom want betrays;
Her who loves loneness best, and her who masks and plays;
Her whom the country form'd, and whom the town;
Her who believes, and her who tries . . .

(John Donne, 'The Indifferent')

The last four lines are all parallel to each other grammatically and can be interpreted as having roughly the same meaning (quasi–synonymy), a meaning which itself involves a contrast (quasi–antonymy) within each line.

The last of a series of three or more items is often perceived as climactic, particularly if it differs in some formal way from the rest of the series through internal deviation (*cf.* my suggestion in 2.2.7 that internal deviation is in some ways the reverse side of the coin from parallelism). A particularly clear example is:

Example 30
She is a woman, therefore may be wooed;
She is a woman, therefore may be won;
She is Lavinia, therefore must be loved.
(William Shakespeare, *Titus Andronicus*, II, i, 82–4)

The syntactic structure is held constant throughout, as is the alliterative relation between the complement of the first clause and the main verb of the last clause in each line. But the last line substitutes the specific *Lavinia* for the more general *woman* and the more insistent *must* for *may*. We thus see Lavinia as more important and paradoxically, because she is such an attractive *individual*, as containing all of the most beguiling attributes of women in general. Indeed, she has all of those qualities *and* something extra – what we might call 'the Lavinia factor'.

On the basis of what we have now seen, we could rewrite the 'parallelism rule' as follows: 'When readers come across parallel structures they try to find an appropriate semantic relationship between the parallel parts.' This is often a relationship of quasi–synonymy or quasi–antonymy, but other relations are also possible. This rule is not a hard and fast one. We can find parallel structures where it is not very easy to perceive the semantic relations I have been talking about. Rather, what we are describing is a *processing tendency* on the part of readers. If a parallelism of a reasonably obvious kind exists, readers will try to find a semantic motivation for that parallelism. Parallelism is an important tool for the writer in exercising control over the reader: (i) it helps readers to perceive some associations and not others, (ii) it pushes readers towards perceiving semantic relations between words and phrases which do not exist as such in the language system as a whole, and (iii) by relating parts of a text together it acts as a powerful force in the cohesion of foregrounding.

Exercise 6

(a) Examine the role which parallelism plays in the following poem:

> Glory be to God for dappled things —
>   For skies of couple–colour as a brinded cow;
>   For rose–moles all in stipple upon trout that swim;
> Fresh–firecoal chestnut–falls; finches' wings;
>   Landscape plotted and pieced – fold, fallow, and plough;
>   And áll trádes, their gear and tackle and trim.
>
> All things counter, original, spare, strange;
>   Whatever is fickle, freckled (who knows how?)
>   With swift, slow; sweet, sour; adazzle, dim;
> He fathers–forth whose beauty is past change:
>   Praise him.
>
>   (Gerard Manley Hopkins, 'Pied Beauty')

(b)   Examine the role which parallelism plays in 'Long–Legged Fly' by W. B. Yeats, which is quoted in full in 2.2.1.

2.4 Meaning, style and choice

If we step back for a moment from what we have discovered about deviation and parallelism, it should become apparent that **linguistic choice** is at the base of what we have been exploring. When authors invent deviant structures they *choose* structures which are outside the bounds of some norm–system, which, very often, is the system of rules provided by their language. When they choose to produce parallel structures, they do not step outside the linguistic norm–system, but instead choose the same structure more than once in a short space. In both cases the choices made produce the effect of foregrounding. But it is important to notice that the phenomenon of linguistic choice does not just relate to foregrounded phenomena. The less foregrounded features of texts still have an important role to play in the generation of meanings and effects, and choosing one word rather than another will certainly make some difference. For example, if I choose to refer to my mother by using the word 'mum' rather than 'mother' I have not necessarily produced a point of foregrounding, but I have made a linguistic choice, which may well affect, for example, the formality of my utterance. It is important, then, when we are analysing texts, to compare what is *actually written* with what *might have been written* – that is, alternative structures which the author could have used to represent roughly the same meaning, but which were rejected in favour of the eventual choice. By comparing what occurs with *what might have occurred* we can arrive at more sensitive interpretations of the texts we read. One way in which we can demonstrate this is by comparing published versions of poems with earlier drafts which the poet discarded. Here is the first few lines of a well known war poem by Wilfred Owen, followed by an earlier draft of the same lines:

Example 31

[1]   **Anthem for Doomed Youth**

>   What passing–bells for these who die as cattle?
>   Only the monstrous anger of the guns.
>   Only the stuttering rifles' rapid rattle
>   Can patter out their hasty orisons.

A previous version of the poem ran as follows:

[2]   **Anthem for Dead Youth**

>   What passing–bells for you who die in herds?
>   – Only the monstrous anger of the guns!
>   And only the stuttering rifles' rattled words
>   Can patter out your hasty orisons.
>
>   (Wilfred Owen, 'Anthem for Doomed Youth')

The change from *dead youth* to *doomed youth* in the title may not seem to be very different at first point. But *doomed* is better for two reasons. Firstly, it provides an assonance relation (a parallelism) with *youth* and thus brings out more forcefully the contrast between the hopeful *youth* and their imminent early death. Secondly, *dead* means that the young men are already dead, but *doomed* presupposes that they are not yet dead but suggests that they are bound to die. The funeral anthem thus becomes more horrific, as it is being presented before the people for whom it is written have actually died

The first line of the earlier version contains a direct address to the young men, whereas in the final version the addressee is someone else, who is, by default, the reader (see Chapter 9.2.3). In the final version, then, the moral and religious questions are addressed more directly at us. The simile at the end of the line is also changed from *in herds* to *as cattle*. The first version, by making the overt comparison with *herds*, suggests that the salient part of the simile is the large quantity involved. But the final version is preferable as it allows a more direct comparison between men and cattle, prompting the reader to conjure up associations from the abattoir. *Herds* are live groups of animals and so tend to be associated with open fields and the rural life. The change from *herds* to *cattle* also entails a change in line 3, because of the rhyme scheme Owen has chosen for the poem. Again, the change is a fortuitous one as it allows a rhyme with *rattle* and forces the deletion of *words* and the insertion of another word before the rhyme—word. This enables Owen to use the noun phrase *stuttering rifles' rapid rattle* which is well known for its startling and sustained onomatopoeia.

By comparing these two versions we can see Owen working his way towards a particularly appropriate and effective set of linguistic choices. Of course we do not always have earlier manuscript versions of poems in front of us when we are analysing them but it should be clear that comparing what the poet writes with related alternatives helps us to be able to express more accurately the meanings and effects which we feel in the lines.

This process of comparison often raises a particular question in my students' minds. Was Owen consciously aware of what he was doing when, for example, he changed *dead* to *doomed*. My reply to that would be 'No, I don't expect that he was, although he could have been.' Although poets weigh their words considerably more carefully than most of us, it is unlikely that Owen could have been consciously aware of all the tiny choices that he made as he wrote, any more than we are aware of choosing between one word and another, or one structure and another, when we speak. But at some sub—conscious, intuitive level he must have made the choices he did, and it is difficult to believe that the choices were made randomly.

In the long run, though, I do not think that it is very important to know whether the choice was conscious, sub–conscious or accidental. What matters rather more is that the choice *was* made. And by comparing what occurs on the page with near equivalents which could have occurred, we can identify more precisely meanings and effects which we can intuitively agree on, but which otherwise we would find difficult to state explicitly.

Exercise 7

Compare the choices made by W. B. Yeats in the three versions of the first stanza of 'Leda and the Swan'. He wrote (A) first, (B) second, and finally the version seen in the complete text of the poem (C):

A Now can the swooping godhead have his will
   Yet hovers, though his helpless thighs are pressed
   By the webbed toes; and that all–powerful bill
   Has suddenly bowed her helpless face upon his breast.

B A rush, a sudden wheel, and hovering still,
   The bird descends, and her frail thighs are pressed
   By the webbed toes, and that all–powerful bill
   Has laid her helpless face upon his breast.

   A sudden blow: the great wings beating still
   Above the staggering girl, her thighs caressed
   By the dark webs, her nape caught in his bill,
   He holds her helpless breast upon his breast.

   How can those terrified vague fingers push
   The feathered glory from her loosening thighs?
   And how can body, laid in that white rush,
   But feel the strange heart beating where it lies?

   A shudder in the loins engenders there
   The broken wall, the burning roof and tower
   And Agamemnon dead.
                        Being so caught up,
   So mastered by the brute blood of the air,
   Did she put on his knowledge with his power
   Before the indifferent beak could let her drop?
                        (W. B. Yeats, 'Leda and the Swan')

Exercise 8

Being as systematic as you can (perhaps using the kind of layout
which I used in Chapter 1 for the analysis of 'Wants' by Philip Larkin,
attempt a full stylistic analysis of one, or more, of the following poems
(not quoted here for reasons of space):

(a) The first of Eliot's 'Preludes'

(b) 'yes is a pleasant country' by e. e. cummings

(c) 'This Bread I Break' by Dylan Thomas

Discussion of exercises

Exercise 1

(a) *The forgettle* is a blend of two words, 'forget' and 'kettle'.
This is made possible because the first syllable of *kettle* and
the last syllable of *forget* are almost identical (even the /g/
and /k/, although not identical sounds, share two out of
three distinctive phonetic features and so are as alike as
two different sounds could possibly be). [5] Given that the
word is a lexical blend and that the picture on the
advertisement is of a well known brand of kettle – one
which switches itself off and has a distinctive shape – the
neologism is understandable as 'the kettle you can forget'.
By using the newly–coined word the advertisement
produces that meaning in a fresh and original way.

(b) *Twindles* is one of Hopkins's neologisms. A likely
interpretation is that it is a blend of the verbs 'twine' and
'dwindle' as it shares their phonetic characteristics and the
meanings of the two verbs are both appropriate. The froth
on the stream is falling down a waterfall into a lake, and so
it can be seen as turning round and round and apparently
dwindling in size as it falls further and further away from
the observer. This poem is discussed in full in Short and
van Peer (1988).

Exercise 2

(a) The following features are typical of 'Poetic' poetry: line–
initial capitalisation; a regular rhyme scheme; inversion of

adjective and noun inside the noun phrase (*e.g.* 'lady fair') and of various phrases within the structure of the clause; use of 'thou', 'thee', 'thy' as second person singular pronouns instead of *you*; particular subject–matters like love, the countryside and the natural world, and appropriate lexical choices; archaic lexis (*e.g.* 'haycock', 'whilom'); poetic spellings (*e.g.* 'ere' instead of 'ever').

(b) The major deviant grammatical feature in the stanzas from 'The Tyger' is that of the deletion of grammatical elements and a concomitant effect of compression and the feeling of hidden power which is reinforced by the lexical choices. The verb *aspire* of line 3 normally requires a following 'to–' phrase. Line 4 can be normalised to something like 'What is the hand which would dare to seize the fire?' or 'What sort of a thing is the hand that would dare to seize the fire?' It is possible to have a stab at what elements are missing because most of the missing information is grammatical in nature, and even in line 3, where we need to provide some lexical information too, the context gives us some indication of what might be appropriate. But in much of the rest of the quotation this is not really the case. A much more dramatic form of syntactic deletion has taken place so that on four occasions sentences are reduced to 'What' plus an associated noun phrase. In other words, we are not given enough information to work out the form of the proposition which is being asked about by the poem's *persona*. Hence we could legitimately ask 'What dread hand and what dread feet *what*?', 'what the hammer *what*?', 'what the chain *what*?', 'what the anvil *what*?' The resultant uncertainty on the part of the reader is likely to increase the sense of fear and awe of the Tyger.

Exercise 3

(a) cummings runs *mountainrange* together as one word presumably because he wants to see what is represented as one undifferentiated concept. This example is not enormously different from the normal construction. More interesting is the running together of *where* and *when* to form a singular concept of time and space. The prefixing of the negation marker *un–* onto *wish* and *self* is also morphologically deviant and helps to prompt the reading that the lenses of the microscope or astro–

telescope led human beings to discover things which they did not want to know about and which then undermine human aspirations.

(b) The first example from *Finnegans Wake* involves a blend of a word (*varicose*) and a phrase (*very coarse*) which are phonetically similar. Hence *varicoarse veins* has an overall meaning which blends the two aspects together: 'very coarse varicose veins.'

(c) *Hither and thither* is run together and then *–ing* is added to the end to turn the whole into a participial adjective which modifies *waters*. The to and fro movement of the water is then seen as one complex movement rather than a series of connected smaller movements. In addition the syntax and graphology are at odds with one another in *waters of. Night!*, helping to give special climactic emphasis to *Night!*

Exercise 4

Let us first of all 'translate' the deviant spelling line by line:

1. you've got to
2. you don't
3. you understand
4. you don't know
5. you understand them
6. you've got to get
7. you understand them dirty
8. you've got to get rid of
9. you don't know nothing
10. listen bud listen
11. them
12. god
13. damn
14. little yellow bas–
15. –tards we are going
16. to civilise them

By 'translating' the written representation in this way we can provide a base for comparison with the poem's deviant graphology. It is then easier to abstract the explicitly racist and antagonist propositions that the *persona* is putting forward, namely 'We've got to get rid of those goddamn dirty little yellow bastards' and 'We are going to civilise them.' The rest of the words of the text represent ripostes to the words of the *persona*'s unknown interlocutor (*e.g.* 'you don't know nothing'), explicit moves to prevent the other person from speaking ('listen bud listen') and repetitions of parts of the formulation of the two very simple statements. It can be seen from this evidence alone that cummings is portraying his racist *persona* in an extremely ironic light. Because we are not given any of the words of the *persona's* interlocutor (see 2.2.1), and because the *persona* explicitly prevents the other person from speaking, the person who is speaking (presumably male, given the use of the male–to–male address form *bud*) is represented as having a closed mind. This, combined with the unreasonableness of what he says, indicates that cummings intends us to disapprove of the *persona* and his views.

The graphological deviations involve mis–spellings (*e.g. sivileyez*), the running of more than word together into one (*e.g. ygUDuh*), the splitting of words across line boundaries (*e.g. bas/tuds*), and improper use of capitalisation (*e.g. ygUDuh*). We infer that these deviations represent (i) pronunciation features of the *persona* (for example splitting up *gudam* across a line boundary helps indicate a slowed–down pronunciation and possible equalised stress; *doidee* represents a working class American (New York?) accent) and (ii) his uneducated (and hence unthinking?) qualities. We know that cummings would have no difficulty spelling 'civilize', and so *SIVILEYEzum* must be a representation of the *persona's* inability to cope with the English spelling system (in spite of the fact that he is talking, not writing). The various graphological infelicities combine with non–standard grammatical features, swear–words and **normally non–fluent speech features**[6] to ram home the uneducated, unthinking qualities of the *person*. Apart from being a very striking example of the use of graphological deviation, this poem is also a good example of a poet's use of stereotypes. There is no necessary relation between being uneducated and being unthinking or being a working–class New Yorker and having racist views. But these features are stereotypically used in setting up the web of disapproval which characterises this poem.

Exercise 5
For an interesting analysis of this poem, with which I largely concur, see Cluysenaar (1976: 68–72). What follows are comments which are additional to Cluysenaar's analysis or help to clarify points that she makes. Her account comments

particularly on the lexical characteristics of the poem and merely presupposes or ignores various important facts of syntactic organisation. From line 5 onwards, each stanza begins with a fronted prepositional phrase acting as an adverbial which contrasts with the normal SVOA order set up in the clauses of the refrain, and the first, introductory stanza. In the next section of the poem the prepositional phrase repeats a word from the right–hand side of the previous stanza in each case, with each new lexical item being inside the previous one in terms of semantic relations. This helps to produce the 'zoom–in' camera effect which Cluysenaar notes, foregrounding the last stanza of the sequence, namely stanza 4, the one where the knight is described. A whole series of changes take place at this point in the poem, making it very foregrounded in terms of internal deviation: the tense of the verbs in the first line of each stanza change from past to present and their aspect changes from simple to continuous; the verb *to be* is replaced by a series of intransitive verbs; the complement of the verb changes from inanimate to animate. From this stanza onwards, in Cluysenaar's terms, the camera 'pans round', and the lexical repetition which takes place is from one stanza–initial fronted prepositional phrase to the next with a semantic progression upwards. This progression, which is also reflected in the verb choice (*lieth, kneeleth, standeth*) produces another climatic focus on the last item in the new series, the final stanza. This stanza in turn deviates internally from previously established patterns. The complement phrase at the end of line 1 reverts from animate back to inanimate, forcing a reinterpretation of the meaning of *standeth*, and the second line of this stanza contains the only passive construction in the poem, forcing *Corpus Christi* into a prominent position at the end of the line. There are thus two major points of foregrounded prominence in the poem, the stanza where the knight is introduced and the last one, where we are told that the knight is Christ.

Exercise 6
'Pied Beauty' is often thought to be a difficult poem, and at first sight it would appear so, with its syntactic compression, metaphors, neologism and relating together of very different things. The key to the poem, however, is a pervasive scheme of parallelism, and once this parallelism has been unlocked much of the poem's difficulty falls away. The first line, *Glory*

be to God for dappled things is simple enough. The next line is a prepositional phrase which parallels the prepositional phrase in the first line. It can be understood as having 'parallel meaning' with that phrase – the sky, like the brindled cow is of two colours (*i.e. dappled*). So are the *rose–moles all in stipple* (the multi–coloured spots on the side of the trout) in line 3. The same parallelism continues in line 4 onwards, except that the initial *for* in each case is deleted and hence 'understood'. Even if you do not know anything about the parti–coloured patterns on finches' wings, it is obvious from the parallel scheme that you need to construe an interpretation where they have at least two colours. The same interpretative parameters apply throughout the first stanza. The head noun of each parallel noun phrase is generic, and in most cases plural, pushing us towards a generalised interpretation.

The second stanza begins a new sentence, but the parallel structure continues. Hence we can understand the first line by 'supplying' *Glory be to God for . . .* , and so on. The reason for the stanza division is to mark a *widening in the scope* of the parallel items. In the first stanza the dappled quality is applied to things which could be visually perceived. That restriction no longer applies, and so the meaning of *dappled* is now widened metaphorically to include many different kinds of multi–facetedness or contrast. The parallel scheme ends at line 9 and is replaced by a series of contrasts themselves embedded in smaller, line–internal parallel constructions, all of which act as rather unusual manner–adverbials related to the neologised verb *fathers–forth*. The command to praise God in the last line is thus predicated on a series of variegated, contrasting and often contradictory attributes of the world which God has created and hence God himself.

This poem also contains an example of the possibility of more than one interpretation at a relatively delicate level of interpretation, where either meaning can be successfully integrated into the overall structure and interpretation of the text. In line 4 the syntactically compressed and reorganised *fresh–firecoal chestnut falls* can be understood to mean either (i) 'chestnuts which have fallen from the firecoals' (*i.e.* roasted chestnuts, which will be a mixture of colours, the brown of the skins, the black of the burnt parts and the red of the still–burning sections), or (ii) 'chestnuts which have fallen from the trees like fresh firecoals' (in this version, the chestnuts are parti–coloured as the husks split when they hit the ground, revealing three colours, the brown of the nuts, and the green (outside) and white (inside) of the husks. Either of these two 'mini–interpretations' fits the scheme of parallels. Whole poems can, of course, have more than one interpretation, but much of what commentators call different interpretations can be accounted for by this kind of variation at a detailed level of analysis.

Exercise 7

A discussion of the differences among the three versions of the first stanza of 'Leda and the Swan' can be found in Greenfield (1967).

Exercise 8

(a) A discussion of this poem can be found in Short (1982a).

(b) A discussion of this poem can be found in van Peer (1986: 70–2).

(c) A discussion of this poem can be found in Leech (1970).

Notes

1. The placing of adjectives after the noun in poetry is often characterised as an archaic usage. However, it appears never actually to have been a feature of English. Rather, it was borrowed from French into *English poetry* after the Norman conquest and can be found as a regular feature in poetry (but not prose) from that time.
2. For a more detailed discussion of the interpretation of various sorts of list construction see Short (1986).
3. For a more advanced discussion of graphological foregrounding in poetry, see van Peer (1993).
4. Prototypically, transitive and intransitive verbs are dynamic, 'referring' to actions. Transitive verbs are 'goal directed' and so take both a subject and an object (*e.g.* 'John ate the banana'), whereas intransitives are not, and so do not take an object (*e.g.* 'John ran'). nothing needs to join.
5. For a description of the articulatory features of English speech sounds, see 4.2 and Knowles (1987: Chs 2–3).

6. Descriptions of the phenomenon of normal non–fluency can be found in Leech, Deuchar and Hoogenraad (1982: 139–43), and Leech and Short (1981: 161–6).

Further reading

The readings for Chapter 1 are also relevant for this one. Leech (1969: Chs 3–5) covers similar ground to this chapter. Van Peer (1986) is an account of an empirical investigation into foregrounding in poetry, and van Peer (1993) looks in particular at graphological foregrounding in poetry.

CHAPTER 3

Style variation in texts

3.1 Style variation in English

In 2.2.3 we noticed that poets can produce surprise effects by importing into a text a word belonging to another variety of language. In this chapter we will examine the way in which some writers make systematic use of such **style variation,** that is, variation from one identifiable kind of English (*e.g.* formal, informal) to another within the same text. In the process we will analyse two relatively simple poems by Philip Larkin and Edward Thomas, and then look at a more complex example by Henry Reed. In carrying out the analyses we will be making use of the intuitive knowledge which we possess of different varieties of language and the linguistic features which distinguish them.

It might be argued that style variation is merely another kind of foregrounding produced through the device of internal deviation discussed in the last chapter, and in a sense it is, as internal deviation clearly occurs. But so far we have used the notion of foregrounding to apply to the perceptual highlighting of very small portions of text (words, phrases or lines) and the idea that a large section of a poem might be foregrounded because it varies in style from previous sections is not so appealing intuitively. The foregrounding effect is likely to be strong in the first few words of the new style, but will then fade away. This makes it difficult to believe that a long stretch of text can all be foregrounded in this way. Consequently, I have decided to treat style variation separately.

Without being consciously aware of it, native speakers of English can perceive language varieties associated with **dialect** (*e.g.* regional dialects, class dialects, men's *vs* women's language, adult *vs* child language), **medium** (*e.g.* written *vs* spoken language), **tenor** (*e.g.* formal *vs* informal language, accessible *vs* inaccessible language) and **domain** (*e.g.* the language of advertising, legal language, the language of instruction and the language of science). I will not provide a comprehensive account of language variation here, but below I give a brief account of the concepts just referred to in order to contextualise the discussion of literary texts which follow in 3.2 onwards. Your intuitive knowledge of language variation should allow you to follow the discussion of the texts without too much difficulty, and if you want to explore language variation more fully, references are provided in the notes and further reading sections at the end of this chapter.[1]

3.1.1 Language variation: dialect

Dialectal variation in relation to what part of the country people come from is probably the most well known kind of language variation. However, there is a tendency for many people to equate dialect with accent (phonetic variation). It is often possible for us to infer roughly where someone comes from by listening to their accent. Just about everybody in England intuitively knows, for example, that Northern and Southern varieties of British English differ in their pronunciation of the 'a' and 'u' vowels. Hence, in general terms, 'bath' is pronounced /baθ/ in the North and /baːθ/ in the South, and 'bus' is pronounced /bus/ and /bʌs/ respectively (see the appendix for a guide to the pronunciation of phonetic symbols). But dialect variation can involve variation at any linguistic level. *Lexical* variation can be illustrated by the fact that the word 'hill' in the South of England may be replaced by 'fell' in the North or 'tor' in the South–west, and *morphological* variation by the fact that although the past tense of the verb 'treat' is generally formed by adding the '–ed' ending it can be 'tret' in some dialects. There is also a striking, though probably apocryphal, tale concerning *grammatical* dialect variation. The word 'while' is a conjunction used to introduce subordinate clauses of time in Southern forms of English, as can be seen in sentences like 'I waited while he fed the cat'. But in many Northern varieties it can also be a preposition with roughly the same meaning as 'until' in Southern varieties. The story goes that just after the traditional crossing gates at rail/road junctions had been replaced by a system of flashing lights to indicate to car drivers that a train was coming, a Northerner driving a car arrived at a rail crossing. The sign next to the lights said 'Wait While Lights Flash', and the driver waited until the lights began to flash before attempting to cross the line, with disastrous consequences.

So far the examples of dialect variation I have used have come from within England. But it should also be remembered that various world varieties of English (*e.g.* Scottish English, American English, Indian English, Australian English) are also essentially dialect forms, and that writers may well make use of our intuitive knowledge of these dialects in their writing, for example in the creation of individual voices for particular characters in novels or plays. The notion of dialect is also not restricted to geographical location. Any group variation which is semi–permanent is dialectal. We also find social–class dialects (note, for example, that /n/ instead of /ŋ/ at the ends of words like 'hunting' is a marker both of some working–class and some upper–class dialects). Arguably, language variation related to gender and age can be thought of as dialectal.

In the terms that I have been using so far, so–called Standard English (the English spoken, for example, on BBC news broadcasts) is also a dialect, if a rather pervasive one. Because it can be found right across Britain it is not particularly related to region (though there is evidence of Northern, Scottish and Irish standards, varying from Standard Southern English mainly in pronunciation). However Standard English is clearly related to education, and hence indirectly to social class. I began life as the son of working–class parents in rural Sussex, and grew up speaking a Sussex country dialect. But the experience of grammar school and university education gradually changed my dialect to Standard English with some residual working–class Sussex country accent characteristics. Thus someone's dialect can change, but the change normally takes a long time. This is why I have called dialect a semi–permanent phenomenon.

3.1.2 Language variation: medium

We have noted that the dialect we speak is a semi–permanent characteristic of our language behaviour. We can change our dialect if we want to, but it takes a lot of time and effort. However, the kind of language we produce also changes from moment to moment during each day, depending upon what we are doing. One example of this more transient kind of variation is variation according to the *language medium being used*. The most pertinent distinction here is that between speech and writing. Spoken language is unrehearsed and produced for external consumption at very high speed. As a consequence it is full of 'performance errors' (*e.g.* hesitation noises like 'um' and 'er', unnecessary pauses and repetitions, and false starts). In writing, which normally takes place at a more leisurely pace, and with the opportunity to rework what we say before it is exposed to others, these performance characteristics of speech are considered to be infelicitous, and so are ironed out. But there are also other systematic differences between speech and writing. Because our short–term memory is only seven or eight words long, there is a tendency for speech to consist of short and relatively simple sentences, and to involve structures like main clause co–ordination, which enable the speaker to finish one part of the sentence as a separate unit before moving on to the next part. Writing, on the other hand, does not involve short–term memory constraints, and so written sentences are often considerably longer and more complex. The opening sentence of Conrad's short story 'The Secret Sharer' is 66 words long, and near the beginning of Act 2 of Faulkner's novel *Requiem for a Nun*, there is a sentence which is more than a page long.

Some speech can be more like writing than ordinary conversation. Political speeches and lectures are often written out in order to be spoken, and so take on some of the characteristics of written language. It is also possible to write in ways which are more like spoken English than normal, and, other things being equal, this kind of writing seems more informal than other written language.

3.1.3   Language variation: tenor

Another way in which our language can vary from one moment and context to another is in relation to the *tenor* of discourse. Leech, Deuchar and Hoogenraad (1982: 9) define tenor as having to do with 'the relationship between a speaker and a hearer, [. . .] often characterised by greater or lesser formality'. Typically, then, we choose our tenor to suit our relationship with the people we are talking to. We will use more technical vocabulary when talking to people who share the same level of understanding, and more accessible, 'common core' vocabulary when talking to those who are not equally qualified (members of the medical profession are thus likely to use, say, 'tibia' when talking to colleagues and 'shin bone' when talking to patients). Similarly, we will use direct and informal language with friends and close family members, and more formal, indirect language with those we are not so close to, or who we feel are in a superior social position. This can be most easily seen when someone uses language inappropriate to a particular social situation. There is a story concerning the philosopher Bertrand Russell's first utterance as a young child when his mother asked him if he was all right after an accident. He is said to have replied, 'The pain, madam, has somewhat abated.' The formal verb 'abated' and the vocative 'madam' suggest a considerably wider social distance than would be normal between a young child and his mother.

Social distance is something which can be negotiated through talk. I remember, some years ago, witnessing a conversation between the Vice–Chancellor of my university and the President of the Students' Union (I have changed the names in what follows to protect the innocent). The Vice–Chancellor repeatedly called the student 'Mr Smith', suggesting a formal and respectful relationship, and the student responded by calling the Vice–Chancellor 'Mick', indicating a much more close and informal relationship. Both participants were obviously engaged in a form of social engineering.

3.1.4   Language variation: domain

Language variation according to domain, that is **subject matter** and/or **function**, is one of the easiest kinds of variation to perceive. Let us begin with subject matter. Legal language automatically involves legal terminology (*e.g.* 'plaintiff', 'tort'), and the language of science is also well known for its specialist lexis (*e.g.* 'neutron', 'positron'). Linguistics, literary theory and stylistics all have their specialist vocabularies too. Much of mine is emboldened and explained in this book, because I am assuming that stylistics is relatively new for many of my readers. In other words, I am trying to make my technical terminology accessible to you.

There is clearly a relationship between subject matter lexis and **accessibility**. Many specialist vocabularies, like the terminology of science, linguistics or the law, will be inaccessible to the ordinary reader. But we should remember that to some extent what counts as technical depends upon who we happen to be. Almost all 'ordinary readers' have access to some specialist vocabularies, as well as to 'common core' words like 'table' and 'chair', but what counts as specialist terminology will vary from one person to another. Many students of literature have become so used to the technical vocabulary of literary criticism (*e.g.* 'genre', 'metaphor') that it no longer seems technical to them, even though many others would find it inaccessible. To accuse someone of 'using too much terminology' is thus a dangerous business. If you are not careful you can, in turn, easily find yourself being accused of the same thing.

Contrary to the belief of many school students, specialist terms are not usually invented to make the life of others difficult, but to help experts be as clear, precise and unambiguous as possible in discussion. For this reason, I would certainly like any surgeon who might operate on me to be fully in command of his technical vocabulary as well as his scalpel – 'tummy' might well not be precise enough. But it is clearly important to make sure that those you communicate with also understand the specialist vocabulary you use.

As with the kinds of style variation discussed above, variation according to domain is not restricted to the lexical level of language. For example, there is a well known tendency in the language of science to use what are called **passive** sentence constructions, with the '*by* + agent' phrase deleted. Hence, at school, when students learn for the first time to write up scientific experiments they have performed in class, they are told not to write **active** sentences like 'John put the copper sulphate in the test–tube', but to replace them with sentences of the form 'The copper sulphate was placed in the test–tube'. It is important for science to stress the fact that experimental results will be the same as long as the experiments are replicated exactly, no matter who performs them. If we use active sentences, the agent responsible for the action is the subject of the sentence, and English grammar makes it very difficult for us to omit the subject. However, passive constructions put the 'receiver' or 'goal' of the action in subject position, the agent appearing in the optional '*by* + agent' phrase, thus allowing the 'personal' aspect of the action to be removed, and the description of the experiment to appear more objective.

To some extent, what counts as a subject matter varies depending upon our knowledge and purposes. The language of science, for example, can easily be subdivided into the language of physics, the language of biology, and so on, even though there will be overlaps. Interestingly, some subject matters and their characteristic language are only available to most of us through verbal art. A good example of this is the language of espionage, to which, by definition, very few of us have access through direct experience, but with which we are now all familiar through spy fiction and spy films.

So far, we have talked of language variation according to domain only in terms of subject matter. But another way in which the domain of language can vary is in terms of the *function*, or purpose to which language is being put. We can talk of the language of advertising, for example, not because there is a particular subject matter associated with advertising – advertisements can be about almost anything: cars, clothes, food, holidays, and so on – but because there is a consistent function, namely to persuade us to buy some product or service. This consistent function leads to typical linguistic characteristics, just as a consistent subject matter will. Hence we expect advertisements to repeat the name of the product, and to contain descriptive words with positive connotations. There are also typical grammatical constructions, for example the uncompared comparative, as in the slogan 'Persil washes whiter'. Here, although we have a comparative construction we are not told what it is that Persil is being compared with. Whiter than what? The power of this kind of construction for the advertising copy writer is that it enables the viewers or readers of the advertisement to complete the comparative construction subconsciously with whatever product they happen to use. Because advertising and poetry share some functional aspects (*e.g.* the need to be striking, and to affect their readers emotionally) they share some typical features, in particular foregrounding effects produced by linguistic deviation and parallelism (see Leech 1966a: Chs 20–22). If we think about passports and identity cards, we can see that their tabular graphological structuring is related to the function of making it easy for an official looking at the document to process rapidly the information it contains. In Leonard Cohen's poem 'All there is to know about Adolph Eichmann', Cohen uses the identity card format in the first part of the poem to describe Eichmann, a Nazi who sent thousands of Jews to their deaths in World War II, as a very ordinary 'Mr Average' in physical terms. He then uses this characterisation to undermine the unthinking assumption that nice people look nice and monsters look monstrous.[2]

3.2 Literature and dialect

The majority of English literature is written in Standard English, which thus counts as the norm. Characters speaking non–standard dialects in novels or plays stand out from the rest, and if a poet chooses to write in a non–standard form this often counts as a socio–political act of some kind. In the advertisement to his collection called *Lyrical Ballads* in 1798, Wordsworth was being revolutionary in his description of his collection of poems as being 'written chiefly with a view to ascertain how far the language of conversation in the middle and lower classes of society is adapted to the purposes of poetic pleasure'. Wordsworth's experiment might seem rather tame when we actually read his poetry, especially when compared with the modern dialect poetry of Tom Leonard or Valerie Bloom, or the first–person working–class Belfast narration of Frances Molloy's *No Mate for the Magpie* (which begins 'Way a wee screwed up protestant face an' a head of black hair a was born, in a state of original sin. Me ma didn't like me, but who's te blame the poor woman, sure a didn't look like a catholic wain atall'). But that is because Wordsworth was one of the first in a long line of writers reacting to the literary dialect norms of their day, and later writers in the tradition can afford to be more adventurous.

In exercise 4 of Chapter 2 we have already noticed that writers of poems and novels can use deviations from the orthographical system to suggest particular accents (the sound stratum of dialect). Not surprisingly, if we look at the texts examined there in terms of other linguistic levels, we find that dialect is represented at those levels too. When the *persona* in cummings's 'ygDUh' says *LISN bud LISN*, for example, readers will recognise the vocative *bud* as a working–class American word, equivalent to 'mate' in many British English dialects. The extract from *No Mate for the Magpie* above also uses orthographical deviation and special lexis (*e.g. wain*), this time to suggest a Northern Ireland dialect. Examples of dialect invocation at the grammatical level can be seen in the following extract :

Example 1

Mrs Bryant:	Time drag heavy then?	(1)
Stan:	Yearp time drag heavy. She do that. Time drag so slow, I get to thinkin' it's Monday when it's still Sunday. Still, I had my day gal I say. Yearp. I had that all right.	(5)
Mrs Bryant:	Yearp. You had that an' a bit more ole son. I shant grumble if I last as long as you.	
Stan:	Yearp. I hed my day. An' I'd do it all the same again, you know that? Do it all the same I would.	(10)
Mrs Bryant:	Blust! All your drinkin' an' that?	
Stan:	Hell! Thaas what kep' me goin' look. Almost anyways. None o' them young 'uns'll do it, hell if they will. There ent much life in the young 'uns. Bunch o' weak–kneed ruffians. None on 'em like livin' look, none on 'em! You read in them ole papers what go on look, an' you wonder if they can see. You do! Wonder if they got eyes to look around them. Think they know where they live? 'Course they don't, they don't you know, not one. Blust! the winter go an' the spring come on after an' they don't see buds an' they don't smell no breeze an' they don't see gals, an' when they see gals they don't know whatta do wi' em. They don't!	(15) (20) (25)

(Arnold Wesker, *Roots*, II, i)

In this conversation the Norfolk dialect of the two characters is indicated not just by deviant spellings, but also by a number of grammatical markers. The third person present tense of the verbs has no final '–s' marker, as it would in Standard English (*time drag heavy*); adverbs are sometimes realised by the corresponding adjective form (*time drag so slow*); the preposition 'of' is replaced by *on* (*none on 'em*); the tag form '(do you) see' is replaced by *look* (*thaas what kep' me goin', look*); and double negatives are introduced (*they don't smell no breeze*).

The above examples of dialect representation suggest characterisation, and are relatively straightforward. More interesting are cases where dialect presentation is used as a vehicle to express thematic meaning. We can see this at work in the following poem by Philip Larkin:

Example 2
On shallow straw, in shadeless glass,
Huddled by empty bowls, they sleep:
No dark, no dam, no earth, no grass –
Mam, get us one of them to keep.

Living toys are something novel,
But it soon wears off somehow.
Fetch the shoebox, fetch the shovel –
Mam, we're playing funerals now.
(Philip Larkin, 'Take One Home for the Kiddies')

This very simple poem explores two attitudes to the treatment of pets. The first viewpoint is that of the adult and the second is that of the child. Through the contrast Larkin implies that the *persona* in the poem feels considerable guilt at his or her proxy involvement in the ill–treatment of the pets at the hands of the children. Part of his mechanism for expressing these contrasts is our intuitive knowledge of the dialect features associated with class, region and age.

The first three lines of each stanza are written in Standard English. If we were trying to place the variety we would be likely to classify it as adult, middle–class, educated language, open to speakers over a wide geographical area in Britain. The last line of each stanza, which in both cases is marked off graphologically from the preceding lines by the use of italics, exhibits a variety of language which is unusual, or **marked**, for poetry It appears to be echoic of the language of working–class, Northern children.

Let us begin with the italicised lines. The fact that the lines are intended to be representative of spoken language is indicated by the use of the vocative construction *Mam* in both lines, the imperative request structure in line 4 and the adverbial *now* in the last line of the poem. The particular vocative used indicates that the speaker in the last line of each stanza is a child addressing his or her mother, and the pronunciation indicates a Northern accent. The grammar of line 4, *get us one of them to keep* instead of 'get us one of those to keep' is consistent with many working–class varieties of English, including those from Yorkshire and Lancashire.

The attitude towards the pets expressed in the italicised lines is typical of young children in its egocentricity. In the first stanza the first three lines indicate from an adult perspective that the life of the pets in the pet shop is uncomfortable. The child in the last line does not notice this, but is entirely consumed by the desire to have a pet. In the second stanza, the third line, *fetch the shoebox, fetch the shovel* assumes as contextual knowledge that the parent in the poem has bought a pet for the child and that the pet has died. This, coupled with the earlier statement indicating that the pet has been ignored as the novelty wore off, leads us to infer guilt on the part of the adult *persona*. The feeling of complicit guilt is contrasted ironically with the attitude of the child, for whom the pet has again become novel. As it is dead, a new game can be played with it, the funeral game.

Exercise 1

Analyse as carefully as you can the features which indicate Mrs Goodall's dialect in the extract below. Is it an accurate reflection of the dialect being represented? Does it matter whether it is or not? What function do you think the dialect representation has in the passage?

Mrs Goodall was a large woman with smooth–parted hair, a common, obstinate woman, who had spoiled her four lads and her one vixen of a married daughter. She was one of those old–fashioned powerful natures that couldn't do with looks or education or any form of showing off. She fairly hated the sound of correct English. She *thee'd* and *tha'd* her prospective daughter–in–law, and said:
   'I'm none as ormin' as I look, seest ta.'
   Fanny did not think her prospective mother–in–law looked at all orming, so the speech was unnecessary.
   'I towd him mysen,' said Mrs Goodall, ''Er's held back all this long, let 'er stop as 'er is. 'E'd none ha' had thee for *my* tellin' – tha hears. No, 'e's a fool, an' I know it. I says to him, "Tha looks a man, doesn't ter, at thy age, goin' an' openin' to her when ter hears her scrat' at th' gate, after she's done gallivantin' round wherever she'd a mind. That looks rare an soft." But it's no use

o' any talking: he answered that letter o' thine and made his
own bad bargain.'

(D. H. Lawrence, 'Fanny and Annie')

3.3   Literature   and   medium

Literature is prototypically written language, but writers often
create special effects by writing in ways which borrow
characteristics associated with speech. Here is an example from
the beginning of a novel where the narrator is apparently
involving himself in a conversation with the reader:

Example 3
You must go back with me to the autumn of 1827.
   My father, as you know, was a sort of gentleman farmer . . .
(Anne Brontë, *The Tenant of Wildfell Hall*, Ch. 1)

The direct address to the reader and the monitoring phrase *as
you know* suggest a conversation between intimates, helping us
to feel close to the narrator.

The most obvious examples of written language trying to
imitate spoken language are, of course, when novels and plays
represent talk between their characters. But we should not
assume that novelistic and dramatic conversations are exactly
like real speech, precisely because the 'speech' is written, not
spoken, and so is bound to take on some of the 'orderliness' of
written language. How realistic conversation in the novel can
be is discussed in Leech and Short (1981: 159–73). How
realistic character talk can be in plays is discussed in 6.3 below.

3.4   Literature   and   tenor

Our knowledge of the **appropriate** variety of language for a
particular situation, formal language for formal situations,
informal language for informal situations and so on, is used to
good effect in Dickens's characterisation of Mr Chadband in
Bleak House. Mr Chadband is a lay preacher who cannot stop
preaching:

Example 4
'My friends,' says Chadband, 'we have partaken in moderation'
(which was certainly not the case so far as he was concerned) 'of
the comforts which have been provided for us. May this house

live upon the fatness of the land; may corn and wine be plentiful
therein; may it grow, may it thrive, may it prosper, may it
advance, may it proceed, may it press forward! But, my friends,
have we partaken of anything else? We have. My friends, of
what else have we partaken? Of spiritual profit? Yes. From
whence have we derived that spiritual profit? My young friend,
stand forth!'

    Jo, thus apostrophized, gives a slouch backward, and another
slouch forward, and another slouch to each side, and confronts
the eloquent Chadband, with evident doubts of his intentions.

    'My young friend,' says Chadband, 'you are to us a pearl,
you are to us a diamond, you are to us a gem, you are to us a
jewel. And why, my young friend?'

    '*I* don't know,' replies Jo. 'I don't know nothink.'

                     (Charles Dickens, *Bleak House*, Ch. 19)

Mr Chadband is at a tea party with his friends, and at this
point he is addressing the crossing–sweeper, Jo, a poor
unfortunate who has been brought in off the street to be
cross–questioned about an incident in which he has been
involved. Even though he is talking first to his friends, the
Snagsbys, and then to Jo, Mr Chadband uses the extremely
formal and rhetorically patterned language associated with the
pulpit. The inappropriateness of the tenor of his speech is
made very clear in the contrast with the simplicity of Jo's reply
to Mr Chadband's rhetorical questions. Besides the lexical and
grammatical indicators of inappropriate formality, Mr
Chadband's speech is discoursally inappropriate, as my use of
the word *speech* shows. We expect conversations between
friends to have short, frequently changing turns. But Mr
Chadband's turns are long speeches, where he positively deters
intervention on the part of others. One indication of this is
his recurrent use of rhetorical questions, which are not meant
to be answered by anyone other than himself. Indeed, some of
the comedy of the piece is provided by Jo's ignorance of the
form. He treats one of those rhetorical questions as if it was a
real one, thus inadvertently interrupting Mr Chadband's flow.

    The notion of tenor can easily be extended to apply to the
relationship between writer and reader, as well as to that
existing between characters in a fictional conversation. The
writer/reader relationship is most easily seen in novels where
the author apparently addresses the reader. In *Tom Jones*,
Henry Fielding talks to his reader formally and respectfully at
the beginning of each book of the novel:

Example 5
The reader will be pleased to remember that at the beginning of
the second book of this history we gave him a hint of our
intention to pass over several large periods of time in which
nothing happened worthy of being recorded in a chronicle of
this kind.

In so doing we do not only consult our own dignity and ease
but the good and advantage of the reader . . .

(Henry Fielding, *Tom Jones*, Book 3)

Fielding's polite attitude towards his reader is seen not just in
the care he apparently takes to look after his reader's best
interests, but also in the formal third person reference to the
reader. Below, however, is a very different writer/reader
relationship:

Example 6
Try to foresee now everything that might make you interrupt
your reading. Cigarettes within reach, if you smoke, and the
ashtray. Anything else? Do you have to pee? All right, you know
best.

(Italo Calvino, *If on a Winter's Night a Traveller*, Ch. 1)

Here the tenor is much more informal, almost impolite. The
writer gives the reader orders about how to get comfortable
before beginning to read, asks very personal questions and uses
informal, even slightly taboo vocabulary. The last sentence also
indicates informality because it pretends that a conversation is
taking place in which the reader has responded to the question
which the writer has just asked. Here, then, we see the
dimensions of tenor and medium interacting. Giving a written
text conversational qualities helps to make it more informal, in
this case engineering a closer relationship between writer and
reader.

3.5 Medium and tenor intertwined

In terms of tenor, poetry prototypically uses formal language.
This is partly because it is expected to be serious, and so a fairly
formal tenor is appropriate. But poetry (particularly short lyric
poetry) is also characteristically a *written* form which does not
attempt to evoke characters and this fact about medium also
pushes poetry towards formality. This does not mean, of

course, that all poems, or all parts of poems, will exhibit only writing characteristics. It is possible for poets to depart to some extent from the language of writing, and as a consequence to alter the tenor of their writing, in order to create particular strategic effects:

Example 7

Yes, I remember Adlestrop –	(1)
The name, because one afternoon	
Of heat the express train drew up there	
Unwontedly. It was late June.	
The steam hissed. Someone cleared his throat.	(5)
No one left and no one came	
On the bare platform. What I saw	
Was Adlestrop – only the name.	
And willows, willow herb, and grass,	
And meadowsweet, and haycocks dry,	(10)
No whit less still and lonely fair	
Than the high cloudlets in the sky.	
And for that minute a blackbird sang	
Close by, and round him, mistier,	
Farther and farther, all the birds	(15)
Of Oxfordshire and Gloucestershire.	

(Edward Thomas, 'Adlestrop')

Although it is a poem, 'Adlestrop' (which we have referred to before in 2.2.1 and 2.2.4) begins with a written representation of relatively informal spoken language, a representation which continues throughout the poem's first stanza. In the first line, the use of the initial *yes*, which normally occurs in a 'second–turn' position in conversation, indicates that spoken language is being represented and that the 'I' of the poem is replying to someone else's question. The dash at the line–end is easily understood as a pause, and the noun phrase at the beginning of line 2 represents a partial reformulation of *Adlestrop* in line 1. The speaker changes his mind. It is not Adlestrop, the place, that he remembers but the rather strange name. This kind of reformulation is typical of spoken language, where we have to produce language very fast and so sometimes have to recast what we say. Written language typically has longer and more complex structures than speech, and it is certainly the case that in the first two stanzas the structures we find are short and simple. In addition, the lexis is simple and everyday (the only exception being *unwonted*), and the line units are broken up by a series of major syntactic boundaries in the middle of the line.

After this 'conversational' tone in the first two stanzas, we find that in the second half of the poem Thomas changes to an overtly poetic style. There is thus a major internal deviation which needs to be explained, which we will return to after noting the linguistic features which mark this more formal, poetic style. The subject matter changes to things pastoral, as shown in lexical items like *willows, meadowsweet* and *blackbird* and an absence of the train terminology seen in the first stanza. Also absent are the positively conversational features of the first stanza, like the reformulations (note that what is *not* present in a text is sometimes as significant as what *is*, particularly if what is missing is something we have been led to expect). The sentences now become longer and a little more complex. Archaic lexis and grammar are present in *haycocks dry, no whit less still* and *cloudlets*.

If you read this poem out loud to yourself you should be able to notice that you react automatically to the change which takes place in the middle of the poem by changing your reading voice. When I read the poem out loud, the second half generally comes out at a slower, more even pace than the first half, a littler higher pitched and with a smoother, less gravelly voice quality than the first half. These are the sorts of voice features which we feel are appropriate to 'poetic' poetry. By way of contrast, the first half of the poem will be read in a voice felt to be appropriate to 'conversational' English, less smooth, less evenly paced, lower pitched and with a more gravelly voice quality. Another interesting difference is that you will tend more towards vowel reduction in unstressed syllables in the first half of the poem than in the rest. The occurrences of vowels in *and* and *was*, for example, will all be reduced to /ə/in the first two stanzas, whereas some of the *and*s in stanzas 3 and 4 will be less reduced, and *than* at the beginning of line 12 is more likely to be pronounced /ðan/ than /ðən/. The fact that others who have read the poem a few times (but have not analysed it)will also produce a voice–quality contrast like the one I have suggested, is evidence that readers react intuitively to the style variation in the poem even though they may not be consciously aware of it.

What is the purpose of this change which takes place half-way through the poem? The answer lies in the change in subject matter and in the syntax of the beginning of stanza 3. This stanza consists of one long noun phrase which we have to integrate into some 'statement' or clause structure to be able to interpret. The easiest way to do this is to 'borrow' the structure of the first stanza. What is described in stanza 2 thus becomes part of a catalogue of *what I saw* which was started in stanza 1 (*cf.* the same kind of interpretative move in my discussion of Hopkins's *Pied Beauty* [Chapter 2, exercise 6]). So, although the poem's *persona* says at first that the only thing he saw was the name *Adlestrop*, he then goes on to indicate that he saw a lot of other things besides, things which, unlike the ordinary, unimportant objects in the railway station itself, have a much larger significance for us, namely the various elements of the natural world in the surrounding idyllic countryside. This interpretative move in turn helps us to see why Thomas makes the stanza divisions he does. The first two stanzas are conversational and about man–made matters, the name *Adlestrop*, the railway station and the train. The midway break between the second and third stanzas marks the change to more pastoral matters. The third stanza describes things close to the railway station, whereas the final stanza expands what is 'seen' to include a wide sweep of the surrounding countryside which could not literally have been perceived by the *persona*. The fields and flowers seen from the train thus become representative of the countryside as a whole, and remind us of the traditional pastoral idyll for which we yearn, particularly in a modern, mechanised age. What was at first sight an insignificant arrival at a small railway station has become an experience to value and remember.

Exercise 2

Return to Mr Chadband's speech quoted in this section and examine it in more detail for linguistic features representative of formal 'pulpit language'.

3.6 Literature and domain

We saw in 3.1.4 that subject matter and function had consequences for linguistic structure. We also noted, with an example from spy fiction, that our assumptions about domain–related language might be formed not from encounters in the real world but from interacting with verbal art. Our reading of John Le Carré and others leads us to assume that fictional spies, and hence real spies, will use the technical terminology of espionage. This assumption in turn means that language variation according to domain can be used for characterisation and also for parody. In the excerpt from a Stephen Fry and Hugh Laurie sketch below, two intelligence officers in London are discussing the fact that Firefly, a secret agent in Berlin, has sent them an urgent message:

Example 8

Hugh: Firefly is under deep cover. Has something quite
             important happened to make him break it like this?
Stephen: Well, that was the first thought that crossed my
             mind, Tony, certainly. It looks as if his network has
             been penetrated by an enemy agent.
Hugh: Oh no.
Stephen: Yes, I'm afraid so. All his men have been arrested.
             Glow–worm was shot attempting to cross over into
             the west and Firefly himself is hiding up somewhere
             in the east.
Hugh: So the whole network has been blown?
Stephen: That's right. It's a thundering nuisance.
Hugh: It certainly is. Thundering.
Stephen: I'm severely vexed, I don't mind telling you.
Hugh: I expect a coffee would come in welcome then.
                 (Stephen Fry and Hugh Laurie, 'Spies One',
                            A Bit of Fry and Laurie, p. 8)

The use of technical lexis like *deep cover* and code names for the agents clearly places us as onlookers of a conversation between intelligence officers. The humour derives from the fact that the code names also allow Hugh and Stephen to distance themselves from the desperate difficulties which the agents are in, so that they can talk about them as if they were two civil servants discussing mere administrative inconveniences.

Metaphorical and humorous effects, can also be achieved through describing something in terms which are normally reserved for another subject domain. For example, in 'she being Brand', e. e. cummings describes the act of sexual intercourse using the kind of language we would normally associate with driving a car, forcing us to see sexual relations in a disturbing and yet amusing new way.

3.7 An extended example of style variation

We have already dealt with language variation according to domain inside a text without noting it explicitly, when we examined 'Adlestrop' in 3.5. The reason that lexical items to do with trains and the countryside respectively occur in the two stanzas is because Thomas has chosen to write about the subject matters with which those items are associated. The grouping of lexical items into associated areas of vocabulary are referred to by linguists as **lexical** or **associative fields**. In 'Naming of Parts', Henry Reed, a World War II poet, produces a systematic series of contrasts between the lexical fields associated with war and the natural world. In so doing he also exploits our intuitive knowledge of military language and the language of instruction:

Example 9

To–day we have naming of parts. Yesterday,	(1)
We had daily cleaning. And to–morrow morning,	
We shall have what to do after firing. But to–day,	
To–day we have naming of parts. Japonica	
Glistens like coral in all of the neighbouring gardens,	(5)
And to–day we have naming of parts.	

This is the lower sling swivel. And this	
Is the upper sling swivel, whose use you will see,	
When you are given your slings. And this is the piling swivel,	
Which in your case you have not got. The branches	(10)
Hold in the gardens their silent, eloquent gestures,	
Which in our case we have not got.	

This is the safety–catch, which is always released	
With an easy flick of the thumb. And please do not let me	
See anyone using his finger. You can do it quite easy	(15)
If you have any strength in your thumb. The blossoms	
Are fragile and motionless, never letting anyone see	
Any of them using their finger.	

And this you can see is the bolt. The purpose of this	
Is to open the breech, as you see. We can slide it	(20)
Rapidly backwards and forwards: we call this	
Easing the spring. And rapidly backwards and forwards	
The early bees are assaulting and fumbling the flowers:	
They call it easing the Spring.	

They call it easing the Spring: it is perfectly easy   (25)
If you have any strength in your thumb: like the bolt,
And the breech, and the cocking–piece, and the point of balance,
Which in our case we have not got; and the almond blossom
Silent in all of the gardens and the bees going backwards
and forwards,   (30)
    For today we have naming of parts.

                              (Henry Reed, 'Naming of Parts')

If we look at the first four verses of this poem we can see that
there is a systematic division which takes place in the middle of
the fourth line of each stanza. Up to that point in each verse
the speaker is a weapons instructor in the army, probably a
sergeant or a corporal, giving instructions on the use of a rifle
to some assembled recruits. However, the remaining part of
each stanza appears to be the unspoken thoughts of one of
those recruits. Alternatively, the recruit could be directly
addressing us, the readers. Often, when the poem is performed
it is read by two people, the first with a working–class
'sergeant major' voice, and the other with voice properties
like those I have already suggested for the second half of
'Adlestrop'.

The most obvious features of the language of instruction
are the use of commands. *And please do not let me/See anyone
using his finger* (14/15) is an imperative command and *and to–
morrow morning,/We shall have what to do after firing* (2/3) can be
interpreted as a combined statement and command. Other, less
obvious features of the language of instruction, are sentences
where the speaker tells the hearers what they must already
know (*e.g. And this is the piling swivel,/Which in your case you
have not got* (9/10) or where he tells them what they are
capable of doing (*e.g. You can do it quite easy/If you have any
strength in your thumb* (15/16)).

These instructions assume an audience which has the rifles
referred to in their possession. We know this for a variety of
reasons. Firstly, there are a number of words or phrases which
refer to items present in the immediate situational context and
code those items in terms of distance from the speaker. Such
expressions are usually called **deictic**.[3] Examples are *this*
(indicating that the item is close to the speaker; *cf.* 'that') in
stanzas 2, 3 and 4 and the close time deictics *to–day, yesterday*
and *to–morrow* in stanza 1 (compare 'that day', 'the day before'
and 'the day after'). In this case, of course, there is no real
situational context; instead we, the readers, have to imagine an

appropriate situation. The use of **deixis** is thus one of the ways in which writers persuade readers to imagine a fictional world when they read poems, novels and plays.

The second reason that we know that the instructor is addressing a set of people present with him is his use of pronouns (*I/me; you* and *we*) referring to himself and his listeners. There is also some verbal indication that he is **monitoring** the reactions of his hearers as he speaks to them (*cf. as you see* in line 20).[4]

The fact that it is military weapon training that the men are being instructed in is made clear by use of the relevant technical terminology, and the status of the instructor as a non–commissioned officer is indicated by the use of the adjective *easy* as an adverb in line 15. This is a grammatical feature associated with various working–class dialects of English, and in World War II the commissioned officers would have been from the middle–classes and above, and the 'lower ranks' would have comprised working–class soldiers.

The poetic description of the natural world in the gardens surrounding the soldiers will not need such detailed examination as we have already covered similar ground in our examination of 'Adlestrop'. In the last two and a half lines of each stanza, starting with the new sentence in the fourth line in each case, the rifle terminology, short sentences and instructional language are replaced by words and phrases referring to the natural world, longer sentences and poetic tropes like simile and metaphor (*e.g. Japonica/Glistens like coral* and *The branches/Hold in the gardens their silent, eloquent gestures*).

The result of all of this is a comparison between war and its accompanying death and destruction on the one hand, and, on the other, the peace of the gardens and the generative qualities of the natural world (*e.g. The early bees are assaulting and fumbling the flowers:/They call it easing the Spring*. This contrast is made more ironic and direct by a complex pattern of lexical repetition. The last line of each of the stanzas, which is thus in the 'natural world' part of the poem in each case, constitutes a repetition of phraseology found in the 'weapon training' section of that stanza. The war world thus appears at first sight to invade the natural world.

I have made a point so far of talking only about the first four stanzas of the poem. This is because the last stanza constitutes a significant and interesting *internal deviation* from the pattern so far described. At first sight its juncture in line 4 also reflects the war/nature division seen in the rest of the poem. But this time the line 4 syntactic division is *not* a sentence division. Indeed, despite a number of major syntactic junctures, the last stanza is one complete sentence. Moreover, this time *the whole stanza* is made up of an amalgam of repetitive echoes from earlier stanzas. Most of the echoes in the first three and a half lines of the stanza come from the war sections of previous stanzas, but not all of them do. In particular, the first clause *They call it easing the Spring* is a repetition from the last line of the previous stanza. We know this must be a nature reference, not a military one because the word *Spring* is capitalised, as it was in the nature section of stanza 4, but *not* in the war section of the stanza where it first appears.

Once we have noticed the point about *Spring* it is easier to see that *Which in our case we have not got* in line 28 is a more exact repetition of the natural world version of line 12 than the war world version in line 10. The 'garden' section of the last stanza, on the other hand, repeats items exclusively from the natural world sections of previous verses, except for the very last line of the poem, which repeats the clause in the first stanza which occurred in both the war and nature parts of the stanza.

What are we to make of these internally deviant features of the last stanza of 'Naming of Parts'? In the first four stanzas it seemed that the pattern of repetition represented the invasion of the natural world by the world of war. But in the last stanza it is the opposite which happens, suggesting a triumph of life over death or at least a hopeful resolution in the 'double' repetition of the poem's last line. Henry Reed thus manipulates style variation in a particularly sophisticated way in order to guide us in interpreting his poem.

3.8 How finicky can you get?

The analysis of Henry Reed's 'Naming of Parts' may well have raised in your mind an issue concerning how much linguistic detail a reader can be expected to pick up. Is it really plausible that readers will notice such a small thing as a capital versus a small 's' and then treat it as interpretatively significant in the way I have just suggested? Surely real readers aren't like that?

Well, what evidence there is suggests that readers (and hearers too, for that matter) do indeed pick up extremely fine nuances and small linguistic details subconsciously, even if they cannot explicitly describe what they have intuitively reacted to. One small difference in pronunciation can help us tell where people come from, even when they are trying to disguise their accents, and governments sometimes suggest changes in policy by very small language changes (*e.g.* 'we' instead of 'them', 'England' instead of 'Britain'). These sorts of changes are certainly noticed by people, and given that the insertion of one frame into a film can produce a subliminal response in spite of the fact that the watchers will not know they have seen the picture involved, there should be nothing surprising in readers picking up very small linguistic details and treating them subconsciously as significant. The task for the stylistic critic is, through analysis, to make those subconscious factors explicitly available for examination to help us debate interpretative disagreements rationally and openly.

The fact that the evidence does appear to be in favour of readers noticing very small–scale linguistic features is extremely fortunate. Although the alternative assumption to that of the **perfect reader**[5] which stylistics normally presupposes (namely the **average reader**[6]) is beguiling at first sight, it turns out to be much more difficult to deal with. If you assume that readers will notice some things but not others the critic is then faced with having to decide where to draw the line for any particular text. This would seem to be impossible to do. For critical purposes, then, it is much more realistic to assume that literally any detail may turn out to be significant, and that readers will be prepared to use any kind of evidence available to turn literature's apparent non–sense and lack of pattern into patterned interpretative sense. As Leech (1974: 7) says, 'the human mind abhors a vacuum of sense'.

Exercise 3

Examine Philip Larkin's use of style variation in his poem 'Vers de Société'.

Discussion of exercises

Exercise 1
Lexis: (*stupid, gormless*)
Grammar: *none* for 'not' (*I'm none as ormin' as I look*); use of a variant of the archaic '–est' ending for second person singular present tense verbs (*seest ta*); addition of the '–s' ending to first person singular present tense verbs (*I says to him*); *her* as subject pronoun instead of 'she' (*'Er's held back all this long*); use of the 'thee'/'thou'/ 'thy' system for second person singular pronouns (*'E'd none ha' had thee for my tellin'; tha looks a man; that letter o' thine*)
Orthographical representation of pronunciation: *ormin'* – use of /n/ instead of /ŋ/ for words ending in '–ing'; removal of /l/ where it occurs before /d/ at the ends of syllables in Standard English plus attendant lip rounding (*I towd him*); *sen* for 'self' (*mysen*); *tha* for 'thou'; dropping of initial /h/ (*'e's a fool*; *scrat* for 'scratch'; dropping of /v/ in word–final position of grammatical words (*'e'd none ha' had thee; that letter o' thine*).

The representation is not an accurate one, but rather a series of deviations which we interpret as representative of the dialect concerned. Some of the deviations will be quite close to the target dialect form, particularly the lexical and grammatical features, but it is not really possible for a writer to produce an accurate representation of the pronunciation of someone *via* our writing system. A phonetic alphabet, specially set up for the purpose, would be needed for that. For example, the 'the' of *at th' gate* would probably disappear entirely in this dialect and be realised by lack of plosion on the glottal stop which would represent the /t/ of *at*. This glottal stop would then be 'converted' into the /g/ at the beginning of *gate*. The *th'*– spelling thus represents a kind of compromise between what can be represented by our spelling system and the phonetic reality. Lawrence's representation is also not entirely consistent. 'Her' turns up as both *'er* and *her*, for example.

But it would be unreasonable to criticise Lawrence for not producing an exact representation of the dialect that Mrs Goodall would have spoken. In essence it is impossible to do, given the constraints of the writing system we use and the author's need to produce a representation which can be read and understood reasonably easily as well as giving the flavour of the dialect. For more discussion of this matter see Leech and Short (1981: 160–70) and 6.3 below.

Exercise 2
Formal lexis (*e.g. we have partaken in moderation*); formal use of vocatives (*my friends, my young friends*); archaisms (*e.g. whence*); rhetorical questions and answers; long strings of overtly parallel structures which merely repeat one another's meaning in other words (*may it grow, may it thrive, may it prosper, may it advance, may it proceed, may it press forward*), frequent use of dead metaphors (*the fatness of the land; you are to us a diamond/gem/jewel*).

Exercise 3
For an extensive discussion of this poem see Trengove (1989).

Notes

1. See, for example Crystal and Davy (1969), O'Donnell and Todd (1980), Leech, Deuchar and Hoogenraad (1982: Chs 8–9) and Freeborn, French and Langford (1986).
2. For a discussion of this poem, see Short and Candlin (1988)
3. See 9.3.5, and Lyons (1981: 228–42).
4. See Leech, Deuchar and Hoogenraad (1982: 139–40).
5. See Leavis (1952: 212–13).
6. ¬See Riffaterre (1965).

Further reading

Accessible introductions to variation in English are Crystal and Davy (1969), O'Donnell and Todd (1980), Leech, Deuchar and Hoogenraad (1982: Chs 8–9) and Freeborn, French and Langford (1986). Leech (1969: Ch. 1 and 49–52) discusses styles and style variation in poetry. O'Donnell and Todd (1980: Ch. 7), Leech, Deuchar and Hoogenraad (1982: Ch. 10) and Freeborn, French and Langford (1986: Ch. 9) discuss English literature in terms of language variation. Short (1993) discusses 'To Paint a Water Lily' by Ted Hughes, a poem which uses the language of instruction as a 'backdrop' for describing how to paint the lily.

CHECKSHEET   2:   STYLE VARIATION

A.   Dialect

(a)   What dialect is the text in? Does it vary from standard written English? If so, what is the purpose of this deviation from the norm for written English?

(b)   What linguistic features (*e.g.* vocabulary, grammar, spelling) indicate the dialect?

(c)   Is there any variation in the text with respect to dialect (for example, do any characters speak in a variety different from the 'default dialect' for the text?)? If so, what effect does this variation produce in terms of interpretation or reader attitude?

B.   Other variation (according to subject matter, function, tenor or medium)

(a)   What linguistic variety does the text you are examining use as its basic style? Is it an unusual one for the literary genre that the text comes from? If so, what effect does this have?

(b)   What are the linguistic features (*e.g.* vocabulary, grammar, spelling) which indicate the variety (or varieties)?

(c)   Are there any parts of the text which have features associated with a different language variety? If so, what are the linguistic features which indicate the change? What consequences does this style variation have for the interpretation of the text as a whole?

CHAPTER 4

Sound, meaning and effect

4.1 Introduction

It will be apparent from the first three chapters of this book
that in order to do stylistic analysis well you need to have at
least some basic abilities in language analysis. So far, though,
even if you have not studied English grammar or vocabulary
(lexis), it should not have been too difficult to understand the
points I have been making and the analyses of texts I have
provided. This is because most educated people have absorbed
a fair amount of unsystematic knowledge about English
grammar and vocabulary through learning foreign languages,
doing English at school and so on. A knowledge of English
sound structure and metrics is also important in analysing
poetry, but the general knowledge that people normally have
of phonetics is small, and so I will need to provide a minimum
of phonetic description in order to ensure broad
understanding. I will introduce this information as and when
needed. The notes and further reading section at the end of
this chapter give some suggestions for those who want to
explore sounds in poetry more fully. At appropriate points in
the following discussion I will make references to relevant
sections of Knowles (1987), which is written for students who
need to know phonetics in order to enhance their study of
English language and literature. I also follow Knowles in his
use of phonetic symbols for English sounds (his key is
reproduced in the appendix at the end of this book).
Remember that the use of phonetic symbols is not entirely
consistent from one phonetics textbook to the next.

4.2   Alliteration, assonance, rhyme and related matters

The terms in the title of this section should be familiar, but it will help us to go over their definitions in some detail. To do so, we will use the examples listed below. It should be borne in mind that these phonetic **schemes** are themselves examples of **phonetic parallelism**, and therefore are often interpretable *via* the 'parallelism rule' described in 2.3. In the examples below, the phonetic schemes which are discussed are emboldened.

4.2.1   Alliteration

Alliteration primarily involves the repetition of **the same or similar consonants**:

> **Example 1**
> A dreadful winter passed, each day severe
> **M**isty when **m**ild, but **c**old when **c**lear.
>   (George Crabbe, 'Tale 17: Resentment', lines 351–2)

Here, the /m/ alliteration in the first half of the second line binds together the concepts of mistiness and mildness and brings out the contrast with the second half of the line, which in turn exhibits alliteration, binding together the words *cold* and *clear*. The next example shows that alliteration primarily involves *sounds* and not spelling:

> **Example 2**
> These fruitful fields, these numerous flocks I see,
> Are others' **g**ain, but **k**illing **c**ares to me:
>   (George Crabbe, 'The Village', I, 216–17)

Killing and *cares* alliterate, and bind the meanings of the words together in spite of the fact that their initial sounds are represented by different letters. If alliterating sounds are also spelled the same this will help to make the alliteration more obvious, but alliteration can occur even when there is no 'spelling alliteration'.

   In general, sounds seem to be more salient than spellings. Critics do sometimes point out **eye rhyme** (*e.g.*

'bough'/'cough'), that is groups of words where there is no phonetic rhyme but where there is graphological parallelism involving *more than one letter in each sequence*. But no one, to my knowledge, has ever wanted to point out 'spelling alliterations' (*e.g.* '**c**orrupt **c**entres') which are not accompanied by sound alliteration.

The second line of example 2 also demonstrates that alliteration can involve *similar but not identical sounds*. Most readers will perceive that *gain* also takes part in the alliterative pattern involving *killing* and *cares*, helping to bring out the contrast of meaning between the first and second half of the line. This is not the **full alliteration** which we have seen in example 1, involving the repetition of identical sounds, but what we could call **loose alliteration**. In the English sound system the consonants /g/ and /k/ are distinctive sounds which are used to distinguish meaningful units (words or morphemes) from one another. 'Got' (/got/) and 'cot' (/kot/), for example, are distinguished by the /g:k/ opposition (distinctive sounds like /k/ and /g/ are called **phonemes**). The difference between the sounds arises because /g/ is **voiced** (*i.e.* the vocal cords in the larynx, or 'Adam's apple', are vibrating when the sound is pronounced), but /k/ is not. However, although they are clearly different sounds, they also seem in some ways to be *alike*. This is because they are pronounced in similar ways: they share two out of three **distinctive pronunciation (articulatory) features**. Although they differ with respect to voicing, they are both **velar** sounds, *i.e.* they are both produced by arching the blade of the tongue up and pushing it against the soft palate (or **velum**) at the back of the roof of the mouth. They are also both **stop consonants**, *i.e.* they are both produced by stopping the air–flow completely on its way out from the lungs. To understand what this description means, make the two sounds, feel carefully what happens in your mouth when you make them, and then compare what happens when you make other consonants, like /t/, /d/, /f/ or /s/.

An interesting combined use of full and loose alliteration is:

Example 3
Here Files of Pins extend their shining Rows,
Puffs, Powders, Patches, Bibles, Billet–doux
$\qquad\qquad$ (Alexander Pope, 'The Rape of the Lock', I, 137–8)

The list of items on the Lady Belinda's boudoir table in the second line of this example are linked together grammatically, because they are all plural generic nouns (see 1.3.2, Grammar) in a list construction. They are also linked phonetically by the loose alliteration which extends along the whole line (/p/ and /b/ are both **bilabial stops** – sounds produced by pressing the two lips together to stop the air flow). But in addition, the line also subdivides into two sections of full alliteration, the /p/–alliterating part and the /b/–alliterating part. Both the loose and full kinds of alliteration are put to work here. The loose alliteration along the whole line, in conjunction with the grammatical parallelism, helps us to infer that for the Lady Belinda all of the items have the same status. This is where the irony in the line comes from: we cannot easily conceive of bibles as having the same sort of value as the rest of the things lying on the table. The /p/ items are all beauty aids, whereas the /b/ items are examples of reading matter. Hence the full alliterative pattern helps bring out more strongly the ironic contrast between bibles and love–letters.[1]

We can also use example 3 to show that alliteration is much more salient on **syllable–initial** sounds than others, particularly when the syllable concerned is itself **word–initial**. There is a loose alliteration on the final /s/ and /z/ sounds for each of the words, but this seems much less important than the alliteration on the bilabial stops. Alliteration is also more noticeable when it involves **stressed** syllables. In the first line of example 3, the word–initial /f/ of *files* and the word–final /v/ of *of* are similar sounds. But readers are very unlikely to perceive this as a significant alliterative pattern because (i) the sounds are similar but not identical, (ii) only one of them occurs in a syllable–initial position, (iii) one of the sounds is in an unstressed syllable and (iv) that unstressed syllable is only a grammatical word (and so does not carry much meaning for us to use interpretatively). However, if an alliterative pattern has already been established on the initial sounds of stressed syllables of lexical words, then identical or similar sounds in other, less prominent positions will also tend to get drawn into the pattern precisely because the reader has been made aware of it. This can be seen in example 2 above, where the /f/ at the beginning of the second, unstressed syllable of *fruitful* will be thought of as part of the pattern already made clear on the initial sounds of *fruitful, fields* and *flocks*.

We have seen that it is important to know when speech sounds are similar, and therefore to recognise the **criteria** by which they are judged to be similar or not. One way to approach this (indeed the way which my discussion of alliteration in examples 2 and 3 assumes) is by examining the way phonemes are pronounced or **articulated** in the mouth. This kind of study is called **articulatory phonetics**. All of the sounds used in the English speech system are produced as the air is expelled from the lungs through the mouth and/or the nose. The thing which distinguishes consonants from vowels is whether we impede the air flow or not. When we produce consonants we physically impede the air–flow in some way, stopping it entirely for a moment, or making it difficult for the air to escape from the mouth. When we produce different vowels we merely alter the general shape of the mouth cavity and the lips.

The majority of consonants are distinguished one from another according to three main sets of features, the place in the mouth where the air–flow is impeded (**place of articulation**), the kind of impediment involved (**manner of articulation**) and whether or not the sounds are **voiced**.

With these distinctions in mind we can explain why /f/ and /v/ are similar sounds. They are produced in the same place in the mouth, by bringing the top teeth and bottom lips together (thus they are **labio–dental** sounds) and they are both **fricative** sounds. Unlike stops, fricatives do not stop the air–flow completely. Instead the parts of the mouth involved are pushed together slightly less firmly, so that the air can get through, but with difficulty, thus producing friction. The only difference between /f/ and /v/ is that /f/ is voiceless and /v/ is voiced. Thus, in:

Example 4
Full fathom five thy father lies;
                    (William Shakespeare, *The Tempest*, I, ii, 396)

the /v/ in *five* will be felt to alliterate as well as the /f/s in the line. You may also feel that the sounds represented by *th* in *fathom*, *thy* and *father*, besides alliterating with one another, alliterate in a looser way with the /f/s. This is because the sound /ð/ which the *th* represents here shares two articulatory features with /v/. Both sounds are fricatives and both are voiced (their voiceless counterparts are /f/ and /θ/, the sound at the beginning of *thin*, which also happens to be represented by the *th* spelling). /v/ and /ð/ only differ with respect to place of articulation (they are both voiced fricatives). /ð/ and /θ/, on the other hand, are both dental fricatives, produced by pushing the tongue tip against the back of the teeth. This description is not enough to enable you to relate all similar consonants together, but it should help you to check that the similarities and differences between sounds can be explained by examining the phonetic facts. If you want to take this kind of examination a step further, see Knowles (1987: Chs 2–3).

4.2.2 Assonance

Assonance is the term traditionally reserved for patterns of repetition between vowel sounds. In example 5 the words *withered, nipped* and *shivering* are connected by assonance:

Example 5
I, like yon wither'd leaf, remain behind,
Nipped by the frost, and shivering in the wind;
                    (George Crabbe, 'The Village', I, 210–11)

Both the speaker and the withered leaf have been affected by the frost (*withered, nipped*) and as a result both appear to be *shivering*. Assonance, like alliteration, connects important words together and helps the reader notice meaning–connections between them. Although there are only five vowel letters in the English spelling system, there are twelve **pure vowel** sounds in 'BBC' English, and even more vowel sounds if we include the **diphthongs** (*e.g.* the vowel sounds in 'play' and 'boy'), sounds which consist of a glide from one pure vowel sound to another. Vowels are distinguished from one another according to whether they are *long* or *short* and *where the highest point of the tongue in the mouth is* along the co–ordinates *low–mid–high* and *front–mid–back*. Thus the /i/ of 'bit' and the /iː/ of 'beet' will be felt to be similar because they are both high front vowels, differing from one another mainly through the feature of length (the symbol ':' after a vowel indicates that it is long).

Vowel length is something which is not difficult to perceive. Vowel positioning is a bit harder. One way of feeling the differences is to hold all of the features constant except one, say vowel height, and then to produce the relevant sounds, making yourself aware of what happens to your tongue as you do so. It is mainly the tongue which is used to alter the shape of your mouth cavity and so change the position in the mouth where vowels are pronounced. Thus, if you pronounce one after another the vowels /i/, /e/ and /a/ of 'bit', 'bet' and 'bat', you should feel your tongue stepping down in your mouth and your mouth becoming more and more open. Try it. All of these vowels are short front vowels, differing from one another with respect to the parameter of height (high–mid–low).[2] If you produce in succession the vowels /e/, /ɜ:/ and /o:/ of 'bet', 'Bert' and 'bought' you should feel your tongue being drawn back in stages allowing the vowels to move from front to mid to back in the mouth. (Again, do it yourself if you have not already done so. There is no substitute for practical, in this case 'tongues on', experience). The feature of length also varies in /e/, /ɜ:/ and /o:/. There is no set of pure vowels moving from front to back in the mouth which differ only with respect to position. An interesting use of assonance can be seen in the following advertising slogan:

Example 6
You'll never get a better bit of butter on your knife
/juːl nevə get ə betə bit əv bʌtə on joː naif/

If we concentrate first on *better bit of butter* it should be clear that there is alliteration on the /b/s and /t/s and assonance on the /ə/s, which occurs in each of the even syllables. This alternation also spreads onto *never get a,* fully in terms of the assonance and loosely in terms of the alliteration (/n/ and /g/, like /b/ and /t/ are both stop consonants). In addition, the vowel alternation from /e/ to /ə/ is itself a form of loose assonance as the vowels concerned are both short mid–vowels in terms of vowel height. They differ only in that one is a front vowel and the other is in the middle on the front/back parameter.

4.2.3   Rhyme

Rhyme is usually reserved to refer to the final syllables of different lines of poetry when the vowel and syllable–final consonants (if any) of the words in question are identical. Thus *five* can rhyme with *live* and *alive*. Slightly looser connections than this (*e.g. five/fife*) are usually called **half–rhymes**, and if the rhymes occur in positions other than at the end of a line, they are usually called **internal rhymes**. Rhymes can also be fuller than usual, and therefore more obvious perceptually, if more than one syllable is included in the rhyme relation. This can be seen in the first and third lines of the following stanza from Hardy's 'The Voice', where the rhyme extends over three syllables:

Example 7
Or is it only the breeze, in its **listlessness**
Travelling across the wet mead to me here,
You being ever dissolved to wan **wistlessness**,
Heard no more again far or near?

> (Thomas Hardy, 'The Voice')

An interesting use by W. H. Auden of fuller than usual internal rhymes is the naming of the protagonists in 'The Three Companions', as can be seen from an examination of the initial lines of the first three stanzas:

Example 8
[1]   'O where are you going?' said **reader** to **rider** . . .
[2]   'O do you imagine,' said **fearer** to **farer** . . .
[3]   'O what was that bird,' said **horror** to **hearer** . . .

> (W. H. Auden, 'The Three Companions')

The contrast between the pairs of people referred to in each line is emphasised by the almost identical phonetic form of their two–syllable names. In each pair the second syllable is identical, and the first syllables differ only with respect to the vowel. In addition, there are obvious phonetic connections among all the names, making the reader suspect that *fearer* and *farer* and *horror* and *hearer* might be alternative names for the people initially referred to as *reader* and *rider*. The various kinds of rhyme, and indeed other sound connections,[3] all help to connect important words together and often submit to the 'parallelism rule' for interpretative purposes, as the above example shows.

Exercise 1

(a) Examine the rhyme–scheme of Hopkins's 'The Windhover', (i) taking into account the last syllable only of each line and then (ii) the penultimate syllable as well.

To Christ our Lord

I caught this morning morning's minion, king–
dom of daylight's dauphin, dapple–dawn–drawn Falcon, in
                                   his riding
Of the rolling level underneath him steady air, and striding
High there, how he rung upon the rein of a wimpling wing

In his ecstasy! then off, off forth on swing,
As a skate's heel sweeps smooth on a bow–bend: the hurl
                                   and gliding
Rebuffed the big wind. My heart in hiding
Stirred for a bird, – the achieve of, the mastery of the thing!

Brute beauty and valour and act, oh, air, pride, plume here
Buckle! AND the fire that breaks from thee then, a billion
Times told lovelier, more dangerous, O my chevalier!

No wonder of it: shéer plód makes plough down sillion
Shine and blue–bleak embers, ah my dear,
Fall, gall themselves, and gash gold–vermilion.
                    (Gerard Manley Hopkins, 'The Windhover').

(b) Examine 'The Windhover' for other phonetic patterns and try to assess their significance.

4.3   Sound   symbolism

In some ways, the phonetic analysis of poetry is dangerous for students of literature as there is a tendency to 'over–milk' the significance of phonetic patterns. This is particularly the case with **sound symbolism**. Linguists generally agree that the sounds that happen to form most words are **arbitrary** – that is, there is no intrinsic relation between their meaning and their phonetic make-up. Hence, for example, there is nothing particularly 'chairy' about the sounds which together make up the word 'chair'. Indeed, if there was, we would be hard put to explain why other languages can use words for the same object which bear very little phonetic resemblance to our word (the Chinese for 'chair' is 'yizi', and the equivalent word in Malay is 'kerusi').

There *are* various words in English where the phonetic make–up *does* appear to bear an intrinsic relation to the thing which the word refers to, and it is for this circumstance that we reserve the term *sound symbolism*. It is seen most clearly in *onomatopoeic* words for sounds like 'miaow', 'bow–wow' and 'crack'. In **onomatopoeia**, the sounds which make up a word are thought to mimic the sound which the word refers to. But sound symbolism is a more general concept, including not just sound–sound mimicry, but also similar relations between the sounds of words and other aspects of the things which the word refers to, like size or brightness. For example, we often feel that there is a sound symbolic relationship between the words 'large' and 'titchy' and what they rep– resent (they 'sound like' what they describe), but not for their rough synonyms 'big' and 'small'.

Linguists have recently begun to see that cases where there is a sound–symbolic connection between a word's meaning and its phonetic characteristics are more prevalent than they first thought, but words which exhibit sound symbolism are still *much less common* than the words with no intrinsic sound–meaning connection like 'chair', 'table', 'settee' and so on.

It is important for me to emphasis this point at the beginning of this section, precisely because we are going to go on to explore the matter of sound–symbolic relations in some detail. As a result, the discussion of sound symbolism will far outweigh that of arbitrariness in terms of the space we devote to it. But we must still remember that arbitrariness is the dominant feature, and keep in check the temptation to see sound symbolism wherever we look, even when it is not there. This is what I mean by 'over–milking' the significance of phonetic structure. As an example of 'over-milking', I will refer to a remark by a well known critic, F. W. Bateson, about the following line from Chaucer's 'Troilus and Criseyde':

Example 9

But nedes day departe hem moste sone

        (Geoffrey Chaucer, 'Troilus and Criseyde', III, 1709)

The lovers, Troilus and Criseyde, have spent the night together, but now that daybreak has come, like Romeo and Juliet in Shakespeare's version of the story, they must part. Bateson comments: 'Here the alliterating *d*s add a certain solemnity and pathos that might be thought appropriate to the introduction of the concept of necessity . . .'[4] But the problem here is that alliterating sounds do not *of themselves* have associations of solemnity or pathos. Rather, the occasion is a sad and solemn one, and the line happens to have alliterating *d*s in it. The reader, on perceiving the *alliterative pattern*, will try to give some significance to it. But we must not fall into the trap of believing, as Bateson appears to, that sounds have inherent meanings. Moreover, because English only has approximately 45 phonemes, there are bound to be a fair number of accidental alliterative and assonantal patterns in any text as a consequence of the chance distribution of sounds in groups of words. So we should not assume that all sound patterns will be significant in terms of interpretation.

Now that I have explicitly stated my warnings about 'over–milking' phonetic structure, we will move on to examine various sound–symbolic relations. Like section 4.1 this section will not be exhaustive. For more discussion of this area see Knowles (1987: 38–42) and Epstein (1978: 25–37).

4.3.1 Length

One obvious way in which sounds might mirror some extra–linguistic reality is in terms of length. Some vowels are long and some are short, and the same is also true of consonants. In particular, stop consonants, the liquid sounds (/l/ and /r/) and the semi–vowels (/w/ and /j/, as at the beginning of words like 'wet' and 'yet') are shorter than the fricatives (*e.g.* /f/, /v/, /s/, /θ/, /ð/), nasals (/n/ and /m/, especially in syllable–final position) and affricates (/tʃ/ as in *church* and /dʒ/ as in *judge*). The sound–symbolic effect enacting the firing guns of Owen's lines in 'Anthem for Doomed Youth' is a consequence of the correlation readers make between the high density of short vowels and consonants and the subject matter being described:

Example 10
Only the stuttering rifles' rapid rattle
/ounli ðə stʌtriŋ   raiflz rapid ratl/
(Wilfred Owen, 'Anthem for Doomed Youth')

In Keats's 'To Autumn', on the other hand, Autumn is personified watching the juice drip out of the cider–press as *watching the last oozings hours by hours* (/wotʃiŋ ðə laːst uːziŋz auəz bai auəz/), where the high incidence of fricatives and long vowels and diphthongs is felt by readers to enact the slowness of the process. Here, notice, there can be no straightforward, onomatopoeic relationship as the speech sounds are being related to a temporal, not a phonetic phenomenon. But readers intuitively perceive the relationship between the drawn–out nature of the process described and the high incidence of long sounds as being *appropriate*. It is this matter of appropriateness which is the key to sound–symbolic relations. If we can find an appropriate connection between sound features and meaning we will; and as a consequence the 'meaning' of the relevant sound feature changes from one context to another. Earlier in the same stanza of 'To Autumn' Keats uses alliteration and assonance on fricatives and long vowels to represent sleepiness: *Drowsed with the fume of poppies* (/drauːzd wiðə fjuːm əv popiːz/). In this case, the relation of appropriateness is a rather more attenuated one. The long sounds can be said to be apposite because if you are drowsy you take longer to realise things and perform actions. Of course, once this kind of thing is allowed for there will be many possible appropriacy relations, with some being felt to be more reasonable than others. The shorter the chain of inference needed to establish the relationship, the more directly appropriate the relationship appears to be.

4.3.2   The relative pitch of different sounds

The pitch level at which sounds are produced varies from one speaker to another and even from one utterance to another for the same speaker. Women generally speak with a higher pitch than men, and if someone is excited, for example, they speak at a higher pitch than normal. But it is still the case that within any speaker's normal pitch range some phonemes will be produced at a higher or lower pitch than others. In particular, vowels produced high and to the front of the mouth tend to be higher pitched than vowels produced lower or further back. This is a consequence of the difference in shape of the mouth cavity involved. So, if we take sequences like 'ding dong', which are usually used to represent the sound of bells, the 'ding' will be associated with higher pitched, and the 'dong' with lower pitched ones. If we take a sequence like 'splish splash', the change from a high vowel to a low vowel is related to differently pitched sounds and hence different object sizes. The word 'splish' is the higher pitched of the two and so is thought to mimic, say, a small stone being dropped into the water. The result of a larger stone being dropped into the water is a lower pitched sound, and so 'splash' is more appropriate. The English comedy duo Little and Large, one of whom is much bigger and fatter than the other, were wise in choosing that stage name rather than 'Big and Small' because the high front vowel in 'Little' and the low back vowel in 'Large' are sound–symbolic of the meanings of the words they are a part of. The vowels in 'big' and 'small' work against the meanings involved. In D. H. Lawrence's poem 'Piano', the contrasting vowel features, long/short and high/low pitch, are used in the words *boom* and *tingling* to represent two alter–native viewpoints on the same event:

Example 11

A child sitting under the piano, in the **boom** of the **tingling**

strings

(D. H. Lawrence, 'Piano')

From the perspective of the adult narrator, who will assume a position away from the piano even if in the same room, the notes of the piano sound relatively highly pitched and distinct. Note also how the word *tingling* is very close phonetically to the conventionally onomatopoeic 'tinkling', which is used to represent piano playing. But from the perspective of the narrator as child, sitting under the piano, near the strings while someone else plays, the sounds appear louder and less distinct. The phrase *the boom of the tingling strings* thus fuses the adult and child viewpoints.

4.3.3 Indistinctness

Short, bright consonants like /t/ and /p/ are usually perceived as clear sounds, and longer voiced consonants will tend to feel more indistinct. Nasals in particular go with indistinctness. So do vowels produced towards the back of the mouth. The words *clunk* and *click* are normally felt to be onomatopoeic, and they were interestingly used in an English advertising slogan trying to persuade people to put on their safety belts when they got into their cars. The slogan was:

Example 12
Clunk Click Every Trip

For many English people at the time, the *clunk* became associated with the sound of the car door shutting and the *click* with the sound of the seat belt being put on. The /ʌ/ vowel and the nasal /ŋ/ made *clunk* in this context feel indistinct, and thus appropriate to the sound of the car door shutting, where a layer of rubber separates the two metal surfaces, thus muffling the sound. *Click*, on the other hand, consists of bright sounds, and so was appropriate for the metal–to–metal sound of the seat belt being fastened. The sequence *clunk click* is also the appropriate sequential ordering (you usually shut the car door before you put your seat belt on), and the assonance and loose alliterative relationships between *trip* and *click* helped to form a close associative link between the *clunk click* slogan and the idea of automatically putting on a seat belt when driving a car.

4.4 Phonaesthemes

As we have already noted, the distinctive speech sounds which do not themselves have meaning, but which are used as sound building blocks in language are usually called *phonemes*. As we noticed in 2.2.5, the smallest linguistic units which actually possess meaning are called *morphemes*. But there are some sequences of phonemes in English which appear to lie somewhere in between phonemic and morphemic status. These sequences are usually called **phonaesthemes**. Consider the word–initial cluster 'gl–'. You may well feel that this sequence of sounds, even though it is not a morpheme like 'un–' or '–kind', is somehow associated with things to do with light, especially if the context is appropriate. This is because a lot of words to do with light and sight happen to begin with 'gl–': 'gleam', 'glimmer', 'glisten', 'glare', 'glint', 'glance'. Words which are associatively related in this way and share a common phoneme sequence are usually referred to as a **phonaesthetic series**. We can see that 'gl–' cannot literally mean 'light' because there are plenty of counter–examples (*cf.* 'glottis', 'gladioli', 'gland',). This particular phonaestheme does not appear to be sound symbolic in any way. The associative meaning is entirely a result of the phonaesthetic series. But some phonaesthemes may also possess sound–symbolic qualities. This appears to be the case with the sequence 'sl–,' which is often associated with wet, vaguely unpleasant things (*cf.* 'slime', 'slippery', 'sludge', 'slug', 'slither' but contrast 'sleep', 'slang', 'slender'). Coleridge uses both the 'gl–' and the 'sl–' phonaesthetic series in 'The Rime of the Ancient Mariner':

Example 13

[1]   It is an ancient Mariner
      And he stoppeth one of three.
      'By thy long gray beard and **gl**ittering eye,
      Now wherefore stopp'st thou me?'

[2]   The very deep did rot: O Christ!
      That ever this should be!
      Yea, **sl**imy things did crawl with legs
      Upon the **sl**imy sea.
                        (Samuel Taylor Coleridge, 'The Rime of the Ancient
                        Mariner', Part I, stanza 1 and Part II, stanza 10)

The word *glittering* is used to portray the fearsome light in the eye of the ancient mariner, and the word *slimy* to characterise the monsters the mariners see on the sea–bed after the ancient mariner has them brought bad luck by killing the albatross

There is not enough space to catalogue every possible sound–symbolic relationship or phonaesthetic series in English.[5] Instead, let us look at a more extended example, from Tennyson's 'The Passing of Arthur'. After the wounded King Arthur, with some difficulty, has persuaded Sir Bedivere to return the magic sword, Excalibur, to the Lady of the Lake, Sir Bedivere has to carry Arthur though the mountains to the

lake where the ladies on the funeral barge are waiting to take
the King to Avilion:

Example 14

Dry clash'd his harness in the icy caves
And barren chasms, and all to left and right
The bare black cliff clang'd round him, as he based
His feet on juts of slippery crag that rang
Sharp—smitten with the dint of armed heels —
And on a sudden, lo! the level lake,
And the long glories of the winter moon.
    (Alfred Lord Tennyson, 'The Passing of Arthur', lines 351–8)

When Bedivere is climbing through the cliffs, Tennyson uses
assonance, alliteration and internal rhyme to foreground a
series of words beginning with stop consonants, many of
which have a bright quality: *clash'd, chasms, cliff, clang'd, crag*.
All but one of these words have the low, open mouth /a/
vowel. They are all short. Low, open vowels are often
associated with loudness. Short open vowels can also be seen
in *barren* (in an assonance relationship with *chasms*), *rang*
(which rhymes internally with *clang'd*) and *black* (which has an
assonance relationship with *clang'd*). These words, connected
together in patterns of sound as they are, bring to the fore
short, loud, bright sounds, which, given the situation being
described, are likely to provide echoes for the reader of the
sound of armour banging against the rocks. In turn, this helps
to suggest the effort involved in climbing the crags.

In marked contrast there is a sudden change (an internal
deviation) when Arthur and Sir Bedivere see the lake. The
alliteration switches to the softer, liquid /l/ sound, and the
vowels become much higher. In the final line the /l/
continues to appear and the incidence of longer vowels and
consonants increases. This series of phonetic contrasts is thus
used to mark the contrast in atmosphere as Arthur reaches his
goal.

Exercise 2

Comment on the sound effects in the underlined section of the
following extract:

Down the road someone is practising scales,
<u>The notes like little fishes vanish with a wink of tails,</u>
<u>Man's heart expands to tinker with his car</u>
For this is Sunday morning, Fate's great bazaar,
            (Louis MacNeice, 'Sunday Morning')

Discussion of exercises

Exercise 1

(a) 'The Windhover' is a Petrarchan sonnet, and divides into
two quatrains and two tercets: ABBA; ABBA; CDC;
DCD. The two quartets of the octet, and the two tercets
of the sestet, are thus joined together by the rhyme
scheme, forcing an interpretation which integrates these
stanza pairs in some way.

    However, if we examine the last syllable of the first
eight lines, we can also see that *all* of them rhyme. If we
also take the penultimate syllables of stanzas 1 and 2 into
account, then we see the ABBA structure referred to
above − /iŋ, aidiŋ, aidiŋ, iŋ/. The evidence so far, then,
suggests that the first two stanzas have to be integrated
together in contrast to the last two, which are themselves
linked together by the rhyme scheme. The octet describes
the beauty and wonder of the falcon in flight. The first
tercet also describes the falcon, this time attacking his
prey. The second tercet, on the other hand, describes
what are at first sight more mundane things, the visual
results of the ploughing of a field and some coals
dropping from a fire onto the hearth. My overall reading
of this poem is that Hopkins is thanking God for the
astounding and fearsome beauty of the windhover, but
goes on to say that it is not surprising that something as
unusual as the windhover should be beautiful. Even the
most mundane things God has created can be beautiful
and remarkable if we take the care to examine them. In
this way the poem becomes a paean of praise to God and
the natural world he has created.

(b) Some of the phonetic patterns and effects in this poem
can be explained in an iconic way at a local level. For
example, *off, off forth* can be seen as representing the pent
up energy of the bird and its release as it begins its sweep

through the air. This can be related to the switch of the fricative /f/ from word–final to word–initial position. Particularly effective is the long frication and its final release as the reader moves from the final /f/ of *off,* through the initial /f/ of *forth* without a break and finally releases the consonant to move into the /o:/ vowel. Similarly, the high incidence of /l/ and /r/ in *riding/Of the rolling level* can be seen as representing the movement of the bird and the air underneath him as he hovers. But by no means all of the phonetic effects can be explained away in this fashion. My view is that Hopkins puts on a display of verbal pyrotechnics (at the phonetic level and others) to help us feel the extraordinariness of the windhover. These pyrotechnics are also carried over into the description of the more mundane things, thus increasing our wonder of them by associating them with the windhover.

Exercise 2
The incidence of short vowels, particularly the short front vowel /i/ in the first of the two emboldened lines is high. The sound–symbolic effect of smallness correlates with the smallness of the fishes and the visual phenomenon of vanishing *with a wink*. In the second line, *man, heart* and *expand* all contain open vowels, suggesting largeness, and mimicking the meaning of *expand*. But ironically the expansion of the human heart is for the mundane purpose of tinkering with the car. *Tinkering* exhibits an internal rhyme with *wink*, and is sound–symbolically related to the smallness already seen in the first line. The sound contrast in the second line thus underlines the contrastive irony seen in the lexis and grammar.

Notes

1. My commentary on this line of Pope's is derived partly from Widdowson (1974). For further commentary, on the line's grammatical structure, see Short (1986).
2. Because vowel height is related to how open or closed your mouth is, you will find that some phoneticians talk about open and closed vowels instead of high and low vowels.

3. For a more detailed account of the sound structure of poetry than is given here, see Leech (1969: Ch. 6). For further commentary on the Auden poem, see Rodger (1982).
4. Bateson (1971).
5. For more discussion of these areas, see Epstein (1978: 25–37) and Nash (1986).

Further reading

Knowles (1987) is an introduction to English phonetics which uses literary examples throughout. Leech (1969: Ch. 6) discusses patterns of sound in poetry.

CHECKSHEET 3: PHONETIC STRUCTURE

A. Phonetic patterns

(a) What patterns of alliteration and loose alliteration are there?
(b) What patterns of assonance and loose assonance are there?
(c) What patterns of rhyme and half–rhyme are there?
(d) What patterns of internal rhyme are there?
(e) Which of the above patterns are stylistically significant at a local level, for example helping to link important words or lines together or producing effects associated with the 'parallelism rule'?
(f) Are there any significant patterns of distribution of kinds of sounds ('phonetic texture'), for example particular kinds of sounds being associated with particular sections of the poem or aspects of meaning?

B. Sound symbolism

(a) Are there any occurrences of sound symbolism?
(b) Are there any occurrences of words belonging to a phonaesthetic series?
(c) What effects can you associate with the sound symbolism and phonaesthesia, either locally, or at a more global interpretative level?

CHAPTER 5

Rhythm and metre in the reading of poetry

5.1 What is rhythm?

The first thing to remember is that rhythm is not special to poetry. We can perceive rhythm in many things (for example, music, dancing, marching, digging, swimming). Even the cycle of the year's seasons can be seen to have a rhythm. The perception of rhythm, then, is a fundamental human ability. All we need to feel a rhythmic effect is to perceive a regular grouping of events in some sequence or other (*e.g.* of sounds, physical actions, periods of the year).

However, a very regular repeated rhythm soon becomes boring, even irritating, as anyone who buys a small child a drum soon discovers. For *interesting* rhythmic effects to occur we need some underlying regularity mixed with variations. Once a regular rhythmical beat in a tune is established, it can be made more interesting by adding cross–rhythms or by modifying the beat in some way (*e.g.* by adding extra beats to, or removing them from, the basic rhythmic pattern). Similarly, dancing can be made more fun by adding variations to the basic steps, and our perception of the annual seasonal cycle is overlaid by our differing perceptions of how long particular seasons are each year, depending upon the weather, how happy we are, and so on.

5.2 Rhythm in language

Languages also have rhythm. The underlying rhythm of English is often said to be based on an assumption by native speakers that the amount of time between strong stresses is roughly equal.[1] In English speech, each **lexically full**, or content word, has a major stress on one of its syllables, even if it only consists of one syllable. Single–syllable grammatical words, like prepositions (*e.g.* 'in', 'on') or articles ('a', 'the'), do not normally take stress, but grammatical words of more than one syllable (*e.g.* 'above', 'upon') will have a major stress.

Let us begin with a straightforward case, a one–word variation on a traditional English proverb. You should be able to say out loud *A **roll**ing **stone gath**ers the **moss*** and make the beat clear by tapping out a regular rhythm with your hand, the beats coinciding with ***roll–***, ***stone***, ***gath–*** and ***moss***. Note that there are eight syllables in the sentence, four with strong and four with weak stresses:

```
1  2  3   4    5  6  7   8
A rolling stone gathers the moss
W  S  W   S    S  W  W   S
```

But although you can beat a regular rhythm with your hand, the weaker syllables are not evenly distributed through the sentence. In other words, when saying the sentence out loud, you will need to vary the speed with which you pronounce the various syllables to make the rhythm clear. This rhythmic effect is not unlike the effect of rhythmic variation in music which I described above. There is a weak syllable before both *roll–* and *stone*, and this gives rise to a regular 'di dum di dum' pattern for the first half of the sentence. But the second half has the two weak stresses next to each other, in between the two strong ones. This means that (i) you will have to pronounce the two syllables *–ers the* fast to reduce the amount of time needed to say them towards that normally reserved for one syllable, and (ii) you will have to produce some kind of delaying effect to help establish a 'di' beat in between the two 'dums' of *stone* and *gath–*. You might do this by lengthening the pronunciation of *stone*, or by inserting a small pause in between *stone* and *gath–*.

I have already assumed in my discussion that *A rolling stone gathers the moss* can be divided into two halves in between *stone* and *gathers*. One reason for saying this is that the four strong beats in the sentence can easily be divided into two equal parts of four syllables with two strong beats. But another factor which reinforces this division into two halves is that the *rhythmic* spacing coincides with an important *grammatical* boundary within the structure of the sentence. The first half is the subject noun phrase of the sentence, and the second is what is said about it (the **predicate**). In other words, the rhythmic division into two halves reinforces the basic subject–predicate structure of the sentence. This helps us to see that interesting rhythmic effects in English can be created by varying the way in which units at other linguistic levels (*e.g.* word structure, grammatical structure) relate to the groupings of strong and weak stresses. Compare, for example, your 'tapping out' readings for *A rolling stone gathers the moss* with the following two sentences, each of which also has eight syllables: (i) *A rolling stone obliterates* (where the last word has four syllables and you are likely to perceive two rhythmic beats within it, one on –*blit*– and one on –*ates*, to preserve the 'two–halves' structure coinciding with the subject–predicate division) and (ii) *A large rolling boulder totters* (where the subject–predicate division no longer coincides with the middle of the sentence, giving rise to two ways of 'reading' the sentence, one with a division after *rolling*, which emphasises the 'two–halves' structure, and one with a division after *boulder*, emphasising the subject–predicate structure).

5.3 Metre

Poetry has more marked, and more complex, rhythmic effects than ordinary language because it has an *extra layer of rhythmic structuring*, which is usually called **metre**. As we will see below, this level of rhythmic structuring is indicated by the fact that lines of poetry, unlike prose, do not extend out to the right-hand edge of the page. Because the possession of metre is one of the basic ways in which poetry can be distinguished from prose, it will be important to examine it in some detail. Some traditional treatments of metre have tended to assume that rhythm and metre are the same thing. But as we saw in 5.2, all language has rhythm, and so although metre is an extremely important aspect of poetic rhythm, it is not the only factor involved.

The study of metre has had contrasting receptions by poets and students of poetry. Many of my students find metrics tedious to study. This is probably because metrical structure is the level of poetic organisation which is least directly con- nected with meaning, and because the study of metre is a complicated, and at times difficult, matter. Indeed, there are still a number of disagreements among experts on rhythm and metre about fairly basic aspects of their study. Poets, on the other hand, appear to find the study of poetic rhythm fascinating and central to their art. An indication of this is the number of well known poets who have written essays or longer works on the subject, Gerard Manley Hopkins, Robert Bridges and T. S. Eliot, for example. D. H. Lawrence, though not an analyst of metre, eloquently captures its rhythmic regularity and his feeling for its importance in the following extract from a letter:

> I think more of a bird with broad wings flying and lapsing through the air, than anything, when I think of metre.
>
> (Letter to Edward Marsh, November 1913)

Why is poetry metred? Firstly, metrication is one of the formal features which sets poetry off from other kinds of writing; and in earlier times particularly, when poetry was reserved for special subject matters like love and nature, metrication was a formal signal of importance. Even today, when the subject matters of poetry are much more various, writing a text in metred lines appears to say 'I have something significant to tell you'. But a more interesting reason is the one mentioned at the beginning of this section: the addition of a background metrical scheme to a text adds a new rhythmical dimension, not generally found in prose,[2] which affords poets all sorts of interesting effects which are not otherwise available.

In the twentieth-century, the linguistic level that has become of primary importance in the study of poetry is meaning. The majority of critical discussions of individual poems revolve around interpretation. But if we look back at earlier periods, the sixteenth- and seventeenth-centuries especially, we find that the notion of *musicality* was much more important than now. Poems did not have to be like cryptic crossword puzzles in order to please. They could also say relatively straightforward things in ways felt to be specially appropriate. The basic idea was that poems should *enact* what they described: 'the sound must seem an echo to the sense' (Alexander Pope, 'An Essay on Criticism', line 365). Musicality revolves around phonetic and rhythmic effects in particular, and it is thus necessary to be able to do metrical analysis in order to be able to explain important effects in many poems. The rest of this chapter will be aimed mainly at helping to elucidate the rhythmic aspect of poetry's 'musicality'. In spite of the modern preoccupation with interpretation, twentieth-century poets also use 'musical' effects, of course, and so our discussion will certainly not be confined to early texts.

Although rhythm and metre are not the same thing, metre is clearly an important contributory factor in the perception of rhythm in poetry. One way in which we can show this is to study the feature of line length. Consider, for example, my previous sentence broken into two lines of 'poetry':

Example 1
One way in which we can show this
Is to study the feature of line length.

All I have done here is to break the sentence into two lines which feel rhythmically equal and to capitalise the word which happens to come at the beginning of the second line. Immediately, the sentence is more easily perceived as having two halves, each with a basic rhythmic pattern of three beats:

One way in **which** we can **show** this
Is to **study** the **feature** of **line** length.

Clearly, writing lines which do not extend to the right–hand edge of the page has an important effect on our perception of rhythmic effects in written texts. We view the above two lines as being equivalent and then impose parallel rhythmic patterns on them. However, it is important to notice that the original prose sentence could also be said to possess this rhythm; the lineation has, in effect, made it more prominent. And as with the *A rolling stone gathers the moss* example, a major grammatical division, the subject–predicate boundary, coincides with a major rhythmic boundary, this time the boundary between the two lines.

There are, of course, other possible rhythmic 'readings' of the above lines. For example, in a context where there was a special communicative need to highlight the word *this* in the first line or *length* in the second (for reasons of contrast with previous things mentioned, for instance) we would find in our pronunciation that the major stress on *show* or *line* would move one word rightwards in each case. We will discuss how these sorts of overall meaning parameters affect rhythm in 5.7, but the major point to note here is that even if the stress was moved onto *this* or *length* above, we would still be able to perceive these readings as variations on the basic 3–beat rhythm of the lines. In other words, we would have an example of the sort of complex rhythmic effect which I referred to in 5.1.

In some ways, though, the two lines in example 1 are not very equal. The first one has 8 syllables and the second has 10. The first line has a pattern whereby the strongly stressed syllable (emboldened) is followed by two lighter syllables in the first two cases and one in the last. But the second line reverses that pattern, having two light syllables followed by the stressed syllable in each case, plus one at the end. There are other differences too, for example the number of words which are lexically full in each line. But in spite of these inequalities, the two lines are still 'equal enough' to be perceived as equivalent.

The concept of 'equal enough' is important here. If I change the line lengths radically, into something more like what is usually called **free verse**, the pattern of equivalence from line to line disappears:

One way in which
We can show
This
Is to study
The feature of line length.

This does not mean that the sentence now has no rhythmic properties at all. We have already noted that we can perceive rhythm in any stretch of language. But because the line lengths are now very irregular we do not feel that the rhythmic properties of each line are parallel to one another. It is this *extra regularity* which makes metre what it is. Metred poems, then, are poems where the line lengths and rhythmical patterns within the lines are close enough for us to feel a basic pattern of equivalence from line to line. This is why explaining how the different poetic metres work is an important aspect of explaining rhythm in poetry.

5.4 Different kinds of metre

Metre in English verse is a level of organisation which is based upon a *two–term* contrast between positions in a line which should contain strong and weak syllables. Let us use the traditional terms **ictus** (/) and **remiss** (X) to refer to these strong and weak positions respectively. If we restrict ourselves for the moment to a situation where these two positions are only allowed to contain one syllable each, we can see that there are two possible patterns of weak and strong events, X / ('di dum') and / X ('dum di'). These two elementary patterns are essential to an understanding of English metrics. The first pattern, X / ('di dum') is traditionally called the **iamb** and the / X ('dum di') pattern is called the **trochee**.

The basic metrical unit of one strong plus one weak (ictus plus remiss) position is traditionally referred to as the **metrical foot**. Thus we can find iambic feet, trochaic feet, and also other combinations when the basic unit is expanded to include more than two syllables in the remiss of the foot (the metrical foot must have *one and only one* ictus syllable, but can normally have from zero to three remiss syllables). Below I list, with illustrative examples, the major foot structures that can be found with any regularity. Some are much more common than others, the iambic foot being by far the most widespread in English verse. The trochee is reasonably common, and the others are more rare:

iamb	X / ('di dum')
trochee	/ X ('dum di')
anapaest	X X / ('di di dum')
dactyl	/ X X ('dum di di')

It is also possible to get poetic feet which have three light syllables in the remiss position, or where the ictus has a light syllable on either side of it, but these foot patterns are too rare to detain us here.

Now let us restrict our discussion for a moment to lines of poetry with iambic ('di dum') feet. Normally, iambic lines will consist of more than one iamb, and poets can choose how many iambs to have as the basic line–template for particular poems. One particular form has dominated English poetry since the fifteenth–century, however, namely a line with *five* iambs, as in the following example:

Example 2

    X   /   X / X   /   X / X   /
    Then tooke the angrie witch her golden cup
    X   / X   /   X /   X / X   /
    Which still she bore, replete with magick artes;
                    (Edmund Spenser, *The Faerie Queene*, I, viii, 14)

This kind of line is found throughout the verse of Shakespeare, Milton and Wordsworth, for example, and is called **iambic pentameter** (literally 'iambic five metre'). We might call the iambic pentameter line the **metrical norm** for English poetry from the fifteenth–century onwards. Other possibilities can, of course, be found:

1. Monometer   one foot line
2. Dimeter   two feet lines
3. Trimeter   three feet lines
4. Tetrameter   four feet lines
5. Pentameter   five feet lines
6. Hexameter   six feet lines

These 'number of feet' combinations can in principle involve any kind of foot as the basic unit, and various stanza forms can have patterns involving differing numbers of feet from line to line (for example, Keats's 'Song', which we analysed in 2.2.7, has *tetrameters* in the first and third lines of each verse and *trimeters* in the second and fourth lines). But it is the iamb in units of five which is the dominant English verse form.

Exercise 1

(a) Re–examine Keats's 'Song' in 2.2.7. What is the rhythmical effect created by having a 'missing foot' in the second and fourth lines?

(b) Below are a series of extracts from poems. Work out, for each example, what the basic foot unit is and how many feet there are to the line.

(i)   Thus I
         Passe by
         And die:
         As One,
         Unknown,
         and gon:
              (Robert Herrick, 'Upon His Departure Hence')

(ii)   My lusts they do me leave,
         My fancies all be fled,
         And tract of time begins to weave
         Grey hairs upon my head.

         For age with stealing steps
         Hath clawed me with his crutch,
         And lusty life away she leaps
         As there had been none such.
             (Thomas, Lord Vaux, 'The Agèd Lover Renounceth
                                  Love')

(iii)   Never weather–beaten Saile more willing bent to shore,
         Never tyred Pilgrim's limbs affected slumber more,
        Than my weary spright now longs to fly out of my troubled
                              breast.
         O come quickly, sweetest Lord, and take my soule to rest.
         Ever blooming are the joys of Heavin's high paradice,
         Cold age deafes not there our eares, nor vapour dims our
                                  eyes;
         Glory there the Sun outshines, whose beames the
                      blessed onlee see.
         O come quickly, glorious Lord and raise my
                            spright to thee.
             (Thomas Campion, 'Never Weather–beaten Sail')

(iv)   All look and likeness caught from earth
         All accident of kin and birth,
         Had passed away. There was no trace
         Of aught on that illumined face,
         Upraised beneath the rifted stone
         But of one spirit all her own –
         She, she herself, and only she,
         Shone through her body visibly.
               (Samuel Taylor Coleridge, 'Phantom')

(v)   She was a gordian shape of dazzling hue,
      Vermilion–spotted, golden, green, and blue;
      Striped like a zebra, freckled like a pard,
      Eyed like a peacock, and all crimson barred;
      And full of silver moons, that, as she breathed,
      Dissolved, or brighter shone, or interwreathed
      Their lusters with the gloomier tapestries –

                              (John Keats, 'Lamia', 47–53)

5.5 Fitting together the metre and what a poet wants to say

5.5.1 How many syllables in the line?

Let's pretend that I am a poet who has chosen the iambic
pentameter form for a poem. Assuming what we have said so
far, this restricts me to adopting a pattern of ten syllables
arranged in a weak + strong ('di dum') pattern. But it may be
that what I want to say and the words I need to say it in do
not fit well into this predetermined pattern. What happens
then? One possibility can be seen in the first line of example 2
above. Spenser rearranges the syntactic form of 'Then the
angry witch took her golden cup' to *Then tooke the angrie witch
her golden cup* in order to conform to the metrical dictates of
the line. In essence, a **tension** has arisen between the metre
and the grammar, and in this case the metre has won the
contest. Notice that although the matter has been resolved, the
tension is still observable in the resulting line as a result of your
knowledge of which ordering is grammatically most normal.
In example 2, then, in order for the metrical system and the
language system to fit together the grammatical rules have been
relaxed. This is probably where the term '**poetic grammar**'
comes from.

There are other possibilities of course. Let us assume that
what you want to say has one too few, or one too many,
syllables. Then there are ways open to you (apart from saying
something else, that is!) to resolve the difficulty. Either you
relax the pentameter rule which says that there should be ten
syllables in the line, five in ictus position and five in remiss
position, or you deform the normal pronunciation of the
words in order to conform to the metrical rule:

Example 3

His garment was disguisèd very vaine,

(Edmund Spenser, *The Faerie Queene*, III, xii, 9)

In this example, the normally two–syllabled word 'disguised' is expanded to three syllables in order to conform to the metrical pattern. Spenser puts a diacritic mark over the vowel symbol at the end of the word to indicate to the reader that this written symbol has to be realised as the vowel at the centre of a syllable in speech. This option is possible because the '–ed' past tense ending is often realised as a syllable in other English words (*e.g.* 'yielded', 'transported'). Parallel with the term 'poetic grammar' we might call the use of special diacritic marks and spellings in poetry '**poetic orthography**'. Another example of poetic orthography, this time used to produce the opposite result from the Spenser example can be seen below:

Example 4

I hang my silenced harp there, wrung and snapt

(Christina Rossetti, 'Mirage')

By deleting the 'e' vowel symbol in 'snapped', and changing the 'd' to a *t*, Christina Rossetti mirrors more closely than the standard orthography the normal pronunciation of the word, thus ensuring that the reader does not 'syllabify' a potential extra syllable at the end of the line. The Spenser and Rossetti examples are interesting not only because they show poetic orthography at work, but also because it can be easily seen that the appropriate rhythmical result would still be achieved by experienced readers even if the standard orthography had *not* been adopted. Although deviant orthography *forces* a particular pronunciation we cannot conclude that if a word is written in the normal way it must be pronounced normally as well. Rather, we have to take into account both the rules of the language and the dictates of the metrical form in any reading. Sometimes the intentions of the writer will be clear without special orthography. But if a poet is in doubt, then he or she may resort to such special devices to make clear what the reader has to do to scan the line.

In the following example the apostrophe is used to indicate that a potential syllable must be suppressed in performance:

Example 5

By foul play, as thou say'st, were we heaved thence
                    (William Shakespeare, *The Tempest*, I, ii, 62)

This example is fairly standard in that it is easy to pronounce 'sayest' with one syllable or two. This is because:

1   the syllable containing the deleted vowel is a tense marker, information which is easily recoverable from the context (it would be unthinkable to elide the first syllable of the word as this carries lexical information, which would be much more difficult to recover contextually);
2   the consonant intervening between two vowels at the centre of the two syllables in the word is /j/, a phoneme which is on the borderline between being a vowel and a consonant (a semi–vowel). It is thus very easy to elide; and
3   the resulting /st/ consonant cluster is a permissible one in syllable–final position in English.

Let us now pretend, however, that the word involved was not *sayest* but 'shouted'. It would be much more difficult to elide this two–syllable word into one syllable. If we tried to get rid of the vowel at the centre of the second syllable ('shout'd') we would end up with a syllable–final cluster (/td/) which is not permissible in English. If, instead, we tried to remove the /t/ between the two vowels we would also be in difficulty because /t/ requires a lot more articulatory effort in its pronunciation than a vowel, and so is less easy to ignore.

From this discussion we can see that there are some general conventions at work when poets decide what to delete or not:

1   Syllables carrying information which is easily deducible from the context are easier to delete than others. This tends to mean that syllables carrying grammatical information are more likely candidates for elision than those which carry lexical information.
2   The resulting phonetic form after elision has to be a permissible sequence of phonemes in English, otherwise elision cannot take place.
3   There appears to be a hierarchy of the ease with which particular consonants can be deleted. Stops and affricates are less easy to elide than fricatives, and fricatives are less easy to

elide than liquids, laterals or semi–vowels. The ease of suppression corresponds with what some phoneticians have called the **scale of obstruence**. This essentially has to do with the force that is needed to hold the various articulators in the mouth (*e.g.* tongue, teeth, lips) together to produce a particular consonant sound. Stops are more obstruent than fricatives, and so on. Even so, it is possible to find consonant elisions fairly high up the obstruent hierarchy. The fricative /v/, for example, can be elided in grammatical words, as the poetic spelling of 'over' as 'o'er' shows.

In the next example a more radical form of elision takes place:

Example 6
So dry he was for sway, wi' th' King of Naples
                    (William Shakespeare, *The Tempest*, I, ii, 112)

The apostrophe seems to indicate at first sight that only the final /ð/ of *with* will disappear. But this would not remove a syllable, which is required if the line is to scan. In fact, if you say this line out loud to yourself rapidly you can make the *with* disappear almost entirely, its only remaining trace being some rounding of the lips (a feature of the pronunciation of the /w/ of *with*) just before you begin to pronounce the /ð/. This elision of a whole word demonstrates the earlier point about the suppression of grammatical information.

Even after the elision, the pentameter line in example 6 still ends up with eleven syllables. One light syllable too many at the end of the line, or one too few, is permissible in a line of poetry, and there are examples of lines with two extra light syllables. But even though such variation is permissible, the resulting tension with the basic metrical form will still be perceptible and add reading interest.

It should be apparent from the foregoing description that the set of decisions involved in getting the right number of syllables into the line can often be very complex indeed. The poet has to choose whether to relax the metrical rules or the language rules in order to fit together metrical form and linguistic content. If the decision is to keep the metrical form stable, then choices will have to be made concerning which aspect of linguistic structure to alter in order to get the line to 'scan'. There is some evidence to suggest (Fowler 1971b) that when iambic pentameter was new as a form, poets did not relax the metrical form much because they needed to establish the pattern. However, after the pattern became established, poets could more easily deviate from the basic metrical structure, thus producing a wider and more interesting range of tension effects.

5.5.2 Metrics and the English stress system

Besides the tensions created by the act of getting the right number of syllables into a line, there is also possible tension between the metrical system and the language system in terms of what we might call *strong and weak events*. Let us pretend that in a slot where the metrical pattern predicts a remiss (weak event) followed by an ictus (strong event), we want to have the word 'summer'. Where the metre predicts a weak event the language rules predict a strong event, and vice–versa. As we noted in 5.1, every lexically full word in English has an **accented syllable**, the syllable which normally takes a strong stress in speech. The same is true of the grammatical words which consist of more than one syllable, like 'upon' and 'below'. If we make the metre overrule the normal stress–assignment dictates for English, we get a highly unnatural, 'metrical' reading, of the sort young children produce when they are beginning to learn to read poetry out loud. If the normal stress–assignment rules are given precedence over the metre, in this case we have what is traditionally known as a **reversed foot** and a correspondingly less metrical reading. A good example of a reversed foot in an iambic pentameter poem would be the first word of '**Trances** of thought and mountings of the mind' (line 20 of the first book of Wordsworth's *Prelude*, my emphasis). A competent reader would need a fairly extraordinary set of contextual communicative circumstances to reverse the strong and weak stresses normally associated with the accented and unaccented syllables respectively of *Trances*.

It should be clear from this that when we read poems out loud we have a whole series of choices open to us depending upon where on the scale from 'heavily metrical' to 'conversational' we wish our reading to be. This decision will depend in part on what we think is appropriate for the particular text, and the rhythmic style may even change within a text if there is some interpretative motivation to prompt such a change (*cf.* the voice quality change half–way through recitations of 'Adlestrop' discussed in 3.5).

But the situation is actually even more complex than this example suggests. The metrical pattern makes a *binary* choice between strong and weak events, which we have called ictus and remiss. But the rules for English stress are not so simple. Linguists disagree over what exactly 'stress' is and how many degrees of stress there are in English, but it is demonstrable that there must be at least three. If we take a four–syllable word like 'unflappable' we can see that normally the heaviest stress would have to be on 'flap', the accented syllable. But the other three syllables do not all appear to have same weight. In particular, the initial 'un–' appears to be more heavily weighted than the remaining two syllables. For our purposes we will ignore any finer stress distinctions, and consider three degrees of stress, from the heaviest to the lightest: primary (1), secondary (2) and tertiary (3). It should be apparent that the rhythmical tensions involved in fitting together a two–term system (the metre) and a three–term system (the English language) will of its own produce a number of interesting possibilities of rhythmical tension. Let us now examine a concrete example of iambic pentameter:

Example 7
Th'expense of spirit in a waste of shame
Is lust in action; and, till action, lust
Is perjured, murd'rous, bloody, full of blame,
Savage, extreme, rude, cruel, not to trust;

(William Shakespeare, 'Sonnet 129')

I will analyse the lines one at a time, indicating the weightings suggested by both the metre (indicated by 'X' and '/') and the stress–assignment rules for English (indicated by '1', '2' and '3'). I will also indicate the foot divisions (|):

```
    X    /   | X /| X /  |X  /    |X    /
    2    1   | 3  1| 3 3 |3  1    | 3   1
    Th'expense |of spi|rit in |a waste |of shame
```

The fit between the basic iambic metre and the stress assignments normally predicted by a non–poetic, ordinary language reading (sometimes referred to as '**prose rhythm**'[3]) is not very difficult in this line. In the first position, Shakespeare has indicated orthographically that the unstressed syllable of *The* is to be elided into the next. This reduces an eleven–syllable line to the requisite ten syllables. Metrically the first syllable should be a remiss, and the secondary stress normally expected for the *ex–* of *expense* is acceptable as it is not a primary stress. The one major point of disagreement between the two systems is over the treatment of *in*. Various possibilities are open to readers. They can let the metre win and produce a highly metrical reading for this part of the line. This seems unacceptable as it would seem childish when compared with the complexity of the poem and what we know about the author. A second possibility is to let the stress– assignment rules for English override the metrical assignment, thus producing a prose rhythm reading. A third possibility is to compromise between the two systems. The metre predicts a strongly weighted syllable and the language system predicts a tertiary stress. A 'secondary stress' realisation would give equal weight to both systems. This would give us a 'scanning' as follows:

```
 2   1   | 3  1| 3  2 |3  1   | 3   1
Th'expense | of spi| rit in |a waste | of shame
```

In the first and third feet, some tension will be felt in this final reading because these are the places where the basic metrical pattern and the stress rules for English have had to accom– modate one another.

There is one other reasonable possibility for scanning this line, which would involve allowing the beat to fall upon a silence in between *spirit* and *in*, and pronouncing *in a* swiftly so that the two unstressed syllables would occupy one remiss position in the metrical scheme. We will discuss what is involved in allowing beats to fall on silences in 5.8.1.

Now let us move on to the second line:

```
X /  |X /| X    | /   X / | X    /
3  1  |3 1 | 3   | 3   2 1 | 3    1
Is lust | in ac| tion;  |and, till ac| tion, lust
```

In this line the metre apparently predicts a heavily weighted syllable for the unstressed *and*. Upgrading *and* to a primary stress will produce an oddly metrical reading. And reversing the foot structure and having a primary stress on *till*, another grammatical word, will not improve matters much. What the reader is most likely to do here is to allow the third ictus in the line to fall on a silence, thus representing orally the juncture indicated in the middle of the line by the semi–colon:

```
3   1  |3 1 | 3   1 |    2    1 | 3    1
Is lust |in ac|tion;  |  and, till ac|tion, lust
```

As a result of this scanning, note that *and till* will need, according to the metrical form, to occupy the space normally filled by just one remiss syllable. The result is that the *and* is almost entirely elided, its only residue being features of the /n/ (in particular nasalisation) turning up as part of the pronunciation of the /t/ of *till* (/n/ and /t/ are both pronounced in the same place in the mouth, and so it is easy in articulatory terms to move from the /n/ to the /t/).

The third line is easy to scan:

```
X   / | X     / | X     / |X   / | X   /
3   1 | 3     1 | 3     1 |3   1 | 3   1
Is per |jured, mur|d'rous,  bloo|dy, full | of blame
```

The line has one too many syllables, but the two systems can be made to fit together almost perfectly if the second syllable of *murderous* is elided, which is easily accomplished:

```
3   1| 3     1 | 3     1 | 3   1 | 3   1
Is per|jured, mur|d'rous, bloo|dy, full | of blame
```

In the next line larger difficulties appear:

```
X / | X   /   | X   | X /?|  X     /
1 3 | 3   1   | 1   | 1   | 2 3  1
Savage,| extreme,| rude,| cruel,| not to trust
```

There is no option but to reverse the first foot. The second foot works well, but the next two words are both lexically full words which are also monosyllabic. Hence there is no choice but to assign a strong stress to each of them. Once this is done, the remaining ictus will have to be taken up by *trust*. But it is difficult to reduce *not* to a tertiary stress, and in any case the line only has nine syllables as it stands. One possible way round this problem is to make *cruel* into two syllables. This produces an odd pronunciation for the word to many modern ears (though it would have been normal in Shakespeare's time). A twentieth–century reading possibility is to realise the comma after *cruel* as a pause equivalent to a weak, remiss beat. This helps take account of the fact that it marks off the last item of the list, but it does not really help us out of the difficulty with *not*. Whatever way we look at it, this line presents difficulties in trying to resolve the metrical and English stress–assignment systems, and this, in turn, will prompt the reader to look for some *reason* for the sudden change at this point in the poem. One good possibility is appropriateness. Shakespeare is listing a particularly unpleasant set of attributes in this line. Metrical disruption can thus be seen as a rhythmic mirror of the disruptive meaning of the words.

5.6 Intonation, or 'sentence stress'

We have seen already that fitting together the chosen metre for a poem with the syllable and stress structure of English words allows for a wide degree of rhythmical variation and interest. But so far we have been discussing the accentuation of words in isolation from the sentences in which they happen to occur; and it is a well known linguistic fact that when words are joined together into phrases, clauses and sentences, certain syllables become even more prominent than others, even those carrying assigned primary stress according to the considerations we have already discussed.

What this means in essence is that what we have called 'prose rhythm' itself has two layers of organisation, (i) the stress–assignment rules for English words and (ii) English intonation patterns and the special 'sentence stresses' which we assign to particular syllables in sentences in order to make our meaning clear in context.

Let us first take a simple sentence like:

Example 8
He's gone to see Mary

in answer to the question 'Where is John?'. The obvious candidates for primary stress are the accented syllables of the lexically full words, *gone, see* and *Ma–*. But these three syllables will not all have the same weight. Because *Mary* is the important piece of new information in the sentence, its accented syllable, *Ma–* will be louder than the other syllables carrying primary stress and will also exhibit a greater degree of pitch movement than any other syllable (***italicised emboldening*** is used below to indicate the syllable with greatest pitch movement):

He's gone to see **Ma**ry

This syllable, then, bears what I have called the 'sentence stress': what phoneticians usually called **tonic syllable** or **nucleus**. In general terms, the nucleus usually falls on the accented syllable of the word which carries the newest or most contrastive information, or for some other reason needs to be highlighted.

When we speak, we chop up portions of what we say into 'information packages', each containing one such nucleus or tonic syllable. Phoneticians usually call these information packages **intonation groups** or **tone groups**. Very often, tone–group boundaries coincide with major syntactic boundaries (*e.g.* clauses or sentences), as indeed happens in the above description for example 8. But this apparently neat fit is not automatic. The person producing the above sentence as a reply might, for example, want to highlight *two* different pieces of information at the same time: (a) that the person referred to has left (thus cancelling a presumed assumption of the hearer that John is still somewhere in the vicinity) and (b) that he has left for the specific purpose of seeing Mary. In this case, the sentence might well be divided into two tone groups with two nuclei ('|' marks tone–group boundaries):

| He's *gone* | to see **Ma**ry |

In the examples we have looked at so far the nucleus has occurred at the end of the tone group concerned, but this does not have to be the case. In answer to the question 'Where are John and Paul?', the following is easily possible:

Example 9
| ***John's*** gone to see Mary | but I've *no* idea | where to find ***Paul*** |

On this reading there are three tone groups with the nucleus in a different position each time. Given the right contextual circumstances, it is possible to chop the above sentence up into even more tone groups. Moreover, the nucleus can be moved onto literally any syllable within a tone group. In answer to the question 'Has John gone to Gressingham?', for example, we could even receive a reply 'No, he's gone to Gressing–**ton**', the second speaker placing the nucleus on what would normally be a syllable with a very low degree of stress in order to correct the first speaker's pronunciation of the village name.

We can see from the above discussion that the splitting up of sentences into tone groups and the assignment of the nucleus within each tone group is closely connected with matters to do with interpretation and the emphasis of particular parts of the message in context. When poetry is read out loud, like all other spoken forms of language, it will be divided up into tone groups with appropriate assignment of nuclei in order to make the reading 'make sense'. And because we all sub–vocalise when we read, a similar process is enacted whenever poetry is read silently.

There can clearly be a lot of variation in the assignment of tone groups and their nuclei in ordinary conversation, let alone poetry. But we should not be led unwarily into thinking that, as a consequence, 'anything goes'. The meanings which speakers or writers convey will have to be contextually appropriate, and so although it is often theoretically possible to assign more than one intonation pattern to stretches of writing, not all such possibilities are reasonable in given circumstances. Hence, if the answer to the question 'Where has Mary gone?' is 'She has gone to see John' it is difficult to assign the nucleus to any of the first three words precisely because they represent information already given in the question. The tendency will clearly be to put the nucleus on 'John' because (i) this word comes in the end–weighted position in the sentence, and (ii) if Mary finds John, in normal circumstances she will automatically see him (unless he is hiding in a cupboard, for example). However, let us now pretend that Mary has been blind and has just recovered her sight. In this case, the nucleus could easily be moved to 'see' and the hearer of the sentence would be alerted to the special aspect of meaning by the unusual intonation pattern.

There will be a strong tendency when reading metred poems for *each line to be represented as a tone group*, and for the nucleus to fall on the accented syllable of a lexically full word at or near the end of the line. But this does not have to be the case, and indeed sometimes *cannot* be so. At the beginning of Act 5, scene 1, of *Othello*, Othello is convinced that his wife, Desdemona, has been unfaithful to him and is working himself up to kill her in spite of the fact that he still loves her dearly:

Example 10
It is the cause, it is the cause, my soul –
Let me not name it to you, you chaste stars –
It is the cause. Yet I'll not shed her blood . . .
(William Shakespeare, *Othello*, V (ii) 1–3)

In the first line there are only three lexically full words and therefore only three easy candidates for syllables to take primary stress. But we know that the play is written in iambic pentameter and so need to find two more syllables to be stressed. Given what we know about the metrical structure, the comma in the middle of the line and the repetitive structure, one obvious strategy is to divide the line into two tone groups and put the nuclei on syllables which do not normally take primary stress:

| It *is* the cause, | it *is* the cause, my soul – |

This reading assigns a regular metrical structuring to the line and also fits in well with the context. Othello is trying to decide what *is*, and is *not* the case. In other words, our knowledge of metre and how the English language works in communicative contexts leads us into a particular reading for the line. There may, of course, be other ways of construing the line, but note that any successful reading of it will need to realise the iambic pentameter template as well as an appropriate meaning in context. In this way, the combination of metrical scansion and interpretation indicate the range of possible performances of the line to us as we read, and to actors playing the part of Othello.

Another interesting example of the interaction between nucleus assignment and the interpretation of poetic lines is the first stanza of Yeats's 'Leda and the Swan' (the whole poem is quoted in Chapter 2, exercise 7):

Example 11
A sudden blow: the great wings beating still
Above the staggering girl, her thighs caressed
By the dark webs, her nape caught in his bill,
He holds her helpless breast upon his breast.
(W. B. Yeats, 'Leda and the Swan')

There are a number of ways of scanning the last line. The first possibility is to have *holds, help, breast, –pon* and *breast* as the ictus positions. A better solution, in my view, is to put the tonic on **his**, bringing out the contrast between *his* and *her* breasts. This makes sense contextually because of the repetition of *breast* and the contrasting roles of Leda and the swan who is raping her, but means that the second instance of *breast* will have to be downplayed as, in spite of the fact that it is a lexically full word, it will not be able to occupy an ictus position. What we see in this example and the line from *Othello* in example 10 is that even though we know the strict 'rules' for the iambic pentameter line, more communicative, rather than more metrical, performances of poetic lines will tend to be favoured. This strategy allows us to capture the meaning sensitively, and at the same time to feel the rhythmic tension between the actual assignment of stress in particular lines and the pattern of the metrical template underlying the verse.

5.7   Metrical and phonetic organisation put to appropriate use

Now that we have established at least an outline of the rules of the metrical game, we can try out what we have learned in conjunction with other levels of stylistic analysis. We will examine two couplet stanzas from Ted Hughes's 'October Dawn':

Example 12
First a skin delicately here
Restraining a ripple from the air,

Soon plate and rivet on pond and brook;
Then tons of chain and massive lock

To hold rivers. . . .

(Ted Hughes, 'October Dawn')

Hughes is describing the increasing strength of winter as it takes hold on the countryside. Although the stanzaic division suggests a two–part structure, the grammar and lexis indicate a threefold one. The sequencing indicators *First . . . Soon . . . Then . . .* occur in clause–initial and line–initial positions. This three–part division is mirrored in the lexis. The entity which is held back increases in size lexically from *a ripple from the air* to *pond and brook* and finally to *rivers*. The restraining force also increases in size and strength. The *skin* in the first unit gives way to metallic objects in the second (*plate, rivet*). The metallic imagery is continued into the third unit, with *chain* and *lock*, unlike the previous 'restrainers', now being pre–modified by indicators of large size (*tons of, massive*). We are now in a position to see that the phonetic and metrical organisation underscores what we have seen at the lexical and grammatical level by being appropriate to what we have seen there. The distinctions which take place relate to the stanza divisions, and hence reinforce the contrast between the tentative start to the freezing process and the later, harsher developments. Let us now examine a phonetic transcription of the two stanzas:

/fɜːst ə skin delikətli hiə
ristreiniŋ ə ripl from ði eə

suːn pleit n rivit on pond ən bruk
ðen tʌnz əv tʃein n masiv lok/

In the first couplet, slightly over half of the vowel sounds involve the high front vowel /i/ which, as we saw in 4.3, is sound–symbolic of smallness and lightness, and thus reinforces the flimsiness of the lexis. There are fifteen vowel sounds, of which seven are instances of the pure vowel /i/ and two others are diphthongs involving /i/. In a poem written in half–rhyming couplets, this couplet is also the only one in the poem to end in an open–syllable rhyme, helping to mirror the lightness in sound–symbolic terms.[4]

The second stanza, by way of contrast, rhymes on the most obstruent of closed syllable rhymes, stop consonants. Of the thirty–one consonants in this stanza, nine, almost a third, are stops. If we take into account the affricate (1) and the nasals (10), which also involve stopping, the figure is approximately 60%. The equivalent figure for the earlier stanza is approx–imately 40%. Moreover, the alliteration which takes place in the second stanza is on stops and affricates, whereas in the first stanza it was on /s/ and /r/.

This phonetic contrast between the stanzas is upheld by the metrics. The poem is written in iambic tetrameters. If we examine the second, 'heavy' stanza first, we find that the metrical form and the stress–assignment rules for English fit together reasonably well:

```
 2    1  | 3  1| 3  2    1   |  3    1
Soon plate| and ri|vet on pond | and brook
```

```
 2    1  | 3   1  | 3    1 | 3    1
Then tons| of chain| and mas|sive lock
```

The stanza's second line has the right number of syllables, and, apart from some downgrading on the initial linker *then*, no adjustments have to be made. This good fit with a regular 1–3 stress contrast enables the line to be read with a strong metrical beat, reinforcing rhythmically the strength seen at the other linguistic levels. Similar comments apply to the first line, except that the second syllable of *rivet* needs to be elided to fit the 8–syllable line structure.

The metrical situation in the lighter, first stanza contrasts with this and instead is more appropriate to the content found there, with considerably less 'fit' between the underlying metrical pattern and the stress–assignment rules for English:

```
 1   | 3  1  |  1 3  3 | 3   1
First| a skin| delicate|ly here
```

The first line has the requisite eight syllables, but, if it was scanned with two syllables to each foot, both *a* and the third syllable of *delicately* would have to receive primary stresses. This would produce an unacceptably heavy metrical reading. To reconcile the two systems in a less metrical way, *first* has to be upgraded to primary stress and given an ictus, thus occupying

a whole foot. *Skin* and *de–* must receive primary stresses as they
are the accented syllables of lexical words, and that leaves the
deictic *here* to occupy the last ictus position. Rhythmically the
result is that the line cannot be read evenly, as the number of
syllables in the metrical feet varies from one to three. Hence
the syllables will have to be pronounced at differing paces if a
roughly equal amount of time is to be allowed for each foot.

Now let us examine the second line:

```
 3  1 | 3  3  1 | 3  1  | 3   1
Restrai|ning a rip|ple from|  the air
```

There are nine syllables to be fitted into eight slots. The
accented syllables *–strai–, rip–* and *air* must receive primary
stress. That leaves one other ictus position to be filled, with *a*
and *from* being the candidates. *From* looks the best bet, and if
you read the line aloud you will probably find that you have
upgraded the vowel in the word from the reduced vowel /ə/
to /o/, which is a sure sign of stress promotion. Contextually
there appears to be even less reason for stressing *a* than *from*.
The result of this assignment is that the second foot has three
syllables, and, like the first line of the stanza, the delivery of
this line will be uneven in terms of speed and provide another
contrast with the regular rhythm of the succeeding stanza.
Notice also that in this couplet the grammar runs over from
one line to the next, whereas this is not the case for the other
couplet (for a discussion of the relationship between line and
grammar, see 5.9).

The discussion of these four lines of verse has proved to be
quite lengthy, but it should give some idea of the subtle way
in which poets can manipulate phonological and metrical
structure in concert to underscore what is happening at those
linguistic levels which carry meaning more directly. As we saw
when we examined F. W. Bateson's discussion of the lines
from Chaucer's 'Troilus and Criseyde' in 4.3, sounds (and
rhythmic patterns) do not possess meaning of their own
accord, but, if we can, we will infer an appropriateness
relationship between the meaning of poetic lines and their
phonetic and metrical structure.

5.8 Rhythm and timing

One obvious thing which affects timing, and therefore rhythm, is the length of syllables. Other things being equal, the word 'big' will take slightly less time to say than 'splurge', for example. Although they each consist of one syllable, the former has a short vowel and *two* short stop consonants, whereas the latter has a long vowel and *four* consonants, one of which is a fricative and one of which is an affricate. These phonetic facts are bound to affect the rhythmical properties of the lines in which they are involved, even though we will try to 'equalise' things when we read poems out loud or in our heads. Similarly, if two poetic lines, or two metrical feet inside a line, have different numbers of syllables in them, this will affect the rhythm of the line, producing the interesting sort of rhythmic effect referred to in 5.1.

We have already seen from the 'October Dawn' example that the rhythmical properties of lines of verse can be arranged in such a way as to be thought to be appropriate to the subject matter contained in them. Now let us look at another appropriateness example, this time from the perspective of timing. I am interested particularly in line three of the stanza below. Before we comment on it, however, I would like you to read the stanza to yourself and answer the following question: How fast is the horse going? If you want to read the stanza in the context of the whole poem, it is reproduced as example 25 in Chapter 2:

Example 10
My lady's maid had a silken scarf,
And a golden ring had she,
And a kiss from the stranger, as off he went
Again on his fair palfrey.

(John Keats, 'Song')

In my experience, when asked about the speed of the horse, most people reply that the horse is galloping or at least moving fairly fast. It cannot be moving slowly, apparently. Yet we are not *told* this. How, then, do we come to know this mysterious fact?

The poem is written in a typical ballad stanza form which has four iambic feet in the first and third lines and three iambic feet in the second and fourth lines. We can predict, therefore, that the third line should have four heavily stressed syllables and roughly four lightly stressed ones, giving a total of approximately eight syllables. However, if we count them, we find that the line actually has eleven:

```
   X   /  |    X      /  |   X   /|  X    /
   3  3  1 |   3     3    1 | 3  3 2 |  2   1
And a kiss|  from the stran|ger as off|  he went
```

Given the stress–timed nature of English rhythm (see 5.2 and note 1 at the end of this chapter) and the extra unstressed syllable in each of the first three feet, they will all have to be enunciated more quickly than the majority of feet in the poem. This speed of delivery can then be 'explained' by the reader as an iconic reflection of the speed of the horse. This first inferential connection between rhythm and subject matter can then, in turn, act as the basis for a further inference. Why is the stranger riding away speedily from the hall where he has made love to the lady? An obvious explanation is that he wants to get away before the lord returns. This suggestion of guilt chimes well with the disapproval of what he has seen by the poem's narrator, see commentary in 2.1.7.

What is of general interest about this particular example is that metrical and rhythmic structure can be the basis for what we might call 'textual magic'. We are not explicitly told about the speed of the horse or the motivations of the stranger, but we can infer them on the basis of metrical and other kinds of evidence. Thus although the rhythmical level is relatively far removed from the semantic level of language, it can have consequences for *meaning* as well as effect.

Exercise 2

In Tennyson's 'The Passing of Arthur', Sir Bedivere is entrusted by his dying King with the task of giving the magic sword back to the Lady of the Lake. He goes to perform the task but does not do so, and instead he hides the sword in the reeds. Strongly feeling his guilt, he returns to Arthur:

> So strode he back slow to the wounded King
>> (Alfred Lord Tennyson, 'The Passing of Arthur')

Examine how the line's rhythmic and phonetic structure enacts the unwillingness of his return.

5.8.1 Silent Stress

So far in our discussion we have tended to assume that strong and light rhythmical beats always fall on some syllable or other. But there is another possibility, namely that a beat will fall on a silence or pause. Consider, for example, the way in which the phrase 'my lords, ladies, and gentlemen' is usually read out by an announcer at the beginning of an important occasion. If you mimic to yourself the way it might be said, it is very likely that you will put pauses in between the phrases at the points where the commas fall in my written version. These pauses are easily perceptible because they occur at points where major rhythmic beats should occur. These stressed pauses are usually called **silent stresses**,[5] and they can be used in ordinary speech for various reasons, for example to highlight the phrase which follows them. In an oral rendering of a poem the number of silent stresses often increases in the last couple of lines of the poem, as a way of indicating to listeners that the end is coming. Silent stresses in poetry can also help us out in the scanning of poetic lines. If we are a syllable short, we can choose to provide a silent stress at an appropriate place in order to make the line scan. When we discussed *A rolling stone gathers the moss* in 5.2 we noticed that one pronunciation possibility which could be used to even out the rhythm of the two halves of the sentence was to 'realise' a minor beat equivalent to an unstressed syllable in between *stone* and *gath–*. And we have already contemplated a silent stress equal to a major beat in a line from Shakespeare's 'Sonnet 129' which we discussed in 5.5.2:

Example 11
Is lust in action; and till action lust
>> (William Shakespeare, 'Sonnet 129')

We realised the semi–colon as a silent stress in order to avoid the heavily metrical reading which would otherwise place an ictus on *and*. Its positioning also helps to bring out the fact that the line has two clauses which express different but related relationships between action and lust.

Silent stresses are often prompted by line ends and significant mid–line punctuation markers (often called *caesurae*), although it is also possible for readers to realise these tension points not by silences but by noticeably lengthened enunciation of the sounds in the words on either side of the juncture. A line end which also has a punctuation marker is more likely to receive a silent stress than one which has no punctuation; and the more major the punctuation mark the more likely it is that a reader will want to insert a silent stress. But these matters are rarely easy to predict in advance. Factors like the style of recitation chosen, the linguistic context of the line in question and the shade of meaning that the reciter wishes to convey all interact in a complex way to produce different outcomes on different occasions.

An example involving silent stresses in which rhythmical factors can be interpreted as appropriate to meaning can be seen in:

Example 12

'Tis the middle of night by the castle clock,
And the owls have awakened the crowing cock;
Tu–whit!——Tu–whoo!

(Samuel Taylor Coleridge, 'Christabel')

In this poem Coleridge uses a very old, accentual verse form[6] which has four strong stresses to the line, no matter how many syllables the line has. The first two lines have eleven and twelve syllables respectively, but the third has only four. How, then, are we to read the line? One possibility is to assume that each monosyllabic word takes a primary stress and that each of those syllables must be lengthened in order to equalise as much as possible the timing of this line with the others. But it is difficult to lengthen *whit* because it has a short vowel and a final stop consonant. An alternative possibility, which also takes account of the long dash in the middle of the line, is to insert silent stresses after *whit* and *whoo*. Read the line to yourself and work out which rendering you intuitively favour.

I prefer the silent stress reading, which I realise by pauses in the relevant places and the downgrading of *tu* to carry a low degree of stress. This is signalled by the reduction of the vowel in *Tu* to /ə/.

One of the most salient places to find silent stresses is in poems with stanzas which have *a regular pattern of uneven line lengths*. This is the case in many traditional ballads, which have a verse pattern of four feet for the first and third lines and three feet for the second and fourth. Keats's 'Song' is one such example (see example 25 in Chapter 2, and the beginning of 5.8 above). In Christina Rossetti's 'Mirage', the repeated last line of each stanza is only two feet long instead of the four found in the other lines. This helps give each stanza a wistful, 'falling away' quality which is appropriate to the content of the lines:

Example 13

The hope I dreamed of was a dream,
Was but a dream; and now I wake,
Exceeding comfortless, and worn, and old,
For a dream's sake.

I hang my harp upon a tree,
A weeping willow in a lake;
I hang my silenced harp there, wrung and snapt
For a dream's sake.

Lie still, lie still, my breaking heart;
My silent heart, lie still and break:
Life, and the world, and mine own self, are changed
For a dream's sake.

(Christina Rossetti, 'Mirage')

Exercise 3

(a) Characterise the rhythmical properties of the final verse of 'The Voice' by Thomas Hardy in relation to the previous stanzas.

(b) Try to explain why Hardy changes the rhythmical structure of his poem at this point.

(c) Characterise the rhymes in the poem and how they contribute to its meaning and effect.

Woman much missed, how you call to me, call to me,
Saying that now you are not as you were
When you had changed from the one who was all to me,
But as at first, when our day was fair.

Can it be you that I hear? Let me view you, then,
Standing as when I drew near to the town
Where you would wait for me: yes, as I knew you then,
Even to the original air–blue gown!

Or is it only the breeze, in its listlessness
Travelling across the wet mead to me here,
Your being ever dissolved to wan wistlessness,
Heard no more again far and near?

Thus I; faltering forward,
Leaves around me falling,
Wind oozing thin through the thorn from norward,
And the woman calling.

(Thomas Hardy, 'The Voice')

5.9 Foot, line and grammar

Much of the discussion so far has centred on how we decide
to distribute syllables along a line of verse and weight them.
We now turn to the interaction between the metrical *line* and
grammatical structure. The simplest situation is that of the
end–stopped line, where the line–end coincides with a major
syntactic boundary, that of a sentence or a clause, thus leading
almost inexorably to a tone–group boundary at the line–end.

The Elizabethan play, *Gorboduc*, one of our earliest secular
plays, is well known in the history of English drama. But it is
not very often performed as it is rather boring. One feature
which makes its verse–structure tedious is the prevalence of
end–stopped lines. Here, Gorboduc is talking about his two
sons, between whom he is about to divide his kingdom:

Example 14
Gorboduc: Their age nowe asketh other place and trade,
            And myne also doth aske another chaunge,
            Theirs to more travaille, myne to greater ease.

(Thomas Sackville and Thomas Norton, *Gorboduc*, I, ii, 55–7)

This quotation is typical. All three lines end at the end of a major clause, the only significant variation being that the last line contains two verbless clauses. Not surprisingly, most later poetry is found to have a significant proportion of **run–on** lines (or **enjambment** as it is sometimes known). This allows rhythmic variation effects involving tone groups and lines, with the tone group carrying on over a line boundary. The cover term 'run–on line' disguises a variety of different effects, however.

Sometimes at the end of a line we know from the structure received so far that the grammatical structure is not complete and that there must be more to come. Consider the last two lines of the first stanza of 'No Road':

Example 15

Since we agreed to let the road between us
Fall to disuse,
And bricked our gates up, planted trees to screen us,
And turned all time's eroding agents loose,
Silence, and space, and strangers – our neglect
Has not had much effect.

(Philip Larkin, 'No Road')

When we get to *our neglect* we know that there is still more information to come because so far we only have the subject of the clause. The line–end thus interrupts the flow of the grammar. John Sinclair has called this kind of effect **arrest**.[7] The arresting variety of enjambment tends to produce two points of foregrounding, one at the end of the line where the arrest occurs, and one at the later point where the arrested structure is **released**, where the predicted information finally occurs. The prevalent use of arrest structures tends to correlate with *tight* poetic writing styles (see also 11.4.4).[8]

What we have said so far also applies to *our neglect/Has not had much effect*. But here Larkin also uses the possibilities of the arrest structure to create surprise. The information built up in the stanza leads us to assume that the couple's neglect of their relationship will have had significant effects, but the last line of the stanza explicitly cancels this assumption.

The lower down the linguistic scale that an arrest in structure takes place, the more foregrounded it appears to be. Thus, when e. e. cummings breaks a noun phrase over a line boundary he produces a more startling effect than Larkin's use of arrest at the boundary between subject and predicate:

Example 16
i like my body when it is with your
body
                    (e. e. cummings 'i like my body when it is with your')

If the break takes effect over a larger unit than the line (*e.g.* a stanza division), then again the degree of foregrounding and possible surprise is also greater.

The second kind of enjambment (for which we can use Sinclair's term **extension**) is where we mistakenly think at the end of the line that the linguistic unit concerned is completed. Then, when we move to the next line, we discover that there is more of that unit to come. Extension thus correlates with *loose* styles of writing (see also 11.4.4). In the following example Philip Larkin uses extension effects across stanza boundaries:

Example 17
Everyone old has dreamed of all their lives –
Bonds and gestures pushed to one side
Like an outdated combine harvester,
And everyone young going down the long slide

To happiness, endlessly.
                    (Philip Larkin, 'High Windows')

Larkin uses the extension structure for a surprise effect, much as he did with the arrest structure in example 15. When we get to the end of the line *And everyone young going down the long slide* the clause appears to be complete. But when we move to the next line we find that it contains two more adverbials at the end of the clause, in the form of the prepositional phrase *to happiness* and the adverb *endlessly*. *To happiness, endlessly* cancels the assumptions that we have made concerning the younger generation going down the long slide. The connotations of *going down the long slide* lead us to assume that the young are heading for misery. But Larkin then tells us that the opposite is in fact the case.

Exercise   4

Examine the way in which Ted Hughes uses arrest and extension
structures in the following extract.

> Terrifying are the attent sleek thrushes on the lawn,
> More coiled steel than living – a poised
> Dark deadly eye, those delicate legs
> Triggered to stirrings beyond sense – with a start, a
> > bounce, a stab
> Overtake the instant and drag out some writhing thing.
> No indolent procrastinations and no yawning stares,
> No sighs or head scratchings. Nothing but bounce and stab
> And a ravening second.
>
> > (Ted Hughes, 'Thrushes')

5.10   An   extended   analysis

Now that we have examined a number of salient features of
the phonetic and metrical structure of English poetry, let us
apply them to a whole poem. In doing so, we will return to
the connection with musicality which is often at the heart of
poetic manipulation of the sound stratum of language:

Example 18

> Rose–cheeked Laura, come;
> Sing thou smoothly with thy beauty's
> Silent music, either other
> > Sweetly gracing.
>
> Lovely forms do flow
> From concent divinely framed;
> Heav'n is music, and thy beauty's
> > Birth is heavenly.
>
> These dull notes we sing
> Discords need for helps to grace them;
> Only beauty purely loving
> > Knows no discord,

But still moves delight,
Like clear springs renewed by flowing,
Ever perfect, ever in themselves
    Eternal.
              (Thomas Campion, 'Rose–cheeked Laura')

This poem is an easy one to understand in general terms. The *persona* links his praise of Laura's beauty with praise of her singing, saying that they perfectly complement one another. This contrasts with the other people present, who cannot sing so well (*These dull notes we sing*), and, by association, are not as attractive. But the poem is also somewhat elusive. Is Laura really singing, or is Campion merely using the notion of music as a metaphor for her beauty? And when he talks about *we* singing, is he really talking about song, or about writing, the notes being metaphors for the poet's words? He may well be saying that Laura is so beautiful that it is not possible to write poems (or songs) to describe her beauty adequately. It appears that these interpretations for the text exist side by side. Individually they all account for the text adequately, and the poem gains from our being able to hold all of these interpretative aspects together in one integrated whole. Whatever is the case, it is clear that the link between music and beauty is an important one, and as we shall see, Campion uses the phonetic and metrical resources at his disposal to enact what he is saying in an interesting way.

Metrically, 'Rose–cheeked Laura' is quite complex. The middle two lines of each stanza are written in trochaic tetrameters (see 5.4). The initial lines of each stanza only have five syllables each, and would appear to be trimeters (the first lines of stanzas 2 and 4 are the clearest examples). But the final line of each stanza is even shorter. These lines have only two feet and because they come at the end of the stanza they exhibit the 'falling away' effect which we saw earlier in Christina Rossetti's 'Mirage'. If we examine the poem more closely we can also observe that in the majority of lines the stress assignments according to the language system and the metrical system coincide remarkably well, with ictus and remiss being filled by primary and tertiary stresses respectively. This regular alternation of obviously contrasting stresses helps to give the verse a dominant 'musical' beat which is appropriate to the subject matter. This character of regular marked alternation also applies at the level of phonetic segments. There is a very strong tendency for the stressed, ictus, syllables to have a long vowel or diphthong and for the unstressed, remiss, syllables to have a short, reduced syllable, usually /i/. This can be seen in lines 3 and 4 for example.

The characteristics we have listed so far apply to four important words in the poem which are phonetically parallel, *music* (/mjuːzik/), *beauty* (/bjuːti/), *smoothly* (/smuːðli/) and *purely* (/pjuəli/). The poem revolves around the integration of the concepts of 'music' and 'beauty', and Campion is able to use the parallel phonetic form of the two words to link the two concepts in the reader's mind. They both possess the 'musical' qualities so far described, they are both repeated in close proximity (in the same phrase in stanza 1 and in the same line in stanza 2) and in addition, they are parallel to two manner adverbs in the poem which suggest harmony and perfection.

Once this pattern has been noticed, other harmony and perfection words can also be seen to parallel (a little more loosely) those already mentioned in that they exhibit this alternation between a long vowel and /i/, as in *sweetly, perfect* and *divinely*. All of the words exhibiting the qualities we have noticed are syntactically related to music or beauty in the poem, and they all apply to Laura.

What we have seen so far helps us to demonstrate the poem's musical texture and to show that the dominant ideas of Laura's singing, beauty, harmony and perfection are related together through phonetic patterning. But another important feature of the poem's organisation is the contrast between Laura and the others, including the narrator, who sing dull notes, and so by inference are also not as physically attractive. This contrast is made clear in lines 9–10, which also turn out to be internally deviant in terms of the features we have been examining:

> These dull notes we sing
> Discords need for helps to grace them

Dull, notes and *sing* must presumably take primary stresses as they are monosyllabic lexically full words. This would appear to 'use up' the three strong beats for a trimeter line. But it is also arguable that, given the context in which they occur, the other two words should also receive primary stresses. *These* and *we* are textually contrastive items (*these notes* versus the given 'those notes' sung by Laura and *we* versus the previously introduced *thou* referring to Laura).

This would give a deviant five major stresses to the line. Whether a particular reader chooses this solution, or prefers to downgrade one or two of the line's syllables, it is obvious that the metrical pattern set up so far is disrupted in a major way at the point that the narrator's dull notes are referred to. Metrically, then, the line *enacts* its discordant content.

The next line, which completes the clause started in the first line of the stanza, has seven stop consonants in it, whereas the other lines only have between one and four each. Lines 9 and 10 together also exhibit a high proportion of monosyllabic words (eleven out of twelve) compared with the rest of the poem. The contrasting unmusical content of these two lines, when compared with the rest of the poem, is thus also brought out in terms of phonetic quality.

The other part of the poem which deviates from the dominant rhythmical pattern is the end (lines 15–16). The only occurrences of the phoneme /ɔː/ occur in these lines, linking together the words *perfect* and *eternal* through a parallelism which also involves the alternation between long and reduced vowels seen elsewhere. These two lines also exhibit metrical peculiarities. The last line has just three syllables, of which only /tɔːn/ can easily take a primary stress. If we see the line as trochaic, it would appear to begin with half a foot, containing only a remiss syllable. One solution to this problem is to see the last line of the poem as containing an extra silent stress compared with those needed to 'equalise' the last lines of the other stanzas. Line 15, on the other hand, has one syllable too many, and it is conceivable that we could read the line so that it contained five major stresses, the last of which (/selvz/) could be 'borrowed' over into the last line from the previous one.

Whatever performance solution a particular reader arrives at, the metrical deviation is very apparent, and occurs at the point in the poem where we are told that Laura's music (and hence her beauty) has eternal qualities, a statement which is also heavily foregrounded by its position at the very end of the poem.

Exercise 5

Examine the phonetic and metrical structure of W. H. Auden's 'In Memory of W. B. Yeats' and how it relates to the poem's meaning. The poem is not reproduced here for reasons of space.

Discussion of exercises

Exercise 1

(a) You should feel a significant pause in your reading of the lines with only three feet, as psychologically you try to equalise the four lines metrically. This metrical structure is quite common in English ballads, and is sometimes used for specific interpretative effect (see 5.8).

(b) 'Upon His Departure Hence' – iambic monometer.
'The Aged Lover Renounceth Love' – iambic trimeter.
'Never Weather–beaten Sail' – trochaic septameter.
'Phantom' – iambic tetrameter.
'Lamia' – iambic pentameter.

Exercise 2

Through its high density of long sounds, *So strode he back slow* enacts the slowness it refers to, and hence by inference, Sir Bedivere's unwillingness to return. The alliteration on *So, strode* and *slow* is on fricatives, which are long consonants. These words also exhibit assonance on a diphthong (/ ou/). All diphthongs are long and *he* also contains a long vowel. Metrically, *strode, back, slow, wound–* and *king* are lexically full and are obvious candidates for primary stress. There are other possibilities, though, which would increase the number of strong stresses to a deviant six, or even seven. It is possible to upgrade *so* to stress the manner of Sir Bedivere's walking. This would also enable all three of the alliterating and 'assonating' words to be parallel in stress terms. It is also conceivable that there could be a silent stress after *slow*, further emphasising the unwillingness. In the case of a reading which gives the line too many syllables, the deviation is likely to be correlated in the reader's mind with the slowness, thus foregrounding Sir Bedivere's unwillingness to return to Arthur. Even if the line is given the standard five–ictus interpretation, *back* and *slow* will each occupy a whole foot, thus forcing a slowed reading which will mirror the content of the lines.

Exercise 3

(a) This poem is one of a series which Hardy wrote about
& his dead wife. Although happy together in the first years
(b) of their marriage, they often quarrelled in later life, and after her death Hardy suffered considerable remorse. The poems about his wife thus try to capture the early happiness of his marriage in contrast to the later bitterness. In this poem he thinks he hears her voice brought to him on the wind. This brings back the pleasant memories of the early marriage. But then, in the last stanza, he realises that he is mistaken, and is returned suddenly to the realisation of the uncomfortable loneliness of life without his wife.

The first three stanzas, with some slight variations, consists of four–beat lines of accentual verse, with a dominant pattern of twelve syllables for the first and third lines and ten syllables for the second and fourth. These lines describe the voice, the early years with his wife and the dawning realisation that he is mistaken. The shorter line lengths of the second and fourth lines have the 'falling away' effect that I have described in 5.8.1, helping to mirror the intangible quality of Hardy's mistaken hearing of his wife's voice and the past memories which are evoked. The last stanza enacts the mental discomfort of finding that he is really alone and that his mistaken perception is a result of the fact that he misses the woman so much that he tries to see her everywhere he looks. The slow, faltering quality of his movement, which in turn represents his mental state, is mimicked by the rhythmical disruption of *Thus I; faltering forward*, with its strong mid–line caesura and a total of seven syllables instead of the normal twelve. The most plausible assignment for the stressed syllables would seem to be one on *I*, a silent stress to represent the caesura and one each on the accented syllables of *faltering* and *forward*. The first two strong stresses will thus fall together, producing a further rhythmical awkwardness. Line three of the last stanza has only nine syllables, and lines two and four have only seven each. The last line has only two syllables which can easily take a primary stress, *wom–* and *call–*. The 'falling away' effect is thus very marked here, helping to characterise the ethereal quality of the experience he has just gone through. The second line can be read as having either two or three major stresses, and so the 'falling away' effect is also discernible there to a lesser extent. This helps us to see the possibility of a symbolic interpretation, where the falling leaves represent old age and imminent death.

(c)   The second and fourth lines have normal rhymes, but the first and third have rhymes extending over three syllables. In the first stanza, the rhyme is an open one, which involves the repeated phrase *call to me*, thus helping to represent the idea of an echo from the past. In the second stanza, *view you then* rhymes with *knew you then*, juxtaposing present hypothetical desire and remembered reality. In the third stanza the effect of the wind and the intangible, ghostly wife is conveyed through polysyllabic words containing a high density of the voiceless fricative /s/, which thus takes on relevant sound–symbolic qualities. The open rhymes of lines two and four are also appropriate to this intangible subject matter. In the last stanza a break in the pattern occurs. The first and fourth lines have only two–syllable rhymes, and of course it is the first line of the last stanza which enacts the author's realisation of his plight. On the other hand, the rhyme of lines 2 and 4 ranges over two syllables instead of the one found in equivalent lines of the other stanzas, and in the second part of this rhyme pair we return to Hardy's characterisation of the ghost calling to him.

Exercise 4

Hughes uses arrest structures in these lines to create tension and suspense. This structuring can then be seen as mirroring the suspense the narrator feels waiting for the birds to strike, a tenseness which itself mirrors that of the thrushes. In the first line the subject phrase is held up until after the verb. In lines 2 and 3, a noun phrase is broken across the line before the occurrence of the head noun. This is very arresting indeed. Note that a break between the head noun and its post–modifying phrase (*e.g.* 'the man/in the moon') is considerably less arresting. In lines 3 and 4 a head noun is broken away from its post–modifying relative clause. The verb *overtake* at the beginning of line 5 does not have an obvious grammatical subject, but given that it has no final 's', the subject must be plural. Hence the subject is either the agglomerated parts of the bird or the legs of line 3, in which case there is another, over-arching arrest structure. Line 5 represents the kill, and so is strongly end–stopped. The next line is also not arrested (although it might appear so at first sight, owing to the verbless nature of the clause) and this is appropriate as it describes non–'attent' qualities opposed to that of the hunting birds. The last line of the stanza is the first true extension structure of the poem, representing, almost as an afterthought, the birds' final eating of the worms after their swoop onto their prey.

Exercise 5
For a discussion of the phonetic and metrical properties of this poem, see Nash (1986).

Notes

1. Not all languages have stress timing. The rhythm of languages like French and Arabic, for example, are said to be syllable timed, because their speakers perceive each syllable, not the interval between each strong stress, to take a roughly equal time. It is also worth remembering that 'equal time' between strong stresses in English is not a precise concept when measured in microseconds. The phenomenon of rhythmic timing appears to have as much to do with our *perceptions* as with measured equality in micro–time.
2. Phonetic and rhythmical patterning is sometimes put to good use by prose writers, however. See, for example, Leech and Short's discussion (1981: 89, 95) of passages from Conrad's 'The Secret Sharer' and Lawrence's 'Odour of Chrysanthemums'.
3. The terminological distinction between prose rhythm and metre derives from Fowler (1966b).
4. An open syllable is one which ends with a vowel. A closed syllable ends with a consonant. In sound–symbolic terms, where relevant, closed syllables will be appropriate to heavier, definite, things, and open syllables to the less lighter and less definite.
5. See Abercrombie (1965 and 1971).

6. See Leech (1969: 118–19). Knowles (1987: 135–9) refers to the same kind of verse structure as 'binary verse'.

7. Sinclair has developed the related notions of arrest, release and extension in a series of three articles, Sinclair (1966, 1968 and 1972).

8. See Sinclair (1972). For more general discussions of loose and tight styles, see Hendricks (1976: Ch. 5).

Further reading

Leech (1969: Ch. 7) discusses metre in poetry and Leech (1986) discusses music in metre. Cureton (1992) is an advanced discussion of rhythm and metre. Haynes (1989) relates metre to viewpoint and ideology (see also Chapter 8 below).

CHECKSHEET 4: METRICAL STRUCTURE

A. Metrical patterns

(a) Is there an identifiable metrical form for the poem as a whole? If so, what is it, and what effects do you associate with it?

(b) Are there any lines where interesting rhythmical effects are created by marked good fit, or marked lack of fit between the dictates of the metrical form and those of the stress assignment rules for English? If so, note down their effect.

(c) Are there any lines in the poem which depart significantly from the overall metrical 'set' for the poem? If so, what meaning and/or effects are connected with this internal metrical deviation?

(d) Examine the relationship between grammatical organisation and line boundaries. Is the dominant pattern end–stopping, arrest–release or extension? Can you determine any significant local meaning effects related to these occurrences? What effect do these structural matters have on the assignment of tone–group boundaries and the positioning of their nuclear syllables?

(e) If there is a consistent pattern revealed by (d) above, are there any significant internal deviations from this overall norm, and what effects are associated with them?

B.   Interpretative integration of metrical and phonetic patterns

Are there any interesting ways in which phonetic and metrical organisation interrelate? How do the sound and rhythmic patterns you have identified integrate with what you have noted about the poem at linguistic levels more directly related to meaning?

CHAPTER 6

Drama: the conversational genre

6.1 Introduction

Drama is the literary genre which is most like naturally occurring conversation (though it is not *exactly* the same, as we shall see in 6.3 – for example, conversations in plays are designed to be 'overheard' by an audience, and this is only true for a small minority of naturally occurring dialogues). Although some *poems* have speaking *personae*, most are authorial monologues. *Novels* typically contain talk between characters, and so they are a bit more like conversation, but they also contain large stretches of narrative description. *Drama*, on the other hand, largely consists of character–to–character interaction, and it is for this reason that the most profitable areas of language analysis to apply to drama are those developed by linguists to describe face–to–face interaction and how we infer meaning in context. This is not to say that what we have learned about poetry has no relevance for prose or drama. The fictional prose of D. H. Lawrence, for example, often uses language features typical of poetry (*e.g.* heavy use of metaphor and lexical repetition) to increase the emotional strength of his descriptions. Poetic drama, like Shakespeare's or Marlowe's, is clearly amenable to the forms of stylistic analysis typically used on poems. And grammatical deviation, phonetic parallelism and style shifts, for example, can all be examined with profit in 'unpoetic' drama or prose texts, even though such features will probably occur with less meaning–related density than in poems. There is a clear general lesson for us here. I am gradually introducing you to what I like to call my 'stylistician's tool–kit', and, in doing so, I am showing you the analytical tools that work best for explaining our understanding of each individual genre. However, it is very important to remember that you will be able to use all the forms of analysis to some extent on any text you choose to examine. What we will learn about drama in the next few chapters can easily be applied to the conversation parts of novels and even to 'conversational' poems, like those we saw in 2.2.1.

6.2 The discourse structure of drama

We noted in 2.2.1 that although there are many poems with *personae*, the *prototypical discourse structure of poetry* has just one discourse level, where authors apparently address readers directly. *Prototypical drama* is more complex discoursally, having at least two levels of discourse, the author–audience/reader level and the character–character level:

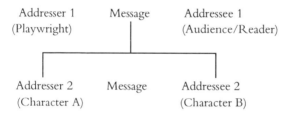

Addresser 1   Message   Addressee 1
(Playwright)   (Audience/Reader)

Addresser 2   Message   Addressee 2
(Character A)   (Character B)

The overarching level of discourse is that between the playwright and the audience. Character talk is embedded in that higher discourse, allowing the audience to 'listen in' to what the characters say. It is this 'doubled' structure which gives rise to the notion of dramatic irony, which typically occurs when the knowledge of some of the characters is less than that of the author and audience at level 1, producing tension for the audience as they wonder what will happen when that knowledge is revealed to the characters. This tension can, in turn, give rise to a range of effects from the tragic to the comic. In Shakespeare's *Othello*, we know that Iago dupes Othello into thinking that his wife, Desdemona, has been unfaithful to him. As Othello's jealousy mounts we hope that he will discover Iago's plot before tragedy arrives, but he does not, and kills Desdemona in spite of her protest–ations of innocence. In the 'Basil the Rat' episode of John Cleese and Connie Booth's television situation comedy, *Fawlty Towers*, the Spanish waiter, Manuel, has a pet rat, secretly named Basil after the hotel's absurd owner, Basil Fawlty. The rat escapes from its cage on the day when the hotel receives a random visit by Mr Carnegie, a food hygiene inspector. Will Manuel, Basil, Sybil, his wife, and Polly, the maid, be able to serve the inspector with his meal without him discovering the rat? There are, of course, a series of hilarious close calls. Then, at the end of the meal, when Mr Carnegie is offered the biscuit tin to select biscuits to go with his cheese, the lid is removed to reveal the rat inside:

Example 1

. . . Mr Carnegie is stunned and continues to stare at the rat.

Basil: . . . Would you care for a rat? Or . . . ? Just . . . just the biscuits then please Polly.

Polly leaves with the tin. Carnegie continues to stare into space.

Sybil: . . . Black or white?

Carnegie: . . . Hmmm?

Sybil: Black or white?

Carnegie: . . . Black, please . . . was that a . . . ?

Sybil: There we are.

Polly: *(coming back)* Here are the biscuits.

She holds the tin out, now minus rat. Mr Carnegie stares at it. He takes a biscuit mechanically and just holds it. In the background Manuel is dragging an unconscious Basil by the heels out of the door into the lobby.

Sybil: *(conversationally)* I'm afraid it's started to rain again

(John Cleese and Connie Booth, *The Complete Fawlty Towers*, 'Basil the Rat', pp. 332–3)

Interestingly, because the programme ends at this point, we never know whether Mr Carnegie discovers the truth or not. Have the others managed to convince him that he was hallucinating? As usual in this programme, the women have managed to keep an air of normality going. Basil Fawlty is not so proficient, asking Carnegie accidentally if he would care for a rat, and then passing out because of the shock. But if Manuel manages to remove Basil before the inspector sees he has fainted, they might just get away with it . . .

Although our account of prototypical drama needs two discourse levels to account sensibly for what goes on, we can also see that there can be many variations on this basic pattern. At the character level we rarely have just two characters talking to one another for the whole play (though it does happen – in *Happy Days* by Samuel Beckett, for example). We normally have a succession of different contexts, with different groupings of characters talking, just as we saw in 2.2.1 with the non–prototypical poem 'Long–Legged Fly' by W. B. Yeats.

There are also examples of plays with more than two discourse levels: usually plays which also have a narrator. This narrator stands outside the action of the play, perhaps completely, perhaps partly. Bertolt Brecht's *Caucasian Chalk Circle* is a clear example of a three–level discourse structure:

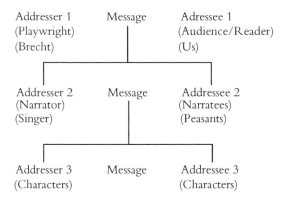

We observe a Singer who 'narrates' a story to a group of peasants. He begins most of the scenes with a mini–narrative about the characters in the story he tells. The characters then act out the story in front of the peasants (and us). Brecht thus has us 'looking in' on a tale which is apparently being told to others. The story is a variation on a very old tale, about the wisdom of Solomon. Choosing this three–level structure, with the peasants on stage 'listening' to the story helps to remind us that we are only watching a fiction, and that we should not be completely enthralled. This is a particularly important matter for Brecht, who, with his theory of *alienation*, wanted his audience not to become completely involved in what they watched, but to distance them to some degree so that they could examine more easily, and more critically, what was happening on the stage. At the same time, this structure helps to remind us of traditional *oral* renderings of stories, making what we see seem basic, fundamental and universal.

There can also be variations on this three–level structure. In Robert Bolt's *A Man for All Seasons.* for example, there is a narrator, but no group of people separate from the audience or the characters for him to talk to. This narrator also happens to be Sir Thomas More's steward in the story from which he steps out to provide narratorial comment. So, he is a dramatic version of a typical first–person narrator in a novel. The structure for *A Man for All Seasons* is thus:

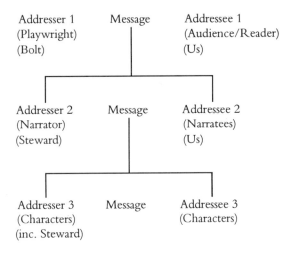

Addresser 1 (Playwright) (Bolt)	Message	Addressee 1 (Audience/Reader) (Us)
Addresser 2 (Narrator) (Steward)	Message	Addressee 2 (Narratees) (Us)
Addresser 3 (Characters) (inc. Steward)	Message	Addressee 3 (Characters)

Hence in this play the three discourse levels are 'collapsed' together in one of two places when the steward is on stage, at levels 1 and 2 on the right–hand side of the diagram and at levels 2 and 3 on the left–hand side. The narrator is also a character, and at times we are the addressees of both the playwright and the narrator. We can see from this that different plays can have what I like to call different 'discourse architectures'. These architectures, which can also change as a play unfolds, are crucial for us to grasp if we are to understand the play and react sensitively to it. For example, plays with narrators have a mechanism for guiding audience reaction which is not present in plays with a more prototypical dramatic discourse structure.

Exercise 1

(a) My intuitions about the prototypical structures of the three major
    literary genres are (i) that poetry typically has *one* discourse level
    (author to reader) but individual poems may have more than one,
    (ii) drama must have *two* discourse levels (author and character
    levels) but particular plays may have more than two, and (iii) prose
    fiction must have *three* (author, narrator and character levels),
    though particular novels or stories may have more than three. So
    for me, Wordsworth's 'The Daffodils' and Shakespeare's *Macbeth*
    have prototypical discourse structures for poems and plays
    respectively but Yeats's 'Long–Legged Fly' and Brecht's *The
    Caucasian Chalk Circle* or Alan Bennett's *Talking Heads* series of TV
    dramatic monologues (which have one actor producing a
    monologue throughout) have non–prototypical structures.
    Working with someone else, check your intuitions against mine,
    and try to think of texts which do not conform to the 'standard' for
    each genre.

(b) Select a representative selection of 10 poems and 10 plays all by
    different authors, and from different periods, and examine them to
    check whether your intuitions about the prototypical structure for
    each genre are borne out. Examine more carefully the texts which
    vary from the prototypes and try to work out why the author has
    chosen the particular variation you find.

6.3   How like real conversation is dramatic dialogue?

I began this chapter by noting that drama was the literary
genre most like naturally–occurring conversation. But it is not
exactly like it, as our discussion in 6.2 has begun to show.
Because I am concentrating on the *language* of literary texts I
am not examining in any detail other aspects of our
understanding of literature, for example socio–cultural setting.
These factors play an important role, of course, and in drama
this is more obvious in terms of the 'conditioning' of the
audience than for the other genres. We can read poems and
novels in our own homes, but theatre audiences often travel
large distances to 'take part' in an act of spoken
communication in which they do not usually get a speaking

turn, and where they know that the actors on stage are saying words which were written by someone else and expressing views which they do not expect to be committed to after the show is over. It is the artificiality of the situation which helps us to be so strongly aware of level 1 in the 'doubled' discourse structure of drama which I have outlined in 6.2.

In any case, most ordinary conversations do not have a 'doubled' discourse structure. In this respect, the rough conversational equivalent of a play would be a conversation where two people, A and B, were talking while a third, C, is overhearing what is being said, and where A, B and C all know that this is the case. Note that in this situation, A and B might well say things for the benefit of C which they might not otherwise mention. Radio and television chat shows have this structure, and in them, the guests are often introduced by the host 'telling' the guests who they are and/or what they do or have just done: 'Madonna, you've just shocked the publishing world with your book of nude pictures.' Clearly, this information is for the immediate benefit of the audience, not the guest.

If dramatic dialogue is both like and unlike ordinary conversation, it is important for us to see where the similarities and dissimilarities lie. We can only apply conversational analysis to drama in relation to those areas where conversation and plays are similar.

6.3.1 How dramatic dialogue is *not* like conversation

Apart from the area we have just explored, the other main way that drama is *not* like conversation stems from the fact that dramatic dialogue is *written to be spoken*. Casual conversation, on the other hand, is unprepared and unrehearsed. There are counter–examples, of course. If you want to ask your employer for a rise in wages you might well run through the arguments in your mind before you ask, and in radio and TV interviews of politicians, the politicians usually demand to know in advance what questions they are going to be asked, so as to avoid being caught out. But when we chat casually, we make up things as we go along, and very fast at that. We can see what differences the spoken/written–to–be–spoken contrast gives rise to by comparing a stretch of tape–recorded conversation with an extract from a dramatic dialogue. The following is a transcript of a tape recording of a dinner conversation between two couples. It is a version, without stress and intonation markings, of an extract transcribed in Crystal and Davy (1975). I have preserved Crystal and Davy's labelling of the participants. A is married to D, B is married to C, and the two couples are old friends. They have been comparing holiday experiences, and A and D have just started to talk about their holiday in Denmark, which involved a sea crossing:

Example 2

A: and it's of course we could say to the children we'll   (1)
     just be upstairs and they knew they just had to k put
     (D: m) their dressing gown on and come up (C: Yeah) if
     they wanted us . and that was super −

C: w were you . did you have a car with you.   (5)

A: m

D: m . it's all (C: how) included in the price

C: I see (A: Oh I <?>) er . how did you get − I mean how
     did you find that side of it because (A: marvellous) you
     know (D: <?>) some people say that (A: <?>) driving (10)
     a car across a ferry is the devil of a job .

D: eh

A: well this was (*clears throat*)

D: across a

C: I mean taking a car across − to the continent (A: no)   (15)
     on on a ferry (A: it's it's) is is hell

A: no it isn't at all

B: why

C: I don't know but <?>

D: well I mean we . we've . done it nu I mean the across (20)
     the channel − is that what you mean

C: yes that's wha (D: in nu) exactly what I mean
     across the channel

                                   (Crystal and Davy, 1975: 52)

This conversation is clearly unscripted, and as a consequence the speakers have to think out what they want to say in a very short space of time. The extract has 14 major conversational turns plus 10 other attempted contributions (represented in brackets in the middle of the major turns). It is 165 words long (plus a number of identifiable noises [e.g. *nu, m*] and uninterpretable contributions [marked <?>]). Yet this part of the tape–recording is only 30 seconds long, an average of more than 5 words a second. Not surprisingly, when a host of linguistic decisions (take your turn at the right time, make your contribution relevant, choose the right words, get your grammar sorted out, get your pronunciation right, and so on) have to be taken at this fantastic speed, mistakes are bound to occur. These mistakes, characteristic of ordinary conversation, are normally referred to by linguists as **normal non–fluency**. They would be edited out if you were writing a speech, for instance. Examples in this extract are:

1 *voiced fillers*, used to give speakers time to work out exactly what they want to say (*e.g. of course* (1), *er* (8), *you know* (9)–(10), and *I mean* (15));

2 small *silent pauses* with a similar function in the transcription (*e.g.*(4), (5), (7)), marked '.';

3 *mispronunciations* (*e.g. w were* (5) and *wha* (22));

4 *unnecessary repetitions* (there are three such cases in line (16): *on on a ferry (A: it's it's) is is hell*;

5 *grammatical structures which are abandoned* part of the way through (*e.g. it's of course we could say to the children* (1) *how did you get – I mean how did you find that side of it* (8)–(9));

6 *attempts at taking conversational turns which are lost* in the general melee (*e.g.* D's attempt to say something or other through three failed turns (10)–(14));

7 *the competition among the speakers to take the conversation off onto a topic of their choosing*: D clearly fails in such an attempt in the example mentioned in (6) above, and C manages from (7) onwards to move the topic from how good the ferry was for keeping an eye on the kids while having fun, to the problems of taking a car on a ferry.

These normal non–fluency features are usually not noticed in the course of ordinary conversation because we all produce them all the time, and because when we listen to others we are more interested in working out (a) what is being said, (b) what the implications might be and (c) getting our own turn (how often have you found yourself not paying enough attention to another speaker because you are concentrating on jumping in yourself at the next permissible juncture?). Unless you are studying them, normal non–fluency features only become noticeable when they occur with unusual frequency. When I was at school we had a Religious Studies teacher who said *um* or *er* every two or three words. He became famous among the boys in the school, and to make the lessons more interesting we invented a secret game of classroom cricket around these and other mannerisms. The batting side scored one run for *um*, two for *er*, and so on. The teacher's raised index finger meant that the batsman was out, clean–bowled, and so on. We played this game undiscovered for some time until, at the climax to one match (three runs to get and one wicket to fall), an unwary boy cried 'Owzat?' at the fall of the last wicket.

Normal non–fluency does not occur in drama dialogue, precisely because that dialogue is written (even though it is written to be spoken). Moreover, if features normally associated with normal non–fluency do occur, they are per-ceived by readers and audience as having a *meaningful* function precisely because we know that the dramatist must have included them *on purpose*. The following extract is from *A Man for All Seasons*, a play which centres on Sir Thomas More's refusal to give his approval to the divorce of Henry VIII from Catherine of Aragon. Henry wants the divorce because Catherine has not borne him any sons and he is worried about the succession to the throne when he dies. Sir Thomas, Henry's Chancellor, does not approve of the divorce as the Pope has not given his dispensation. Here, the career diplomat, Chapuys has been trying to edge More to resign as Lord Chancellor if the Church in Convocation agrees to Henry's proposed divorce, a decision which will set the English Church and Government at odds with Rome. Lord Norfolk then rushes in with the news that Convocation has agreed to the divorce:

Example 3

Norfolk: One moment, Roper, I'll do this! Thomas — (*Sees CHAPUYS*) Oh. (*He stares at CHAPUYS, hostile*)

Chapuys: I was on the point of leaving, your Grace. Just a personal call. I have been trying . . . er to borrow a book – but without success – you're sure you've no copy, my lord?

(Robert Bolt, *A Man for All Seasons*, Act II)

Norfolk's incomplete sentence is not to be ignored, but interpreted as his coming to a dead stop at the sight of

Chapuys, who he distrusts. Similarly, Chapuys's voiced and unvoiced fillers in the middle of his speech are not to be perceived as normal non–fluency either. They clearly represent his discomfort as he comes up with a flimsy excuse for visiting More. He apparently does not want Norfolk to know why he has come, and Bolt ensures that we come to this conclusion about his motives through this conversational behaviour. In well–constructed dramatic dialogue everything is meant by the playwright, even when it is apparently unintended by the character.[1]

Another way in which dramatic conversation is not like ordinary conversation relates to what is often called *feedback*. When someone is talking to us it is important that we give regular indications, while they are talking, to the effect that we are still listening, and understand what is being said. Such feedback can take the form of movements, like head nods, selecting appropriate expressions (*e.g.* raising the eyebrows to indicate surprise at what you have just been told, or pulling a funny face to indicate displeasure) and appropriate response noises (*e.g.* D's *m* and C's *yeah* in the middle of A's first turn in example 2 above). The extent of the need for such feedback signals can be seen if you watch someone listening to what is being said on the other end of a telephone line. Telephonic addressees will use head nods, facial expressions and so forth, even though the people they are listening to can't possibly see them. Moreover, if you make a point of withholding feedback noises completely it is only a few seconds before the person talking at the other end begins to ask if you've been cut off. Try it when you next phone your parents or a friend, and time how long it takes before you are asked 'are you still there?'.

Clearly, feedback does take place in drama conversation, and sometimes it may be indicated in the script. But it certainly won't occur anything like as regularly as it does in real life, and often when one character is talking on stage the other characters stand completely still and expressionless. This sort of convention ensures that the attention of the audience is focused on whoever is speaking. It would be distracting if the other characters nodded furiously and made continual 'uh–uh' noises. Moreover, as with the normal non–fluency features, we would almost certainly treat such movements and noises as unusually repetitive and begin to *interpret* them, for example, by hypothesising that the character listening was feigning enthusiasm for some reason.

Exercise 2

Look again at the extract from *Fawlty Towers* in example 1, isolating the features that look like the equivalent of normal non–fluency and feedback in real conversation. How do you interpret them?

6.3.2 How dramatic conversation *is* like real conversation

What we have seen so far in this chapter might lead us to the conclusion that drama conversation is completely unlike real conversation. Clearly, the doubled discourse structure and the fact that dialogue is written to be spoken mean that we must be continually aware of the fact that drama conversations and our understanding of them are dependent on special 'stage conventions'. But we must also remember that in a number of other respects real conversation and drama are similar. For example, in both real and dramatic talk we use our observation of conversational behaviour to infer the things people suggest (as opposed to what they state) when they talk, and we also use such behaviour to infer things about people (or characters) which they might not even intend us to realise. Indeed, if there were no communicative correspondences between ordinary conversation and drama, it would be difficult to see how dramatists could write plays and have us understand them. Below we look at some of the similarities, as they will indicate the most useful methods of conversational analysis when looking at drama:

1 In real conversation people take turns at talking, and by and large, apart from the feedback mechanisms we have already noticed, people do not talk at the same time. Drama conversation also exhibits turn–taking, and apart from small overlaps between the end of one speech and the beginning of another to give a 'realistic feel' to the conversation (usually conversations do not have silences in between speech contributions), the 'don't talk at the same time rule' is fairly strictly observed. Among other things, if it were not, there would be difficulties for the audience in hearing

what was being said. This is why asides are often produced on stage with other characters silently mouthing their talk for a few moments. Turn–taking patterns have similar meanings in ordinary and dramatic conversation. So, if one person or character talks significantly more than the others, we will infer, depending upon other contextual infor–mation, that the person/ character involved is dominating the conversation, likes the sound of his or her own voice, or whatever.

2   Within each turn, the speech produced counts as one or more *acts* performed by the person/character, and the act(s) which the speech performs will vary from one context to another, depending upon what is assumed. For instance, in example 1, as Mr Carnegie has already asked for coffee when Sybil says *Black or white?*, her utterance counts as a request for information about whether Mr Carnegie wants his coffee with or without milk. And said in a real–life conversation where coffee was being served, the same sentence would have the same meaning. But at the beginning of a game of chess the same utterance might well count not as a *question* about whether someone wants milk in their coffee, but as an *offer* that an opponent can choose whether to play with the black or the white pieces. The same would be true if the sentence was uttered at the beginning of a game of chess in a play.

3   Another thing which can be seen if we think a bit harder about Sybil's utterance of *Black or white?* is that much of what is meant when we talk about *context* relates to the assumptions which people bring along to situations because of their previous experience from a series of other, similar situations. So, the reason we can interpret Sybil's speech correctly has to do with the fact that when we have coffee we normally get to choose whether to drink it black or white, and that in restaurants we might well expect a waiter or waitress to bring the milk or cream so that we can make our choice.

4   In dramatic conversation characters often *say* one thing but *mean* another. When, near the beginning of *Romeo and Juliet*, Benvolio asks the love–sick Romeo who he is in love with, Romeo replies '. . . in sadness, cousin, I do love a woman'. Assuming that Romeo is heterosexual, he is clearly telling Benvolio something Benvolio already knows, and hence, by implication, it is clear that Romeo is really

telling Benvolio to go away and leave him alone. Dramatic critics have often suggested that this sort of thing is special to drama, referring to it as the meaning 'behind' or 'between' the lines. It is part of what Stanislawski and his followers mean when they talk about the *sub–text* of play conversations. But this 'say/mean' distinction is clearly important in ordinary conversation too. You might well use Romeo's conversational strategy to put off an enquiring friend, and it is not at all uncommon to hear someone complain 'It's not what he said, but what he implied that worries me'.

There are even more similarities between ordinary and dramatic conversation than the ones mentioned here (for example, how we are polite or impolite appear to be the same in real life and drama). The factors which I have outlined here are particularly important for explaining how we understand drama, and will form the basis of the next two chapters.

6.3.3   A scale of realism for dramatic dialogue?

Before we leave the issue of how like one another real conversation and drama are, it is interesting to note that we have intuitions about how realistic particular dramatists are in their presentation of conversational interaction. Harold Pinter, for example is often said to have an 'ear' for how people talk, whereas a playwright like George Bernard Shaw would be thought to be more stilted in his presentation of conversation among characters even though the conversational style of his characters varies to some extent from play to play. There is more to the issue of the 'realistic illusion' than conversational realism, of course, for example how credible the plots and the characters are. But it will be interesting to see how what we have noticed so far relates to our intuitions about how realistic the dialogue of different dramatists is. I would expect most people to agree with what I have said about Pinter and Shaw. Let us compare two short extracts from the works of these dramatists to see if what I suggest is borne out:

Example 4
Ben: Kaw!   (1)
He picks up the paper.

What about this? Listen to this!

He refers to the paper.

  A man of eighty–seven wanted to cross the road. But (5)
  there was a lot of traffic, see? He couldn't see how
  he was going to squeeze through. So he crawled
  under a lorry.

Gus: He what?

Ben: He crawled under a lorry. A stationary lorry. (10)

Gus: No?

Ben: The lorry started and ran over him.

Gus: Go on!

Ben: That's what it says here.

Gus: Get away. (15)

Ben: It's enough to make you want to puke, isn't it?

Gus: Who advised him to do a thing like that?

Ben: A man of eighty–seven crawling under a
  lorry!

Gus: It's unbelievable. (20)

Ben: It's down here in black and white.

Gus: Incredible.

Silence

*Gus shakes his head and exits. Ben lies back and reads. The
lavatory chain is pulled once off left, but the lavatory does not flush.* (25)
Ben whistles at an item in the paper.

Gus re–enters

  I want to ask you something.

Ben: What are you doing out there?

Gus: Well, I was just— (30)

Ben: What about the tea?

Gus: I'm just going to make it.

Ben: Well, go on, make it.

Gus: Yes I will (*He sits in a chair. Ruminatively*). He's laid on
  some very nice crockery this time, I'll say that. It's (35)
  sort of striped. There's a white stripe.

       (Harold Pinter, *The Dumb Waiter*)

This extract comes from the beginning of the play. Let us first
look at possible candidates for normal non–fluency. In 35–6
there is an apparently unnecessary quasi–repetition (*It's sort of
striped. There's a white strip.*). In theory Gus could be sorting
out the exact formulation he needs, but I suspect that most
readers or watchers of the play would interpret the quasi–
repetition as expressing his initial uncertainty about what

pattern was on the cup. In the same piece of text there are two potential candidates for voiced fillers, *I'll say that* and *sort of*, though the audience is more likely, I think, to see the first as an indication of the firmness of Gus's approval for the crockery and the latter as an another marker of his uncertainty about what to call the pattern he sees on it. There is also an indication that Ben monitors Gus to see whether he is getting feedback from him in line (6). It is sometimes possible to invest expressions like 'sort of' with meaning in ordinary conversation too, but real conversation's normal non–fluency, which is ignored in terms of generating meaning, just does not occur here. Hence, if this sort of dialogue is felt to be more like real conversation than most, it must be other features which are contributing to the effect.

Ben and Gus appear to be ordinary, working–class people, and one aspect of potential realism is their informal, common core, and sometimes decidedly idiomatic vocabulary (*e.g. kaw!* (1), *puke* (16)). Elliptical sentences are common in this extract, and the speeches are all short, unlike the set speeches associated with Shakespearian drama, for instance. Nothing of any real importance appears to happen in the conversation, which does correspond with the ritualistic, or phatic, function that much ordinary talk has (*cf.* conversations about the weather, or how late the train is). The characters are also in the middle of what–ever they are up to, and yet there is no obvious attempt to indicate artificially to the audience who the characters are, where they are and what they are doing. These features all help the realistic effect to some extent. But perhaps the most important is the fact that the dialogue appears to be 'unaimed', unrelated to some obvious strategic or thematic purpose of the author's design. After the discussion of the apparently trivial newspaper report of the man who crawled under a lorry and died, the conversation moves to tea–making and from there to the crockery in the room. Ben and Gus, it gradually transpires, are hit–men, waiting to discover who they are to kill next, and to be provided with the weapons. The talk wanders, apparently aimlessly, from one topic to another, with only the occasional intervention from outside, in the form of messages delivered to the room by a small mechanical lift of the sort used in restaurants to transport food and crockery from one floor to another (the dumb waiter of the title). At the end of the play, Gus is out of the room and Ben is apparently ordered to kill the next person who enters the room. Gus, stripped of his jacket and gun, then enters, and the play ends in frozen silence, as the characters and the audience realise that Ben is meant to kill Gus. Even though some of the talk in the play is about random killing, as reported, for example, in the newspapers the characters read, the aimless, almost domestic feel to the conversation provides a contrastive background for the major occurrence which concludes the play.

Now let us compare Pinter's dialogue with Shaw's:

Example 5

Catherine:	(*entering hastily, full of good news*) Raina! She	(1)
	pronounces it Rah–eena, with the stress on the ee).	
	Raina! (*She goes to the bed, expecting to find*	
	Raina there). Why, where –? (*Raina looks into the*	
	room). Heavens, child! are you out in the night air	(5)
	instead of in your bed? You'll catch your death.	
	Louka told me you were asleep.	
Raina:	(*dreamily*) I sent her away. I wanted to be alone.	
	The stars are so beautiful! What is the matter?	
Catherine:	Such news! There has been a battle.	(10)
Raina:	(*her eyes dilating*) Ah! (*She comes eagerly to Catherine*)	
Catherine:	A great battle at Slivnitza! A victory! And it was	
	won by Sergius.	
Raina:	(*with a cry of delight*) Ah! (*They embrace rapturously*)	
	Oh, mother! (*Then, with sudden anxiety*)	(15)
	Is father safe?	
Catherine:	Of course! he sends me the news. Sergius is the	
	hero of the hour, the idol of the regiment.	
Raina:	Tell me, tell me. How was it? (*Ecstatically*) Oh,	
	mother! mother! mother! (*She pulls her mother*	(20)
	down on the ottoman; and they kiss one another	
	frantically)	
Catherine:	(*with surging enthusiasm*) You can't guess how	
	splendid it is. A cavalry charge! think of that!	
	He defied our Russian commanders – acted	(25)
	without orders – led a charge of his own	
	responsibility – headed it himself – was the first	
	man to sweep through their guns. Can't you see it,	
	Raina: our gallant splendid Bulgarians with their	
	swords and eyes flashing, thundering down	(30)
	like an avalanche and scattering the wretched	
	Serbs and their dandified Austrian officers like	

chaff. And you! you kept Sergius waiting a year
before you would be betrothed to him. Oh, if
you have a drop of Bulgarian blood in your   (35)
veins, you will worship him when he comes back.

(George Bernard Shaw, *Arms and the Man*, Act I)

Like the excerpt from *The Dumb Waiter* in example 4, this extract is from the opening of the play. The only potential
normal–non–fluency feature is the incomplete sentence in line
(4). But this is clearly not because Catherine is having
problems working out what to say. Rather, she appears to
work out the answer to the question she is asking while asking
it, and so does not need to complete it. Like example 4, this
extract has a number of elliptical sentences, but this time they
are all clearly used to indicate the exclamatory nature of the
utterances performed.

This play also opens in the middle of an action, but this
time we know Raina's name from the play's first utterance,
and are sure that Catherine is her mother by line (15) at the
latest. In just over 200 words we also learn that they are
Bulgarian, Raina has a maidservant called Louka, that Raina's
father is in the army, who are fighting the Serbs, that Sergius
wants to marry Raina and that they are now betrothed, but
that Raina made him wait for a year before agreeing to the
betrothal. And, of course, we also learn, among other things,
that the Bulgarians have just defeated the Serbs at Slivnitza and
that Sergius was a hero in the battle. This conversation is
clearly set up for the purpose of filling in the audience on the
information they need to get the character relationships right,
understand the context of the ensuing action and so on.

In this extract, the characters often talk in a way that feels
rather unnatural when compared with example 4. A clear
example is the unnecessary use of terms of address like *child* in
line (5) and *mother* in (15) and (20). Given that the characters
know one another well and that they are the only people
present, this incidence of vocatives would be very unlikely in
real life, even given the emotional intensity of the scene.

Another unnaturalness factor is seen in the last speech,
which is significantly longer than the others, and displays a
syntactic length and complexity more often associated with
writing than speech. In fact, the short speeches of the play's
beginning are somewhat untypical, giving way to a pattern of
talk much more consistent with what we see in this last speech

of the extract. These characters give speeches in a manner reminiscent of more traditional drama and unlike Pinter. Finally, we should not forget how significant what we learn at the beginning of this play appears to be, when compared with the beginning of *The Dumb Waiter*. This family is clearly important socially, and involved in significant national affairs. As a consequence, the fairly contentless chit–chat that most of us indulge in socially is replaced with talk about big things – battles, heroism, society weddings, and so on. At the end of the Pinter extract we have very little information on which to base predictions about what will happen later in the play. But at the beginning of *Arms and the Man*, we can already guess that there may be an issue about whether Raina will marry Sergius or not, and about the role of Sergius in the battle at Slivnitza. This dialogue is considerably more aimed, and hence appears more organised. In fact, Raina does not marry Sergius. Instead, she opts for a markedly unheroic Swiss mercenary who is not really cut out to be a soldier and is an expert in the hotel business. Bluntschli may not be heroic, like Sergius, but, in addition to the out–spokenness suggested by his name, he is eminently practical, and efficient at getting things done and what he wants. What happens at the beginning of the play is thus clearly the background preparation for a comic critique of the idealistic values of heroism and romantic love.

To arrive at a general judgement about how realistic the dialogue of Pinter and Shaw is, we would need to examine more texts to see how representative these extracts are. And we may also find other textual features which give play dialogues a realistic or unnatural feel. But it would appear that the difference in appearance of realism between these two passages has to do with (a) the length and complexity of speeches (whether the organisation internal to the speeches is more reminiscent of writing or speech) and (b) how organised the conversation is at a more tactical level, how aimed it is towards particular plot and thematic ends, and how much it takes into account the 'overhearing' audience. All dramatists have to take their audience into account,. But there are clearly more obvious and less obvious ways of catering for one's audience.

Exercise 3

After you have checked your intuitions abut the Pinter and Shaw
passages, to see if they correspond with my findings, examine the
following extracts from the beginning of Shakespeare's *Measure for
Measure*, and from the middle of Caryl Churchill's *Hot Fudge*, working
out where they would come on a scale of realism in comparison with
the Pinter and Shaw extracts, and detailing the evidence for your
conclusion:

(a) *The Duke's palace. Enter DUKE, ESCALUS, Lords and
    Attendants.*

Duke:	Escalus!	(1)
Escalus:	My lord.	
Duke:	Of government the properties to unfold	
	Would seem in me t'affect speech and discourse,	
	Since I am put to know that your own science	(5)
	Exceeds, in that, the lists of all advice	
	My strength can give you; then no more remains	
	But that to your sufficiency – as your worth is able –	
	And let them work. The nature of our people,	
	Our city's institutions, and the terms	(10)
	For common justice, y'are as pregnant in	
	As art and practice hath enriched any	
	That we remember. There is our commission,	
	From which we would not have you warp. Call hither,	
	I say, bid come before us Angelo.	(15)
	[Exit an Attendant]	
	What figure of us think you he will bear?	
	For you must know we have with special soul	
	Elected him our absence to supply;	
	Lent him our terror, dress'd him with our love,	
	And given his deputation all the organs	(20)
	Of our own power. What think you of it?	
Escalus:	If any in Vienna be of worth	
	To undergo such ample grace and honour,	
	It is Lord Angelo.	
	Enter ANGELO	
Duke:	Look where he comes.	(25)
Angelo:	Always obedient to your Grace's will,	
	I come to know your pleasure.	

Duke: Angelo,
        There is a kind of character in thy life
        That to th'observer doth thy history   (30)
        Fully unfold . . .
                (William Shakespeare, *Measure for Measure*, I, i, 1–31)

(b)   *Club, 11 pm*

Jerry: I feel that a career in global industry offers a   (1)
        lifetime package as exciting as it is possible to
        conceive.
Colin: You need flexibility.
Grace: You need interpersonal skills.   (5)
Hugh: The world is certainly getting smaller.
Grace: And you must find that, Colin, with all the world
        news pouring into your / office.
Colin: Yes, I'm certainly very aware of the village /
        aspect.
Grace: You must feel like you're the nerve centre.*   (10)
Hugh: We'll soon be able to drive anywhere in France
        within twelve hours but I could still offer you a
        watermill with conversion potential of fifteen
        bedrooms for just under eighty–five thousand.
Ruby: If someone acquired it as a hotel you could   (15)
        put me in touch –
Hugh: And you could arrange the holidays.
Colin: *It is exciting / making the connections.
Grace: And exhausting.
                        (Caryl Churchill, 'Hot Fudge', scene 3,
                                Churchill: Shorts, pp. 290–1)

[NOTE: The '/'' mark indicates that the next speaker starts speaking at
this point, overlapping with the previous speaker, perhaps entirely. A
'*' at the end of one speech and at the beginning of a subsequent,
non-adjacent speech indicates that the two contributions are integrally
connected, even though they are some lines apart. These marks are
inserted by Caryl Churchill and thus constitute instructions to the
actors about timing etc.]

Discussion of exercises

Exercise 1

I have already made my views in the first part of this exercise clear, and I can't really give answers to the second part, as I don't know what texts you have looked at. Instead, let me describe one early comedy attributed to Francis Beaumont, a contemporary of Shakespeare. The play was very innovative in its day and gets many of its laughs from the way in which it manipulates our prototypical assumptions about the discourse structure of the play. Below is a diagram of the discourse architecture of *The Knight of the Burning Pestle*:

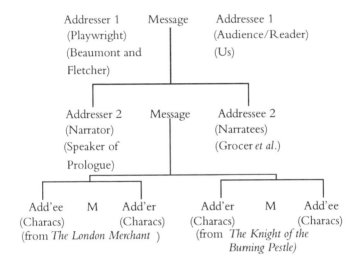

[Note: At level 3, words have been abbreviated in order to save enough space to make the diagram clear.]

At the beginning of *The Knight of the Burning Pestle*, we witness an 'audience' on stage who are about to watch a play called *The London Merchant*, which begins with a speech by a narrator, the speaker of the prologue. But the 'audience' includes a grocer and his wife, who interrupt the play because they do not think that *The London Merchant* will show grocers in a good enough light. After some negotiation it is agreed that they will lend to the performers an apprentice of theirs, Ralph, who they claim is a good actor. For the rest of the performance, two plays are presented, interleaved, Ralph and others performing *The Knight of the Burning Pestle* and the original company performing *The London Merchant*. Meanwhile, the grocer and his wife in the on–stage audience interrupt, demanding that the plays be performed in ways that please them. These are the sorts of techniques used by Brecht, but well before his time, and in the service of comedy. And this kind of experiment would also be immediately recognised by modern 'fringe' dramatists.

But note that the diagram as it stands is inadequate. First of all, *The London Merchant* has a Prologue but *The Knight of the Burning Pestle* does not. So we have two discourse structures, one with two levels and one with three levels, intertwined. Secondly, there is a 'semi–collapsing' between the narrator level and the 'audience' level of *The London Merchant* in that the grocer and his wife interfere with the progress of the play. And thirdly there are two different sorts of 'semi–collapsing' in *The Knight of the Burning Pestle*, both of which are different in kind from the one seen in *The London Merchant*: (a) Ralph, the grocer's apprentice, becomes one of the characters in the play and (b) the grocer and his wife interfere with that play too by speaking directly to the actor–characters rather than the narrator. There is clearly much in this play which is being rediscovered by today's *avant garde* theatre.

Exercise 2

One interpretation of Basil's first utterance is that he makes the lexical selection error of *rat* for *biscuit*. If so, this presumably counts as normal non–fluency on Basil's part, but clearly John Cleese and Connie Booth will have intended it, in order to get the laugh and to show how much Basil has been put off his stroke by the appearance of the rat. The ensuing pauses and repetition of *just* are interpretable in exactly the same way: normal non–fluency for Basil but intended by Cleese and Booth to show how much he has been affected by the rat in the biscuit tin. Sybil's only example of normal non–fluency is the pause before her first utterance of *black or white?* and Polly does not trip up at all. Mr Carnegie, on the other hand, who is clearly as affected as Basil – to the extent that he can't really believe his eyes – pauses twice, has an obviously incomplete utterance and produces what would normally be a feedback noise, *ummm* as a positively inadequate response to Sybil's question. Finally, Sybil quickly takes the conversation off into a topic area as far removed from that of rats as possible, the weather — a topic which is well known for its phatic, non-conflictual qualities and which is thus, particularly when compared with the topic of rats, very unlikely to cause upset. This is another demonstration of the conversational efficiency of the two women.

An alternative interpretation for Basil's first utterance is that he has not made a lexical selection error, but is ludicrously trying to get out of the embarrassing situation he finds himself in by passing the rat off as a normal thing to serve with the cheese at the end of a meal. His subsequent normal non-fluency will still contrast with the coolness of the women.

Exercise 3

This play beginning is even less realistic than *Arms and the Man*, and purposely so. Shakespeare's major characters speak in iambic pentameter verse, something which no one normally does in real life. Most of his lower characters, by way of contrast, speak in prose. Hence we can see that the point is to give the major characters a *gravitas* appropriate to their importance and the affairs of state they deal with. The Duke, in particular, as well as speaking verse, also produces sentences of a length and complexity that few people could manage in extempore conversation. The first sentence of his first major speech is 56 words long and syntactically complex. The second, which is a mere 29 words long by comparison, has, when unravelled, a simple subject (y') verb (*are*) complement (the rest of the sentence) construction. But the complement, which is in any case a very complex comparative construction, is split up so that the majority of the first term of the comparison is moved away from the rest of the complement to the very beginning of the sentence. Re-ordered, the sentence would read 'Y'are as pregnant in the nature of our people, our city's institutions, and the terms for common justice, as art and practice hath enriched any that we remember.' The point here is that it is not just its length and complexity which makes the original sentence unlikely to be used in casual conversation. Also important is the fact that the particular construction and ordering used is one which cannot be entered into unless its producer already has a syntactic 'plan' for the whole sentence before embarking on it. In other words, the sentence has an **anticipatory** rather than a **trailing** construction (for a detailed discussion of these terms see 11.4.4). Trailing constructions are more common in casual speech precisely because they allow speakers to complete a construction and then add extra bits on, in a chain. Anticipatory reordering, which is much more commonly found in writing, prevents this 'add–on' strategy and involves considerably more planning. Compare, for example 'We bought the red dress for Janet's birthday because red is her favourite colour and because it was reduced in price' (trailing) with 'Because it was reduced in price and because red is her favourite colour we bought the red dress for Janet's birthday' (anticipatory). The second sentence is much less likely to occur in ordinary talk than the first.

The features so far discussed are additional to those we noticed from the beginning of *Arms and the Man*. Otherwise, the features found are very reminiscent of Shaw's play. From the first three words of the play we know Escalus's name, and that the other character is his lord. By the end of the extract we also know that the Duke is going away for a while and that he has decided that Angelo, of whom he thinks very highly, will take his place. The scene is thus already set for trials and tribulations of some sort when Angelo takes over, perhaps involving his character and judgement. And this, of course, is exactly what happens. It is also very convenient dramatically that Angelo can be found so quickly by the servant sent to find him, arriving just as the Duke and Escalus finish talking about him. This extract is clearly less realistic even than the beginning of *Arms and the Man*.

The Churchill extract is more like Pinter than Shakespeare or Shaw. But the topics discussed seem rather more purposeful, and clearly related to the yuppie, business–oriented world that these characters live in. The main point for us is that Caryl Churchill is a dramatist who seems particularly interested in controlling the timing of characters' speeches, producing overlaps by her use of the slash marks which are reminiscent of what we saw in the tape–recorded extract in 6.3.1.

Churchill has also fastened onto another feature which discourse analysts have noticed about ordinary conversation, called *skip–connecting*. What happens in skip–connecting relates to the battle for the conversational floor typical of conversations and which we noticed in the transcript of the tape–recording in example 2 (section 6.3.1). With, say, four people in a conversation, you can have what amount to two separate conversations being interleaved. And this is what happens in the extract from *Hot Fudge*. Although the topics being discussed are related in various ways, it is clear that (a) the marked overlaps occur only between Grace and Colin, (b) Grace uses Colin's name when she does not really need to single him out for conversational purposes, and (c) the skip-connecting involves Colin linking up with a speech of Grace's some turns before. These features tell the actors not just when to make their contributions, but also imply appropriate facial expressions, gestures and body movements to go with the special interest that these two characters are displaying in each other.

There is probably no point in trying to work out whether Pinter's or Churchill's dialogue is more realistic. They are fairly close to one another on the scale, and concentrate on different aspects of conversational behaviour for their own particular textual purposes. In any case, there are no automatic ticks or crosses to be awarded just for being realistic. First of all, as our examination of the Pinter showed, even so-called realistic dialogue is far removed from what casual conversation is really like. Being realistic in literature is thus to some degree a matter of convention. Secondly, and more importantly, being realistic is not a very interesting end in itself. Shakespeare makes his characters talk in particular ways because of the importance he wants us to accord them. Pinter and Churchill, at the other extreme, make their dialogues feel more realistic, but, again, they do so for tactical and thematic purposes.

Note

1. Of course it is also possible for us to make inferences which the writer did not apparently intend either. This is what 'deconstructionist' and 'post-structuralist' kinds of criticism often engage in.

Further reading

Leech and Short examine discourse structure in the novel (1981: Ch. 8) and also the issue of realism in conversation in the novel (1981: 159–73). Fowler (1986: 109–18) compares dialogic techniques in *Look Back in Anger* by John Osborne and *Waiting for Godot* by Samuel Beckett. Birch (1991: Chs 2–3) discusses multiple voices in drama, realism and making sense of dramatic dialogue. Simpson (1989a) explores phatic communion in fictional dialogue. Freeborn, French and Langford (1986: Chs 5 and 7), Leech, Deuchar and Hoogenraad (1982: Ch. 8) and Traugott and Pratt (1980: 41–8) discuss speech and writing.

CHECKSHEET 5: DISCOURSE STRUCTURE AND SPEECH REALISM

A. Discourse structure

Draw a diagram to represent the discourse structure of the text you are examining. Does the discourse structure remain constant throughout the whole text, or does it vary? Are there any significant discoursal 'collapsings' (*i.e.* where the same individual occurs at more than one discourse level in your diagram)? What interpretative consequences does the 'discourse architecture' of the text have?

B. Speech realism

How realistic is the speech in the text you are examining?

(a) Is the lexis formal or informal?

(b) How complex is the grammatical structure of sentences? Is the dominant syntactic pattern for complex sentences anticipatory or trailing?

(c) To what extent are there graphological contractions (like 'I'll')?

(d) What features associated with normal non–fluency are present? How are they to be interpreted in context?

(e) Are there any other significant features to be noted?

How do your findings affect your overall interpretation of the text or your response to it? Do any of the features you have noted have specific local interpretative effects at the point they occur in the text?

CHAPTER 7

The meaning of speech acts, turn–taking and politeness

7.1 Speech acts

When people say things, they don't *just* say things. They also perform *acts* by saying what they do. Let us pretend that I tell my daughter 'I will collect you and your belongings from university at the end of term'. By uttering these words in an appropriate context I perform the act of promising, and if I don't subsequently do what I have promised I will have some explaining to do. Writing things also constitutes action. If I write '60%' at the bottom of one of my students' essays, I have performed the action of grading the essay and have, to a small extent, determined the eventual degree which that student will be awarded. These linguistic acts are actions just as much as cooking the dinner or kicking the cat. What is more, by observing the speech acts which different people perform we can infer things about them and their relations with others. Someone who habitually performs the speech act of ordering others to do things will be thought of as bossy. On the other hand, someone who always obeys the commands of others and who only timidly requests others to do things in return will be thought of as a wimp. What works for the real world also works for the fictional world of the play. By observing patterns of speech act use (as well as physical actions, of course) we can begin to understand the characters on stage and how they relate to one another.[1] A clear example can be found in Shakespeare's *King Lear*.

Example 1

Lear: Attend the Lords of France and Burgundy, Gloucester.
Glos: I shall, my liege.
Lear: Meantime we shall express our darker purpose.
   Give me the map there. Know that we have divided
   In three our kingdom; and 'tis our fast intent
   To shake all cares and business from our age,
   Conferring them on younger strengths, while we
   Unburden'd crawl toward death . . .
               (William Shakespeare, *King Lear*, I, i, 33–40)

Lear's absolute power as King is reflected in the fact that he tells others what to do and they do it immediately and unquestioningly. For Lear, telling the Earl of Gloucester to go and meet the Lords of France and Burgundy is a trifling example of his power. However, by saying that he has divided up his kingdom, Lear actually creates the division publicly – a much more important matter. Later in this first scene, of course, he changes his mind about the exact nature of the division. His loving daughter, Cordelia, refuses to perform a pretty speech saying how much she loves him, and so he naively divides the state equally between his two wicked daughters, Goneril and Regan, who are prepared to lie and flatter to get their hands on the reins of power. At this point in the play, Lear's whim is law: for him, saying something makes it so. But by Act II the awful consequences of Lear's foolishness in giving away his power become apparent. Although Goneril and Regan have agreed to have him and his retinue live with each of them for half the year, they soon tell him that he can have no retinue at all and force him out onto the heath. Lear is reduced to alternately pleading with, and railing at, Goneril and Regan, and all to no avail. He has no authority in their world. They now have all the power, and the speech acts he uses and their intended effects all come to naught. For the Elizabethans all this presented a powerful conundrum. If Lear is King, ordained by God, then he is King, whatever happens. But if he is King he has the power to do anything he wants, including giving his kingdom away. The play thus pulls apart two apparently inextricably intertwined aspects of kingship. Lear has no practical power once he has given his kingdom away, and Goneril and Regan demonstrate this fact in the clearest possible terms. But for the Fool, Edgar and Kent, who follow him onto the heath, Lear is clearly still the King. The play thus explores a central paradox for the Elizabethan audience, and explores it through the way in which Lear, and others, use speech acts.

Speech acts, like other acts, change the world we inhabit. They have *effects* on people and, in turn, make them do things. I can frighten others by threatening them with a knife or by telling them that I will make their illicit love affair public. I can make them feel loved by sending them flowers or telling them how much I think of them. I can get someone to open the front door by standing next to it with my arms full of groceries or by saying 'could you open the door, please'. Though we should note that, like Lear when he tries to get Goneril and Regan to keep their promises, the effects I *intend* by my speech acts may not necessarily be those I achieve. If I threaten someone, I might accidentally induce that person to laugh. This is another aspect of speech act analysis which we will be able to apply to dramatic texts, using it to understand what is happening on stage, the relations between characters and so on.

It is clear, though, that if we want to talk about this area with any clarity, we need some terms to distinguish the various aspects we have talked about so far. These are the terms linguists usually use:

Act performed by speaking:	speech act/illocutionary force
Intended effect as a consequence of performing a speech act:	intended perlocutionary force/effect
Actual effect caused by the act:	actual perlocutionary force/effect

In the *King Lear* example discussed above, the intended perlocutionary effects of Lear's utterances at the very beginning of the play are almost always the same as the actual effects. But by the end of Act II there is almost no match at all between his intended and actual perlocutionary effects.

In plays, speech acts, like other acts, usually only operate inside one of the levels of discourse we described in 6.2. If a character on stage says 'it's chilly in here' we would be very surprised if one of the audience got up and shut the window. You can sometimes get cross–discourse–level interaction, though, as the account of the example from *The Knight of the Burning Pestle* in the discussion of exercise 1 at the end of Chapter 6 shows. Another, better–known, example would be the way that in Christmas pantomimes some characters get the audience to shout out and warn other characters of some impending disaster (*e.g.* to tell Aladdin that his wicked uncle is coming). Here, the speech act of telling the audience to shout out is performed at the character level but the perlocutionary effect obtains at the audience level. Then, when the audience shouts out to warn Aladdin, the speech act is performed at the audience level and the intended perlocutionary effect is within the character level. Moreover, the actors can also make play with the intended/actual distinction within the notion of perlocutionary effect. The person playing Aladdin can, for example, pretend not to hear the warnings shouted by the audience. But this sort of interaction across discourse levels is relatively rare. Speech act patterns usually tell us about the social relations among characters in the play's fictional world.

7.1.1   How do we define or describe particular speech acts?

For some speech acts there appears at first sight to be quite a good fit between grammatical structure and illocutionary force. Indeed, the fit between these structures and the acts they realise is so good that teachers often use 'interrogative' interchangeably with 'question', 'imperative' 'command' and so on. When I was at school I was puzzled that we had two sets of terms to refer to the same things, a puzzlement that was not resolved until I realised many years later that one set of labels related to grammar and the other to illocutionary force:

Grammatical structure	Speech act	Example
Interrogative structures	Questions	'Is he singing?'
Imperative structures	Commands	'Sing!'
Declarative structures	Statements	'He is singing.'

Although declaratives typically realise statements, they do not have to. 'Jones can swim a length' will, out of context, most likely be understood as a statement. But by specifying the context carefully I can make it into a command. Imagine that a class of school children are standing in their swimming costumes at one end of the school swimming pool. If the teacher says 'Jones can swim a length' in this context, the illocutionary force is more likely to be that of a command than anything else, and if Jones responds not by diving in and swimming, but by saying 'yes, that's right sir' he is very likely to incur the teacher's displeasure.

There are not many different basic types of sentence structures, but there are very many different kinds of speech act: promising, threatening, pleading, stating, suggesting, asking, challenging, contradicting and so on. Indeed, no one is completely sure how many there are. This is why we cannot associate each speech act uniquely with a particular kind of grammatical structure.

Although the structure of the utterance is one speech act indicator, it is by no means the only one. As we saw from the swimming pool example above, certain contextual conditions (often called happiness or **felicity conditions**) have to be in place for an utterance to function properly as a particular speech act. 'Jones can swim a length' can only be a command if the speaker (the teacher here) and the hearer (Jones) are in an appropriate social relationship. Jones could not order his teacher to swim a length. And the teacher could not order Jones to swim a length if he knew Jones could not swim, or if they were in the Art Room and not next to the swimming pool. Relevant contextual conditions for the adequate performance of particular speech acts include speaker/hearer intentions as well as states of affairs in the world. If you say that you promise to do the washing up but don't really intend to, you haven't really promised to wash up at all, but merely pretended to do so.

One clear way to see that speech act definitions are affected by felicity conditions is to note how they can be used to distinguish one speech act from another. Consider promising and threatening. If I say I will pay you a visit tomorrow, that counts as a promise on the assumption that (a) you want me to come and (b) I know that you do. However, if you don't want me to come (because, for example, you will have to pay me the money you owe me) and I know that, my statement of my future intentions can quickly become a threat. This explains why a mother, after saying that she will tidy up a child's bedroom, can add 'and that's a threat, not a promise!' Although promises and threats are opposites in terms of their illocutionary force and intended perlocutionary effect, they share a large number of linguistic and contextual features, and the change of just one feature can result in an utterance moving from one speech act category to its opposite.[2]

The reason that I have explored at some length the contextual aspects of speech acts is that we can use this context–boundness to infer <u>important unstated aspects of</u> <u>context</u>, including social relations between characters, when we read literary texts. This is a particularly important matter at the beginning of plays. Most ordinary *spoken* language behaviour takes place in a firmly grounded situational context, where relations between speakers are already known. However, writing in general, and literature in particular, is more decontextualised than most speech, and this decontextualised aspect is at its strongest at the beginning of texts, when the writer has had no chance to provide us with details of the textual world we are about to step into. Consider the following beginning of a sketch by Harold Pinter:

Example 2

An office in a factory. Mr. Fibbs at the desk. A knock at the
door. Enter Mr. Wills.

Fibbs:	Ah, Wills. Good. Come in. Sit down, will you?	(1)
Wills:	Thanks, Mr Fibbs.	
Fibbs:	You got my message?	
Wills:	I just got it	
Fibbs:	Good. Good.	(5)
	Pause	
	Good. Well now . . . Have a cigar?	
Wills:	No, thanks, not for me, Mr Fibbs.	
Fibbs:	Well, now, Wills, I hear there's been a little trouble in the factory.	

(Harold Pinter, 'Trouble in the Works')

From the very beginning of this sketch we can infer that Fibbs is part of the management of the factory and that Wills is an employee. We can also begin to sense that although he is apparently totally in control of the situation, things might not be quite as they seem, a situation which might well have consequences later in the sketch. Let us explicate these first steps towards interpretation, concentrating on what we learn from the speech acts. There are other factors which help us to build our interpretation, of course, and I will take account of these as I go along.

We know from the stage directions that the context is a factory. This brings some background assumptions (something which we will explore more fully in Chapter 8) into play even before the characters start talking. The fact that Fibbs is sitting at a desk clearly makes him part of the office staff at least, not a factory worker, and will lead us to suspect even on first reading that he is a manager of some kind. Wills, on the other hand, has to knock before he can come in, is addressed by Fibbs using last name only (*Wills*) and addresses Fibbs with the more polite 'title + last name' formula, *Mr Fibbs*. When I saw this sketch produced some years ago, this relationship was marked by dressing Fibbs in a suit and Wills in workman's overalls, and by having Fibbs's desk on a raised dais to indicate his status. Clear speech act indications of this master–servant relationship are Fibbs's commands (*Come in . . . Sit down . . .*) and the fact that Wills obeys them immediately. This even applies to what must have happened immediately prior to the sketch's opening. The message which Fibbs sent to Wills was clearly telling Wills to come and see him, a command which Wills has obviously obeyed straight away (*I just got it*). This fact also helps to explain the first part of Fibbs's first speech. *Ah, Wills* is a recognition that Wills has arrived, and the act of evaluation, *Good*, clearly relates to the fact that Wills has done his bidding. It also explains the form of Fibbs's second speech *You got my message?* In speech act terms, the sentence's declarative structure in combination with a question mark makes it look like a hybrid between a statement and a question. Presumably Fibbs has good grounds to believe Wills has received his message, otherwise he would not have come. Hence the declarative form. But why the question mark? This seems to indicate that Fibbs is not completely sure of himself. Logically, Wills might have come for some other reason, and so we might think that Fibbs is just making sure before he goes any further. Another possibility is that Fibbs is not completely sure of his ground for some other reason, not yet revealed (but which begins to become clear in the last line of the extract). And, of course, there is no reason why both of these things should not be true at the same time.

Another indication of Fibbs's unsure attitude towards Wills occurs in his first speech, *Sit down, will you?* This is another hybrid speech act. The first part looks like a command, but the interrogative tag edges the utterance towards being a more polite request or suggestion. This movement away from a straightforward dominating–dominated relationship goes a little further when Fibbs says *Have a cigar?.* Although this sentence is imperative in structure it is an offer, not a command. The question mark at the end helps us in this interpretation, as does the fact that Fibbs appears to want Wills to do something which he thinks of as being beneficial to Wills and having cost to himself (cigars are expensive, after all). Moreover, Wills feels able to refuse this offer, even though he has obeyed all the commands so far. Fibbs also makes a point of continually evaluating Wills's actions positively, thus playing down any possible dissonance between them. He uses the word *good* four times in his first three speeches, or once every 5.25 words, a very high incidence. The last instance of *good* is part of a string of three such instances, broken only by a pause in the middle of Fibbs's speech. This suggests that Fibbs is having some difficulty in embarking on the topic for which he has summoned Wills. This interpretation is strengthened by Fibbs's repeated use of the filler *well now* at the beginning of two of his eight speech acts in example 2, and the fact that when he finally mentions the trouble at the factory he plays down its importance by using the adjective *little* and grammatically embedding *there's been a little trouble in the factory* under *I hear.*

From a very short stretch of text we have begun to see a quite complex relationship through the way the characters, Fibbs in particular, use speech acts in connection with other language features. Fibbs's relationship with Wills does not appear to be a straightforward master–servant one, and whatever is going on appears to be related to the trouble mentioned in the last line of the extract, and in the title of the sketch.

The dramatic interest which Pinter has set up, then, is in what the trouble is and how it affects the relationship between the two men. It transpires that Fibbs is the owner of the factory, and that the factory workers no longer want to make engineering products because they have 'taken a turn' against them. As the discussion unfolds, the power relation between the two men changes, so that by the end of the sketch the workers' representative dominates completely the owner of the factory, who is now a broken man.

Fibbs clearly thinks that the engineering products his factory produces are not just useful but objects of beauty, which his workers ought to appreciate too:

Example 3

Fibbs: But not, surely not, my lovely parallel male stud
         couplings.

                    (Harold Pinter, 'Trouble in the Works')

But Wills responds with an utterance which is a cross between statement, abuse and threat:

Example 4

Wills: They hate and detest your lovely parallel male stud
         couplings . . .

                    (Harold Pinter, 'Trouble in the Works')

and the sketch ends with Wills telling Fibbs that the workers want to make sweets instead. In the performance I saw, the two men got up and, in unison, gradually moved clockwise round the set as the sketch unfolded. By the end of the sketch Wills was sitting in Fibbs's place and vice versa, thus instantiating visually the power change that had taken place discoursally.

When we read or watch Pinter's sketch we interpret what happens very quickly indeed. The whole sequence which I have analysed so painstakingly (but even so, not exhaustively) will flash by in about 20 seconds in the theatre. But although what we come to know seems to be achieved effortlessly, even such a short stretch of dialogue conveys an enormous amount of information, some direct and some unstated (and which we therefore have to infer). Deducing situation and character relations through our knowledge of how speech acts work is one important aspect of the complex inferential process of textual understanding.

Our discussion of the Pinter extract also reveals some other important things about speech acts and how they work. First of all, we can see that there is no straightforward one–to–one relationship between a sentence or clause and a speech act. A clause might contain more than one speech act, or be a hybrid of two or three speech acts at the same time. This kind of ambiguity is often extremely useful in social terms. If I say 'the washing up needs doing' (which is ambiguous between a statement and a suggestion that you do the washing up), and you object that I am pressurising you into doing the work, I can always retreat verbally by saying that it was the statement interpretation I intended all along.

At the other end of the scale, a whole set of sentences may consist of a series of speech acts which all add up to one overarching macro speech act. An example would be the long speeches by Goneril and Regan in the first scene of *King Lear* which both count overall as overt declarations of their love for their father.

The speech act value of an utterance might also be different for different characters on stage, or for the characters on the one hand and the audience on the other, leading to differing understandings, and hence to situations of dramatic irony. Goneril's and Regan's speeches referred to above count as declarations of love for Lear. But for almost everyone else on stage and also for the audience, they count as lies which are designed to dupe Lear into handing over his kingdom. Speech acts are thus quite a flexible and powerful mechanism in helping us to interpret what we hear and read.

Exercise 1

Examine how the comedy in the extract below revolves around the different possible speech act values of the utterance 'fire'.

[*Context: The guests at the Fawlty Towers hotel have just been through a rather chaotic fire drill, and are just coming back into the hotel when Basil Fawlty discovers there is a real fire.*]

Large Woman: What is it?
Basil: Well . . . the point is . . . er . . . can I put it this way . . . fire!
Large Woman: What?
Basil: F–f–f–f–f–f–f–fire!
Mrs Sharp: Fire?
Mr Sharp: Where?
Basil: Fire! . . . Fire!!! Fire!!! Fire!!!

The guests move yet again towards the main doors
(John Cleese and Connie Booth, 'The Germans', *The Complete Fawlty Towers*, pp. 148–9)

7.2 Turn–taking and topic control

One last thing which we can begin to notice as a consequence of the examination of example 2 is that speech acts are often connected together into sequences of turns in conversation. Fibbs asks Wills whether he received his message, and Wills confirms that he has. Fibbs offers Wills a cigar, and Fibbs declines. These sequences are examples of conversational turns being 'chained together' as a consequence of their speech act values. The occurrence of a speech act by one speaker enables us to predict with a fair degree of certainty the occurrence of another speech act by another speaker. We expect a question to be followed by an answer, an offer by its acceptance or refusal, an order by that order being carried out, and so on. Patterns of linkage like this are part of the normal 'glue' of conversation. These patterns do not have to consist exclusively of *pairs* of utterances (though many do). In classrooms, for example, the expected pattern is a triple of turns. The teacher asks a question, a student responds and, finally, the teacher will evaluate the student's response in some way before moving on to the next question. Similarly, a complaint will usually be followed by an apology, which can then, in turn, be followed by a statement of forgiveness. More complex patterns are also possible. Imagine, for example, that I ask you a question which you take to be ambiguous. You would probably feel the need to ask me a question to solve the ambiguity before finally giving me your answer. In this case one question–answer pair of turns would be embedded inside another, similar pair.

Turn–taking patterns and deviations from relevant turn–taking norms can easily become meaningful in texts. In 'Trouble in the Works' we expect Fibbs to use commands. He is the factory owner, after all. But the fact that he uses a pattern of more polite speech acts (*e.g. offering* Wills a cigar) is significant for us in interpreting his behaviour. Similarly, because it is polite to accept an offer, particularly when it is made by someone you think of as your superior, the fact that Wills declines the cigar is likely to be read as indicating that he will not automatically accede to all of his boss's wishes in the ensuing conversation.

But there is more to turn–taking and its interpretation than noting what speech acts are used. It is rare for just one person to speak, and when two or more people are talking, it is rare for more than one person to speak at the same time. Everyone seems to know instinctively when and how to swap turns, and consequently there is remarkably little overlap between turns by two different speakers, even when the conversation becomes very animated. Moreover, pat–terns of turn–taking have clear general connections with conversational power, as you will see when you do Exercise 2 below.

Exercise 2

Look at the questions below and decide whether they apply best, other things being equal, to more powerful or less powerful interactants in conversations . I have indicated my intuitions with an 'X' in the columns below. See if your intuitions about what is typical coincide with mine:

	Powerful speakers	Powerless speakers
Who has most turns?	X	
Who has the least?		X
Who has the longest turns?	X	
Who has the shortest?		X
Who initiates conversational exchanges?	X	
Who responds?		X
Who controls the conversational topic?	X	
Who follows the topics of others?		X
Who interrupts?	X	
Who is interrupted?		X
Who uses terms of address not marked for respect (e.g. first name only)?	X	
Who uses terms of address marked for respect (e.g. title + last name)?		X
Who allocates turns to others?	X	

All other things being equal, powerful speakers in conversations have the most turns, have the longest turns, initiate conversational exchanges, control what is talked about and who talks when, and interrupt others. Note, though, that the point about the number of turns per speaker only applies to conversations with more than two participants: by definition, two–character conversations will have roughly equal numbers of turns for each speaker (though the size of the turns may well differ significantly). Imagine a conversation between one of your teachers and yourself, and the patterns outlined above should become abundantly clear.

This does not mean, however, that all conversations follow this general pattern exactly. The worm can turn, at least to some degree. Students can break out from class conversation 'regulations', for example, and in more informal classes may well be encouraged to do so. But the room for manoeuvre from the norm is not large (in even the most informal of classes the teacher will speak much more than all the students combined), and if a student exhibits too many powerful conversational features, he or she will almost certainly be seen as pushy, even rude, by everyone else – a perception which has clear consequences for social relations.

Particular functional and contextual circumstances for conversations (often called **activity types**) also demand some variation from these general rules. In the interview activity type, for example, the least powerful person, the interviewee, will be expected to take the longest turns precisely because the purpose of the interview is to judge the candidate on the basis of what he or she says. But in all other respects the conversational power rules will be followed. Let us examine them at work in a conversation from Shakespeare's *Richard III* between the Duke of Buckingham and King Richard in the presence of Lord Stanley:[3]

Example 5

Buck:	My lord, I have consider'd in my mind	(87)
	The late request that you did sound me in.	
K. Rich:	Well, let that rest. Dorset is fled to Richmond.	
Buck:	I hear the news, my lord.	(90)
K. Rich:	Stanley, he is your wife's son: well, look unto it.	
Buck:	My lord, I claim the gift, my due by promise,	
	For which your honour and your faith is pawn'd:	
	Th'earldom of Hereford, and the moveables	
	Which you have promised I shall possess.	(95)
K. Rich:	Stanley, look to your wife; if she convey	

> Letters to Richmond, you shall answer it.
> Buck: What says your Highness to my just request?
> K. Rich: I do remember me; Henry the Sixth
>   Did prophesy that Richmond should be King,   (100)
>   When Richmond was a little peevish boy.
>   A king! – perhaps
> Buck: My lord—
> K. Rich: How chance the prophet could not, at that time,
>   Have told me, I being by, that I should kill him? (105)
> Buck: My lord, your promise for the earldom—
> K. Rich: Richmond! When last I was at Exeter,
>   The Mayor in courtesy show'd me the castle,
>   And call'd it Rugemont, at which name I started,
>   Because a bard of Ireland told me once   (110)
>   I should not live long after I saw Richmond.
> Buck: My lord—
> K. Rich: Ay – what's o'clock?
> Buck: I am thus bold to put your Grace in mind
>   Of what you promis'd me.
> K. Rich: Well, but what's o'clock?   (115)
> Buck: Upon the stroke of ten.
> K. Rich: Well, let it strike.
> Buck: Why let it strike?
> K. Rich: Because that like a Jack thou keep'st the stroke
>   Betwixt thy begging and my meditation.
>   I am not in the giving vein to–day.   (120)
> Buck: May it please you to resolve me in my suit.
> K. Rich: Thou troublest me; I am not in the vein.
>   *Exit [followed by all save Buckingham]*
>   (William Shakespeare, *Richard III,* IV, ii, 87–122)

Buckingham has helped Richard to murder his way to the throne of England and comes to claim his reward. He has high status and Richard is in debt to him. But Richard treats him badly. How does the discourse structure of the extract show this?

As there are only two characters talking, the number of turns each has is equal. However, Richard dominates the word count with 164 words to Buckingham's 107, 53% more than Buckingham. Buckingham uses a stream of status–marked address terms (*my lord* [six times], *your Highness* and *your Grace*) to be polite and defer to Richard's power. Richard only once bothers to address Buckingham directly, when he uses *thou* in contrast to Buckingham's consistent use of *you* to Richard.[4] Buckingham's use of status–marked vocatives stops in the last quarter of the interchange, as he begins to realise he is not getting anywhere. Richard also clearly interrupts Buckingham three times. Buckingham conceivably interrupts Richard in lines 103–4, but it is equally possible to see this interchange as a point where Richard just happens to stop in his reverie and Buckingham merely seizes the chance to ask for his reward again.

Buckingham sticks to his request because it is so important to him. In spite of the fact that he is not as powerful as Richard, it is he who initiates the large majority of the conversational exchanges, and each time with the same topic, his unfulfilled reward for services rendered. But Richard deflects him time and again, mainly by changing the topic and by addressing Stanley when in conversational terms he should be responding to Buckingham's just requests. In his first speech Richard explicitly tells Buckingham not to pursue the topic he has raised, and begins a new one, Richmond's flight. The next time Buckingham asks for his reward, Richard ignores him and addresses Stanley instead. The third time Buckingham tries, Richard apparently goes off into a reverie about Richmond, a tactic he continues over Buckingham's next two attempts to get the topic back to what Richard owes him. At Buckingham's next try, Richard changes the topic again, asking what the time is, and when Buckingham ignores this request for comparatively trivial information, by returning to the topic of Richard's promise, Richard forces Buckingham to answer his question about the time, even though he almost certainly knows the answer already. Richard follows this up by openly telling Buckingham that he is getting in his way, and then saying he is not in a giving mood, which clearly entails that he won't give anything to Buckingham. Even then, Buckingham insists on raising the issue one last time, only to be told that he is a nuisance, with Richard repeating that he is not in the giving mood. It is hardly surprising that, when everyone except Buckingham leaves the stage after Richard's last put–down, Buckingham decides to flee.

We can also use the speech act analysis developed in 7.1 to elucidate further the interactional patterns we have noticed in this extract. Given Buckingham's polite use of status–marked address terms at the beginning of the interchange, we might well expect to see other examples of politeness in his language.

One indication of this in his first speech is his use of an *indirect* speech act:

> My lord, I have consider'd in my mind
> The late request that you did sound me in.

Buckingham *states* that he has thought about Richard's request to him, which he has carried out. The stating of a felicity condition that needs to be in place for another speech act to work usually counts as an indirect way of performing the relevant speech act indirectly. This is why saying 'I am hungry' counts as a request to be given food, or 'Can you reach the top shelf?' counts as a request for you to get something down from that shelf. Hence Buckingham's statement clearly counts as an *indirect request* to Richard to honour his promise – his thinking about Richard's original request, now fulfilled, is a statement of one of the felicity conditions which need to be in place for Buckingham to try to call in payment for the debt which Richard owes him, but which Richard is studiously avoiding.

In his longest speech of the extract, his next attempt at the request, Buckingham makes what he wants very explicit, stating clearly both what he is claiming and his grounds for claiming it. In sequencing terms this should clearly lead to Richard saying either that he will, or will not, grant the request, the clearly preferred option in terms of honour and the preservation of social relations being Richard's agreeing to do what he originally promised. Richard changes the topic, however, and Buckingham has to make the matter even more explicit, by asking Richard how he responds to the request.

From now on, Buckingham hardly manages to say much more about the matter until his last turn, which is no more than a polite reformulation of his last request. He has clearly lost. Richard has all the power and Buckingham has no more conversational armoury with which to confront him.

Exercise 3

Take the questions about turn–taking from exercise 2, and apply them to the beginning of Shaw's *Major Barbara*, to see what they show us about the characters and how they relate to one another:

[*Context: Lady Britomart, a woman of about fifty, is writing at her writing desk in a rather grand room Her son, Stephen, a young man, comes in.*]

Stephen: What's the matter?   (1)
Lady B: Presently, Stephen.
[*Stephen walks submissively to the settee and sits down.*
He takes up a Liberal weekly called The Speaker.]
Lady B: Don't begin to read, Stephen. I shall require all   (5)
          your attention.
Stephen: It was only while I was waiting—
Lady B: Don't make excuses, Stephen. [*He puts down* The
          Speaker]. Now! [*She finishes her writing; rises; and*
          comes to the settee].I have not kept you waiting   (10)
          very long, I think.
Stephen: Not at all, mother.
Lady B   Bring me my cushion. [*He takes the cushion*
          from the chair at the desk and arranges it for
          her as she sits down on the settee.]. Sit down.   (15)
          [*He sits down and fingers his tie nervously.*]
          Don't fiddle with your tie, Stephen: there is
          nothing the matter with it.
Stephen: I beg your pardon. [*He fiddles with his watch*
          chain instead.]   (20)
Lady B: Now are you attending to me, Stephen?
Stephen: Of course, mother.
Lady B: No: it's not of course. I want something much
          more than your everyday matter–of–course
          attention. I am going to speak to you very   (25)
          seriously, Stephen. I wish you would let that
          watch–chain alone.
Stephen: [*Hastily relinquishing the chain.*] Have I done
          anything to annoy you, mother? If so, it was
          quite unintentional.   (30)
Lady B: [*astonished*] Nonsense! [*With some remorse.*]
          My poor boy, did you think I was angry with
          you?
Stephen: What is it then, mother? You are making me
          very uneasy.   (35)
Lady B: [*squaring herself at him rather aggressively*]
          Stephen: may I ask how soon you intend to
          realize that you are a grown–up man, and that
          I am only a woman?

Stephen: [*amazed*]: Only a—   (40)

Lady B: Don't repeat my words, please: it is a most
          aggravating habit. You must learn to face life
          seriously, Stephen. I really cannot bear the
          whole burden of our family affairs any longer.
          You must advise me: you must assume the   (45)
          responsibility.

Stephen: I!

Lady B: Yes, you, of course. You were 24 last June.
          You've been at Harrow and Cambridge. You've
          been to India and Japan. You must know a lot   (50)
          of things, now; unless you have wasted your
          time most scandalously. Well, advise me.

                    (George Bernard Shaw, *Major Barbara*, pp. 51–3)

— 7.3   Politeness

In the discussions of examples 2–5 in this chapter I have made
a number of informal remarks about **politeness** in regard to
relationships between characters. For example we noted that
the variant forms of the vocatives which characters use to
address one another have different effects in terms of politeness
(*cf.* the vocative *Wills* vs *Mr Fibbs* in 'Trouble in the Works'
and Buckingham's repeated use of *my Lord* when addressing
Richard III). Similarly, we noticed that offering to perform an
action beneficial to someone else (*e.g.* Fibbs offering Wills a
cigar) is polite to that person, and ignoring the needs and
wishes of a person (*e.g.* Richard III ignoring and deflecting
Buckingham's just request for his reward) is very impolite.
Because politeness is an important aspect of human social
interaction and therefore plays an important role in plays, it
will also be helpful to examine politeness phenomena carefully.

Perhaps the most well known account of politeness is that
provided by Brown and Levinson (1978, 1987).[5] They suggest
that politeness is a universal phenomenon, affecting linguistic
and other social behaviour. We all want other people to be
polite to us, and in turn we are polite to others (a) because we
recognise the same need in them and (b) because if we don't
pay attention to the politeness needs of others we are unlikely
to be very efficient in getting things done. Imagine, for
example, how difficult it would be to persuade your father to

lend you some money while at the same time telling him he has not been a good father to you.

Brown and Levinson's account of politeness is built around the concept of **face**. Your face is your public self–image, and has two components, **positive face** and **negative face**.

Positive face is our need for our actions and wants to be desirable to other people as well as ourselves. This is why being told 'well done' or being clapped at the end of a performance is important for us, and it also explains why the receiving of essay marks is such an emotional matter. A low mark does not just reduce your chances of doing well educationally. It also threatens your positive face because it counts as criticism on the part of someone in authority, criticism which will also damage your status among your peers. Conversely, a high mark enhances your positive face as well as your educational chances.

Negative face is the wish that our actions should be unimpeded by others. This is why being asked (or even worse, *told*) to do the washing up when you want to watch television is so annoying.

In example 5, Buckingham politely attends to Richard's positive face by calling him *my Lord*. Richard, on the other hand, threatens Buckingham's negative and positive face at the same time when he interrupts him (threatening Buckingham's negative face by impeding his desire to speak) and at the same time makes it clear that he will not give Buckingham his reward (threatening Buckingham's positive face by making it clear that he does not want what Buckingham wants). Richard threatens Buckingham's negative and positive face again and again during the interaction in example 5, which explains why his behaviour appears so markedly rude.

In Brown and Levinson's terms, many quite trivial acts are face threatening to some degree. They use the term **Face Threatening Acts** (or **FTAs**) to refer to such activity. Even asking someone to open the window threatens that person's negative face, if only slightly, because it impedes their wish to do something else (negative face). Avoiding face threat altogether is thus virtually impossible in normal social interaction. If you want to be polite, then, you avoid and/or minimise the *number* and *size* of your FTAs as much as you can, given whatever needs to be done. And if you *can't* avoid an FTA you try to **mitigate** the amount of threat by the way in which you say, or do, what you do. This is why it seems more polite, when visiting someone, to open the door to their room gently rather than abruptly, and to *ask* rather than *order* someone to do the washing up. Asking gives your inter-locutor the choice of saying 'no' without social disruption, but ordering makes saying 'no' much more difficult.

'I know you are interested in that TV programme, but can you do the washing up please?' *mitigates* the FTA (i) by taking account of the other person's face wants in the first clause, (ii) by apparently asking a question about his or her ability to do the washing up in the second (*i.e.* by using an *indirect* speech act) and (iii) by adding the politeness marker 'please'. You could make your request even more polite if you wanted by making it what Brown and Levinson call *off–record*. Hence if you say 'There's a bit of washing up to be done' you perform the FTA off–record by merely stating what is the case rather than asking or telling someone to get on with the work, and you mitigate the FTA further by using a minimising phrase like 'a bit of'.

If, on the other hand, you want to be **impolite** (or downright rude), you can reverse the above social 'rules'. Maximise the number and size of your FTAs, make a point of performing them *on record* and perform those FTAs without any mitigation at all (that is, **baldly**, or **without redress**): 'Dig out the cesspit, damn you!'

Although politeness is in our general social interests, there tends to be quite a lot of *impoliteness* around in dramatic texts. If plays are to be interesting dramatically, we need to see situations of conflict arise and be dealt with, and impoliteness is a way of indicating social conflict. In the extract below, Juliet, who is, by now, secretly in love with Romeo, has told her mother, Lady Capulet, that she no longer agrees to her arranged marriage with Paris. Juliet's parents have only just arranged for the wedding to take place on the following Thursday, and Lady Capulet now passes on the news to Lord Capulet in Juliet's presence:

Example 6

Capulet:	. . . How now, wife!
	Have you delivered to her our decree?
Lady Cap.:	Ay, sir; but she will none, she gives you thanks.
	I would the fool were married to her grave!
Capulet:	Soft! take me with you, take me with you, wife.
	How will she none? Doth she not give us thanks?

> Is she not proud? Doth she not count her blest,
> Unworthy as she is, that we have wrought
> So worthy a gentleman to be her bridegroom?

Juliet: Not proud you have, but thankful that you have.
> Proud can I never be of what I hate.
> But thankful even for hate that is meant love.

Capulet: How how, how how, chopt logic! What is this?
> 'Proud' – and 'I thank you' – and 'I thank you
>   not' –
> And yet 'not proud'? Mistress minion, you,
> Thank me no thankings, nor proud me no prouds,
> But fettle your fine joints 'gainst Thursday next,
> To go with Paris to Saint Peter's Church,
> Or I will drag you on a hurdle thither.
> Out, you green–sickness carrion! Out you baggage!
> You tallow–face!

(William Shakespeare, *Romeo and Juliet*, III, v, 137–57)

When Capulet first talks of his *decree* to Juliet to marry Paris in a few days' time, he can speak in such a bald way because he thinks that Juliet wants to marry Paris. After all, she has earlier said that she would be very happy with the marriage. Hence he assumes that he is not threatening her negative *or* her positive face. Lady Capulet's reply on Juliet's behalf reports the dramatic news that she has suddenly refused to marry Paris. This decision clearly threatens her parents' positive and negative face, and in turn, Lady Capulet's reaction that she wishes Juliet dead threatens both aspects of Juliet's face. Consequently, it would appear that when she tells Capulet that *she gives you thanks* her report of Juliet's polite conversational behaviour in refusing the marriage is almost certainly ironic. Indeed, just before this extract begins, when Juliet told her mother that she would not marry Paris she was extremely direct about it and thanked no one.

Capulet's next speech is rude to Juliet in that he asks Lady Capulet questions he should really be asking of Juliet, thus apparently depriving her of the right to speak. His flurry of questions, which come too fast for anyone to respond to, are all about Juliet's sudden lack of positive politeness towards her parents (why does she not want what they want?), and clearly indicate his shock, as well as his anger, at what he has just heard.

By responding to her father's questions Juliet takes a turn which has been offered by Capulet to his wife. This threatens her parents' negative face, and of course she is bound to threaten both their positive and their negative faces by restating her refusal to marry Paris. Thus she tries to *mitigate* the FTA by making the distinction between being proud and being thankful. By stating her thanks for what she characterises as misplaced love she is attempting to be positively polite, and thus to get out of the bind in which she finds herself. However, Capulet is very angry indeed. The first part of his response to his daughter indicates his extreme dissatisfaction with her attempts to engineer a way out of the social dislocation she has produced, and which, from his viewpoint, has no reason. From then on he produces a stream of FTAs without redress against Juliet. Ordering her to attend the marriage ceremony, and threatening to force her if she refuses, attacks her *negative* face. Juliet clearly does not want to do what her father orders, and the imposition is high as who she marries is clearly a matter of considerable importance to her. At the same time, his stream of vocatives of extreme abuse repeatedly attack her *positive* face. It thus becomes clear, despite Juliet's attempt to mend her fences, that in a very short space the previous family harmony over the proposed marriage has quickly degenerated to such a point that repair is unthinkable. This disharmony, of course, leads directly to the tragedy at the end of the play.

Exercise 4

Examine the politeness strategies employed by the two characters in the extract below (they have just met for the first time). What can you deduce about their attitudes towards one another?

Professor: Good morning, good morning . . . You are . . . er . . . I suppose you really are . . . the new pupil?
[*The Pupil turns round briskly and easily, very much the young lady: she gets up and goes towards the Professor, holding out her hand.*]

Pupil: Yes, Sir. Good morning, Sir. You see I came at the right time. I didn't want to be late.

Professor: Good. Yes, that's very good. Thank you. But you shouldn't have hurried too much, you know. I don't know quite how to apologise to you for having kept you waiting . . . I was just finishing . . . you understand, I was just . . . er . . . I do beg your pardon . . . I hope you will forgive me . . .

Pupil: Oh, but you mustn't, Sir. It's perfectly all right, Sir.

Professor: My apologies

(Eugene Ionesco, *The Lesson*, pp. 183–4)

Discussion of exercises

Exercise 1

It is clear that when Basil says 'fire' he intends it as a warning, and that the desired perlocutionary effect is to get his guests to leave the hotel as quickly as possible. However, because he has just put them all to the trouble of the fire drill he cannot stop himself from being obsequiously polite when he warns them. The guests, having just gone through the fire drill, obviously have some difficulty interpreting 'fire'. It could be a command to fire something, for example, but they do not have guns. Alternatively, 'fire' could merely be a remark – 'Look, there's a fire' – which is how Mr Sharp appears to interpret it. In the end Basil has to resort to shouting the word over and over, getting louder and more animated each time until he gets his desired perlocutionary effect.

Exercise 2

Commentary is provided in the text, immediately after the exercise.

Exercise 3

An analysis of this extract can be found in Short (1990).

Exercise 4

This passage is analysed in detail in Simpson (1989b).

Notes

1. These comments about conversation in plays clearly apply just as well to conversations between characters in novels,

and even to the character talk in some poems. Leech and Short (1981: 290–4) discuss speech acts in and extract from Jane Austen's *Pride and Prejudice*.

2. The fact that linguistic opposites often share a number of important features and differ only in respect to one also applies to many lexical antonyms (*e.g.* 'boy' and 'girl' which contrast with respect to male/female, but share the features concrete, animate and human).

3. I would like to thank Jonathan Culpeper for pointing out this interesting passage to me (which he discusses in Culpeper 1994: 115–21), and for allowing me to make use of our discussions on it.

4. In Elizabethan English the use of the second–person pronouns 'thou' and 'you' was not unlike 'tu' and 'vous' in modern French. The singular subject pronoun 'thou' (and its associated object pronoun 'thee') was often used to indicate social solidarity when addressing a single intimate or equal. The plural 'you', on the other hand, connoted social distance when addressed to one person. In unequal social encounters 'you' was often used by a social inferior when addressing a superior, to indicate respect. Conversely 'you' could be employed by social superiors as an indication of power, to put other people 'in their social place'. This asymmetric patterning, with its clearly contrasting over–tones, is what appears to be happening in the conversation between Richard and Buckingham. In modern English the singular/plural distinction in the second–person pronouns has virtually disappeared (though the 'thou'/'you' distinction still exists in some dialects of British English, for example some Yorkshire dialects, and a newer version based on 'you'/'you–all' can be found in some American dialects). The fact that we no longer have the same pronoun system makes it hard for us to perceive the exact social nuances of the use of second–person pronouns in Shakespearian and other Early Modern English texts, particularly as there is evidence to suggest that the apparently regular social values of the use 'thee' suggested above is complicated by other discoursal and pragmatic factors in particular social contexts. Wales (1983) and Calvo (1992) explore some of these complexities.

5. An alternative general account of politeness can be found in Leech (1983: 104–51). Leech 1992 uses this approach to examine character relations in Shaw's *You Never Can Tell*.

Further reading

Elam (1980: Ch. 5) is a general account of dramatic discourse and Fowler (1986: Ch. 8) is a general discoursal and pragmatic account of dialogue. Short (1989) explores the application of these approaches to dramatic texts (including 'Trouble in the Works') and Nash (1989) uses similar techniques when discussing the opening of *Hamlet*. Herman (1991) explores turn–taking in dramatic dialogue. Downes (1988) examines discourse structure (including speech acts) in relation to other levels of linguistic analysis, particularly grammar, in an account of the first scene of *King Lear*. Burton (1980) is a book–length application of the Birmingham model of discourse analysis to dramatic discourse. Burton (1979) and Burton (1982) contain parallel work related to particular dramatic texts. Coulthard (1977: Ch. 9) analyses conversational strategies in a scene from *Othello*. Lowe (1994) uses speech act analysis to elucidate an extract from *The Crucible* by Henry Miller. Bennison (1993) uses a wide range of pragmatic and discoursal approaches, including turn–taking and speech act analysis to examine characterisation in Tom Stoppard's *Professional Foul*. Hurst (1987) uses speech act analysis to discuss *A Family and Fortune* by Ivy Compton–Burnett, and Leech and Short (1981: 288–94) apply speech act analysis to a passage from Jane Austen's *Pride and Prejudice* and other texts. Simpson (1989b) discusses politeness phenomena in Ionesco's *The Lesson*. Leech (1983: 104–51) contains an alternative approach to politeness from that of Brown and Levinson, and Leech (1992) uses the Leech (1983) approach to examine politeness phenomena in Shaw's *You Never Can Tell*.

CHECKSHEET 6: TURN–TAKING, SPEECH ACTS AND POLITENESS

A. Turn–taking patterns

(a)   Does one character have significantly more turns than the others? [Note that if two characters only are present, the number of turns for each will automatically be more or less equal.]

(b)   Are the turns the same length, or does one character have longer turns than the others?

(c)   Are the patterns of initiating turns roughly equal for each character, or are there significant disparities?

(d)   Similarly, are there disparities in terms of which character(s) take up the response position in the conversation?

(e)   Does one of the characters allocate turns to others?

(f)   Are there any interruptions? If so, who interrupts who, and why?

(g)   Which characters initiate new topics and which do not? Are there any significant patterns of topic–control?

(h)   Are there any differences in the terms of address, or other markers of power and/or solidarity which the characters use for one another?

(i)   Are there any other interesting turn–taking patterns (politeness routines, for instance)?

Now that you have collected the data, can you discern any patterns among the categories which help distinguish the roles or functions of the characters? How do the turn–taking patterns relate to your overall interpretation of the text analysed, and what light do they throw on the personalities of the characters and how they relate to one another?

B.   Speech acts

(a)   Are there typical kinds of speech acts used by the different characters? If so, what does this tell you about them?

(b)   Examining each speech act in turn, decide whether it is a direct or indirect speech act.

(c)   Are any of the speech acts ambiguous?

What can you deduce from this information about the characters and their interrelationships and/or the thematic concerns of the text?

(d)   Now consider the felicity conditions for the various speech acts. What do these tell you about the fictional world or about the characters and their relations?

(e)   Do the intended perlocutionary effects of the speech acts succeed, or are there cases where they fail? If so, what are the consequences of these failures?

How does what you have found out through speech act analysis affect your understanding of the play and your reaction to the relationships between the characters?

C.   Politeness

(a)   Are the characters' politeness behaviours reciprocal?

(b)   Are the characters *polite* towards one another? In what ways are FTAs mitigated?

(c)   Are there any examples of *impoliteness*?

(d)   Now examine the politeness strategies of the various characters in more detail. Try to measure the number of politenesses or impolitenesses and the extent of the (im)politeness in each instance. Are there any patterns in terms of strategies of positive politeness, negative politeness, or in terms of bald or mitigated FTAs?

If the characters are not acting reciprocally, in what ways are they acting differently from one another? What do your detailed answers to questions (a)–(d) above tell you about the relationships between the characters? Are there any examples of particular styles of politeness behaviour for particular characters? How do the patterns of (im)politeness you have discerned relate to the plot and thematic development of the play?

CHAPTER 8

Assumptions, presuppositions and the inferring of meaning

8.1 Introduction

It appears at first sight that words and sentences possess meaning in some inherent way (everybody knows what 'tree' and 'Oak trees have green leaves' mean). But in addition, to infer appropriate meaning from what is said or written often crucially depends upon applying relevant assumptions about the world (including language itself) to the linguistic 'message'. Pretend, for example that someone says to you 'Go on, then'. If you are playing cards and the other person has had a turn, you will interpret the phrase as meaning that it is your turn to play and that you have not noticed that the other person has already played. If you are a child who has been asking to be allowed to play with your friends outside, the same sentence can be used to give permission, even in a situation where the immediately preceding conversation has not been related to your request.

Thus the context which we assume when interpreting an utterance can affect its meaning or significance. It is important to remember, however, that in real life these contexts will often be provided by the situations we find ourselves in, and that when we read texts this 'situationality' is prompted by clues from within the text. We have to construct meaning 'behind the words' or 'between the lines', as drama critics often say. But we can't construct anything we like. In the middle of a game of poker, 'Go on then' is very unlikely to be construable as the giving of permission for one of the participants to play with a friend outside. When we read, we are prompted in what we construct not by the situation we are in, but by the text itself, and the situations which that text sets up, as we will see below.

A dramatic example of assumptions being used to produce relevant understanding would be the following excerpt from a speech of Lady Bracknell's in Oscar Wilde's *The Importance of Being Earnest*:

Example 1

I'm sorry if we are a little late, Algernon, but I was obliged to call on dear Lady Harbury. I hadn't been there since her poor husband's death. I never saw a woman so altered . . .

(Oscar Wilde, *The Importance of Being Earnest*, Act 1)

We take along to this speech a set of assumptions *triggered by* the reference to Lord Harbury's death. We are not told why Lady Bracknell visited Lady Harbury, but we are likely to infer that it was to convey her condolences. It is a normal thing to express sadness and give support when close relatives of our acquaintances die. Moreover, we assume that Lady Harbury will be grieving over the loss of her late husband, particularly given Lady Bracknell's use of the phrase *her **poor** husband's death*. It would appear that Lord Harbury's death is definitely to be regretted, and the final part of the quotation above seems to confirm this – we assume that Lady Harbury is very upset at her husband's death.

This, then, is the process by which we infer 'the meaning between the lines'. Prompted by the text, we infer relevant meaning through a wide variety of devices, including the foregrounding devices discussed in Chapters 1 and 2, the filling-in of assumptions which we have begun to explore here. However, meaning 'between the lines' is not a special property of drama. We arrive at understanding in the same way for all literary texts, and indeed for all meaningful behaviour, including ordinary language behaviour.

I recently saw a British TV comedy programme starring Rowan Atkinson and called *Mr Bean's Christmas*. The Mr Bean programmes consist almost entirely of mime. In this episode, Mr Bean writes some Christmas cards, puts them into envelopes and then goes out of the bed–sitting room where he lives. Because of what we know about the giving of Christmas cards, we assume he is going to post them to some friends. But Mr Bean immediately posts them through his own letter box, comes back inside, opens the envelopes and puts the cards on his mantelpiece. Comedy is produced here through defeated expectations based on assumptions about normal situations prompted by, and contrasting with, what we see on the screen. But this time no language is used. Many of the things we have noticed about how we understand the language of literature can also be applied to non–linguistic situations, including actions on stage.

But now let us see the rest of the Lady Bracknell's speech which we began to explore above:

Example 2

. . . she looks quite twenty years younger. And now I'll have a cup of tea, and one of those nice cucumber sandwiches you promised me.

(Oscar Wilde, *The Importance of Being Earnest*, Act 1)

We can see now that Oscar Wilde has led us up the garden path. Lady Harbury appears not to regret Lord Harbury's death at all. We have been drawn into using our normal assumptions to make what turn out to be false inferences, thus producing the humorous reaction to Lady Bracknell's line cancelling them. Lady Bracknell appears not to be very much bothered about the demise of Lord Harbury either, as she immediately changes the topic from his death to tea and cucumber sandwiches.

The last sentence in the above quotation is a command to Algernon, in the form of an assertion about the immediate future, to produce the tea and sandwiches forthwith. It gives Algernon no room for negotiation, a big difficulty for him as he and his friend, Jack, ate the sandwiches just before Lady Bracknell arrived. Lady Bracknell's sentence also has embedded within it (in the relative clause post–modifying s*andwiches*) a presupposition that at some point in the recent past Algernon *promised* Lady Bracknell cucumber sandwiches when she next came to tea. In turn, the speech act of promising has, as one of its felicity conditions, the assumption that the speaker can deliver what is promised, but we know from earlier in the scene that Algernon cannot deliver, and this increases the comedy.

In the above examples, I have used two terms, **assumption** and **presupposition** for what might appear to be the same thing. In ordinary speech, indeed, the words can often be used interchangeably. But I have made the terminological distinction on purpose because they relate to rather different domains. At one extreme we have general *assumptions* based upon situations or activities we have repeatedly experienced or observed in literature and life (for example our assumptions about what happens when people die applied to the Lord Harbury example, Christmas card–giving applied to Mr Bean's actions or factories and their organisation as seen in 7.1.1). At the other extreme there are *presuppositions*, specific assumptions of rather precise matters that are embedded inside sentences, like the fact that Algernon had promised Lady Bracknell some cucumber sandwiches. In the middle, there are assumptions tied to a particular utterance, but where what is assumed is not expressed explicitly in that utterance. Examples of this would be what we have noticed above about the speech act of promising and what we generally saw about felicity conditions 'behind' speech acts in Chapter 7. For example, if a character uses a threat in a play we must normally assume that he or she has the ability to carry it out, or if character A apologises to character B it must be because character A has done something harmful or unhelpful to character B, whether or not the original unhelpful act is mentioned in the sentences concerned.

Distinctions along the cline of assumptions which I have referred to above, with general schematic knowledge about how the world works at one end and presuppositions embedded in individual sentences at the other, may be easy to make in some cases, but more difficult in others. If I say 'Three of John's children are in hospital' it is clear that the fact that John has at least four children is presupposed by the sentence, and could not be accessed through general schematic knowledge about the world. On the other hand, the assumption that John's children will have been examined and tended by nurses and doctors, will probably be lying in a hospital bed, and so on, come from schematic knowledge. But it is difficult to know whether the associations for the word 'hospital' (for example that it will be a large building and that it is where people are treated for illness) are part of the presuppositions associated with the term (part of word meaning) or part of our general knowledge about the world. It is in cases like this that language and the world are inextricably interfused, and it is important to remember that although it is helpful to be clear whenever we can about how the 'meaning between the lines' comes about, we will not always be able to do so.

Exercise 1

(a) What do you infer to be the social and personal relationship between the two men in the extract below? How do you know this? What else can you infer which is not explicitly stated?

(b) Using what you know about the men's relationship, and anything else you know which you think is relevant, explain why the last speech is funny:

Algernon:	. . . by the way, Lane, I see from your book that on Thursday night, when Lord Shoreman and Mr Worthing were dining with me, eight bottles of champagne are entered as having been consumed.	(1) (5)
Lane:	Yes, sir; eight bottles and a pint.	
Algernon:	Why is it that at a bachelor's establishment the servants invariably drink the champagne? I ask merely for information.	
Lane:	I attribute it to the superior quality of the wine, sir. I have often observed that in married households the champagne is rarely of a first–rate brand.	(10)

(Oscar Wilde, *The Importance of Being Earnest*, Act 1)

Although we have already looked in some detail at speech acts in 7.1, we have not looked at the other sorts of assumptions referred to above. The sets of background assumptions related to particular situations are usually called 'schemas', and assumptions embedded inside the structure of particular sentences are usually called 'presuppositions'.

8.2 Schema theory

We know a multitude of things about the world and how it works, and we bring to bear *relevant parts* of this knowledge when we understand what other people say or do. These facts have led psychologists and linguists to wonder how we manage to do this. It is unlikely that we store all the facts we know about the world and how it works as an unordered list in our brains. The list would be massively long, and without some sort of organisation of the information it would be difficult to see how we manage so quickly to retrieve the relevant pieces of information from memory and apply them sensibly to whatever situation we find ourselves in. As a consequence, psychologists have argued that connected bits of information are stored as packages, or **schemas**. A helpful analogy might be that of a filing cabinet. When we come across a reference to a situation we have come across before, we access the relevant 'file' in the 'filing cabinet', which consists of an organised inventory of all the sorts of thing related to that situation which we have previously experienced. These schemas get updated from time to time, as new information comes to hand. Let us use the lecture schema as an example. When I was first an undergraduate, my university insisted that staff and students wore gowns to lectures. I accepted this as the norm, which coincided with what I had seen in films and books where universities were depicted. It is interesting to note that fictions play a large part in the establishment of our schemas; for example I have never seen beyond the front desk of a police station, but I have a good idea, from reading novels and watching plays and films, of how those arrested are interviewed, charged and put in the cells.

During my time as an undergraduate we successfully revolted against the wearing of gowns in lectures, and I thus had to adjust my lecture schema to account for this. When I first went to lecture in China my students provided me with a cup of green tea to drink while I lectured, which they continually topped up from a large vacuum flask. At first I did not know whether this phenomenon was general or merely idiosyncratic, but when it happened at other Chinese universities too I had to develop a special sub–schema for lectures in China. Now when I go to lecture in China I automatically expect lecture–tea and would feel deprived if none were to hand. I have even suggested to some of my British students that they might institute the tea–giving tradition, but they have never taken it up, perhaps because it contrasts too strongly with their lecture schema.

Schema theorists make a useful distinction between information stored which is ordered *sequentially* (in a sort of narrative) and that which is not. Non–sequentially ordered information is said to be stored as a **frame** (Minsky 1975), and sequentially ordered information as a **script** (see Schank and Abelson 1977: 36–46).

Sticking with the lecture example, my *frame assumptions* include the fact that most lectures have one lecturer but many listeners, the lecture theatre might well have banked rows of seats and something to rest writing pads on, and the lecturer will normally lecture standing up, facing the students, who will sitting listening. I would expect there to be a blackboard and/or overhead projector near the lecturer, and so on.

My *script assumptions* are that when the students enter the lecture hall they will sit in groups together, probably not using the front few rows unless they have to (do all lecturers have halitosis?). They will talk among themselves, while any handouts will be distributed, and until the lecturer indicates that he or she is ready to start. The lecturer will begin by stating in general terms what will happen in the lecture. When the lecture is nearly at an end the lecturer will probably sum up what has been said. These words will be a signal to the students to start getting ready to leave, and the preparations may well drown the lecturer's last few sentences. The lecturer will finish and the students will rush for the door, except for a few, who will stay behind to ask questions.

Your lecture frame and script might be slightly different from mine, but it will almost certainly share many of the features I have mentioned, and is very unlikely to include a snooker tournament or the entrance of someone with a martini on a silver tray. This shared packaged experience of the world into schemas helps us to interpret what is said and done in ways very similar to one another. And where things occur which go against these expected norms they become foregrounded, and hence *highly interpretable*, just as we noticed in Chapter 1 that the breaking of linguistic rules became foregrounded and thus important for textual interpretation (for a discussion of schema foregrounding, or what he calls 'schema refreshment' see Cook 1994: Ch. 7).

Actually, there is one week every year when someone with a martini on a silver tray might well interrupt my lecture to present the martini to some embarrassed student. It is in Rag Week, when student fund–raising stunts in aid of charity abound. Much of the fun (and money–raising potential) in Rag Week comes from turning schemas upside down, like ordering a drink to be delivered to a friend in the middle of a lecture. In this one week of the year, then, my lecture schema and my Rag Week scheme compete with one another in forming my expectations of what might happen. Note, however, that I am unlikely to adjust my overall lecture schema to include martinis, since they will be irrelevant for most of the time.

The following passage is from near the beginning of *Educating Rita* by Willy Russell. Frank is a university lecturer, and Rita is a mature student at the Open University, coming to see him in his room for the first time for a tutorial on English literature. She has just arrived:

Example 3

Frank looks up and then returns to the papers as Rita goes to		(1)
hang her coat on the door hooks.		

Rita: (*Noticing the picture*) That's a nice picture, isn't it? (*She goes up to it*)

Frank: Erm – yes, I suppose it is – nice . . .   (5)

Rita: (*studying the picture*) It's very erotic.

Frank: (*looking up*) Actually I don't think I've looked at it for about ten years, but yes, I suppose it is.

Rita: There's no suppose about it. Look at those tits.

He coughs and goes back to looking for the admission paper.   (10)

        Is it supposed to be erotic? I mean when he painted it do y' think he wanted to turn people on?

Frank: Erm – probably.

Rita: I'll bet he did y'know. Y' don't paint pictures like that just so that people can admire the brush   (15) strokes, do y'?

Frank: (*giving a short laugh*) No – no – you're probably right.

Rita: This was the pornography of its day, wasn't it? It's sort of like *Men Only*, isn't it? But in those   (20) days they had to pretend it wasn't erotic so they made it religious, didn't they? Do *you* think it's erotic?

Frank: (*taking a look*) I think it's very beautiful.

Rita: I didn't ask y' if it was beautiful.   (25)

(Willy Russell, *Educating Rita*, Act 1, Scene 1)

Frank is the tutor and Rita the new student. But the way Rita behaves clashes violently with our schema for this relationship. First of all, our turn–taking script for this situation is flouted. It is as if Rita has taken over the tutor role and Frank is placed in the student position. She controls the topic of the conversation. She speaks first, and asks Frank questions which he finds difficult to answer. And when he answers the embarrassing question about whether he finds the painting erotic by saying that he finds it beautiful, she indicates that his answer is inappropriate by drawing him back to the question asked, as often happens in seminars and tutorials. The turn–taking script is roughly what we would expect for this situation, but the participants are in the wrong roles.

We can see from this example that the turn–taking patterns we noticed in 7.2 are explainable in part by reference to schema theory. But there are also other ways in which our schemas are turned upside down in this extract. Rita brings up the taboo subject of sex in her first tutorial, and uses the word *tits* instead of the more polite 'breasts'. The subject matter and the way she talks about it seem inappropriate (a) because of the tutorial situation and (b) because we expect women to talk about such things even less than men. All of this is particularly 'upside–down' when we remember that the tutorial is meant to be on English Literature. The subject of painting is not strictly relevant, but you would expect such tutors and students, if they were involved in a discussion about nude painting, to take the aesthetic line which Frank tries, and which Rita explicitly rejects. There is also clearly a sense, though, in which Rita has got it as right as the embarrassed Frank. It is likely that such paintings were produced to fulfil a pornographic role as well as the religious and aesthetic functions more often referred to in polite society. Or, as Rita puts it, *Y' don't paint pictures like that just so that people can admire the brush strokes, do y'*? Rita is clearly turning her first tutorial with Frank, and hence their entire relationship on its head, and she is by no means naive about what has been discussed. So, in spite of her statement, a few lines later, that she was *dead surprised when they took me* and the fact that the play is called *Educating Rita*, it would appear that Frank is likely to learn as much from Rita, if rather more unconventionally, as she is from him.

Schemas are organised representations of background knowledge which readers bring along to texts. As your schemas, although similar, may not be identical with those of other people, this is one of the ways in which we can see that both shared meaning and different meanings might be extractable from the same text. Note, however, that in most cases the schemas which we invoke as part of the process of understanding must be prompted in some way by the text itself. This is clearly the case with the *Educating Rita* example. The relevant context is made very clear at the beginning of the play, and if I tried to interpret the text with another conceivably relevant schema, for example doctor–patient interviews, I would soon find myself in interpretative difficulties. Moreover, somebody with no 'university schema' or 'tutorial schema' to bring along would also miss much of the humour. This is one of the ways in which texts 'position' readers. If you wanted to arrive at a sensitive appreciation of the play and did not have a tutorial schema you would feel that you had to go out and get one. One important aspect of the work of English departments revolves around giving students the requisite schematic knowledge–base for responding sensitively to texts distant from them historically and/or culturally.

Exercise 2

(a) What are your assumptions about how two people would decide to get married? Would there be a specific act of proposal or not? If so, what would the circumstances be? Who would propose to who, or doesn't it matter? Write your answers down.

(b) After you have completed (a) above, read the following extract and consider how your assumptions about proposals compare (i) with Jack's and (ii) with Gwendolen's:

Jack: . . . we must get married at once. There is no   (1)
               time to be lost.
Gwendolen: Married, Mr Worthing?
Jack: (*astounded*) Well . . . surely. You know that I

love you, and you led me to believe, Miss   (5)
Fairfax, that you were not absolutely indifferent
to me.

Gwendolen: I adore you. But you haven't proposed to me
yet. Nothing has been said at all about
marriage. The subject has not even been   (10)
touched on.

Jack: Well . . . may I propose to you now?

Gwendolen: I think it would be an admirable opportunity.
And to spare you any possible
disappointment, Mr Worthing, I think it only   (15)
fair to tell you quite frankly beforehand that
I am fully determined to accept you.

Jack: Gwendolen!

Gwendolen: Yes, Mr Worthing, what have you got to
say to me?   (20)

Jack: You know what I have got to say to you.

Gwendolen: Yes, but you don't say it.

Jack: Gwendolen, will you marry me? (*Goes
to his knees*)

Gwendolen: Of course I will, darling. How long you have   (25)
been about it!

(Oscar Wilde, *The Importance of Being Earnest*, Act 1)

8.3   Presuppositions

Let us now turn from macro background assumptions to the
micro assumptions, or **presuppositions**, held by particular
sentences in texts. The sentence 'The England cricket team has
lost again' *presupposes* the existence of an entity called the
England cricket team, and *asserts* that it has lost again. In this
case, there is no existential problem, as the existential
presupposition coincides with what we know about the real
world. But in many texts, the existential presuppositions
behind particular sentences do not coincide with reality. This
is true of most (but not all) literary texts, but also other
discourses, *e.g.* jokes and stories told in pubs. In this sort of
case, we use the presuppositions held by the sentences to help
us create the fictional world which lies 'behind' the poem,
play or novel. Consider the beginning of 'The Owl and the
Pussy–Cat':

Example 4

The owl and the pussy–cat went to sea
In a beautiful pea–green boat.

(Edward Lear, 'The Owl and the Pussy–Cat')

This sentence presupposes the existence of a specific owl, a specific pussy–cat and the sea, and asserts that the owl and the pussy–cat went to sea in a beautiful pea–green boat. In order to 'take part' in the poem, for the duration of our reading we have to pretend to ourselves that these entities, and various others mentioned in the text, exist, even though we know they do not really. And once we have read the first sentence of the poem, our 'presuppositional pool' for the text is widened to include what has just been asserted, namely that the owl and the pussy–cat went to sea in the boat. As the text unwinds, our pool of presuppositions gets larger and larger. Because 'The Owl and the Pussy–Cat' is far removed from our experience of the real world we are unlikely to add items from our presuppositional pool for the text to our schematic organisation about the world. But if a text appears to coincide rather better with our assumptions about what the real world is like, we might well add aspects of it to our schemas precisely because we have no real–life experience to replace it by. This explains how we can possess schematic knowledge of situations we have not directly experienced. The police station example I mentioned in 8.2 is one such example. Another for me would be bank vaults. I have never seen a bank vault, but through watching films and reading novels I assume that they are large rooms with heavily constructed metal doors. I also assume that they are manually opened, probably by turning a big metal wheel after codes have been punched into the locking device on the door by at least two senior people in the bank. All this could, of course, be wrong. Bank vault locks might all be controlled these days by the use of electronic 'swipe cards' or by a computer from which authorisation has to be gained. Whatever is actually the case, as I am very unlikely ever to see a bank vault 'in the flesh', I will update my schematic knowledge only through access to TV thrillers and the like.

If, in real life, people utter sentences which are false or *presuppose* things which are false, it is open to us to challenge them. But if we objected to 'The Owl and the Pussy–Cat' by saying that the individuals referred to didn't exist, our objections would seem inappropriate, precisely because the object of the text is not to make a series of true statements about the world. Indeed, if we objected to Shakespeare's spirit–character Ariel in *The Tempest* by saying that there are no such things as spirits, we would probably be accused of being insensitive to the play. This sort of thing is part of the motivation behind the critical assumption that when we read literature we have, for the duration of our reading, to 'become' someone we are not: a reader 'implied' by the text (in the case of *The Tempest*, someone who believes in spirits).

As I hinted above, we should not assume that the creation of fictions is something special to literature. Some works classed as literature are factual (many literary essays, for example), and we play the fictional game in ordinary discourse too. In my university's Rag Week a few years ago, the students went out during the night and re–painted the university sign so that it read 'University of Wallamaloo' instead of 'University of Lancaster'. Although the university authorities quickly corrected the prank, the fictional damage was already done, and for some months afterwards people in the university talked about the University of Wallamaloo as if it really existed. In particular, when they came across anything in the University of Lancaster which they did not like, they compared the situation with the University of Wallamaloo, which was always arranged in a more harmonious and beneficial way.

Most fictional texts create their fictional worlds through a relatively standard use of presupposition, schematic assumption and the like. But some texts, particularly comic and absurd works, create special effects by assuming 'facts' that are so at odds with our normal assumptions that we cannot 'take them on', in the normal way. Consider, for example, the sketch by Harold Pinter called 'Applicant'. This is one of Pinter's early works, but we can already see in it elements of the absurdity which characterise much of his mature work. A young man, Mr Lamb, is interviewed by Miss Piffs for a post:

Example 5

(*An office. Lamb, a young man, eager, cheerful, enthusiastic, is*   (1)
striding nervously, alone. The door opens. Miss Piffs comes in.
She is the essence of efficiency.)
Piffs: Ah, good morning.
Lamb: Oh, good morning, miss.   (5)
Piffs: Are you Mr. Lamb?

Lamb: That's right.
Piffs: (*studying a piece of paper*) Yes. You're applying for
         this vacant post, aren't you?
Lamb: I am actually, yes.   (10)
                                   (Harold Pinter, 'Applicant')

Our schemas for interviews are thus activated. But the
interview in this sketch quickly becomes a torture and inter–
rogation session. Saying that he must submit himself to a
psychological test, Miss Piffs attaches electrodes to Lamb and
gives him a series of severe electrical shocks. She also harangues
him, asking him a series of questions which she does not allow
him to answer. This 'interview' clearly clashes with our
interview schema, but Miss Piffs also asks some questions
which presuppose 'facts' which are at odds with our basic
conceptualisation of the world and how it works:

Example 6

Piffs: Are you a good mixer?   (1)
Lamb: Well, you've touched on quite an interesting
         point there—
Piffs: Do you suffer from eczema, listlessness, or falling
         coat?   (5)
Lamb: Er . . .
Piffs: Are you virgo intacta?
Lamb: I beg your pardon?
Piffs: Are you virgo intacta?
Lamb: Oh, I say, that's rather embarrassing. I mean—   (10)
         in front of a lady—
Piffs: Are you virgo intacta?
Lamb: Yes, I am, actually. I'll make no secret of it.
Piffs: Have you always been virgo intacta?
Lamb: Oh yes, always. Always.   (15)
                                   (Harold Pinter, 'Applicant')

When Miss Piffs asks Lamb whether he suffers from eczema or
listlessness, she is asking him about medical conditions it is
possible for him to have, even if our interview schema
indicates that these are not the sort of questions that it is
normally appropriate to ask. But the question about falling
coat is significantly different. This condition is normally
related to animals with fur, not human beings. Moreover,
after Lamb admits to being a virgin, Miss Piffs asks whether he

has always been *virgo intacta*. This question apparently presupposes that being a virgin is a state you can switch in and out of, like being a member of the local dramatic society. But it is part of the concept of virginity that you remain one until you have sexual intercourse for the first time, and that from then on you can never return to that original state. Miss Piffs's presuppositions thus clash with ours in a dramatic way, one that it is difficult to 'make good' by the normal fictional pretence. It is difficult to know whether Lamb shares our presuppositions or those of Miss Piffs. In his last response above he could merely be agreeing with his interviewer in the hope of respite, for example. But whatever is the case for him, it is clear that Miss Piffs holds assumptions, both pre–suppositional and schematic, which clash dramatically with ours. This is one of the major comic mechanisms in the sketch, and one which clearly contributes to the sense of absurdity in it (we can now begin to see why absurdity and comedy often go hand–in–hand). Of course there are other ways in which absurdity can be created, but presuppositional clashes between the character–character and playwright–audience levels of plays is one rich source of possibilities.

Moreover, these presuppositional clashes are part of the mechanism by which we *interpret* this sort of text. Another aspect of this sketch seen in example 6 is the way in which it explores how our society tends to treat men and women differently with respect to sexual matters. It is still more common to ask the sorts of questions Miss Piffs asks in relation to women than men. An obvious interpretative issue is why Miss Piffs, a woman, pointedly asks these questions of Mr Lamb, a young man in a distinctly less powerful position. We can then notice that this part of the sketch is consistent with many other stretches, where Miss Piffs makes a point of dominating Lamb conversationally, often using questions about his attitude towards women to do it:

Example 7
Piffs: Do women frighten you?   (1)
(*She presses a button on the other side of her stool. The stage is plunged into redness, which flashes on and off in time with her questions.*)
Piffs: (*building*) Their clothes? Their shoes? Their voices?
              Their laughter? Their stares? Their way of walking?   (5)
              Their way of sitting? Their way of smiling? Their

way of talking? Their mouths? Their hands? Their
feet? Their shins? Their thighs? Their knees? Their
eyes? Their (*Drumbeat*). Their (*Drumbeat*). Their
(*Cymbal bang*). Their (*Trombone chord*). Their (*Bass*   (10)
note).

(Harold Pinter, 'Applicant')

Here, towards the end of the sketch, Miss Piffs asks whether
women, and their various aspects, frighten Lamb. She is clearly
not interested in his answers, as she asks 22 questions in quick
succession without giving Lamb a chance to reply. Indeed, the
last five questions are questions in form only, deprived entirely
of lexical content. This comic, even ludicrous (absurdist?),
reversal of stereotypical assumptions concerning power in
relation to men and women clearly has male/female relations
at the centre of its discoursal concerns, and so it can be seen
that Pinter is exploring the issue of unequal power relations
between men and women some years before feminism became
politically correct.

Exercise 3

(a) Just after the section quoted immediately above, Miss Piffs
switches on the electric current again, propelling Lamb from his
chair and leaving him unconscious on the floor. The sketch then
ends, with the following lines:

[*He lies face upwards. Miss Piffs looks at him then walks to Lamb
and bends over him.*]
Piffs: Thank you very much, Mr. Lamb. We'll let you know.

(Harold Pinter, 'Applicant')

How would you explain the humour in the sketch's last line?

(b) In the following extract from Oscar Wilde's *The Importance of
Being Earnest*, Jack, who wants to marry Lady Bracknell's
daughter, Gwendolen, has admitted that he does not know who
his parents are, as he was abandoned when a baby in a large
handbag left in the cloakroom at Victoria station. Lady Bracknell
then states her baseline conditions for allowing the marriage to go
ahead:

I would strongly advise you, Mr Worthing, to try and acquire
some relations as soon as possible, and to make a definite
effort to produce at any rate one parent, of either sex, before
the season is quite over . . . You can hardly imagine that I
and Lord Bracknell would dream of allowing our only
daughter – a girl brought up with the utmost care – to marry
into a cloak–room, and form an alliance with a parcel.

(Oscar Wilde, *The Importance of Being Earnest*, Act 1)

How would you explain the humour of these lines?

8.4   Inference

So far, I have tried to explain how meanings end up 'between
the lines' in plays by reference to assumptions (*via* schemas)
which are brought along to texts by readers as a consequence
of some textual cue, or to presuppositions embedded in the
structure of sentences. Another way in which philosophers
and linguists have shown that we can arrive at meanings not
explicitly stated is through the notion of **inference**. Our
understanding of all human behaviour, linguistic or non–
linguistic, appears to involve processes of inference, and
indeed, inference is involved in those aspects of understanding
based on the different sorts of assumption we have already
discussed in this chapter. To show you what I mean, I will
take a couple of non–linguistic examples. Imagine that you see
a friend of yours leaving your local bank, and putting some
£10 notes into her purse. You will infer that she has just
withdrawn the money from her bank account. This inference
comes partly from the fact that she is leaving the bank and
your general schematic assumptions about banks, how they
work and what they are for. But your bank schema alone
could not explain the particularity of the above inference,
because you can use banks for other things besides
withdrawing money (depositing it, paying credit–card bills,
and so on). The other element that is crucial, is the specific
activity involving the money and the purse. If she is putting
the money into her purse we can infer that she must just have
got it from somewhere (note that this inference based on a
small action detail looks rather like the behavioural equivalent
of presuppositions 'embedded' in sentences of texts). It is the
linking together of our schematic knowledge and 'action–

presupposition' that allows us to arrive at our interpretation of this event. The main trigger for inference in literature is, of course, the text itself.

In normal circumstances, we make the kinds of inferences described above so quickly and automatically that we would not even notice that we had been involved in inferential work (this is also true, note, of our interpretation of the language of texts). But we can see from the example that inference is an essential and remarkably general aspect of our understanding of just about anything.

Although inference is usually very automatic and unconscious, it does sometimes get raised nearer to the conscious surface of our thinking. It happens, for example, when we are thinking through a difficult problem, like understanding a complex argument or learning to use a piece of computer software for the first time, and it is not accidental that we often talk to ourselves, or other people, in this kind of situation. Linguistic realisation appears to be an important aspect of conscious thinking. Another example of less automatic inferencing involves the behavioural equivalent of linguistic deviation and the consequent psychological foregrounding which we examined in some detail in Chapters 1 and 2. Imagine, for example, that you see your next–door neighbour fiddling with the lock to his front door with a piece of wire. This is deviant behaviour, as you would normally expect him to have the key to his own door and to use it to unlock the door. You are thus likely to infer that he has lost his key, and because the situation is unusual you may well offer to help, or tell another friend about the incident. This is an indication that your process of understanding has been more conscious than in the bank example.

I have discussed these behavioural examples at some length as they help us to understand how we can produce rich interpretations of actions in performances of plays and their equivalents in the script, stage directions and speeches which imply actions. Consider, for example, the combination of a stage direction and a speech in example 5 (reproduced below):

Example 8

Piffs: (*studying a piece of paper*) Yes. You're applying for this vacant post, aren't you?

(Harold Pinter, 'Applicant')

Because we know, from what Miss Piffs says, and from his own previous nervous behaviour, that Lamb has applied for the post, we can infer that the paper Miss Piffs is studying is an application letter or *curriculum vitae* of Lamb's, even though this fact is not explicitly mentioned in the text. This also allows us to infer that Lamb must previously have sent the paper in the post as part of his application. This is a relatively trivial example, of course, but it should be easy for you to see how the principle can be applied generally and to more significant stage directions and actions. In effect, we are, in part, explaining the 'magic of the text' in the sense that texts 'contain' aspects of meaning which are not explicitly mentioned. But the most important thing to notice is that the 'magic' is only metaphorical. We can explain how these unstated meanings get into texts through our understanding of how inference, and other related phenomena, work.

8.4.1 Inferences based on 'conversational rules'

So far, the inferencing we have noted has all been related to more specific (text–based) or less specific (general) background assumptions. Another very important source of inference in conversation, which thus has direct relevance to our understanding of play talk is our set of 'baseline' assumptions concerning the 'rules' of conversational behaviour. Imagine that some friends ask you about what happened to you when you were at a dance the previous evening. They would normally expect you to try to:

1 tell the truth (*i.e.* not lie);
2 describe what happened at an appropriate level of detail, that is not be too general (*e.g. by* merely saying 'we went to the dance and then came home') or too detailed (*e.g. by* describing what happened minute by minute for the entire evening);
3 say things which are relevant to the topic (*i.e.* not go 'off the topic');
4 say what you need to say in a brief, direct and un– ambiguous way (*i.e.* not be over–loquacious, obscure or confusing).

These rules of conversational cooperation were first spelled out by a philosopher called Paul Grice (1975). He referred to them as 'maxims':

1 The quality maxim (say what you believe to be true);
2 The quantity maxim (give an appropriate amount of information);
3 The relation maxim (be relevant);
4 The manner maxim (avoid obscurity, ambiguity and using two words where one will do).

These maxims, notice, are extremely good maxims to follow not just to be an efficient and reasonable conversationalist, but also if you want to write essays which those who mark them will approve of (or if you want to write books which your readers will approve of, for that matter!). In other words, they apply in general terms to both speech and writing.

Breaking the maxims covertly

Of course, if you have something to hide (if you had acted unacceptably at a social occasion, for example, or spent the evening with someone you are attracted to but do not want your friends to know about), you could conceal what you do not want your friends to know by breaking the above conversational maxims in a *surreptitious*, or *covert*, way by:

1′ lying (breaking the quality maxim);
2′ being 'economical with the truth' (breaking the quality and/or manner maxims);
3′ talking about something else (breaking the relation maxim).

If your friends do not notice your unreasonable conversational behaviour, you will have got away with it. But if they do spot that you are not abiding by the conversational maxims (noticing that you keep going off the topic or are being more obscure than normal, for example), they will probably infer some reason for your less than cooperative behaviour, for example that you are trying to hide something. In the British Houses of Parliament, the biggest crime that a Prime Minister can commit is to lie to the House (break the quality maxim). Being 'economical with the truth' (breaking the quantity and/or manner maxims) is usually thought of as not being quite so bad. And moving the ground of debate away from difficult areas (breaking the relation maxim) appears to be a perfectly acceptable tactic for all politicians. Sessions of Prime Minister's Question Time are full of questions which the Prime Minister avoids answering by changing the topic, usually to some short–coming of the Opposition Party.

Does Juliet's nurse break the maxims covertly or overtly?

An interesting example of teasing conversational behaviour occurs in *Romeo and Juliet*. Juliet has sent the nurse to find out what arrangements Romeo has made for their secret marriage. On her return the nurse playfully delays telling Juliet the news:

Example 9

Juliet:	. . . Let me be satisfied, is't good or bad?	(37)
Nurse:	Well, you have made a simple choice; you know	
	not how to choose a man. Romeo! no, not he;	
	though his face be better than any man's, yet his	(40)
	leg excels all man's; and for a hand, and a foot,	
	and a body, though they be not to be talk'd on, yet	
	they are past compare. He is not the flower of courtesy,	
	but I'll warrant him as gentle as a lamb. Go thy ways,	
	wench; serve God. What, have you din'd at home?	(45)
Juliet:	No, no. But all this did I know before.	
	What says he of our marriage? What of that?	
Nurse:	Lord, how my head aches! What a head have I!	
	It beats as it would fall in twenty pieces.	
	My back a t'other side – ah, my back, my back!	(50)
	Beshrew your heart for sending me about	
	To catch my death with jauncing up and down!	
Juliet:	I'faith, I am sorry that thou art not well.	
	Sweet, sweet, sweet nurse, tell me, what says my love?	
Nurse:	Your love says like an honest gentleman, and a	(55)
	courteous, and a kind, and a handsome, and, I	
	warrant, a virtuous – Where is your mother?	

(William Shakespeare, *Romeo and Juliet*, II, v, 37–57)

And so it goes on for more than 50 lines. In the first of the nurse's speeches above, her answer is not relevant to Juliet's question about whether the news concerning her and Romeo is good or not. The form of this irrelevant response, which is mainly about what Romeo is like, in turn breaks the conversational maxims in two other ways. First, it is much too detailed: it unnecessarily considers Romeo's bodily parts one at a time. Secondly, the manner in which the description of him is given is obscure: the nurse says a number of things which appear to contradict one another (*e.g.* that he is *not the flower of courtesy*, but that he is also *as gentle as a lamb*). Juliet's response makes it clear that the nurse has broken the quantity maxim by saying that the nurse has told her what she already knows. Juliet now asks directly about the issue of the marriage, but the nurse's next speech, instead of answering the question, relates the nurse's ailments, again in excessive detail. Juliet says that she is sorry about the nurse's ailments, and then asks again what Romeo has said. The nurse now apparently begins to answer the question, but instead of indicating the content of what Romeo said, she talks at some length about the *manner* in which he said what he did (breaking the quantity and relation maxims). Then, when she finally gets round to the *content* of Romeo's speech, she switches to the question about Juliet's mother.

There are a number of conceivable ways for the actors to play this scene. Does the nurse act as she does knowingly, or is she by nature a rambling conversationalist? And does Juliet think that the nurse is acting innocently or that she is playing games with her? Elsewhere in the play the nurse can talk to the purpose when she wants to. Hence, Juliet is likely at first to assume that the nurse is behaving reasonably in conversational terms. But as the conversation proceeds, there will have to come a point (to be determined by the director and actresses, but likely to be within two or three exchanges) where Juliet realises that the nurse is teasing her. From then on, the scene would have to be played as a battle of wits which the nurse wins (because she holds all the cards) keeping the game going until she finally chooses to end it, telling Juliet to go to Friar Lawrence's cell to be married.

Flouting the maxims overtly

We began this discussion of the maxims of cooperative conversational behaviour by noting the consequences of infringing them covertly (by lying, being economical with the truth, etc.), and the inferences that might then be made as a consequence of your strategy being 'twigged' by those you talk to. The *Romeo and Juliet* example is interesting because there is an issue about whether both the nurse and Juliet know what is going on. It is also possible, and indeed normal, as we will see below, to have conversations where everyone knows that the maxims are being broken. In such conversations speakers have the ability to 'pass messages' to hearers without saying what they mean explicitly.

THE RELATION (OR RELEVANCE) MAXIM

Imagine, for example, that you and I are just coming out of the theatre. You ask me what I thought of the play and I reply by saying that I thought the costumes were nice. You are likely to conclude (using the maxim of relation) that I am saying in an indirect way that I did not think much of the play. How does this work? My reply is not maximally relevant to your question. I could have replied either by saying that I did, or did not, like the play. I could also, if I had wanted, have commented on some more important aspect of the play or its performance (for example, whether the plot hung together well, or how good the acting was). Given normal polite behaviour, the fact that I choose to say something positive about a relatively minor matter should lead you to infer that I felt I could not be positive about more major matters, and that therefore my view about them was negative. As a consequence, you can infer my intended meaning even though I have said something else. I will thus have conveyed my meaning in an indirect and apparently positive way, something which might be useful if I know that the playwright or director is in earshot, for example. The name which Grice gives to this kind of meaning, where the hearer can easily infer the unstated meaning of the hearer, is **conversational implicature**.

This *ostentatious* breaking (**flouting**) of the maxims is something which we do regularly in conversation and in writing, and it is clearly an important way in which we can explicate 'the meaning between the lines' in texts. It accounts for much of what is involved when ordinary people say things like 'yes, I know what he said, but I'm not sure that I like what he implied'. The relation maxim is probably the maxim which is flouted most commonly in order to generate implicatures. Indeed some linguists (*e.g.* Sperber and Wilson

1986: Ch. 1) believe that it subsumes all of Grice's maxims. They thus raise Grice's maxim of relation to a general Principle of Relevance.

THE QUALITY MAXIM

Imagine a situation where A knows that B has spent the afternoon peeling potatoes for a celebratory family meal:

A 'How many potatoes did you peel?'
B 'Millions!'

Clearly the answer cannot literally be true, and so B appears to want to implicate that he or she peeled an indefinitely large number of potatoes, and that the experience was time–consuming and probably not very entertaining.

THE QUANTITY MAXIM

Assume that A comes into a room where B is sitting, reading a book:

A 'What are you doing?'
B 'Reading.'

In a situation like this it will be obvious that B is reading, and hence the quantity maxim is clearly flouted. Because the answer could easily have been less obstructive (*e.g.* 'I am pre–paring for an essay I have to write') it is very likely that A will infer that B is saying that he or she wants to be left alone.

THE MANNER MAXIM

Imagine a situation where the next day is a child's birthday party. Parents and children are present, and one parent says to another:

'I've arranged the prestidigitator.'

The first parent tells the other (by using obscure lexis) that the magician has been booked, without giving the game away to the children.

An interesting historical example of the breaking of the manner maxim was when General Sir Charles Napier captured Hyderabad, which was the capital of the province of Scinde, in the nineteenth–century. He wanted to inform the Foreign Office that he had been successful, but without others knowing. So, he sent a one–word Latin telegram: *Peccavi*, on the assumption that his masters, but not others, would be able to translate the Latin as 'I have sinned', spot the homophony with 'Scinde' and work out that he had been victorious. In this example like the parents at the birthday party, the manner maxim was broken overtly for some but covertly for others, with interesting communicative results.

8.5　An example analysis

In the brief analysis which follows, where necessary I will use, in addition to the Gricean account of conversational implicature and other aspects of inference, relevant aspects of the forms of analysis outlined in Chapters 6 and 7. The extract below comes from Robert Bolt's *A Man for all Seasons*, a play we have already looked at in Chapter 6. Sir Thomas More is now in the Tower of London because he has refused to swear the oath related to Henry VIII's Act of Succession. This Act established the succession to the throne so as to include other children than those from Henry's first marriage, to Catherine of Aragon, which the Pope had refused to annul. More's daughter, Margaret and the man she is to marry, Will Roper, have come to visit More in the hope of persuading him to change his mind and 'rescue' him from prison.

Example 10

Roper:　Sir, come out! Swear to the Act! Take the oath　(1)
　　　　and come out!

More:　Is this why they let you come?

Roper:　Yes . . . Meg's under oath to persuade you.

More:　(*Coldly*) That was silly, Meg. How did you come　(5)
　　　　to do that?

Margaret: I wanted to!

More:　You want me to swear to the Act of Succession?

Margaret: 'God more regards the thoughts of the heart than
　　　　the words of the mouth' or so you've always told (10)
　　　　me.

More: Yes.
Margaret: Then say the words of the oath and in your heart
            think otherwise.
More: What is an oath then but words we say to God?   (15)
Margaret: That's very neat.
More: Do you mean it isn't true?
Margaret: No, it's true.
More: Then it's a poor argument to call it 'neat', Meg.
            When a man takes an oath, Meg, he's holding   (20)
            his own self in his own hands. Like water (*cups
            hands*) and if he opens his fingers *then* – he
            needn't hope to find himself again. Some men
            aren't capable of this, but I'd be loathe to think
            your father one of them.   (25)
                    (Robert Bolt, *A Man for all Seasons*, Act II)

Roper's first utterance breaks the quantity maxim through its
repetition. To swear to the Act and to take the oath are
effectively the same thing, as they all know. Moreover, given
that he cannot leave prison until he has sworn, the last two
sentences effectively spell out a felicity condition that Roper
must be assuming when he says *Sir, come out*. All this implicates
the fervour with which Roper is making his entreaty. In
speech act terms, Roper is making a request or plea, which is
clearly, from his perspective at least, in More's interest. Hence
we can infer that his fervour is engendered by his attachment
to More and his family.

   More's response breaks the maxim of relation, as it is not
directly relevant to Roper's utterance. It thus implicates (a) that
he is ignoring Roper (who he knows, after all, has provided
the authorities with the excuse to imprison him) in order to
talk to Margaret, and (b) that he has not changed his mind
about the oath. In turn, Roper breaks the turn–taking rules by
answering for Margaret. The two parts of his utterance clearly
need a relation to be inferred between them in order to
connect them together properly. The authorities have let them
come *because* Margaret has sworn an oath to persuade More.
The first sentence of More's response is rude to his daughter,
but mitigates the rudeness by using the shortened form of her
personal name. The question with which he follows this
sentence arguably breaks the manner maxim, in that he could
have asked the question more directly (*cf.* 'why did you do
that?'). The implicature that is generated is that she may not

have intended to do what she has apparently been persuaded to do, something which can be inferred, from More's perspective, to take some blame away from her. His use of conversational implicature thus appears to be related to a strategy of kindness towards his daughter. However, Meg's utterance very directly cancels the implied explanation on More's part. Although she avoids breaking the Gricean maxims in order to indicate her willingness to do what she has done, we can infer that if she wanted to take her oath to persuade her father, it must be because she truly wants him to take the oath of the Act of Succession.

More spells out this inference in his next question, and so effectively challenges Margaret as she, and we, know that because he is a devout Catholic, such a move is bound to be against More's wishes. Margaret then responds by using a quotation which clearly breaks the maxim of relation. From this we can infer that what she says is offered as a reason for her wanting him to swear to the act in spite of what he believes. It thus also restates indirectly her wish that More should sign.

More's direct response *yes* makes it look at first as if he is going to agree with her, and that therefore he should swear to the oath, and Margaret spells out this inference in her next utterance. But More's response cancels this hope. If an oath is the words we say to God, then Margaret's distinction effectively disappears. Margaret's response breaks the relation maxim, and we can infer that it implicates that she has seen the logic of his new argument. It does not, however, commit her to agreeing with him. But More forces her into the open with his next question. He is thus being rather ruthless towards her, even though she is trying to persuade him to agree to something she thinks is in his best interests. This becomes very clear in More's last speech. In addition, in this speech he breaks the quality maxim (a man cannot literally hold himself in his own hands) as a way of implicating the personal and spiritual importance of the issue with respect to the oath. Then, finally, he breaks the maxim of manner by being less clear and direct than he could be. He could have said 'Some men aren't capable of this, but I am not one of them'. Instead, he refers to himself in the third person and embeds the most important content of the sentence under I'*d be loathe to think*. This helps us to infer (i) his modesty, an aspect of his character seen elsewhere in the play, and (ii) the indirect suggestion that it is the fact that he is Margaret's father which leads him to have the quality whereby he can 'find himself', thus giving her face.

From this analysis and the others in this chapter I hope it will be clear how much inferential work the audience or readers have to do when experiencing a play if they are to understand it fully. Moreover, although we have explored the issue of inference in relation to drama, we should not forget that inference is an important aspect of our understanding of all texts (and indeed of all human behaviour). What we have said about drama will also apply in a very straightforward way to character conversation in the novel (see Leech and Short 1981: Ch. 8), but will also be applicable to the narrative portions of novels and to poetry.

Exercise 4

Using what you have learned from this chapter and anything relevant from Chapters 6 and 7, examine the extract below from *Othello* in order to work out how it is that Iago engineers Othello to believe that his wife, Desdemona, has been unfaithful to him with Michael Cassio.

Iago:	My noble lord!	(93)
Othello:	What dost thou say Iago?	
Iago:	Did Michael Cassio, when you woo'd my lady.	(95)
	Know of your love?	
Othello:	He did, from first to last. Why dost thou ask?	
Iago:	But for a satisfaction of my thought –	
	No further harm.	
Othello:	Why of thy thought, Iago?	(100)
Iago:	I did not think he had been acquainted with her.	
Othello:	O, yes; and went between us very often.	
Iago:	Indeed!	
Othello:	Indeed? Ay, indeed. Discerns't thou aught in	
	that?	
	Is he not honest?	(105)
Iago:	Honest, my lord?	
Othello:	Honest? Ay, honest.	
Iago:	My lord, for aught I know.	
Othello:	What dost thou think?	
Iago:	Think, my lord?	(110)

Othello: Think, my lord! By heaven, he echoes me,
         As if there were some monster in his thought
         Too hideous to be shown . . .
                        (Shakespeare, *Othello*, III, iii, 93–113)

Discussion of exercises

Exercise 1

Algernon addresses Lane by his last name only, and Lane addresses him as 'sir', indicating a master–manservant relationship, which is consistent with Algernon asking him about the record of how many bottles of champagne were drunk at dinner. That eight bottles and a pint of champagne were consumed by three men in one evening seems rather excessive, and so when Algernon asks why it is that servants invariably drink the champagne at bachelors' establishments, we can infer that Algernon assumes that Lane must have drunk some of the champagne. This utterance of Algernon's looks as if it could be an indirect accusation. Algernon owned the champagne, and Lane has apparently drunk it without being invited. But it is quite clear from what Lane says about married and bachelor households that he does not interpret Algernon's remark as an accusation, but merely as a request for information. This sentence also presupposes that Algernon is a bachelor, a presupposition which the audience will take on if it has not already realised the fact. Algernon's household seems rather unusual in that master and manservant seem to be on an oddly equal footing. Although Lane is the servant he can drink the champagne, and also offer advice and opinions in the manner of an equal or a superior.

Exercise 2

(a) My schematic assumptions are that the man would make the proposal, not the woman, but that the proposal itself could be very informal in type, not unlike a *suggestion* in speech act terms (as a way of reducing the face–threat to the proposer if he is turned down). I would normally expect the two people involved to love each other, even though I know of marriages of convenience, arranged marriages and so on. The proposal would take place in private, but would not have to be a formal proposal of marriage involving the proposer getting down on one knee and asking 'Will you marry me?'. Hence for me a proposal from a woman to a man, or from one person to another of the same sex, would seem unusual, as would a proposal at a football match or a very formal proposal of marriage preceded by the man gaining consent from the woman's father (although this would have been normal in earlier times).

(b) Jack's assumptions about the marriage proposal seem nearer to my assumptions than Gwendolen's. For him, the suggestion in (1) counts as a proposal, but it doesn't for Gwendolen, who clearly expects Jack to produce a formal proposal on bended knee. Jack assumes that if they establish that they are in love with one another and that they both think marriage is a good idea, the contract is more or less signed. His suggestion, based on a reasonably firm idea that he understands how Gwendolen feels, is aimed at establishing that understanding beyond doubt, although he cannot be completely sure until Gwendolen responds to the proposal. Gwendolen, on the other hand, although demanding the formal ritual, has no qualms about making it clear in advance that if Jack asks the question he will get the right answer. All this is actually based on her understanding that Jack is called Ernest, and she later threatens to call the marriage off when she discovers that he is really called Jack. Although Jack's assumptions about marriage proposals may seem a bit modern for the time when the play was written, Gwendolen's are much more peculiar.

Exercise 3

(a) Miss Piffs has just put Lamb through a session of systematic interrogation and abuse, including physical torture. Now that he is lying unconscious on the ground she reverts to the interview format with which the sketch opened. She thanks him, addresses him by the polite 'title + last name' formula, and uses a locution which has become so much a part of our interview schemas that it has become a stereotype to be played off in comedy shows. These wild swings, from normal to absurd and back to normal again, are not unlike the events in cartoon comedies.

(b) If Jack is a foundling he clearly will not be able to produce his parents. But Lady Bracknell tells him he has to. For me,

relations are something you have inexorably as a consequence of your birth, not something you can acquire,
like land or housing. Lady Bracknell's presuppositions thus
clash dramatically with mine, leading to the effect of
absurdity as well as comedy. Her hypothetical statements
about marrying into a cloakroom or forming an alliance
with a parcel are absurd because she uses the kind of
language connected with the description of high–society
marriages when talking about considerably more mundane
things.

Exercise 4
There is not space to discuss this extract here. It is analysed in
some detail in Coulthard (1977: Ch. 9)

Further reading

Brown and Yule (1983: Ch. 2) is a good general introduction
to this area. Cook (1994), a book–length study, contains clear
summaries of the schema theory approach and applies it,
through an extension of foregrounding theory, to literary
texts in general, and poetry in particular. Short (1989) discusses
the use of presuppositional and conversational implicature
analysis in drama, and Cooper (1981) examines conversational
implicature in Shakespeare's *The Taming of the Shrew*.
Bennison (1993) uses pragmatic analysis in a discussion of
characterisation in Tom Stoppard's *Professional Foul*. Simpson
(1989b) discusses politeness phenomena in Ionesco's *The Lesson*
and Leech (1992) looks at the pragmatic interaction between
conversational implicature and politeness phenomena in
Shaw's *You Never Can Tell*.

CHECKSHEET 7: INFERRING MEANING

A.   Schemas

(a)   Establish the schemas (including both frames and scripts) that
are being relied upon in the text you are examining. Do
they allow you to infer things which are not stated in the
text? If so, make a note of them.

(b)   Do those schemas interact with one another in interesting ways? If so, how?

(c)   Are any of the states of affairs or happenings in the text at odds with the schemas which are invoked? If so, what are the interpretative consequences?

B.   Presuppositions

(a)   Do the presuppositions held by the sentences which the characters utter tell you anything interesting about the fictional world they inhabit and/or about their relationships with one another?

(b)   Are any of those presuppositions at odds with those of speeches uttered by other characters in the same text? If so, what does this tell you about the characters and the text?

(c)   Are any of the presuppositions markedly at odds with those we would normally hold? If so, what does this tell us about the text?

C.   Conversational implicature

(a)   Are there any examples of the *covert breaking* of the conversational maxims? If so, are they covert for all of the other characters or only some of them. Given that the breaks are covert for (some) other characters, but not for the reader/audience, what can you deduce about what the author is telling you about the characters and their relations?

(b)   Are there any examples where the author breaks a maxim in a way which is covert for you? If so, you must presumably discover this at some later point in the text. What effect does this have on the relationships between you and the text and you and the author?

(c)   Are there any examples of the obvious *flouting* of conversational maxims by characters? If so, what implicatures are passed from character to character, and what does this tell you about their relationships?

(d)   Are there any cases where the author flouts a maxim in his or her 'conversation' with you? If so, what implicatures flow, and what does this tell you about your relationship with the author?

Are there any significant patterns in the text in relation to your findings under A, B and C? How do they help you to frame a global interpretation for the text?

CHAPTER 9

Fictional prose and point of view

9.1 Introduction

The last main section of this book will be devoted to the study of fiction: novels and short stories. Much of what I will say can also be applied to non–fictional prose, essays for example; but we will concentrate on fictional prose because it is studied much more than non–fictional writing, and novel–buying far outweighs the buying of poetry collections and play texts. There is a tendency in criticism to use the term 'fiction' interchangeably with 'novel', but we should not forget that many poems, most plays and quite a lot of non–literary texts (*e.g.* joke books, comic strips and some stories in the modern tabloid press) are also fictional. As the analyses I will provide apply equally to novels and short stories, I will use the term 'novel' as a shorthand for both forms in my discussion.

In general, the novel is much more accessible than the other two major literary genres. Poetry is often said to be hard to understand, and most people prefer to watch plays than read them; but everyone likes to read stories. However, in spite of its accessibility, the novel is probably the most difficult genre to analyse stylistically. Firstly, novels are long, and the kind of close linguistic scrutiny which we have been exploring in this book could only conceivably be applied to short extracts. Analysing a long novel in close stylistic detail could take a lifetime. As a consequence, we can only analyse particularly interesting, representative or significant extracts. Secondly, the novel is by far the most complex genre in terms of discourse structure, which leads to its complexity in terms of viewpoint. Indeed, study of the novel in the twentieth–century has to a very large extent been the study of point of view. In this chapter we will explore general discoursal (macro) aspects of point of view in 9.2 and then go on to explore how writers control viewpoint at a more detailed (micro) level through choosing particular words, constructions, etc., in 9.3.

Before we do that, however, it will be helpful to make a basic distinction between *what* is described (*e.g.* a house or a football match) and *from what perspective* it is described. Hence a house can be described from the outside by someone walking past it, or from inside by someone who lives in it. The descriptions will clearly be very different. The same will be true of a football match described by a spectator, a player or the referee. The equivalent in the novel of this distinction is the **fictional world** and how it is portrayed: from what *perspective*. For example, in *The Collector* by John Fowles, which we will discuss in more detail in 9.2, the same event, the kidnapping of a young woman, is portrayed first from the perspective of the kidnapper and secondly from the point of view of the victim.

There is, though, an important distinction to be made between non–fictional and fictional writing. With non–fiction, we can perceive things for ourselves and then compare with the descriptions of others. In fiction, the events and conditions of the fictional world are always construed by the reader from the description itself and cannot be independently verified. Nonetheless, the basic distinction between what happens and how it is described is useful if we are to understand how viewpoint in the novel works.

9.2 The discourse structure of fictional prose

In 2.1 we noticed that *one* layer of discourse structure (poet–reader) was adequate to characterise the prototypical poem (though not all poems, of course). And in Chapter 6 we saw that we needed at least *two* levels of discourse structure to describe the prototypical play (the playwright–audience/reader level and the character–character level). But to account for the prototypical novel or short story we need at least *three* levels of discourse, because there is a narrator–narratee level intervening between the character–character level and the author–reader level:

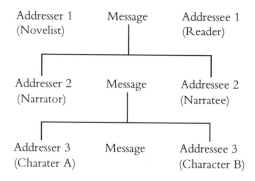

Addresser 1 (Novelist) — Message — Addressee 1 (Reader)

Addresser 2 (Narrator) — Message — Addressee 2 (Narratee)

Addresser 3 (Charater A) — Message — Addressee 3 (Character B)

The above diagram only accounts for the novel 'in general' in the sense that all three levels, and all six participants are needed to explain how 'the novel' works as a form. But any particular novel may neutralise some of the distinctions, multiply others, or do both at the same time. The fact that there are six participants in the basic discourse structure for the novel automatically means that there are more viewpoints to be taken into account in the novel than in the other genres. But as we will see in the rest of this section, the opportunities in particular novels for multiplying the number of viewpoints to be considered, and related to one another, are myriad. It is thus hardly surprising that the novel has become the genre where writers have explored viewpoint extensively.

9.2.1 I–Narrators

The person who tells the story may also be a character in the fictional world of the story, relating the story after the event. In this case critics call the narrator a first–person or I–narrator (because when the narrator refers to himself or herself in the story the first–person pronoun 'I' is used). Since the narrator is a character looking back on events, but often representing them as if they were happening for the first time, first–person narrators are often said to be 'limited' (they don't know all the facts) or 'unreliable' (they trick the reader by withholding information or telling untruths). This sort of thing often happens in murder and mystery stories. For example in Agatha

Christie's *The Murder of Roger Ackroyd*, the reader finds it difficult to guess the identity of the murderer not just because he is a vicar (and our schema for the behaviour of vicars strongly rules out anti–social acts), but also because the vicar himself is narrating the story (from a prison–cell, after his conviction).

Another example of an unreliable narrator is Chief Bromden, the I–narrator in Ken Kesey's *One Flew Over the Cuckoo's Nest*. Here, the unreliability comes about not because the narrator wants to trick the reader deliberately, as in Agatha Christie's *The Murder of Roger Ackroyd*, but because he is mentally disadvantaged. Chief Bromden, a half American–Indian is an inmate of a mental institution. As he is the novel's first–person narrator we sympathise with him, and his account of how he and the other inmates are badly treated by, and try to escape from, the fearsome *Big Nurse* and her nursing staff. But we are also constantly reminded that he is the inmate of an asylum and so is not entirely to be trusted in his views. For instance, he thinks that the asylum has 'special sensitive equipment' which can detect his fear, and a machine to produce fog (which appears to be an external 'explanation' of the odd perceptions he sometimes has when he is feeling particularly stressed). Thus, when he escapes from the institution at the end of the novel we share his feeling of liberation, while worrying at the same time about what the consequences of his escape might be.

9.2.2 Third–person narrators

If the narrator is *not* a character in the fictional world, he or she is usually called a 'third–person' narrator, because reference to all the characters in the fictional world of the story will involve the use of the third–person pronouns, 'he', 'she' 'it' or 'they'. This second main type of narrator is arguably the dominant narrator type. Most narrations are third–person, and this type of narration allows the strong 'default assumption' which most readers appear to hold, namely that, other things being equal, we should assume that the narrator and the author are the same person.

But there is no *necessary* reason for this to be the case. Authors do tend to use third–person narrations to narrate attitudes with which they sympathise, for example, but they don't *have to*. And in any case, our view of an author who has written a number of novels over time is almost certainly an amalgam covering a wide period, and, over time, authors do change their minds about what they believe. This lack of a straightforward identity relation between a third–person narrator and the author is matched on the 'addressee' side of the above diagram by the fact that we often take on, during the reading of a fiction, a set of attitudes and assumptions which may be different, even markedly so, from those we normally hold. In science fiction, for example, we assume that things can happen which patently cannot in the world we normally inhabit (*e.g.* the transportation of people from one place to another by a process which does not involve travel in the normal sense of the term – as encapsulated in the catch–phrase 'beam me up Scotty' from the *Star Trek* TV programmes and books). This lack of fit between the assumptions of the real author and third–person narrators, and between the normal assumptions of real readers and what they assume during the process of reading has led many critics (see Booth 1961: 71–6, 137–9, Leech and Short 1981: 259–62) to interpose another layer of discourse structure between the author–reader and narrator–narratee levels as mapped out in the above diagram. This extra layer involves an 'implied author' (that is, the author implied by our understanding of the text) and an 'implied reader' (that is, the reader we have to 'become' in order to read and react sensitively to the text). Certainly we have to take account of the processes by which, for example, we take on assumptions and attitudes we would not normally hold. Coleridge was clearly trying to capture something like this when he talked about a 'willing suspension of disbelief' (*Biographia Literaria*, Ch. 14, p. 2). But whether we need an entirely separate level of discourse to account for it is less clear (see Toolan 1988: 77–80, Fludernik 1993: 61–4). Whatever we read (or indeed listen to) we have, to some extent, to take on the viewpoint of those producing the discourse, whether it is fictional or not.

   It is because first–person narrators can also be characters that they can easily be unreliable. Third–person narrators, because they can often be assumed to be the author, are much more usually omniscient. Hence when a third–person narrator is limited or unreliable the effect is very heavily foregrounded. Narrators usually tell us things, and so most of the sentences in novels are statements. Narrator questions about the fictional world they are describing thus indicate knowledge limitation. In *Bleak House* by Charles Dickens, when the lawyer, Mr Tulkinghorn, has been shot, the normally omniscient third-person narrator asks questions to create mystery and suspense when he should, according to convention, merely tell us what has happened:

Example 1
What's that? Who fired a gun or a pistol? Where was it?
                        (Charles Dickens, *Bleak House*, Ch. 48)

9.2.3 Collapsing discourse levels together and resulting 'discourse architectures'

We have assumed so far that the narrator–narratee level of discourse is potentially collapsible into the character–character level when the narration is in the first person, and collapsible into the author–reader level when the narration is in the third person. It is also possible under some conditions for all three levels to collapse together. In autobiographies (which are non-fictional), the narrator is the author who is also a 'character' in the story he or she tells, thus explaining the rather straightforward viewpoint relations in standard autobiographies ('I' = author = main character). But it is also possible even for autobiographical accounts to be less straightforward. In *The Armies of the Night: history as a novel, the novel as history*, Norman Mailer describes the protest march on the Pentagon in 1967 against the USA's war with Vietnam, a march in which he took part. In spite of the fact that the march really took place, and that he was in it, he adopts a third–person narrator and refers to himself in the third person, thus blurring the border between fiction and reality into what has come to be referred to as 'faction'.

   The last general point about collapsing that we need to note is that although you may get collapsing between two levels at one side of the diagram in 9.2, you do not necessarily get it at the other side for the same levels. In Charlotte Brontë's *Jane Eyre*, for example, as Jane is both narrator and character there is collapsing on the addresser side between levels 2 and 3. But there is no such collapsing on the addressee side. Instead, on the addressee side collapsing occurs between levels 1 and 2. The narratee appears by default to become the reader in most novels. But this is made explicit, for example, towards the end of *Jane Eyre*, when Jane says 'Reader, I married him' (Ch. 38). Of course, not all novels collapse levels 1 and 2 together at the addressee side. To see this, we have only to think of some of the sea–stories by Joseph Conrad, where the narrator, Marlow, narrates stories to his shipmates in which he is not a character.

The fact that the novel has at least six viewpoints to represent, but that these viewpoints can be collapsed together clearly indicates that the form will be ideal for exploring viewpoint. And, so far, we have conveniently assumed in our discussion that although we need at least three levels of discourse to understand the novel, novels and stories are straightforward in that once you have mapped out a discourse structure for a particular novel it will stay the same throughout. But although many novels do have the same discourse structure for the whole book (*e.g. Jane Eyre* [first–person narration], *Women in Love* [third–person narration]), others do not. For example *Bleak House* has two interwoven narrations, a third–person narration, told in the present tense, and a first–person narration, told in the past tense, by the character Esther Summerson. The following diagram gives an idea of the overall discourse structure:

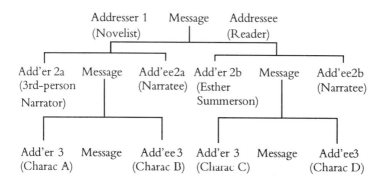

[Note: At levels 2 and 3 words have been abbreviated in order to save enough space to make the diagram clear.]

Bleak House thus has a variation on the basic 'discourse architecture' of the novel with which we started. Under–standing the overall discourse architecture of an individual novel is an important aspect of understanding it. In *Bleak House*, for example, although there is a need to differentiate level 1 and level 2 on the addressee side for the Esther Summerson narration, it is not necessary most of the time for the third–person narration; and it would seem that *both* reader narratees can be collapsed together with the reader for most of the story. In addition, because we assume third–person narrators to be more reliable than first–person ones, the third–person narration is likely to take precedence over the first–person narration if there are any inconsistencies between them over what happened or how whatever happened should be evaluated. The discourse relations across the novel as a whole thus become complex, and will clearly affect viewpoint relations.

In *As I Lay Dying* by William Faulkner there are fifteen first–person narrators, all of which 'tell' sections of the novel. Some of the narrators narrate more than one section. Thus, to produce a discourse structure like the one we have done for *Bleak House* above would entail using a very wide piece of paper! The number of narrator viewpoints is very large, but as there is no third–person narration, the author never appears, even by default. However, we can still discern to some extent the organiser sitting above all these narrations, as we can compare one narration with another and reject some narratorial views in favour of others by reacting to what they say, and comparing them.

I will close this section on the novel's discourse structure with a brief discussion of a novel with two I–narrators and three narrations (the first narrator has another 'go' after the second narrator has finished) in order to explore through a particular example how narrations and their interrelations affect viewpoint and our reactions as readers. In *The Collector*, by John Fowles, an uneducated working–class man, Frederick Clegg, uses his winnings on the football pools to 'collect' an attractive middle–class art student, called Miranda Grey, rather like some people collect stamps or butterflies. He imprisons her in the cellar of a house he has bought, and is eventually the accidental instrument of her death. Told this baldly, it is difficult to feel anything other than revulsion for Clegg and sympathy for Miranda. But actually the story is written in a way which makes the reader feel considerable sympathy for Clegg, helping us to some extent to suspend or mitigate our moral judgements. Although we may not be able to *condone* what he does, we can *understand* why he does it. The first part of the story is an I–narration from Clegg's perspective. We learn that he loves Miranda from afar in the manner of the traditional romance, but feels that she is unattainable. Indeed, she does not treat him well, and is clearly rather a snob. When he imprisons her, he specially prepares a set of plush living quarters for her, and tries to give her everything she could want, apart from her freedom, in order to try to persuade her to love him. When she dies it is not because he kills her, but because she becomes ill and he panics. He is afraid to call a doctor because he might be found out, and tries to cure her with inadequate medicines bought over the counter in a chemist's shop. Later in the story we get the events narrated from Miranda's viewpoint, but sympathy for Clegg still seeps through, even when she dies. Indeed, this sympathy relation is important in Fowles's conclusion to the novel, which switches back to a short I–narration from Clegg. Because he is so in love with Miranda, we have assumed that what has happened is a one–off thing, and indeed Clegg himself tells us this. But in this final narration it gradually becomes clear that, in spite of what he is telling himself and us, subconsciously he is preparing to repeat the process with another young woman. This final, horrific, twist in the tail of the novel, which depends on our normal attitudes towards the criminal acts of sexual perverts, can only be achieved if we have come to like and understand Clegg during the rest of the novel.

Exercise 1

Read the short story 'The Man Who Would Be King' by Rudyard Kipling, and draw a general discourse structure diagram for it, working out what the diagram tells you about possible viewpoint relations. Do the same set of relations pertain throughout the story? If not, what consequences do the changes you notice have?

9.3 Linguistic indicators of viewpoint

Now that we have seen how viewpoint is related to general discourse relations in the novel, we can go to the other end of the telescope, and see how viewpoint is controlled by small–scale linguistic choices on the part of the author. In the rest of this section we will examine eight different linguistic means of indicating and manipulating viewpoint.

9.3.1 Schema–oriented language

We have already noted in 8.2 how the schemas we bring along to texts and situations help us to understand them. It is also worth noting that different participants in the same situation will have different schemas, related to their different viewpoints. Hence shopkeepers and their customers will have shop schemas which in many respects will be mirror images of one another, and the success of shopkeepers will depend in part on their being able to take into account the schemas and points of view of their customers. The situation sometimes seen in comedy films, where a men's outfitter tells his customer looking in the mirror how well a jacket fits, while pulling in the excess material behind his back, depends on the contrast in viewpoint.

One way in which viewpoint can be controlled, then, is through choosing to describe only what could be seen from a particular position. The following example is from David Lodge's *Nice Work*, which is about a young feminist English lecturer, Robyn Penrose, and a bluff engineering works manager, Vic Wilcox. They have to 'shadow' one another in their jobs as part of a scheme to help university and industry understand one another better. Here, much to her annoyance, Robyn's car won't start:

Example 2
. . . Wilcox told her to get in and release the bonnet catch. He opened the bonnet and disappeared behind it. After a moment or two she heard him call, 'Turn the ignition key', and when she did so, the engine fired.

> (David Lodge, *Nice Work*, Section 2, Ch. 3)

It is clear that what is happening is described from Robyn's viewpoint. This is partly controlled through the schematic information we have for what cars are like. We all know, for example, that if you are sitting in the driver's seat you can't see the engine and that once the bonnet is up you also cannot see someone working on the engine. As a consequence, the engine, and what Wilcox does to it, is not described.

Moreover, we know, without being told so, that Robyn
released the bonnet catch, because our car schema tells us that
car bonnets cannot be opened until the catch is released from
inside the car (where Robyn is positioned).

Exercise 2

Another way in which schema–related language can indicate
viewpoint is through the kind of vocabulary typically used by different
people in the same situation. Examine the way in which contrasting
vocabulary indicates contrasting viewpoints on the same objects in
the following conversation, from when Robyn visits the engineering
works which Vic Wilcox manages:

> 'There you are,' said Wilcox. 'Our one and only CNC machine.'
> 'What?'
> Computer–numerically controlled machine. See how quickly it
> changes tools?'
> Robyn peered through a Perspex window and watched things
> moving round and going in and out in sudden spasms,
> lubricated by spurts of liquid that looked like milky coffee.
>> (David Lodge, *Nice Work*, Section 2, Ch. 3)

9.3.2   Value–laden expressions

Besides indicating viewpoint by choosing *what* to describe,
novelists can also indicate it by *how* it is described, particularly
through expressions which are evaluative in nature:

Example 3
She opened the door of her grimy, branch–line carriage, and
began to get down her bags. The porter was nowhere, of course,
but there was Harry . . . There, on the sordid little station under
the furnaces . . .
>> (D. H. Lawrence, 'Fanny and Annie')

The adjectives *grimy* and *sordid* in *grimy branch–line carriage* and
sordid little station under the furnaces help mark the description of
Morley railway station as being from the viewpoint of Fanny,
who clearly disapproves.

9.3.3   Given *vs* new information

Linguists make a distinction between what they call **given** and **new information**, in terms of how information is 'packaged' by speakers. If you want to refer to something which is not already known to your addressee, you will typically use indefinite reference, whereas if what you want to refer to is already known to your addressee, you will use definite reference. In other words, you take your addressee's viewpoint into account. This explains the difference in meaning between the following sentences, which differ only with respect to whether the indefinite ('a') or definite ('the') article is used:

Example 4
[1]   I saw a helicopter yesterday
[2]   I saw the helicopter yesterday

In the second case, but not the first, the helicopter is something which the speaker assumes the hearer already has knowledge of. Other given/new information indicators of viewpoint are whether reference is made through full noun phrases (*e.g.* 'a large man with a wart on his nose') or pronominal reference ('he'/'him'). 'Givenness' can come about for a variety of reasons. The most obvious reason is because something has been previously mentioned in the relevant text or discourse. But if what is referred to can be assumed to be part of our general background knowledge, it will receive definite reference even if it has not been previously mentioned. The sun is usually referred to definitely because everyone has previous knowledge of it, and a reference to 'a sun' will normally be interpreted as 'some other sun than the one which the earth revolves around'. Similarly, I can begin a conversation with my wife about what has just happened at 'the university' and expect her to understand the phrase as referring, by default, to Lancaster University because it is the university with which we have constant dealings. If I wanted to refer to a different university which had not already been mentioned in the conversation, even one which we also know quite well, I would need to use a full noun phrase in order to avoid confusion.

At the very beginning of a story, we should thus be able to predict that narrative reference to everything in the fiction except items generally assumed by everyone in our culture (*e.g.* the sun, the Houses of Parliament) must be new, and hence should display indefinite reference. This is what happens, for example, at the beginning of *The Mayor of Casterbridge*.

Example 5

One evening of late summer, before the nineteenth century had reached one third of its span, a young man and woman, the latter carrying a child, were approaching the large village of Weydon–Priors, in Upper Wessex, on foot.

(Thomas Hardy, *The Mayor of Casterbridge*, Ch. 1)

The first mention of the man (and by implication the woman) and the child have indefinite reference (*a young man and woman, a child*) because we have not met them before. As a consequence, we tend to get a distanced 'bird's–eye view' of the characters. *The nineteenth century* has definite reference because Hardy can assume that his readers will all already know what the phrase refers to. But note that even in this straightforward description, the village of Weydon–Priors gets definite reference for its first mention, encouraging us to pretend to ourselves that we are already familiar with it. Hardy is thus 'positioning' his readers as people who are familiar to some extent with the village (and hence the area) but not the characters.

Many modern novels and stories begin with definite reference, even though in theory they should not. This technique, positioning readers as already 'in the know', even though they are not really, is one aspect of a technique which has come to be called '***in medias res***' (Latin for 'into the middle of things'), which helps us to feel intimately involved with what is going on at the beginning of a story. There are other ways of producing the *in medias res* effect, for example by beginning a story with unintroduced speech.

The following sentence opens *The Little Drummer Girl*:

Example 6

It was the Bad Godesberg incident that gave the proof, though the German authorities had no earthly means of knowing this:

(John Le Carré, *The Little Drummer Girl*, Ch. 1)

Here, the use of the definite article for t*he Bad Godesberg incident* and *the proof* forces us to take on the position of people who know what these phrases refer to, even though we do not ('proof of *what*?', we might well ask), and thus share the perspective of the authorities who are trying to understand a terrorist bombing which has taken place.

Note that here the *in medias res* beginning has a very different viewpoint effect from that noticed at the beginning of Hardy's *The Mayor of Casterbridge*. Instead of having a bird's–eye view, we appear to be much closer to what is going on. We have to position ourselves as if we are right there with the German authorities, trying to work out what has happened.

Perhaps the most startling of *in medias res* novel openings is that of Ken Kesey's *One Flew Over the Cuckoo's Nest*, a novel which we noticed in 9.2 had an unreliable first–person narrator:

Example 7
They're out there.
    (Ken Kesey, *One Flew Over the Cuckoo's Nest*, Picador, p.9)

We don't know who *they* are or where *there* is, and, as a consequence, the sentence helps us very little indeed. We could be witnessing the portrayal of a mind in the middle of thought, or possibly a narrator who, for some reason not yet clear, does not properly take the point of view of his addressees (us, the readers) into account. At this point it is difficult to tell. We later learn that in a sense both explanations are right as we are witnessing the narrated perspective of an inmate of a mental institution, with whom we sympathise but whose views and descriptions are not entirely to be trusted, as we saw in 9.2.1. The *in medias res* effect is thus instrumental in beginning to establish an interesting viewpoint tension which the novel explores throughout its course.

9.3.4 Indicators of a particular character's thoughts or perceptions

In Chapter 9 we will explore how novelists can manipulate the representation of the speech and thought of their characters, but here we can notice that character viewpoint can be indicated in descriptions through the use of (a) verbs of perception and cognition ('see', 'hear', 'imagine', 'think', 'believe') and (b) verbs and adverbs related to factivity. If we compare:

Example 8
[1]   'I know he was ill'
[2]   'I believe he was ill'
[3]   'He pretended he was ill'

we can see that the truth status (**factivity**) of the embedded clause 'he was ill' changes depending upon the verb of the main clause. If 'he was ill' is embedded under a **factive** verb (here 'know') then it is presented as true. If it is embedded under a **counter–factual** verb (here 'pretend') it is presented as false, and if it is embedded under a **non–factive** verb (here 'believe') we cannot tell for certain whether he was really ill or not. Adverbs like 'actually' and 'apparently' also display fac–tivity and hence viewpoint relations.

In the following quotation from *Empire of the Sun*, the verb of perception ('looking') and the non–factive cognition verb 'wondered' establish the viewpoint for the description of the scene as that of Jim, the main character:

Example 9
Looking at this powerful ship, Jim wondered if it had been damaged during its patrol of the Yangtze gorges.
                    (J. G. Ballard, *Empire of the Sun*, Ch. 4)

9.3.5   Deixis

Deixis is the term which linguists use to denote 'pointing expressions' like 'this' and 'that' or 'here' and 'there' which are speaker–related. Imagine that two people, A and B, are standing at opposite sides of a room, each behind a chair. In the diagram below, if A refers to the chair nearest him, he can use the expression 'this chair'. But if he wanted to refer to the one immediately in front of speaker B he would have to use 'that chair'. If B refers to the same objects, the use of the deictic expressions would have to be reversed. In general terms, we have one set of expressions to refer to objects near to the speaker and another to refer to objects which are more remote:

A   B

In psychological terms we each tend to assume that we are the deictic centre of the world we inhabit, and that everything else radiates out from us. This explains not just linguistic behaviour in relation to terms like 'here' and 'there' but many other things too. For example, the various countries of the world tend to draw maps of the world with their own country more or less in the centre of the map. It also helps to explain why a common way of referring to an attempt to understand other people is to 'put yourself in their position'.

Deictic expressions cut across the grammar of English. For example, 'this' and 'that' are demonstrative (deictic) determiners or pronouns, 'here' and 'there' are deictic adverbs and 'come' (movement towards the speaker) and 'go' (movement not towards the speaker) are deictic verbs. Deixis applies to time as well as space, as the contrasts between the adverbs 'now' (time close to the speaker) and 'then' (time remote from the speaker) show. Tense also has a deictic function, and the concept of deixis explains the difference between 'yesterday, today and tomorrow' (a close time frame, appropriate to the speaker at the time of utterance) and 'the day before, that day and the day after' (a time frame remote to the moment of utterance).

Because deixis is speaker–related it can easily be used to indicate particular, and changing, viewpoints. If we reconsider the example from *One Flew Over the Cuckoo's Nest*, we can now see not just that it is odd in terms of given/new structure, but that the people and place mentioned are being referred to as deictically remote ('they' and 'there'). This makes it easy for us to infer the Chief's attitude. He appears to perceive *they* and *there* as 'remote' in psychological terms too, and indeed it soon becomes clear in the novel that the Chief is hostile both to his 'carers' and to the mental hospital in which they are located.

In the following example, from *The Secret Agent*, we see Mrs Verloc's actions from Mr Verloc's viewpoint:

Example 10
Mr Verloc heard the creaky plank in the floor and was content. He waited. Mrs Verloc was coming.
(Joseph Conrad, *The Secret Agent*, Ch. 11)

In addition to the perception and cognition verbs *heard* and *waited* and the indication of his inner mental state (*was content*) we can see that Mrs Verloc's movement towards her husband is viewed from Mr Verloc's position (*coming*). The fact that the events are only seen from Mr Verloc's viewpoint is strategically important at this point in the novel. He does not realise what his wife is about to do to him.

Mr Verloc has had a bad day. Unbeknown to his wife, he is a secret agent who has been given the task of blowing up the Greenwich Observatory. When he left that morning to undertake the task, his wife had insisted that her husband take her younger brother, Stevie, with him. Stevie is mentally subnormal, and Mrs Verloc wants Mr Verloc to like him, so that when her mother dies Mr Verloc will agree to have Stevie come and live with them. Stevie has been primed to help Mr Verloc whenever he can, and innocently insists, in spite of Mr Verloc's protests, on carrying the case with the bomb in it. Mr Verloc finally agrees to let Stevie carry the case to the Observatory, and waits in the park for him to return. But Stevie trips over a tree root while crossing the park, and blows himself to smithereens. Having broken the bad news to his wife, Mr Verloc is having a rest while waiting for his evening meal. What the reader realises, but Mr Verloc does not, is that his wife is bringing not his food, but a carving knife to plunge in his chest. *The Secret Agent* is a novel about isolation, and the way in which Mr Verloc's viewpoint is so restricted at this crucial point in the story is one poignant encapsulation of this theme.

Exercise 3

In the extract below, the two characters and their circumstances are being referred to for the first time. Colonel Fergusson is dying, and his dutiful daughter is by his bedside. How is Colonel Fergusson's viewpoint and his attitude towards his daughter conveyed?

> Colonel Fergusson lay in the cold bedroom of his cold square house three miles outside Dublin and listened to the clicking overhead. It was one o'clock in the morning on a windless November night of 1837. His daughter Amanda sat at his bedside in stiff, pout–lipped profile, reading some piece of religious mumbo–jumbo. At her elbow the candle burned with a steady flame, which was more than that perspiring fool of a doctor with letters after his name had been able to say about the Colonel's heart.
>
> It was a provocation, that's what it was, thought the Colonel. Here he was on his deathbed, preparing for oblivion, and she sits over there reading Parson Noah's latest pamphlet.
>
> (Julian Barnes, *A History of the World in 10 $\frac{1}{2}$ Chapters*, Ch. 6)

9.3.6 'Social' deixis

With the example from *One Flew Over the Cuckoo's Nest* we saw that place deixis could be used to infer psychological attitudes. It is possible, analogously, to view social relations as 'deictic'. We can feel 'close' or 'remote' to other people in social terms. Someone to whom you refer with 'title + last name' would be remote socially, and you would normally refer to those with whom you are close by their first name (see 7.1.1 and the discussion of Exercise 3 at the end of Chapter 8).

In the extracts from David Lodge's *Nice Work*, quoted above, it would appear that the narrator assumes different social relations with Robyn Penrose and Vic Wilcox, because he refers to the former by her first name, 'Robyn', and to the latter by his last name, 'Wilcox'. In the first part of the novel when the two characters are together, their attitudes and behaviour correlate with our stereotypes for their professional and gender roles. Vic Wilcox, the male manager of the engineering firm, is brusque and macho. Robyn Penrose, the female English lecturer, is more humane and 'sympathique'.

This contrast is clearly reflected in the narrator's naming strategy, and as we normally feel that we should 'equalise' our attitudes to, and relationship with, the characters, so that it mirrors the attitude of the narrator to the characters, we will tend to feel closer to Robyn Penrose than to Vic Wilcox.

However, it is important to note that from the beginning of the novel, when Vic Wilcox is portrayed in scenes from which Robyn Penrose is absent, he is usually referred to as 'Vic', thus helping us to feel closer to him. And later in the novel, as the two characters become romantically entwined, the narrator consistently refers to him as 'Vic', including those occasions when Robyn is also present. We can thus see that the social deixis of the naming system in English is being used dynamically to encapsulate the fluctuating relationships between the characters, and between us and them.

The use of varying expressions to refer to the same person, usually called 'elegant variation', is, in part, a consequence of the fact that in English (but not in all languages, by any means), repetition of the same phrase over and over again is deemed to be inelegant. But the Lodge example shows that it is possible for novelists to use such variation for the purposes of viewpoint manipulation, and some writers (for example Henry James – see Leech and Short 1981: 107) make significant or complex use of elegant variation.

In D. H. Lawrence's 'Fanny and Annie', Fanny's decision at the end of the story to marry Harry, in spite of her reservations, is not stated, but implied by the fact that Fanny addresses Harry's mother not as Mrs Goodall but as 'Mother'. The use of names in James Joyce's 'The Dead' is more complex in viewpoint terms, as the following short extract shows:

Example 11

. . . Miss Kate and Miss Julia were there, gossiping and laughing and fussing, walking after each other to the head of the stairs, peering down over the banisters and calling down to Lily to ask her who had come.

It was always a great affair, the Misses Morkan's annual dance. Everybody who knew them came to it, members of the family, old friends of the family, the members of Julia's choir, any of Kate's pupils that were grown up enough . . .

(James Joyce, 'The Dead')

In this short extract, variation in the narrative of expressions referring to the Misses Morkan encapsulate the viewpoints of different people on the two women. 'Miss Kate and Miss Julia', both 'title + first name' formulations, are clearly expressions appropriate for Lily, their maid, to use. 'Kate' and 'Julia', on the other hand, are more likely to be used by social equals who are guests at the dance, and the more formal and inclusive phrase 'the Misses Morkan' could easily be used by outsiders who would not know them very well at all. Later in the story the narrator also refers to them as 'Aunt Kate' and 'Aunt Julia' to mark the viewpoint of the main character, Gabriel, who is their nephew. Hence elegant variation is being used both to vary our relationships with the characters and also to indicate that at different points in the story they are being viewed from the perspective of different characters.

Exercise 4

In the description of a field at harvest time below, there are four characters mentioned (they are underlined for ease of reference). Taking into account how they are referred to, what do you think the social relations are between them, and what relationship do you and the narrator appear to have with them?

There are four figures in the field, besides Lewis on the reaper-binder. Mr Luscombe: red-faced and crooked-grinning, one eye with a cast behind his steel-rimmed spectacles, a collarless shirt with a thin grey stripe, darned, the cuffs worn, cord trousers with peaks at the back for braces, but held up also by a thick leather belt. Bill, his younger son, nineteen, capped and massive, six inches taller than anyone else on the field, arms like hams, a slow giant, clumsy at all but his work . . . but see him scythe, dwarf the distort handle and the blade, the swaling drive and unstopping rhythm, pure and princely force of craft. Old Sam in breeches, braces, boots and gaiters, his face forgotten, though not his limp; a collarless shirt also, a straw hat with the crown detached on one side ('lets in th'ole air a bit, doan'ee see') and a tuft of wilted heart's-ease tucked in the black band. And finally a boy in his mid-teens, his clothes unsuited, a mere harvest helper: cotton trousers, an apple-green Aertex shirt, old gym shoes . . .

(John Fowles, *Daniel Martin*, Ch. 1)

9.3.7   The sequencing and organisation of actions and events to indicate viewpoint

If we consider the sentence 'Horatio opened the door' we know who opened the door, and so it is possible to assume that we are viewing the action from the same side of the door as Horatio. But if the same event is represented by the sentence 'The door opened' we have no knowledge of who is opening the door, and will be likely to feel that we have been positioned on the other side of the door, where, clearly, we cannot see who has opened the door until after the event. We can thus see that the grammatical organisation of clauses can be used by writers for viewpoint manipulation. The same can be said of relationships between sentences or clauses. In 'Robin Hood ran past me', we know the identity of the person at the point when the action of running is described. But in 'A man ran past me. It was Robin Hood', we will infer that although the same event has occurred, the narrator witnessing the event perceived it differently. This time, apparently, the narrator first merely perceived that some unidentified person was running past, and then, a moment later, that the person was Robin Hood. What we have here is an effect called 'psychological sequencing' (Leech and Short 1981: 177). Information which would normally be supplied straight away is withheld for a moment. This prompts us to infer that the narrator must have departed from the norm for some reason, to represent the narrator's perceptions, rather than the fictional reality, which we can still see behind the represented perception. It is exactly this effect which occurs in the following extract from *The Magus* by John Fowles, where the perceptions of the I–narrator, Nicholas, are represented:

Example 12

A figure appeared in the door. It was Conchis.

(John Fowles, *The Magus* (1st edn), Ch. 62)

A more complex example from the same novel can be seen below. Nicholas is about to make love to Julie in a darkened room, thinking that the door is locked. Suddenly two men burst in and attack him. It transpires that Julie must have duped him, and unlocked the door from the inside to let his attackers in:

Example 13

The door was flung wide open, the light came on, there were
two black figures, two tall men in black trousers and shirts. One
was the Negro and the other was 'Anton'. Joe came first, so fast
at me that I had no time to do anything but convulsively grip the
bedspread over my loins. I tried to see Julie, her face, because I
still could not accept what I knew: that she had turned the key,
and opened the door. Anton flung her something that she
caught and quickly put on – a deep red towel bathrobe.

(John Fowles, *The Magus* (1st edn), Ch. 59)

Psychological sequencing is used extensively here to recreate
the perceptions of the I–narrator/character at the time the
events happened. The use of the passive construction with the
agent deleted (*The door was flung wide open . . .*) clearly puts us
with Nicholas, on the inside of the room, where he could not
see who opened the door. The appositional sequence at the
end of the first sentence (*two black figures, two tall men in black
trousers and shirts*), moving from a vague to a more precise
formulation, representing the process whereby Nicholas strives
rapidly to work out who is attacking him. This process,
continues into the next sentence, when he finally works out
the identity of his attackers and we are given their names. In *I
tried to see Julie, her face* we again have an appositional structure
where the second noun phrase is more precise than the first.
From this we can infer that his first urge is to see Julie, but
that this desire is rapidly focused to become a wish to see her
face (presumably because the face is the best indicator of a
person's emotions and attitudes, and he needs to see her
reactions in order to make sense of what is going on). He is
trying to come to terms with the fact that the woman who
was apparently about to make love to him has now betrayed
him. The change from *something that she caught and quickly put
on* to *a deep red towel bathrobe* similarly marks his attempts to
'catch up' with reality, this time in visual terms. There are
other viewpoint controllers in this short passage (verbs of
cognition and perception, deictic markers and variation in
referring expressions, for example), but psychological
sequencing within and across sentences is an important aspect
here of Fowles's narrative technique.

9.3.8   Ideological viewpoint

The final topic that I would like to explore in terms of linguistic indicators of viewpoint is not another kind of indicator but one of the ways in which groups of indicators can be linked together interpretatively, namely in terms of **ideological viewpoint**, or 'world–view' (see Fowler 1986: 130–4 for a helpful discussion). In this case viewpoint has less to do with an individual's spatio–temporal location in some particular scene, but with a generalised mind–set or outlook on the world that a person, often as a representative of a *group* of people, might have. This mind–set or world–view might manifest itself linguistically in a number of ways. Consider the value–laden expressions 'terrorist' and 'freedom–fighter'. They could refer to the same person if uttered by people with radically opposed socio–political views of the world.

The next example involve a kind of world–deixis. Assume that John is leaving tomorrow for Saudi Arabia. Either of the following sentences could be used by someone living in Europe to represent that fact:

Example 14
[1]   John is going to the Middle East tomorrow.

[2]   John is going to North Africa tomorrow.

The first of these sentences assumes a world–deictic centre which has Saudi Arabia to the East, and in the middle distance – not as far as China (*cf.* the 'Far East'), but nearer than Morocco. Not surprisingly, the Saudi Arabians and the Chinese might well get a bit upset by being told they live in the Middle or Far East, and accuse the speaker of being Euro–centric in attitude. They, like the rest of us, tend to assume that they live in the middle of the world. The Chinese word for China literally means 'middle kingdom', most countries produce maps of the world with their own country more or less at the centre of the map and sixteenth–century European explorers worried about falling off the edge of the world. The term 'Eurocentric' brings with it considerably more than world–deixis, of course. It also suggests uncritical assumptions of social and political importance on the part of the speaker, which is presumably why such terms are rather controversial in the modern world.

The second sentence above might look at first sight less ideologically constrained. But that, too, carries socio–political assumptions. A Saudi–Arabian might well have preferred 'the Arab world' to *North Africa* as the latter expresses Africanness and so links Saudi Arabia terminologically with sub–Saharan countries like Kenya rather than with other Arab countries like Egypt and Syria. Many expressions contain hidden ideological assumptions. We tend not to notice the ideological underpinning of our own words because they are 'naturalised' for each of us. This is one of the reasons why extended contact with people from other parts of the world, or with very different outlooks from our own, is good for us. It helps us to see more clearly what we assume without realising it.

In the last example in this section, we will examine a description of some Africans from the viewpoint of Europeans visiting Africa (sentences are numbered for ease of reference):

Example 15

(1) We were wanderers on prehistoric earth, on an earth that wore the aspect of an unknown planet. (2) We could have fancied ourselves the first of men taking possession of an accursed inheritance, to be subdued at the cost of profound anguish and of excessive toil. (3) But suddenly, as we struggled round a bend, there would be a glimpse of rush walls, of peaked grass–roofs, a burst of yells, a whirl of black limbs, a mass of hands clapping, of feet stamping, of bodies swaying, of eyes rolling, under the droop of heavy and motionless foliage. (4) The steamer toiled along slowly on the edge of a black and incomprehensible frenzy. (5) The prehistoric man was cursing us, praying to us, welcoming us – who could tell?

(Joseph Conrad, *Heart of Darkness*)

The title of this novella, *Heart of Darkness*, suggests that it will be about an alien experience, because we tend to assume that light symbolises our world, and darkness the worlds beyond our own. Here, the visitors are on a river steamboat, experiencing Africa for the first time. The first sentence suggests that they are visiting prehistoric earth, and the last sentence refers to prehistoric man. But this is not literally true as both visitors and visited are from the twentieth–century. The term *prehistoric* brings with it here a set of assumptions about cultural naïvety which are clearly connected to the Eurocentric attitude we began to explore above. The extreme, value–laden expressions (*accursed inheritance, profound anguish, excessive toil*) in sentence (2) make it clear that what in the nineteenth–century was referred to as the 'white man's burden' of 'civilising' Africa is to be seen as extremely onerous and unpleasant (but by implication something which must morally be done, nonetheless).

The ideological assumptions of this description are not carried only by overt value–laden expressions. The perceptual centre of the description, as indicated by the verbs of perception, is from the boat, and the scene described is perceptually remote and yet only the edge of a new and frightening world. Moreover, the villagers and villages are depicted in sentence (3) as if they consist of disaggregated parts. We don't see houses or huts, but just walls and roofs. Similarly, we don't see people, but hands, feet and eyes, apparently acting of their own volition. Conrad has restricted the lexical items to parts of buildings and people; and the bodily parts of the people, rather than the people themselves, are subjects of the dynamic verbs. This description of the villagers thus suggests uncontrolled and disorganised activity which it is easy to correlate with the associations we have noted for *prehistoric,* and with verbalised nouns like *burst, whirl* and *frenzy*, referring to rapid and uncontrolled movement. The steamer, by way of contrast, moves extremely slowly and with difficulty. The boat is the deictic centre for the description, and it is made clear that the European perceivers do not understand what they see. This is already implied by the reference to bodily parts acting apparently of their own volition, but is made clear in *incomprehensible frenzy* at the end of sentence (4), which indicates only that the actions of the black man are incomprehensible to the white man, although presumably the reverse would also be true. Finally, this incomprehensibility is enacted by the unresolved alternative interpretations of the villagers' actions presented in the thoughts of the people on the boat: *cursing us, praying to us, welcoming us – who could tell?* (for a discussion of techniques of thought presentation, see 10.4).

9.4   A more extended example

The passage below is from near the beginning of 'The Ebony Tower' by John Fowles. David, an art critic, has just arrived

to interview an English artist who lives in a cottage in rural
France. The scene from the cottage is described more or less
exclusively from David's viewpoint as he looks out over the
lawn. I have numbered the sentences for ease of reference:

Example 16

(1) A wide lawn stretched away, flowerbeds, banks of shrubs,
some ornamental trees. (2) It was protected from the north by a
high wall, and David saw another line back there of lower
buildings, hidden from the front of the house; barns and byres
when the place was a farm. (3) In mid–lawn there was a catalpa
pruned into a huge green mushroom; in its shade sat, as if posed,
conversing, a garden table and three wicker chairs. (4) Beyond,
in a close pool of heat, two naked girls lay side by side on the
grass. (5) The further, half hidden, was on her back, as if asleep.
(6) The nearer was on her stomach, chin propped on her hands,
reading a book. (7) She wore a wide–brimmed straw hat, its
crown loosely sashed with some deep red material. (8) Both
bodies were very brown, uniformly brown, and apparently
oblivious of the stranger in the shadowed doorway thirty yards
away. (9) He could not understand that they had not heard his
car in the forest silence. (10) But he really was earlier than the
'tea–time' he had proposed in his letter, or perhaps there had after
all been a bell at the door, a servant who should have heard. (11)
For a brief few seconds he registered the warm tones of the two
indolent female figures, the catalpa–shade green and the grass
green, the intense carmine of the hat–sash, the pink wall beyond
with its ancient espalier fruit–trees. (12) Then he turned and
went back again to the main door, feeling more amused than
embarrassed.

(John Fowles, 'The Ebony Tower', 1974 Cape edn, p.12)

Perhaps the first thing to notice is how we infer the
geography of the fictional world from the description. David,
standing at the house, sees the lawn stretching away in front
of him. In the middle of the lawn there is a catalpa tree with
garden furniture underneath it. Beyond, two girls lie, sun–
bathing on the lawn. Over at the far side of the lawn, are the
flowerbeds, then the banks of shrubs, and then the ornamental
trees. Beyond the trees there is a wall, and beyond that are the
old farm buildings. In other words, the whole scene is
described as if David were at the deictic centre, with
everything radiating out further and further away from him.

However, although most of the elements in the scene are described in David's 'deictic order', the sunbathing girls (and the catalpa tree and garden furniture used to locate them in the scene) are described *after* the plants, garden wall and buildings which are further away. This ordering would appear to be unusual, and therefore foregrounded, in terms of psycho-logical sequencing as well as deixis (I think I would notice the naked women rather earlier than the nearer flowerbeds!), and therefore needs interpretation. One possibility is that male art critics observe such scenes more dispassionately than other men, but perhaps a more likely explanation is that the girls are going to turn out to be the most significant story elements in the scene, and so are placed in a climactic position, at the end of the description.

In sentence (1) the verb phrase *stretched away* allows us to infer that the ordering of the flowerbeds, shrubs and trees in the sentence reflects their distance from David. This ordering of elements continues through the next sentence, and is reinforced by the deictic phrase *back there*. The next four sentences each begin with words or phrases which spell out the location of what is described in relation to David: *in mid-lawn . . . beyond . . . the further . . . the nearer*. Sentence (2) has a perception verb with David as subject, and this allows us to infer that succeeding descriptive sentences also depict what he saw. Sentence (7) refers vaguely to *some deep red material*, which is consistent with the fact that he is probably too far away to be able to identify the type of material. In sentence (8) there is an indication of the mental state of the girls, who are *oblivious of the stranger in the shadowed doorway thirty yards away*. The term *stranger* is obviously an appropriate lexical item for David in relation to them, as they have not yet met him, and the doorway is described in terms of their deictic centre, not David's. But all of this is, in turn, modified by the non-factive adverb *apparently*, indicating that really this is all David's per-ception, as he tries to put himself in the position of the girls, who have not yet seen him. This is reinforced in sentence (9), where the clause containing the perception verb with the girls as subject is dominated by a main clause with a cognition verb with David as subject. What we see, then, is a description very much from David's viewpoint, consistent with him being the major protagonist in the story. However, the ordering of the items seen from David's deictic centre is rearranged to put the girls last in the sequence, and there is some effort on David's part to see things from their perspective, all of which suggests that they will also be important in the story, and that they will interact with him in significant ways. Now read on!

Discussion of exercises

Exercise 1

'The Man Who Would Be King' is a 'framed story'. There is a first–person narrator, the correspondent of the *Back-woodsman*, who is never named. He tells a story in which he is also a character. He meets two men, Daniel Dravot and Peachey Carnehan, who tell him that they are going to Kafiristan to become Kings. Some years later, Carnehan returns in a very poor state, tells the story of what happened to him and Dravot, and then dies:

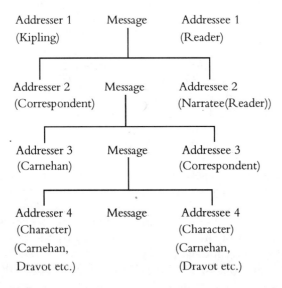

Addresser 1	Message	Addressee 1
(Kipling)		(Reader)
Addresser 2	Message	Addressee 2
(Correspondent)		(Narratee(Reader))
Addresser 3	Message	Addressee 3
(Carnehan)		(Correspondent)
Addresser 4	Message	Addressee 4
(Character)		(Character)
(Carnehan,		(Carnehan,
Dravot etc.)		(Dravot etc.)

The central story is thus embedded deep in the discourse structure of the work, and both the Correspondent of the *Backwoodsman* and Carnehan are narrators who are also characters in their own story. This is important because although we have no reason to doubt the sincerity of either narrator, the events which are described are fantastic in the extreme.

Carnehan claims that Dravot did indeed become King of Kafiristan, because the natives believed that he and Carnehan were Gods. However, Dravot tries to take a wife, in spite of an agreement between him and Carnehan that they would have nothing to do with women or drink until after they had finished being Kings. This action turns out to be their undoing, as it convinces the natives that Dravot is not a God after all. Dravot is killed and Carnehan is crucified. He comes back to tell the tale, although he also states that he was killed himself. Given that he is alive but says that he died, there is clearly some worry about his sanity and hence the veracity of his story. But he shows the Correspondent of the *Backwoodsman* a shrunken skull of Dravot's head. Carnehan leaves, and dies the next day, apparently of sunstroke, but possibly as the result of his experiences. Dravot's skull is not on him, and so there is no way of knowing whether the story is true or not. Kipling is using the multiple discourse layering and the collapsing possibilities in relation to the two narrator-characters to create a situation where we want to believe the story but find it incredible, and finally have no evidence to decide the matter.

Exercise 2
The main point of view contrast here, apart from the differential use of names to refer to the two characters (see the section on 'social deixis' in 9.3.6), is the vocabulary used to refer to the objects described. Their schemas differ in how detailed they are. Wilcox clearly knows the specific lexical items needed to refer to each thing, and indeed, in his use of the initial letters *CNC* instead of 'computer-numerically controlled' shows that he is very familiar with the terms and assumes that others are too. Robyn, of course, does not know what the letters stand for, and in the description of what the machine does from her point of view we see that she is severely underlexicalised in this context. She uses the vague word *things* instead of naming the items of machinery used. Similarly, we infer from her use of *liquid* instead of a more precise term that she does not know what the liquid is. Instead, she describes it by using a simile which analogises what is going on in the factory to a household item, milky coffee. In technical terms, Robyn is **underlexicalised** (see Fowler 1986: 152–4 for other examples). It is also possible to be **overlexicalised** (Fowler 1986: 154–6), as trying to learn

how to do something from an expert who is not a good teacher soon reveals. If you are doing a course in stylistic analysis and have friends studying English literature who are not, you can probably look impressive in the coffee bar by dropping terms like 'underlexicalisation' and 'overlexical— isation' into the conversation. Note that from their point of view you are overlexicalised and from yours they are underlexicalised. This shows how important these concepts can be in the understanding of viewpoint!

Finally, we can use underlexicalisation to show that viewpoint matters are important to all of the literary genres. Craig Raine's poem 'A Martian Sends a Postcard Home' describes the earth from an alien perspective. Here is the Martian's description of the telephone, its dialling tone, its ringing tone, responding to a telephone call and dialling to make one:

> In homes, a haunted apparatus sleeps,
> that snores when you pick it up.
> If the ghost cries, they carry it
> to their lips and soothe it to sleep
>
> with sounds. And yet, they wake it up
> deliberately, by tickling with a finger.

Raine's poem helps us to see the telephone in a new light. The Martian has no experience of it, and so no relevant technical vocabulary. Instead he uses non–technical words in a way which is literal for him but non–literal for us, and thus helps us to see our world afresh.

Exercise 3

It should be clear that this third–person description is told from a viewpoint consistent with Colonel Fergusson's perspective (in fact it contrasts with another description of the scene less than a page later from Amanda's viewpoint). This section of the novel begins with a sentence with the Colonel as subject to the perception verb *listened*, and the adverb *overhead*, by inference, must be over *his* head. As a consequence we may also decide that the repetition of the adjective *cold* is a value– laden characterisation of his view (and so an indication of his emotional attitude towards his surroundings as much as a fact about temperature told to us by the narrator), even though other pieces of information appear to be included by the narrator solely for our benefit. *His daughter Amanda*, for example, is not an expression that the Colonel would use, because he would not use third–person reference for himself and because he would already know that Amanda was his daughter, and so would not need to make the relationship explicit.

The expressions which are overtly value–laden all appear to represent the Colonel's viewpoint. *Some piece of religious mumbo–jumbo* (later referred to for our benefit as *Parson Noah's latest pamphlet*) lets us see that the Colonel disapproves of his daughter's religious beliefs, and *that perspiring fool of a doctor* also makes his view of his physician clear. Other clear indications of the Colonel's viewpoint are the near and remote deictic adverbials *here* and *over there* in the last sentence, which are related to him as deictic centre, and the penultimate sentence, which gives us a privileged representation of him thinking, and helps to establish the strength of his disapproval of his daughter. This third–person representation of a man on his deathbed thus helps us to sympathise with him while at the same time allowing us to take a more 'objective', ironic view. To be that unforgiving so close to the moment of death is, after all, something which most people would not want to be.

In addition to the viewpoint markers already discussed, this passage presents the Colonel's thoughts in a form of thought presentation called 'Free Indirect Thought'. This will be explored in 10.4.

Exercise 4

These figures are not all equal socially, and we appear to be somewhere in the middle of the social hierarchy, above some but below others, and closer to some than others. We adopt the position which the narrator appears to adopt through use of his different conventions for referring to the characters. Lewis is referred to by his last name only. This indicates that we and the narrator are probably above him: he is a farm worker, low in the social hierarchy. On the other hand, Mr Luscombe, the farm owner, appears to be above us. This explains why he is referred to by 'title + last name'. We appear to be closer to Bill, the farmer's younger son, as he is referred to by first name only. Old Sam is clearly another farm worker, but he is described by first name and the adjective *old*, indicating that he probably has more status than Lewis, the status that comes with age and experience. The final figure is not given a name at all – *a boy in his mid–teens*. Apparently we do not know him, and the fact that he is not given a name suggests that he is unimportant. Yet this treatment of the boy is inconsistent with the fact that he appears in the climactic position, at the end of the list of characters, and with the fact that he also gets extensive description. We will learn later that this boy is actually the narrator of much of the story, the Daniel Martin of the book's title, who looks back on his own childhood. Some of the later chapters of the novel use first–person narration from Daniel Martin's viewpoint, but here third–person narration is used as a device to 'trick' us, so that when we do understand the relationship at the end of the chapter an effect of surprise and revelation is produced. There is, however, a clue in the naming relationships we have just explored. In essence our positioning as readers appears to be consistent with that of the anonymous young boy who we will later realise is Daniel Martin, the novel's I–narrator.

Further reading

Fowler (1986: Ch. 9) and Leech and Short (1981: 173–85) contain useful introductory material. Mason (1982) examines point of view at the beginning of *Little Dorrit* by Charles Dickens, and Sasaki (1994) compares two different accounts of viewpoint and applies them to 'The Blind Man' by D. H. Lawrence. Simpson (1993) and Fludernik (1993) contain comprehensive accounts of different aspects of viewpoint.

CHECKSHEET 8: LINGUISTIC INDICATORS OF POINT OF VIEW

A.   Is there evidence of schema–oriented language?
    Which details are observed, which 'facts' presented?

B.   What value–laden or ideologically slanted expressions are used?

C.   What role is played by Given vs New information? *e.g.*
    (a)   definite/indefinite articles ('a'/'the');

(b) textually referring (anaphoric) pronouns ('you', 'it', 'they', etc.).

D. Are there any deictic expressions related to place? *e.g.*
   (a) adverbials ('here'/'there', 'to his left', etc.);
   (b) demonstrative pronouns ('this 'that', etc.);
   (c) verbs ('come'/ go', etc.).

E. Are there any deictic expressions relating to time? *e.g.*
   (a) adverbials ('now'/'then', 'today'/'that day', etc.);
   (b) past and present tenses.

F. Are there any 'socially deictic' expressions? *e.g.*
   (a) personal and possessive pronouns ('I', 'you', 'he', 'mine', 'yours', etc.);
   (b) variant socially relevant expressions for the same person, *e.g.*
       (i) the naming system: 'Mick', 'Dr Short', 'dad'
       (ii) varying expressions in third person reference (some−times called 'elegant variation'): 'Mrs Thatcher', 'the Iron Lady', 'the Witch of Westminster'.

G. Are there any indicators of the internal representation of a particular character's thoughts or perceptions, *e.g.*
   (a) verbs of perception and cognition ('see', 'hear', 'imagine', 'think', 'believe', etc.);
   (b) verbs related to factivity (*cf.* 'It was obvious that he was ill' vs 'It seems that he was ill' vs 'He pretended to be ill');
   (c) modal verbs ('can', 'could', 'may', 'might' 'must', etc.)
   (d) adverbs related to factivity ('actually', 'apparently', etc.).

H. Is there any event coding within or across sentences? *e.g.*
   'The man burst the door open' vs 'The door burst open'; 'Robin Hood ran past me' vs 'Someone ran past me. It was Robin Hood.'

CHAPTER 10

Speech and thought presentation

10.1 Introduction

We saw in 9.3 that the occurrence within a narration of a thought or perception verb with a character as its subject indicated that the narrator was taking on that character's viewpoint (and the same can clearly be said of character speech). However, we have not yet examined the choices which authors have available to represent character speech and thought and how these choices affect meaning and viewpoint. Consider the following constructed example:

Example 1
'Oliver must have seen me,' Ermintrude said.

You will probably recognise this as an example of **Direct Speech**, and be able to contrast it with its **Indirect Speech** version:

Example 2
Ermintrude said that Oliver must have seen her.

What makes Direct Speech direct and Indirect Speech indirect? Examples 1 and 2 differ from one another in two important respects: (i) their linguistic form (*e.g.* only example 1 has inverted commas and only example 2 has explicit grammatical subordination of the reported clause to the reporting clause) and (ii) their effects and functions. If we turn first to effect and function, we can notice, for example, that the Direct Speech version appears to commit the person reporting the speech to the claim that Ermintrude actually uttered the words 'Oliver must have seen me'. As a consequence, inside the inverted commas we have what she said *unmediated by the reporter.* Indeed, this explains the meaning of the term 'Direct Speech'. In example 2, what Ermintrude said (its propositional content) is apparently given to us through the words of the reporter (*i.e. indirectly*). She could actually have said 'He's spotted me' and example 2 could still be said to be a reasonable Indirect Speech representation of what she said. But example 1 would no longer be a reasonable *Direct Speech* representation. Direct Speech, then, claims to represent accurately the propositional content *and* the words originally used to utter that content, whereas Indirect Speech claims only to represent the original propositional content, using instead the words of the person reporting the speech.[1] In the novel, the words of Direct Speech are clearly those of the character concerned. The words of Indirect Speech, on the other hand, usually belong to the narrator.

Direct Speech and Indirect Speech are, in fact, only two places on a continuum, or cline, of **speech presentation** in the novel which blends the contributions of character and narrator, in different proportions at different points on the scale. One of the purposes of this chapter is to explore (in 10.2 and 10.3) how we isolate or define the major places on the speech presentation continuum and how the different effects and meanings which are associated with them are achieved. We will also explore equivalent matters in relation to the presentation of character *thought*, because it turns out that the categories of **thought presentation** are the same as for speech presentation (although they have different meanings and effects, as we will see in 10.4).[2] We can show that the same scale is used to present speech and thought by turning examples 1 and 2 into representations of thought merely by changing the speech act verb to a thought act verb:

Example 3
'Oliver must have seen me,' Ermintrude decided.

Example 4
Ermintrude decided that Oliver must have seen her.

Thus in *formal linguistic terms* the speech and thought presentation categories are the same. However they do not have exactly the same effects. For instance the **Direct Thought** in example 3 looks as if it must be conscious, as opposed to subconscious, reasoning (which turns out to be indicated by another thought presentation category – see 10.4.2 below), and this kind of distinction does not sensibly apply to speech. Hence it will be important to examine the presentation of speech and thought separately, even though the formal mechanisms for their presentation are the same.

Exercise   1

Look more closely at examples 1 and 2, and write down in detail all the changes which take place as you 'translate' the Direct Speech form into Indirect Speech. Then compare it with my account given at the end of the chapter.

Before we have a look at an extract from a novel to see variation in speech presentation at work, it will be important to make clear some general matters relating to speech presentation:

1 In real life when a person reports what someone else said on a previous occasion, there are two speech situations involved, the original, anterior or *reported* speech situation, where the person being reported originally said what is now being reported, and the posterior, or *reporting* situation where the person doing the reporting presents (or represents) what was said, choosing, say, Direct, or Indirect, Speech to do it. This explains why in example 1 grammarians call the first clause the *reported clause* and the second the *reporting clause*. In real life it is possible, at least in theory, to compare for accuracy what was actually· said with what is reported as having been said (for example in newspaper reports of Parliament).

2 However, in the novel there is *no* anterior speech situation. The novelist makes it all up. When we read, we pretend to ourselves that a character whose speech is being reported said the words at some previous point in the fictional world of the novel. But in principle our only access to the words is through the report; veracity cannot be checked. This

difference helps to explain why linguists looking at speech in fiction tend to talk of speech *presentation* while those looking at non–fictional discourse tend to talk of speech *representation*. I will use the two terms interchangeably below.

3   Although, in real life, the veracity of a speech report can be checked *in principle*, it often can't be checked *in practice* (for example if no audio or written record was made at the time). People often use Direct Speech to report words they cannot possibly remember accurately (for example, because they were uttered too long ago, or because what is being 'reported' could not have been heard by the reporter at all, *e.g.* the Direct Speech in 'And then she must have said "Drop dead" because he walked away with a really thunderous look on his face'). The main purpose in these cases appears to be to dramatise what is 'reported' rather than to make a claim about the words used. What this signals for our investigation of the novel is that we should be on the look–out for authors using speech and thought presentation for tactical or strategic purposes.

10.2   An example of variation in speech presentation

I will describe the speech presentation categories in detail in 10.3, but this area is fairly complicated and there are quite a lot of categories involved. So it will help you to understand what is involved if we first explore rather more informally a short passage which contains some variation in the way character speech can be presented. We will examine an extract from *The Old Curiosity Shop* by Charles Dickens (sentences are numbered for convenience of reference). In the discussion of the passage I will begin to introduce the terminology which I will explain more precisely in 10.3, so do not worry if the description of the speech presentation categories below is not absolutely transparent. Little Nell enquires of the schoolmaster she is staying with about a pupil of his who is ill:

Example 5
(1) As the schoolmaster had already left his bed and gone out, she [Little Nell] bestirred herself to make it neat and comfortable, and had just finished its arrangement when the kind host returned.

(2) He thanked her many times, and said that the old dame who usually did such offices for him had gone to nurse the little scholar whom he had told her of. (3) The child asked how he was, and hoped he was better.

(4) 'No,' rejoined the schoolmaster, shaking his head sorrowfully, 'No better. (5) They even say he is worse.'

(6) 'I am very sorry for that, Sir,' said the child.

(7) The poor schoolmaster appeared to be gratified by her earnest manner, but yet rendered more uneasy by it, for he added hastily that anxious people often magnified an evil and thought it greater than it was; 'for my part,' he said, in his quiet, patient way, 'I hope it's not so. (8) I don't think he can be worse.'

(Charles Dickens, *The Old Curiosity Shop*, Ch. 25)

The first point that needs to be made is that not all of the sentences, or parts of sentences, in example 5 represent speech. Sentence (1) and the first part of (7) represent actions or states of being in relation to the characters. One of the purposes of narratives, of course, is to represent actions, perceptions, events and states which occur in the world of the fiction. For convenience, as we are mainly interested in speech presentation, I will lump these other, non–speech phenomena together under the term **Narrator's Representation of Action (NRA)**.

The Direct Speech items are clear enough. They appear within inverted commas in sentences (4)–(8). But sentences (2) and (3), and the part of (7) which comes immediately before the Direct Speech are in a more indirect form. The first question to ask, then, is why some of the speech is represented in Direct Speech and some more indirectly. One answer in this passage is that Direct Speech is being reserved for the more important and more dramatic, heart–tugging information. So Little Nell's enquiry about the little scholar (who we already know to be ill) is in a less direct form than the reply, which tells us that his condition has worsened. Similarly, in (7), when the schoolmaster is talking about generalities (. . . *anxious people often magnified an evil and thought it greater than it was* . . .) his speech is represented indirectly, but when the schoolmaster returns to the particular issue of how ill the little scholar is, Dickens switches the speech presentation to Direct Speech again. One obvious reason for variation in speech presentation, then, is that it allows authors to indicate how important a piece of speech is. In general terms, Indirect

Speech appears to be a backgrounding, and Direct Speech a foregrounding, device.

The next thing to notice is that the various representations of speech in the passage other than Direct Speech are not all the same. Typical Indirect Speech can be seen in sentence (3): *The child asked how he was.* . . . It gives us the propositional content of what Little Nell said, but not the words she used to utter that content. But in *He thanked her many times* . . . at the beginning of (2) we do not even know what statements the schoolmaster made, let alone what words he uttered to make those statements. All we know is that he repeatedly used the speech act of thanking. As a consequence, this part of the passage can be seen as a summary of a longer piece of discourse, and is therefore even more backgrounded than an Indirect Speech representation would be. I call this minimalist kind of presentation the **Narrator's Representation of Speech Acts (NRSA)**. As we will see in 10.3, NRSA is near one extreme of the speech presentation continuum, the end which connects it to the narration of actions events and states (NRA). There is only one possibility of speech presentation which is more minimalist than NRSA, namely a sentence which merely tells us that speech occurred, and which does not even specify the speech act(s) involved, *e.g.* 'We talked for an hour'. For completeness' sake I will call this the **Narrator's Representation of Speech (NRS)**.

So far we have seen that the speech presentation continuum has the following possibilities:

1 Direct Speech (DS)
2 Indirect Speech (IS)
3 Narrator's Representation of Speech Acts (NRSA)
4 Narrator's Representation of Speech (NRS).

Moreover, with the DS in (1) we have what the character said in its fullest form, and as we move from (1) to (4) the contribution of the character becomes more and more muted.

There is, one further category which can occur, which is an amalgam of DS and IS features and is called **Free Indirect Speech (FIS)**. It comes between DS and IS on the speech presentation cline:

NRS   NRSA   IS   FIS   DS

This extra category is called 'Free Indirect Speech' because it usually occurs in a form which appears at first sight to be IS but also has DS features. The clearest example of FIS in the passage is the second half of sentence (3), which I reproduce below:

> The child asked how he was, and hoped he was better.

The child asked how he was . . . is clearly IS, giving the propositional content of the utterance but not the words used, and it could even be seen as a summary[3] of what was said. But you may well feel that . . . *and hoped he was better*, although it is certainly not Direct Speech, does have *some* of the flavour of the words which Little Nell herself used. The reason for this is that although it is coordinated to the IS of the first part of the sentence (which leads us to expect it will have the same status), it omits the reporting clause, which can easily be deduced from the context. A more explicit version of it would be '. . . and said that she hoped he was better'. In line with the above foreground/background account of the speech in the passage, we could interpret Little Nell's FIS here as being more emotionally charged than her IS immediately before, but not as intense as the DS in the passage, almost all of which is a representation of the words of the schoolmaster, the person most involved emotionally in the fate of the little scholar.

The last general thing we can notice from this passage, once we have seen the possibility of the FIS category, is that some of the speech presentation is ambiguous. If we look carefully at part of sentence (7), . . . *he added hastily that anxious people often magnified an evil and thought it greater than it was*, we can see that it could be IS or FIS. In normal circumstances it would be IS, but given the emotional implications of the adverb *hastily* and the example of FIS, on which I have already commented, it would be possible to see some flavour of the schoolmaster's words here as well.

Exercise 2

For each extract, work out what forms of speech presentation are used (some extracts have more than one) and the meaning or effect of each choice:

(a) When the porter had withdrawn, he expressed his regret.

> (David Lodge, *How Far Can You Go?*, Ch. 2)

(b) I asked him whether he wanted to be executed sitting or standing.

> 'Ah, let me think,' he said. 'It is not an easy question . . .
>
> (Vladimir Nabokov, *Lolita*, Part 2, Ch. 35)

(c) Greta was standing at the stove, stirring tinned rice pudding, when Maureen crashed through the kitchen door; coming from darkness into sudden fluorescent light.

> 'Coventry has killed Gerald Fox!'
> *'Coventry?'*
> 'Yes!'
> *'Killed?'*
> 'Yes!'
> *'Gerald Fox?'*
> 'YES!'
> *'Coventry has killed Gerald Fox?'*
> *'YES!'*
>
> An explosion of enjoyment filled the kitchen. The two women, trembling and shocked, but also excited and happy, began to talk. Coventry's life was examined for previous displays of aggression. Greta remembered the time that Coventry had spoken to her sharply once.
>
> (Sue Townsend, *Rebuilding Coventry*, Ch. 4)

(d) 'So that was the first part of the story. Czech troops out, Russian troops in. Got it?'

> Smiley said yes, he thought he had his mind round it so far.
>
> (John Le Carré, *Tinker, Tailor, Soldier, Spy*, Ch. 28)

10.3   The categories of speech presentation discussed in detail

Although they will not all be completely clear yet, we have seen examples of all the categories of speech presentation which novelists have at their disposal, along with the category relating to the presentation of physical actions, events etc., which I have given the shorthand term the 'Narrator's

Representation of Action' (NRA). The scale of speech presentation is connected to NRA as follows:

NRA   NRS   NRSA   IS   FIS   DS

I will now examine each of the above categories, explaining them in detail. I will move from left to right along the scale, up to and including NRSA. Then, because the remaining categories need to be characterised in relation to one another in terms of their detailed linguistic features, and can be understood most clearly if we begin with Direct Speech, I will describe DS next, then IS. Finally, after looking at the general nature of the speech presentation continuum, I will describe FIS, which contains both DS and IS features.

10.3.1 Narrator's Representation of Action (NRA)

This category is to account for sentences of physical description and action, where speech is not presented at all:

1 *Actions* by characters: (*e.g.* 'They embraced one another passionately'; 'Agatha dived into the pond'; 'Lassie barked');
2 *Events*, or happenings caused by agents (usually inanimate) who are not characters: (*e.g.* 'It began to rain'; 'The picture fell off the wall');
3 Descriptions of *states* (including *internal* states): (*e.g.* 'The road was wet'; 'Clarence was wearing a bow tie'; 'She felt furious');
4 *Character perceptions* of any of (1)–(3): (*e.g.* 'She saw Agatha dive into the pond'; 'She saw it had begun to rain'; 'She saw Clarence was wearing a bow tie').

Now let us see these possibilities illustrated in the beginning of a short story (sentences are numbered for ease of reference):

Example 6
(1) There was thin, crisp snow on the ground, the sky was blue, the wind very cold, the air clear. (2) Farmers were just turning out the cows for an hour or so in the midday, and the smell of cow–sheds was unendurable as I entered Tible. (3) I noticed the ash–twigs up in the sky were pale and luminous, passing into the blue. (4) And then I saw the peacocks. (5) There they were in the

road before me, three of them, and tailless, brown, speckled birds, with dark–blue necks and ragged crests. (6) They stepped archly over the filigree snow, and their bodies moved with slow motion, like small, flat–bottomed boats.

(D. H. Lawrence, 'Wintry Peacock')

All of the clauses of sentence (1) are state descriptions. Sentence (2) begins with an action, is followed by a state description and then has another action, which this time has the I–narrator/character as subject. Sentence (3) represents the narrator's perception of a state, anchoring the description from his viewpoint, and so, by inference, the first two sentences (and the later ones) can now be seen as re–presentations of his perceptions too, even though (1) and (2) contain no perception verbs. Sentence (4) represents the narrator's perception of the peacocks, and (5) gives a further state description of them, followed by event descriptions of the peacocks' movements in (6). Given the title of the story and the extensive description of the peacocks at its opening, we are bound to look for their significance as we continue to read.

10.3.2 Narrator's Representation of Speech (NRS)

This category merely tells us that speech occurred, without any indication of what was said. See the emboldened part of the extract below:

Example 7
Gabriel went to the stairs and listened over the banisters. **He could hear two persons talking in the pantry**. Then he recognised Freddy Malin's laugh.

(James Joyce, 'The Dead')

This story, which describes the evening of a large society dinner party in Dublin, is seen almost entirely from the perspective of Gabriel Conroy, whose wife, Gretta, tells him at the end of the evening that before she met him she knew a young man with a fine singing voice, Michael Furey, who died for love of her. He was unwell, and pined away because they had not been allowed to see each other by her family. At the end of the story Gabriel has to come to terms with the fact that although he is fond of his wife, he has never experienced true feelings of love like those of Michael Furey. The trivial social whirl of the evening contrasts with this moment of self–realisation, while establishing Gabriel's viewpoint and our sympathy for him. In the above extract Gabriel is so far away from the conversation described that at first all he knows is that talk is taking place, and then the identity of only one of the speakers.

10.3.3   Narrator's Representation of Speech Acts (NRSA)

With this category we get a little closer to what is said. We are given what speech acts are performed, and perhaps some indication of the topic of the talk. Later in the story from which example 7 is taken, we briefly meet a rather pompous opera singer, Mr D'Arcy, who refuses to sing because he has a cold. At the end of the story we will be able to contrast the triviality of Mr D'Arcy's situation with that of Michael Furey. Here is Mr D'Arcy leaving the party (the significant part of the quotation is emboldened):

> **Example 8**
> Mr D'Arcy came from the pantry, fully swathed and buttoned,
> and in a repentant tone **told them the history of his cold**.
> **Everyone gave him advice** . . .
> (James Joyce, 'The Dead')

When Mr D'Arcy talks we are given an indication of the speech acts he uses and the topic he talks about, but nothing more. In the response of the others still at the party we are only given the speech act force of a series of utterances. This device helps us to feel distanced from Mr D'Arcy and to see him in an ironic light. It also allows Joyce to summarise a fairly trivial piece of conversation in order to move more quickly to the conversation between Gabriel and his wife on the way home from the party, when all is revealed.

10.3.4   Direct Speech (DS)

Having established the minimalist end of the speech presentation continuum, let us now move to the other end, where characters speak directly for themselves, without being 'filtered' through the narrator. Here is the moment when Michael Furey's death is described:

Example 9

She paused for a moment to get her voice under control, and then went on:

'Then the night before I left, I was in my grandmother's house in Nuns' Island, packing up, and I heard gravel thrown up against the window. The window was so wet I couldn't see, so I ran downstairs as I was and slipped out the back into the garden and there was the poor fellow at the end of the garden, shivering.'

'And did you not tell him to go back?' asked Gabriel.

'I implored of him to go home at once and told him he would get his death in the rain. But he said he did not want to live. I can see his eyes as well as well! He was standing at the end of the wall where there was a tree.'

'And did he go home?' asked Gabriel.

'Yes, he went home. And when I was only a week in the convent he died and he was buried in Oughterard, where his people came from. O, the day I heard that, that he was dead!'

(James Joyce, 'The Dead')

This is the most important conversational moment in the story, and not surprisingly, it is all in DS, with very little narrative intervention. It is full of emotion, as shown in the elliptical sentence structure, exclamation marks, exclamatory *O* and the repetition of *that* in the climactic *O, the day that I heard that, that he was dead!* Because some of the things presented in the DS are themselves pieces of remembered conversation, we also have speech presentation embedded inside speech presentation here.

In reported clauses using DS (*i.e.* everything within quotation marks in example 9), all the linguistic features used must be related to the speaker's viewpoint. These could involve any of the viewpoint markers discussed in Chapter 9. In this passage they include:

1 tense (past tense here, as Gabriel and Gretta are referring to what is past time for them: *I implored of him to go home*);

2 pronouns (first– and second–person pronouns for Gabriel and Gretta and third–person reference for Michael Furey, his family and Gretta's grandmother: *I implored of* **him**);

3 other deictic markers besides tense and pronouns (*e.g.* when Gretta describes herself going out to the garden she sees Michael Furey at what must have been some distance: *and* **there** *was the poor fellow at the end of the garden*);

4 speech act indicators (*e.g.* the interrogative grammar and question mark for Gabriel's question: *And did he go home?*);

5 indications of voice quality and other phonetic aspects (*e.g.* the exclamation marks for Gretta's utterances help us to infer that they will have been said with passion, probably involving a louder voice and a wider pitch range than normal: *O, the day I heard that, that he was dead!*);

6 colloquial lexis (*e.g. the poor fellow*).

When Indirect Speech is used, any of the above features which indicate viewpoint relative to the character–speaker will have to be altered so that they are related instead to the narrator, who is reporting the speech. But before we look at IS let us continue with our exploration of DS.

More free forms of direct speech

First of all, we should remember that in the sentence–parts surrounding the typical DS of example 9 there are some indications of the presence of the narrator, helping to keep the represented speech connected to the narrative of the story. These are the quotation marks, which must belong to the narrator–reporter, not Gretta or Gabriel, and any *reporting clauses* (in this case two instances of the clause 'asked Gabriel'). Logically it should also be possible to find examples of DS with even less trace of the narrator: (i) DS without a reporting clause, (ii) DS without quotation marks, and (iii) DS without either reporting clause or quotation marks. In each of these cases the narrator will be even less visibly present than in prototypical Direct Speech.[4]

We have already seen an example of DS without reporting clauses in extract (c) of exercise 2. Here is another from the same novel. Police Sergeant Horsefield concludes a con–versation he has been having on the telephone with his young son:

Example 10

'Bye Matthew, see you tomorrow.'
'Why?'
Because I'm far away, in London.'
'Why?'
'Because I'm at work.'
'Why?'
'To get money to buy you new boots. That's *it*. Matthew,
don't ask any more questions.
'Why?'
'Because it drives me mad, you know it does. I'm going now.
Tell Mummy I love her.'
'Tell Mummy I love her,' Matthew repeated.
'No, tell Mummy *I* love her. Not you.'
His wife came back on the phone. 'You've made him cry!
What did you say?'

> (Sue Townsend, *Rebuilding Coventry*, Ch. 33)

For most of this extract there are only two characters speaking,
and the context makes it clear which is which. So Sue
Townsend can omit any reporting clauses or other narrative
intervention to help capture the quick–fire nature of the
conversation and bring out the humorous repetitive
patterning so typical of this sort of parent–child interaction. A
reporting clause (*Matthew repeated*) only appears when the
author needs to underline the change in the pattern which
brings about Sergeant Horsefield's downfall in his role as
caring parent.

Direct Speech with a reporting clause but no inverted
commas, and sometimes neither, is common in the writing of
James Joyce, particularly his later work:

Example 11

—Then what is it? Buck Mulligan asked impatiently. Cough it
up. I'm quite frank with you. What have you against me now?

> (James Joyce, *Ulysses*, Bodley Head Cheap Edn, p. 5)

Joyce marks off speech at line–beginnings, but nowhere else,
with a long dash. This means that the boundary between
speech and the reporting clause in the first sentence is not
marked off in the normal way. Context and the presence of
deictic changes like tense allow us to see clearly what is DS and
what is not. The next three sentences of the extract are also

DS but Joyce does not mark them with quotation marks *or* a reporting clause. The reporting clause of the first sentence does duty for the other DS sentences too. Of course we have to work a bit harder to see what is what in this sort of speech representation, and this is presumably one small but pervasive contribution to the renowned difficulty of Joyce's later writing.

Let us now explore some more complex matters in the passage leading up to the above extract. Buck Mulligan and Stephen Dedalus live in a tower. Mulligan is trying to persuade Stephen to let his friend Haines (who has rather noisy nightmares) stay with them for a while. Sentences are numbered for ease of reference:

Example 12
(1) —And to think of your having to beg from these swine.
(2) I'm the only one that knows what you are. (3) Why don't you trust me more? (4) What have you up your nose against me? (5) Is it Haines? (6) If he makes any noise here I'll bring down Seymour and we'll give him a ragging worse than they gave Clive Kempthorne.

(7) Young shouts of moneyed voices in Clive Kempthorne's rooms. (8) Palefaces: they hold their ribs with laughter, one clasping another, O, I shall expire! (9) Break the news to her gently, Aubrey! (10) I shall die! (11) With slit ribbons of his shirt whipping the air, he hops and hobbles round the table, with trousers down at heels, chased by Ades of Magdalen with the tailor's shears. (12) A sacred calf's face gilded with marmalade. (13) I don't want to be debagged! (14) Don't you play the giddy ox with me!

(15) Shouts from the open window startling evening in the quadrangle. (16) A deaf gardener, aproned, masked with Matthew Arnold's face, pushes his mower on the sombre lawn watching narrowly the dancing motes of grasshalms.

(17) To ourselves . . . new paganism . . . omphalos.

(18) —Let him stay, Stephen said. (19) There's nothing wrong with him except at night. (17)

(20)—Then what is it? (21) Buck Mulligan asked impatiently. (22) Cough it up. I'm quite frank with you. (23) What have you against me now?

(James Joyce, *Ulysses*, Bodley Head Cheap Edn, p. 5)

The first paragraph, as indicated by the dash, is Buck Mulligan's Direct Speech. From then on we have to work rather harder to understand what is going on, but in return we get a real sense of the seamless flow from speech to narration to thought and back again that Joyce is striving for.

The next paragraph does not begin with a dash, and so is not DS. Given the comment about Clive Kempthorne's rooms, however, the most likely interpretation is that it is an evocation of Stephen's thought, as he remembers the incident involving Kempthorne from his student days. This memory contains remembered speech from that scene: sentence (8) begins with more description, but then moves, unintroduced by either reporting clause or punctuation, into DS. As a consequence we do not know who said the words. Again unmarked, sentence (11) returns to the narration of Stephen's memory of events. From the context we can deduce that (13) and (14) must be speech uttered by Kempthorne, as he is the one being ragged, but part of the effect here is presumably to give a sense of the chaos and confusion of the incident. Sentence (12) would appear to be Stephen's memory of Kempthorne's face (or possibly Ades's?), but could be something Kempthorne said. The fact that the remembered incidents are narrated in the present tense, and are therefore consistent in tense terms with the DS, adds to the reading difficulty and the evocation of chaos and excitement.

In (15) the scene suddenly switches to a narratorial viewpoint from outside the room. *Shouts from the open window* assumes that the hearer could not hear what was said or even know who was shouting. (16) represents the visual perception of the deaf gardener mowing the lawn while at the same time describing his face in studied, and ironic, literary terms. Then, before we finally return to the safe ground of the fictional present, and the conversation between Mulligan and Stephen in (18)–(22), we get the passage's most enigmatic sentence, (17). This could be what someone said at the time of the event, what Stephen thought at the time, what Stephen thinks now or even a remark of the omniscient narrator.

We can see from this section that (i) most authors use both reporting clauses and punctuation marks to delineate DS, (ii) contextual information can sometimes enable a novelist to omit the reporting clause and/or the punctuation marks which connect DS to narration without causing confusion or reader difficulty, but that (iii) once this possibility has been noticed, more experimental authors can then use these freer forms of DS to create special effects, bordering on bewilderment for the reader in some cases, but also allowing the delicate perceptual membranes which separate what is *done*, what is *said* and what is *thought* to be explored in interesting new ways.

10.3.5 Indirect Speech (IS)

Now let us return to more straightforward ground and explore how IS is constituted. The easiest way to see this is to take a prototypical case of DS and observe what happens when we 'translate' it into IS, as in the following constructed example:

Example 13
[1] 'Oh, Oliver please clear up this mess you have just made!'
    Ermintrude demanded. (DS)

[2] Ermintrude demanded that Oliver should clear up the mess he
    had just made. (IS)

Let us first look at the relationship between the reporting and reported clauses. As we move from DS to IS, the following changes take place:

1 the DS quotation marks (and associated comma, if there is one) are removed;
2 the grammatical relationship of semi–independence between the reporting clause and the reported clause in DS becomes one where the reported clause is subordinated to the reporting clause (this is made clear in [2] above by the introduction of the conjunction *that*; but even if the conjunction were not added, the subordination would still remain);
3 it is common in DS for the reporting clause to come *after* the reported clause, whereas in IS the opposite order is typical. 'Demoted'

Now let us look at the changes that take place *inside* the reported clause. As we noted in 10.3.4, in DS we would expect any deictic markers to be related to the speaker of the words. But in IS, the speaker is the person doing the reporting. In the novel the reporter is usually the narrator, and so the various markers of time, place and social relation will have to be changed to relate to the narrator, not Ermintrude. This explains the following changes as we move from [1] to [2] in example 13:

1 *you* becomes *he*, as the narrator is not addressing Oliver;
2 the tense is backshifted to be consistent with the tense of the reporting clause;
3 the proximal deictic in *this mess* becomes neutralised to *the mess*.

The other changes inside the reporting clause which take place are that the initial exclamatory *Oh*, the exclamation mark and the word *please* are removed. These changes can also be explained in terms of appropriateness to the narrator rather than Ermintrude. It was Ermintrude who was annoyed, not the narrator, so the emotion markers need to be expunged. Moreover, narrators usually 'speak' in statements, as they narrate events occurring in the world of the fiction; so other sentence types are rare in 'narrator–speak'.

10.3.6 The speech presentation continuum re–examined

I will not discuss more examples of IS to illustrate its function as the distancing effect we saw in examples 2 and 5 is typical. But it can now be seen why it is that when IS is used in the novel, readers feel that they are receiving what the character said filtered through the narrator. DS represents a character's speech as fully as possible and thus includes: (a) the speech acts used, (b) the propositions stated and (c) the words used to produce those speech acts and propositions. IS, on the other hand, claims to represent (a) and (b), but *not* (c). We can also see why NRSA appears to be even less full than IS. It claims to represent (a), but *not* (b) and (c). And NRS puts even more distance between us and what the character says as it does not reproduce (a), (b) or (c), but merely tells us that talk occurred.

What all this adds up to is that the scale of speech presentation is a scale of the relative weighting of the apparent influence of the character and the narrator over what is reported. I say 'apparent', because in the novel everything is appearance. The novelist makes it all up, after all. But with the most extreme form of DS (DS with no quotation marks or reporting clause), we feel that we are witnessing what the character says with no interference at all from the narrator. The rest of the scale, even prototypical DS, is a *mixture of the contributions of character and narrator*. As we move along the scale from DS to NRS the control and influence of the narrator's viewpoint over the reporting of what the character said gets stronger and stronger. Moreover, NRS and NRSA are the speech equivalents of the narration of actions and events (this is presumably where speech *acts* get their name from), and so it is at the NRS/NRSA end of the speech presentation continuum that speech presentation is integrated with the rest of the narration of what happens in the novel. This can all be summed up in the following diagram:

Event Narration

| NRA | NRS   NRSA | IS   FIS   DS |

Speech Presentation

10.3.7 Free Indirect Speech (FIS)

The one category on the above speech presentation continuum that we have not discussed in detail is Free Indirect Speech (FIS). I have left the Free Indirect category to last partly because of its importance in nineteenth– and twentieth–century fiction (this is particularly true of Free Indirect *Thought*, as we shall see in 10.4.2 below), and partly because in order to understand FIS and how it works we first of all have to understand the DS and IS forms in some detail.

FIS lies between DS and IS on the speech presentation scales because in both formal and functional terms it is a *mixture* of DS and IS features. Typically it has the grammatical characteristics of IS, but some of the 'production flavour' and deictic properties of DS. However, any mix of DS and IS features can produce the intermediate FIS category. As a consequence of its mixed form it is often difficult to ascribe with any certainty which words are the character's and which the narrator's in FIS.

Because we know that novelists can always use the full DS form if they choose, FIS is a category which indicates a move towards narrator control and narrator viewpoint. In other words, we assume that DS is the *norm* in the novelist's representation of speech, and that any movement towards the narrator end of the scale (and FIS is the next possibility leftwards on that scale) represents narratorial interference in the representation of what characters say in the fictional world.

Now let us look at some typical examples. The first is part of a conversation in a well known cold war spy novel by John Le Carré. George Smiley, a self–effacing senior figure in British intelligence, is trying secretly to discover the identity of the 'mole' who is giving information to the Russians. Here, another intelligence officer, the bluff and hearty Jerry Westerby, is telling Smiley about a disastrous event a couple of years earlier when a British spy, Jim Prideaux, who had been sent on a secret operation to Czechoslovakia, was caught and tortured:

Example 14

'So that was the first part of the story. Czech troops out, Russian troops in. Got it?'

　　Smiley said yes, he thought he had his mind round it so far.
　　　　　　　　(John Le Carré, *Tinker, Tailor, Soldier Spy*, Ch. 28)

Jerry Westerby's DS report, that the Czech troops had been replaced by Russians before Prideaux's capture, turns out to be highly significant. It indicates to Smiley that the Russians must have known about the secret operation before Prideaux was 'discovered', and eventually leads Smiley to the identity of the 'mole'. Yet Smiley's response to the information is extremely muted. This is because it is important to him that he does not reveal his interest in the news he has just received. He will only catch the 'mole' if no one else realises the significance of what he has just learned. In addition, the speech presentation contrast for the two utterances helps us to infer that Smiley is being ironic when he says that he has *got his mind round* something which is, in fact, rather straightforward, and which Jerry Westerby has reported in his typically direct, no–nonsense conversational style.

We can show that what Smiley says is in FIS by comparing it with the Direct and Indirect equivalents:

[1]   'Yes, I've got my mind round it so far,' Smiley said. (DS)

[2]   Smiley said that he had understood it that far. (IS)

We can now see that the original has the subordination, tense and pronoun appropriate to IS, but that the initial verbal response word *yes* and the informal lexis of *had his mind round it* is reminiscent of DS. This mixed form allows Le Carré to represent what Smiley said with some of the apparent flavour of the original (*via* the DS features), while using the narrator filtration indicated by the typically IS features to help us to infer the muted, guarded, and ironic tone in which he speaks.

This 'distancing with original flavour' effect is also used for ironic purposes in the next example. Bar and his friends, who are social climbers, are sucking up to Lord Decimus (sentences are numbered for ease of reference):

Example 15
(1) Bar said that he was told (as everybody always is told, though who tells them, and why, will for ever remain a mystery) that there was to be no wall fruit this year. (2) Lord Decimus had not heard anything amiss of his peaches, but rather believed, if his people were correct, he was to have no apples. (3) No apples? (4) Bar was lost in astonishment and concern. (5) It would have been all one to him, in reality, if there had not been a pippin on the surface of the earth, but his show of interest in this apple question was positively painful.

(Charles Dickens, *Little Dorrit*, Bk II, Ch. 12)

Dickens is poking fun at Bar, as the explicit narrator comment of sentences (4)–(5) makes clear. Sentence (1) also contains (in brackets) narratorial comment at Bar's expense. The re-presentation of Bar's speech before the brackets looks like IS, but after the brackets it slips into FIS through the use of the near deictic phrase *this year*. Note that using FIS is not in itself ironic, but its use in this context clearly helps us to interpret it in this manner. In general terms, the mixed character/narrator form of FIS makes it an ideal vehicle for irony. The response of Lord Decimus to Bar's trivial remark is also ironic and in FIS. He apparently takes Bar's insignificant point extremely seriously. Bar then responds to Lord Decimus with the freest form of DS (*No apples?*), indicating in an exclamatory manner his consuming interest in the Lord's reply.

I have assumed that *No apples?* is DS. My arguments for this are twofold: (i) it is most normal to find exclamatory utter-ances in DS, and (ii) when we process sentences with no verb we tend to infer an 'understood' verb in the *present* tense, if one is needed. Note, however, that some readers may interpret this utterance as an exclamatory form of FIS.

Let us look at the FIS representation of what Lord Decimus says in more detail. The pronouns and tense used are what we would expect for IS, but the attitudinal adverb *rather* reminds us of DS. The other significant feature we normally associate with the DS end of the scale is that there is no reporting clause (*e.g.* 'Lord Decimus said that . . .'), and so the reported clause is not subordinated, as it would be in IS, but has instead the main clause status typical of DS.

The two FIS examples which we have examined so far have looked at first sight like IS, and this is by far the most common form. However, we can also find FIS masquerading as DS. The writer who makes most use of this version of FIS is Jane Austen, who is well known for her acerbic ironic presentation of the characters she disapproves of. Here is an example from *Persuasion*, where the boorish Charles Musgrove is apparently much more worried about striking up a social relationship with Captain Wentworth than the health of his youngest son, who has just dislocated his shoulder:

Example 16
. . . 'the child was going on so well – and he wished so much to be introduced to Captain Wentworth, that, perhaps, he might join them in the evening; he would not dine from home, but he might walk in for half an hour.'

(Jane Austen, *Persuasion*, Ch. 7)

The quotation marks make this speech presentation look like DS, but the tense and pronoun selection is characteristic of IS. The resulting FIS form is an ideal vehicle for the ironic accounts of her characters which Jane Austen uses to such effect.

FIS in I–narration and present tense novels

So far, all the examples we have used in our discussion of speech presentation have been from third–person narration novels written in the past tense, the novel's 'default' form. But it is important to note that if a novel has an I—narrator or a present tense narration, our description of the speech presentation categories will need to be somewhat altered. In present tense narration the present tense will often be appropriate *both* to DS *and* to narration, and so will not be available to mark FIS. Similarly, in I—narration novels the first—person pronoun will be relevant to the narrator *and* the character—speaker.[5]

Exercise 3

Examine carefully the variation in forms of speech presentation in the following extract, and work out the effects of the presentational choices Dickens makes in this conversation between Oliver Twist and Mr Brownlow, with whom he is staying. The conversation, which begins with a discussion of books whose best part are the covers, takes place in Mr Brownlow's study. The sentences are numbered for ease of reference:

(1) 'I suppose they are those heavy ones, sir,' said Oliver, pointing to some large quartos, with a good deal of gilding about the binding.

(2) 'Not always those,' said the old gentleman, patting Oliver on the head, and smiling as he did so; 'there are other equally heavy ones, though of a much smaller size. (3) How should you like to grow up a clever man, and write books, eh?'

(4) 'I think I would rather read them, sir,' replied Oliver.

(5) 'What! wouldn't you like to be a book writer?' said the old gentleman.

(6) Oliver considered a little while; and at last said, he should think it would be a much better thing to be a book–seller; upon which the old gentleman laughed heartily, and declared he had said a very good thing. (7) Which Oliver felt glad to have done, though he by no means knew what it was.

(8) 'Well, well,' said the old gentleman, composing his features. (9) 'Don't be afraid! (10) We won't make an author of you, while there's an honest trade to be learnt, or brick–making to turn to.'

(11) 'Thank you, sir,' said Oliver. (12) At the earnest manner of his reply, the old gentleman laughed again; and said

something about a curious instinct, which Oliver, not
understanding, paid no very great attention to.

(Charles Dickens, *Oliver Twist*, Ch. 14)

10.4   Thought   presentation

The categories used by novelists to represent the thoughts of
their characters are exactly the same as those used to represent
character speech. However, the effects associated with two of
the categories, **Direct Thought (DT)** and **Free Indirect
Thought (FIT)**, turn out to be different. This fact clearly
needs some explanation, and will be the main topic of this
section. But let us first establish clearly with constructed
examples that the categories we have used to account for
speech do indeed apply when character thought is being
presented:

Example 17

[1]   He spent the day thinking.
       (Narrator's Representation of Thought [NRT])

[2]   She considered his unpunctuality.
       (Narrator's Representation of Thought Acts [NRTA])

[3]   She thought that he would be late.
       (Indirect Thought [IT])

[4]   He was bound to be late!
       (Free Indirect Thought [FIT])

[5]   'He will be late', she thought.
       (Direct Thought [DT])

I will not discuss NRT, NRTA or IT in detail as the effects
associated with them are roughly the same as for speech
presentation. In any case, these three categories are relatively
rare; if an author has decided to present, and therefore
foreground, the thoughts of a particular character the more
minimal forms of presentation are unlikely to be appropriate.
FIT turns out to be the most common form of thought
presentation, and we will see why in 10.4.2.

10.4.1 Direct Thought (DT)

We can see in the following extract, from *The Old Curiosity Shop*, that DT tends to be used for presenting conscious, deliberative thought. Dick Swiveller, who has been danger-ously ill for some weeks, has just regained consciousness:

Example 18

'I'm dreaming,' thought Richard, 'that's clear. When I went to bed, my hands were not made of egg shells; and now I can almost see through 'em. If this is not a dream, I have woke up by mistake in an Arabian Night, instead of a London one. But I have no doubt I'm asleep. Not the least.'

Here the small servant had another cough.

'Very remarkable!' thought Mr Swiveller. 'I never dreamt such a real cough as that before. I don't know, indeed, that I ever dreamt either a cough or a sneeze. Perhaps it's part of the philosophy of dreams that one never does. There's another – and another – I say, – I'm dreaming rather fast!'

(Charles Dickens, *The Old Curiosity Shop*, Ch. 64)

The humour of the account comes from the fact that Dick thinks he is dreaming but we know that he is thinking rather deliberately as he comes out of his coma. His 'rather fast' dreaming is merely everyday reality impinging on his consciousness, as the intervening sentence of narration makes clear.

DT has the same linguistic form as the soliloquy in drama, which is notoriously ambiguous as to whether the character involved is thinking aloud or talking to the audience. In the novel there is no audience to talk to, and so thought presentation must be DT's sole purpose. However, DT is quite often used to represent imaginary conversations which characters have with themselves or others, which is presumably why it so often has the flavour of conscious thinking.

In the following extract, Mary Pym is worrying over the disappearance of her husband, Magnus, a senior intelligence officer who has deserted his post in Vienna:

Example 19

Her worship, her dinner parties, her life with Pym, had all been conducted on this same sturdy principle [of supporting her husband unquestioningly].

Until last July. Until our holiday in Lesbos. Magnus, come home. I'm sorry I raised a stink at the airport when you didn't show up. I'm sorry I bellowed at the British Airways clerk in what you call my six–acre voice and I'm sorry I waved my diplomatic pass around And I'm sorry – terribly sorry – I phoned Jack to say where the hell's my husband? So please – just come home and tell me what to do.

(John Le Carré, *A Perfect Spy*, Ch. 1)

In the second paragraph Mary is thinking in direct address mode even though it is obvious that the person she is 'addressing' is not there. Her thoughts are presented in the freest form of DT, with no reporting clauses or quotation marks. In addition to the typical features we have seen when discussing DS, this stream of thought is full of interactive markers: the direct address pronouns and address term, the speech acts of apology, and request and the emphatic repetition of *I'm sorry*.

DT is often presented without quotation marks to distinguish it from DS presented with them. This technique is used throughout Hemingway's *The Old Man and the Sea*, where the two sides of the old man's character are juxtaposed as he struggles for survival. When he speaks aloud, in DS, he is usually impulsive and full of action, but when DT is used he is more reflective and thoughtful. Here he is after he has killed the shark which has attacked his boat:

Example 20

. . . You loved him when he was alive and you loved him after. If you love him, it is not a sin to kill him. Or is it more?

'You think too much, old man,' he said aloud.

But you enjoyed killing the *dentuso*, he thought.

(Ernest Hemingway, *The Old Man and the Sea*, Triad Panther edn (1976), p. 91)

Other novelists also use the same DS/DT contrast to bring out the internal/external world distinction. Here is Mary Pym again, being interrogated by Jack Brotherhood (the Jack referred to in example 19), who has been sent from London to investigate the disappearance of Magnus (sentences are numbered for ease of reference):

Example 21
(1) Brotherhood pulled open a drawer.

(2) 'That's for the book he was writing,' she said as he extracted a meagre file. (3) Magnus keeps everything inside something. (4) Everything must wear a disguise in order to be real.

(5) 'Is it though?' (6) He was pulling on his glasses, one red ear at a time. (7) He knows about the novel too, she thought, watching him. (8) He's not even pretending to be surprised.

(9) 'Yes.' (10) And you can put his bloody papers back where you got them from, she thought.

(John Le Carré, A Perfect Spy, Ch. 3)

As in example 20, the DS is in quotation marks, and the fact that the other Direct strings (sentences 3, 4, 7, 8 and 10,) are *not* is what signals that they are Mary's thoughts. Mary is apparently obedient and helpful when speaking, but secretly rebellious.

10.4.2 Free Indirect Thought (FIT)

Let us begin this section by examining a brief example of FIT which you have already come across in exercise 3 of Chapter 9. Colonel Fergusson is lying on his deathbed, annoyed with his daughter, who is reading a religious pamphlet while waiting for him to die. The Colonel, an atheist, is annoyed because he cannot comprehend his daughter's belief in God:

Example 22
It was a provocation, that's what it was, thought the Colonel. Here he was on his deathbed, preparing for oblivion, and she sits over there reading Parson Noah's latest pamphlet.

(Julian Barnes, A History of the World in 10$\frac{1}{2}$ Chapters)

The reported clauses in the first sentence and the first half of the second sentence are in FIT. They contain a mixture of Direct and Indirect features, as we can show by 'translating' them first into IT and then into DT:

[1] The Colonel thought that it was a provocation that while he was on his deathbed, preparing for oblivion, she was reading Parson Noah's latest pamphlet. (IT)

[2]   'It is a provocation, that's what it is,' thought the Colonel.
      'I am on my deathbed, preparing for oblivion and she sits
      over there reading Parson Noah's latest pamphlet.' (DT)

In this example we can see the typical effect of FIT. We feel
close to the character, almost inside his head as he thinks, and
sympathise with his viewpoint. This 'close' effect is more or
less the opposite of the effect of FIS, which makes us feel
distanced from the character and is often a vehicle for irony.
How is it that FIS and FIT have such markedly different
effects?

One reason is that although DS can reasonably be assumed
to be the norm for speech presentation, it is much more
difficult to hold the same view for DT. The thoughts of
others, unlike their speech, are never directly accessible to us.
We can only *infer* what people might be thinking from their
speech, actions, facial expression and so on. It is thus much
more plausible to think of IT as our norm for thought
presentation. In this case, the use of FIT constitutes a move
away from the norm towards the *character* end of the scale,
whereas FIS constitutes a move in the opposite direction.[6]

We can see another reason for the close–up, sympathetic
feel which FIT has from example 23, which is also a
description of a dying man (sentences are numbered for ease of
reference):

Example 23
(1) His hands were weary. (2) He brooded over his long, white
body, marking the ribs stick through the sides. (3) The hands had
held other hands and thrown a ball high into the air. (4) Now
they were dead hands. (5) He could wind them about his hair
and let them rest untingling on his belly or lose them in the valley
between Rhianon's breasts. (6) It did not matter what he did
with them. (7) They were as dead as the hands of the clock, and
moved to clockwork.

                              (Dylan Thomas, 'The Visitor')

The first two sentences of this extract appear to be narration,
but because sentence (2) narrates an internal, cognitive action
of the dying man, we can interpret the rest of the extract as a
representation of his thoughts. They are in Free Indirect mode
because they contain a mix of Indirect and Direct features.
They are all in the past tense, the tense of the narrative, and

they are characterised by third–person reference for the man thinking. But there are no reporting verbs (and so the reported clauses are not subordinated), sentence (4) begins with the near deictic *now*, and (5) contains the modal verb *could*, both of which can be easily related to the man's viewpoint.

Once we have noticed that sentences (3)–(7) are FIT, it is also possible to 'back–project' onto sentence (1) and see that as FIT as well. This is possible because FIT without a reporting clause is often indistinguishable in formal linguistic terms from NRA. Sentence (1) is thus potentially ambiguous in terms of its source – narrator or character – and this fact helps us to explain the peculiar effect of FIT. We noticed in Chapter 8 that readers feel a need to sympathise with the views and position of the narrator. And because the FIT form combines the position of the character and narrator we are bound to want to sympathise with the character's position.

10.4.3   Stream of consciousness writing

The term '**stream of consciousness**' was originally coined by the philosopher William James in his *Principle of Psychology* (1890)[7] to describe the free association of ideas and impressions in the mind. It was later applied to the writing of William Faulkner, James Joyce, Virginia Woolf and others experi–menting early in the twentieth–century with the novelistic portrayal of the free flow of thought. Note, however, that the majority of thought presentation in novels is *not* stream of consciousness writing. The examples we have discussed in 10.4.1 and 10.4.2 are not stream of consciousness writing because they are too orderly to constitute the free association of ideas. Perhaps the most famous piece of stream of consciousness writing is that associated with Leopold Bloom in Joyce's *Ulysses*. Here he is in a restaurant thinking about oysters:

Example 24
Filthy shells. Devil to open them too. Who found them out?
Garbage, sewage they feed on. Fizz and Red bank oysters. Effect
on the sexual. Aphrodis. He was in the Red bank this morning.
Was he oyster old fish at table. Perhaps he young flesh in bed.
No. June has no ar no oysters. But there are people like tainted
game. Jugged hare. First catch your hare. Chinese eating eggs

fifty years old, blue and green again. Dinner of thirty courses.
Each dish harmless might mix inside. Idea for a poison mystery.
(James Joyce, *Ulysses*, Bodley Head Cheap Edn, p. 163)

This cognitive meandering is all in the most free version of DT. It is also characterised by a highly elliptical sentence structure, with as many grammatical words as possible being removed consistent with allowing the reader to be able to infer what is going on. Even the one–word sentence 'Aphrodisiac.' is reduced to *Aphrodis.*, because it is such a distinctive word in English and can be recognised even without the last two syllables. The passage's other characteristic feature, also associated with the extreme ellipsis, is the way in which new aspects or new topics are introduced suddenly and in an apparently semi–random way. The language is thus not very cohesive, and breaks the Gricean maxims of Quantity and Manner. But, as I pointed out in 8.4, we must assume that apparently unreasonable writing behaviour is related to a relevant authorial purpose. It is the assumption that Joyce is really cooperating with us at a deeper level, even though he is apparently making our lives difficult, that leads us to conclude that he is trying to evoke a mind working associatively.

Let us now go through the extract to see the way in which the extraordinary topic changes can be accounted for. A little earlier Bloom has been thinking about things which are poisonous, and has proposed to himself the hypothesis that poisonous objects are brightly coloured in order to warn off prospective consumers. From there he has moved to thinking about other brightly coloured things, and has now come up with the fact that oysters are a counter–example to his bright colour theory in that they can sometimes poison you but are coloured black and green. Thinking of their colour involves their shells, and explains the associative move to thinking about opening them. Because they are difficult to open he then wonders how oysters were discovered as a food source. The reference to sewage can in part be explained in relation to his earlier thoughts about poison. Because oysters feed on sewage they can be thought of as feeding on poison. Thinking about oysters feeding reminds him of people eating, and because oysters are often eaten while drinking champagne, we can also make sense of the *fizz* reference. Oysters are also commonly said to be an aphrodisiac, which explains the next jump. He then thinks about a particular fresh oyster and where it has come from, harking back to the sewage reference. Noticing an older man eating at another table, he wonders whether he is having oysters and hence whether they have aphrodisiac properties for him. He decides that the man cannot be eating oysters after all, because *June has no ar,* an allusion to the saying that you should not eat oysters unless there is an 'R' in the month (which happens to debar all the summer months, when the hot weather is likely to make them go off more quickly). This brings us back to the idea of food going off, and the hanging of game as a counter–example to the idea that you should not eat tainted food. Jugged hare is an example of a dish made from game, and this reminds him of the beginning of a traditional recipe for jugged hare starting with the words *first catch your hare.* Delaying the eating of fresh food also reminds Bloom of Chinese preserved eggs, which are also black and green, and this brings him back to his colour theory. Finally, he begins to think about another way of being poisoned – by happening to eat a combination of things which interact chemically with disastrous results. This, in turn, prompts the idea of the plot for a murder mystery.

Stream of consciousness writing can be in FIT as well as DT, and does not have to consist of the short, elliptical sentences we have seen here. Here is a description from the very end of Lowry's *Under the Volcano*. The main character, Geoffrey Firmin, the ex–consul of a British embassy in a Latin American country, is dying. Now an alcoholic, and in a very bad state, he has been shot as a thief while incapably drunk in a bar in a small village. In his distressed condition he thinks he has just reached the summit of a volcanic mountain, although we can infer from the last sentence that the villagers must have carried him up a hillside in order to throw him down a ravine and so dispose of the evidence of the killing:

Example 25
It was crumbling too, whatever it was, collapsing, while he was falling, falling into the volcano, he must have climbed it after all, though now there was this noise of foisting lava in his ears, horribly, it was in eruption, yet no, it wasn't the volcano, the world itself was bursting, bursting into black spouts of villages catapulted into space, with himself falling through it all, through the inconceivable pandemonium of a million tanks, through the blazing of ten million burning bodies, falling, into a forest, falling
—Suddenly he screamed, and it was as though this scream were

> being tossed from one tree to another, as its echoes returned,
> then, as though the trees themselves were crowding nearer,
> huddled together, closing over him, pitying . . .
>   Somebody threw a dead dog after him down the ravine.
>   (Malcolm Lowry, *Under the Volcano*, Penguin Modern Classics
>   edn, pp. 375–6)

The sentences of this FIT representation are long, rambling and complex, but share the sudden topic shifts characteristic of Leopold Bloom's theorising about oysters and poison. The drunk and dying man's thoughts appear to be an incoherent attempt to make sense of what is happening to him, so incoherent that it is difficult to be sure that we understand in any exact way his individual thoughts and perceptions, and how they relate to one another. In this sense, Lowry's writing here is even more extreme than the extract from *Ulysses*.

Being carried up the hill makes the Consul think he must have climbed a mountain, and his being thrown down the ravine, which we can only infer from the presupposition contained in the final NRA sentence of the novel, makes him think that he is falling into a volcano. The *noise of foisting lava* could be the wind rushing past his ears as he falls down the ravine, or noises inside his own head as his brain functions begin to give out. The latter explanation seems to make better sense of the extraordinary characterisation of the world exploding around him as if he were in an almost unimaginably large and fierce armoured battle.

This discussion of stream of consciousness writing, which brings us to the end of our examination of thought presentation in the novel, has needed to be detailed in order to describe the phenomenon adequately. But it should now be clear that the term 'stream of consciousness' should be used carefully. Although the vast majority of modern novelists present the thoughts of their characters using DT and FIT, they do not indulge in stream of consciousness writing. That is a term we must reserve for more radical experimentation in the presentation of character thought.

Exercise 4

Examine carefully the speech and thought presentation in the passage below. Katherine Hilbery and Ralph Denham are walking in

Kew Gardens when Katherine realises she has lost her handbag. Note that in this passage it is not always easy to decide whether speech or thought is being represented (sentences are numbered for ease of reference):

> (1) But though she did not speak, Katherine had an uneasy sense that silence on her part was selfishness. (2) It was selfish of her to continue, as she wished to do, a discussion of subjects not remotely connected with any human beings. (3) She roused herself to consider their exact position upon the turbulent map of the emotions. (4) Oh yes – it was a question whether Ralph Denham should live in the country and write a book; it was getting late; they must waste no more time; Cassandra arrived to–night for dinner; she flinched and roused herself, and discovered that she ought to be holding something in her hands. (5) But they were empty. (6) She held them out with an exclamation.
>
> (7) 'I've left my bag somewhere – where?' (8) The gardens had no points of the compass, so far as she was concerned. (9) She had been walking for the most part on grass – that was all she knew. (10) Even the road to the Orchid House had now split itself into three. (11) But there was no bag in the Orchid House. (12) It must, therefore, have been left upon the seat. (13) They retraced their steps in the preoccupied manner of people who have to think about something that is lost. (14) What did this bag look like? (15) What did it contain?
>
> (16) 'A purse – a ticket – some letters, papers' Katherine counted, becoming more agitated as she recalled the list. (17) Denham went on quickly in advance of her, and she heard him shout that he had found it before she reached the seat. (18) In order to make sure that all was safe she spread the contents on her knee. (19) It was a queer collection, Denham thought, gazing with the deepest interest.
>
> (Virginia Woolf, *Night and Day*, Ch. 25)

Discussion of exercises

Exercise 1
The comma and inverted commas round the reported clause of the Direct Speech are removed, and the order of the reporting and reported clauses are reversed. The reported clause is explicitly subordinated to the reporting clause in the

Indirect Speech version, as indicated by the conjunction *that*. Inside the reported clause, the first–person pronoun *me* becomes third–person *her*. A more expanded discussion of what is involved in 'translating' Direct Speech into Indirect Speech can be found in 10.3.5.

Exercise 2

(a) The first clause is NRA and the second NRSA. We are thus distanced from the character and what he said (the character is actually apologising in a rather dispirited manner to his wife on their wedding night for forgetting to book a room with a double bed in their hotel).

(b) The first sentence is in IS and the second in DS. There is an ironic flavour because (i) such an important question is represented in a very indirect form, and (ii) the content of the DS response is so laconical.

(c) The first clause is NRA, and that is followed by a string of short utterances all in DS, and without reporting clauses. This form helps to indicate the quick–fire nature of the conversation and the repeated pattern of a statement of disbelief followed by a positive response. The affirmative responses clearly increase in 'size', as indicated typo–graphically, helping us to imagine an increase in volume, width of pitch and other performance features indicating the rising excitement. Given that (i) the first two *Yes* responses are in lower case, (ii) the last two are in upper case and (iii) the fourth response is indicated as being 'higher' than the third by its italicised representation, it could well be that the lack of italicisation for the second response is a printer's error. If it had been italicised, a continually rising crescendo would have been represented across all four utterances of *Yes*. After the DS turns, the next paragraph goes to the opposite end of the scale, the first two sentences being a mixture of NRA and NRS, the third NRSA and the fourth IS. Whereas Coventry's foregrounded maximally uncooperative behaviour has been discussed in DS, her previously supportive discourse role, where only one small indication of dissent can be remembered, is represented through a combination of 'moves' at the indirect, narrator–controlled end of the scale.

(d) This quotation is discussed as example 14 in 10.3.7.

Exercise 3

The speech presentation of the first five sentences is all in DS, as Dickens establishes, and foregrounds the conversational harmony between Oliver and Mr Brownlow in contrast with Oliver's relationship with the monstrous Fagin. However, Oliver's answer to the question as to whether he would like to be an author is in FIS and underlines his naïvety. Mr Brownlow's light–hearted response can also be seen as FIS or possibly IS. Sentence (7) tells us about Oliver's internal state of mind. Mr Brownlow's reassuring remarks to Oliver, again foregrounding his kindness, are in DS, as is Oliver's expression of thanks. The last part of (12) is in NRSA, however, because Dickens now takes on Oliver's viewpoint. The old man presumably says something that the young boy cannot understand, and by switching to the narrator–dominated end of the scale Dickens again underlines Oliver's innocence. This naïvety has already got him into difficulty in his relationship with Fagin, who has taught him to be a thief, but in this more supportive context it becomes an endearing rather than a dangerous trait.

Exercise 4

This passage is characterised by ambiguity in terms of discourse representation. Virginia Woolf almost always omits reporting clauses in the passage. As a consequence there are various possible speech/thought presentation ambiguities, and sometimes ambiguities about *which character's* speech or thoughts are being represented. In addition, a number of sentences are potentially ambiguous between narration and Free Indirect forms. As a consequence, we feel that Virginia Woolf is blurring the boundaries between speech and thought, and in particular between Katherine's internal and external worlds.

Sentence (1) begins with NRA, and the second clause could also be seen as an NRA statement of her inner state of mind. But because of the way in which narration and the Free Indirect category can be formally identical, this second clause could also conceivably be an FIT representation of Katherine's thought process. Sentence (2) is similarly ambiguous. (3) would appear to be the NRA of her internal state, and the first half of (4), with its *Oh yes* beginning is most easily interpreted as the FIT of a series of thoughts. Though with the various topic switches within it, it might conceivably be a Free Indirect representation of snatches of conversation between Katherine and Denham, or it could even be that some of the clauses are speech and some Katherine's thoughts. However the material after the last semi–colon is clearly NRA of Katherine's internal world. Sentence (5) is most likely NRA, but could also be Katherine's FIT, and (6) is NRS. The inverted commas around (7) suggest that this is Katherine's DS, and when we read on further this would appear to be confirmed, as Denham presumably needs to know she has lost her bag in order to be involved in the search for it. But at this point in the reading process it would even be possible to see (7) as Katherine's DT. (8) looks like NRA of Katherine's internal state, but could also be FIT. (9) is most likely FIT, given the status of the previous sentence, but it could just about be Katherine's FIS in reply to something Denham asked. Sentences (10) and (11) are most likely NRA but could be FIT, and (12) could be NRA, FIT or an FIS representation of what either character might have said. (13) is clearly NRA, and (14) and (15) are most likely to be FIS representations of questions Denham asked Katherine, but could just about be construed as his FIT. The first part of sentence (16) must be DS for Katherine, and the rest is NRA. (17) is NRA, mainly from Katherine's viewpoint, (18) is most likely NRA but could be Katherine's FIT, and the last sentence is Denham's DT. With so few of the sentences easily falling into one or another presentation category, the reflective reader is likely to be less and less certain about what is inside and outside Katherine's mind.

Notes

1. For example, 'It's raining cats and dogs' and 'It's pouring' are alternative ways of expressing the same proposition.
2. A number of other writers on speech and thought presentation (*e.g.* Herman 1993 and McHale 1978) do not always distinguish terminologically between speech and thought presentation, and talk instead of discourse presentation. But to my mind this yoking together terminologically of the two areas disguises some systematic differences in effect among the presentational categories when applied to speech and thought (see 10.4).
3. For a discussion of speech summary see Short (1988).

4. Most earlier accounts, including Leech and Short (1981) and Short (1982b), describe the freer forms of DS as a separate category, Free Direct Speech (FDS), but Short (1988) argues the case for the view assumed here. The same arguments apply to thought presentation (see 10.4).

5. This general point about Free Indirect Speech in relation to I–narration and present tense narration is argued in more detail in Leech and Short (1981: 325–34). Similar considerations apply to Free Indirect Thought (see 10.4).

6. For a more detailed discussion see Leech and Short (1981: 325–34)

7. As Wales (1989: 431) points out, William James was the brother of Henry James.

Further reading

The account of speech and thought presentation given in this chapter is based on Leech and Short (1981: Ch. 10) and Short (1988). An analysis of a section from Joyce's *Portrait of the Artist as a Young Man* can be found in Short (1982b). Simpson (1993: Ch. 2) and Toolan (1988: Ch. 4) contain relevant and accessible introductory accounts. Fludernik (1993) is an excellent and compendious advanced treatment of the whole area, and Tannen (1989: Ch. 4) is an interesting discussion of speech presentation in conversation in the context of a more generalised book on spoken discourse.

CHECKSHEET 9: SPEECH AND THOUGHT PRESENTATION

A. Is speech or thought being presented? For each sentence, and sometimes for parts of sentences as they 'slip' from one mode to another, you will need to decide whether action, speech or thought is being presented, and whether there is any ambiguity about possible decisions.

B. Now categorise each sentence or sentence–part using the categorisation system described in the chapter, and noting down, where necessary, the reasons for each decision:

Narration					
NRA	NRS	NRSA	IS	FIS	DS
NRA	NRT	NRTA	IT	FIT	DT

Speech/Thought Presentation

Is there any of the cohesive disjunction associated with stream of consciousness writing? If so, examine its form.

C.   Now examine the functions and effects of each change of category, and any stream of consciousness effects, in order to characterise the detailed flow of presentation and relate your overall conclusions to the overall purposes which you think the author has in mind.

CHAPTER 11

Prose style

11.1 Introduction: authorial style and text style

In Chapters 9 and 10 we have examined various aspects of the
linguistic control of viewpoint, a concept which is central to
twentieth–century criticism of the novel. Other chapters,
devoted primarily to the other literary genres, are also relevant
to the stylistic analysis of prose. Chapters 1 and 2 can help us
to analyse passages of prose, as well as poems; and the forms of
analysis for dramatic speech in Chapters 6 and 7 are also
applicable to the novel, particularly dialogue. Even the
phonetic and rhythmic patterning discussed in relation to
poetry in chapters 4 and 5 will sometimes be relevant in the
analysis of fiction and drama. Indeed, as I said in the preface to
this book, although particular methods of analysis have been
explored in relation to the genre, where they happen to have
most analytical 'payoff', they will be helpful in the
examination of texts from the other literary genres, and indeed
all texts.

But if we were to add together all of the forms of analysis
embodied in the various checksheets at the ends of chapters of
this book, there would be one obvious area which we have
not yet addressed in the criticism of prose, namely the notion
of **style**. It is to style in its various aspects that this chapter, and
the checksheet at the end of it, is devoted.

11.1.1   Authorial style 1: style related to meaning in a general way

When people talk of style they usually mean **authorial style**: in other words a way of writing which recognisably belongs to a particular writer, say Jane Austen or Ernest Hemingway. This way of writing distinguishes one author's writing from that of others, and is felt to be recognisable across a range of texts written by the same writer, even though those writings are bound to vary as a consequence of being about different topics, describing different things, having different purposes and so on. It is this ability to perceive authorial style in the writings of a particular author that enables us to write pastiches and parodies.

In *The British Museum is Falling Down* David Lodge writes various passages in the style of other novelists, usually for humorous effect. Part of the enjoyment in reading this novel is to spot the pastiches. Here is part of his Virginia Woolf passage, which is signalled by the allusion to her novel *Mrs Dalloway* by the mention of her clock (each pastiche in the novel is accompanied by a similar clue). Adam Appleby, an English Literature Ph.D. student at the University of London, is stuck in a traffic jam on his scooter as he tries to get to the British Museum one morning:

Example 1

From near–by Westminster, Mrs Dalloway's clock boomed out
the half hour. It partook, he thought, shifting his height in the
saddle of metempsychosis, the way his humble life fell into moulds
prepared by literature. Or was it, he wondered, picking his nose,
the result of closely studying the sentence structure of the English
novelists? One had resigned oneself to having no private
language any more, but one had clung wistfully to the illusion of
a personal property of events. A fond and fruitless illusion, it
seemed, for here, inevitably came the limousine with its Very
Important Personage, or Personages, dimly visible in the interior.
(David Lodge, *The British Museum is Falling Down*, Ch. 2)

Anyone familiar with Virginia Woolf's novels will recognise this passage as reminiscent of her writing, and in particular the way in which the character's internal philosophical musings are juxtaposed with descriptions of external reality (we have seen an example of it already in the passage from *Night and*

Day, the text for exercise 4 in Chapter 9). Lodge makes fun of Woolf's juxtaposition of inner and outer reality through the extreme disparity between the two modes. Adam muses philosophically about the relations between literature and life while picking his nose. In addition to the reference to Mrs Dalloway's clock, Woolf devotees will recognise the phrase *Very Important Personage or Personages* as an allusion to *Mrs Dalloway*. The title–character of that novel, while walking through the streets of London, glimpses *a face of the very greatest importance* in the window of a large car, and then spends some time trying to work out who the very important person was, ranging through a list of famous politicians and members of the royal family. In Lodge's novel guesses very similar to Mrs Dalloway's are made, but the car's occupants turn out to be a pop group.

So far we have looked at the Lodge pastiche mainly from the point of view of content. But what about style? Here is an extract to compare it with, chosen almost at random from *Orlando*:

Example 2
Yes, she thought, heaving a deep sigh of relief, as she turned from the carpenter's shop to climb the hill, I can begin to live again. I am by the Serpentine, she thought, the little boat is climbing through the white arch of a thousand deaths. I am about to understand . . .
   (Virginia Woolf, *Orlando*, Penguin Twentieth Century Classics
edn, p. 223)

We can see now that it is not just the juxtaposition of internal and external reality which makes Lodge's passage reminiscent of Virginia Woolf, but also the typical use of particular linguistic constructions. Grammatically, he has mimicked the way in which she interposes a reporting clause in the middle of sentences of thought presentation. Although the speech presentation category is different in the two examples (FIT in example 1 and DT in example 2), the thought is presented without quotation marks, helping to juxtapose dramatically character thought and external description. This juxtaposition in turn brings with it contrasting sets of lexical items, more concrete and down–to earth for the external reality, and more abstract for the thoughts.

Exercise   1

Another way in which we can see authorial style at work is by
comparing accounts of the same, or similar, things by two different
authors.[1] Take two authors you are familiar with and whose style
contrasts, and write two pastiche descriptions of the same character or
setting.

Note: there is no discussion of this exercise at the end of the chapter
as I cannot know what authors you will use for your comparative
work.

In our discussion of example 2 we traced the interface
between Virginia Woolf's overall thematic and strategic aims
and the linguistic means through which those aims are
achieved. We perceive the former through our interaction
with the latter. In this kind of example, then, our notion of
authorial style is inextricably linked with meaning, but in a
rather general way. Writing style is seen as symptomatic of
what might be called the **mind style** or *world view* of the
writer (see 9.3.8).[2] The linguistic choices made are thus both
evidence of authorial style and evidence of textual meaning at
the same time.

11.1.2   Authorial style 2: style completely unrelated to meaning: fingerprinting

The notion of style as an indication of an author's world
view, although very important, is merely one of a myriad of
definitions of style, both literary and non–literary. Style can be
perceived in any consistent writing, literary or otherwise, or,
indeed, in *any consistent behaviour*, linguistic or otherwise.
Individual novelists can be said to have styles, but so can
weather forecasters, singers or runners. It is also possible for
groups to possess a common style (think of stream–of–
consciousness novelists or punk rock groups in contrast to
other kinds of novelists or pop groups).[3]
Some of the individual styles I have just outlined, however,
are completely independent of meaning. A running style is just
a running style, which will help you to recognise a particular

runner in a race. It doesn't tell you anything about the runner's world view.

An equivalent of this in terms of writing style is what is sometimes called 'fingerprinting'. Imagine, for example, that you are interested, as some literary scholars have been, in determining whether particular scenes in Shakespeare's plays were really written by Shakespeare or by other writers (*e.g.* Bacon). To do this you will need to take long stretches of writing, preferably in the same genre, which are definitely by (i) Shakespeare and (ii) Bacon, and compare, through an examination of statistical frequencies, the linguistic make–up of those pieces of writing with the text whose authorship is in doubt. To do this, you will have to count language items which are as *unrelated to meaning* as possible, in order to make sure that you are examining personal style indicators and not linguistic choices determined by the topic or textual purpose (*e.g.* description, action) of the particular text or extract. In fingerprinting studies, then, scholars examine linguistic features such as average sentence–length, the average number of morphemes or syllables per word or the average instance of grammatical words like 'of' per thousand words.

Because most students are not interested in issues of authorship, but in aspects of language which are more meaningful, they are not particularly 'turned on' by counting the incidence of 'of' in texts. But if you did want to deter–mine the authorship of a text you would have to use this sort of technique, and it is important to notice that to isolate style of any kind must involve *some* statistical work, because style can only be isolated by examining typical choices, and therefore frequencies. We can see from the style/world view and style/fingerprinting examples that the kind of style you want to characterise determines the kind of linguistic items you decide to count.

11.1.3 Authorial style 3: style intrinsically related to meaning: text style

Just as authors can be said to have style, so can *texts*. Critics can talk of the style of *Middlemarch*, or even parts of it, as well as the style of George Eliot. When the style of texts or extracts from texts is examined we are even more centrally concerned with meaning than with the 'world view' version of authorial style discussed above, and so when we examine **text style** we will need to examine linguistic choices which are intrinsically connected with meaning and effect on the reader. All of the areas we have looked at so far in this book could be relevant to the meaning of a particular text and its style; as can areas like lexical and grammatical patterning, which we have not yet covered in detail, but which will be dealt with later in this chapter. Even the positioning of something as apparently insignificant as a comma can sometimes be very important in interpretative terms.

To summarise, there are many versions of the notion of style, and as a consequence 'style' is a rather slippery term. Fingerprinting counts frequencies of items which are as meaningless as possible. At the other extreme, text style looks closely at how linguistic choices help to construct textual meaning. The versions of style which critics and students of English literature feel most at home with are the 'world view' kind of authorial style, and text style. As this book is concerned with understanding the part that language plays in the creation of textual meaning and effect, the rest of this chapter will be mainly concerned with text style.

11.2 Lies, damned lies and statistics

Most people in the Humanities feel more at home with reading than counting, and many of my students ask whether they really need to do statistical analysis as part of stylistic analysis. In addition, they have all heard of the saying (usually attributed to Disraeli) that there are three kinds of lies: lies, damned lies and statistics. This saying helps bolster their hope that if they close their eyes the statistics will go away.

My answer to my students' question is that sometimes statistics can be useful, in which case we need to do statistical work. And if we need to do it, like everything else, we should do it well. But it is also important to have a properly balanced view of what statistics can and cannot do. Statistics appears at first sight to be precise and objective, but the apparent objectivity is not so hard–edged when we remember that (i) analysts choose what they will count, which brings in one element of subjectivity, and (ii) the *interpretation* of the statistics can vary from one person to another, depending upon the initial assumptions they bring along to the figures. In spite of the saying alluded to in the title of this section, the statistics themselves are not lies, it is the way people *interpret* and *use* them which usually turns out to be illicit.

Clearly, we are not allowed to fiddle the evidence, but it is also important to make sure that we don't arrive at the wrong conclusions by accident. Hence we need to be careful in providing statistical evidence in stylistic analysis, and it is best if the quantitative work points in the same interpretative direction as the qualitative analysis seen in the rest of this book. I often think that interpretation is a bit like laying bets on a horse race, but under a convention whereby you are allowed to continue betting during the race. The more evidence you amass as you read and analyse, the safer your interpretative hypothesis, or reading bet, becomes.

Luckily, the kind of statistical analysis needed for textual work is not very complex. But it will be helpful if I spell out some general 'rules':

1　We can count anything that is countable, but we should not assume that quantitative analysis leads to automatic conclusions. They always have to be interpreted, and we need to take into account as many kinds of evidence as we can muster in doing stylistic analysis, both quantitative and non–quantitative.
2　Statistical work is essentially comparative. To have a set of statistics for a passage or an author does not really tell us anything until we have figures relating to *relevant com–parators* with which to contrast those statistics. The best comparators are near equivalents. For example, if we are analysing a prose text then we need other prose comparators. Comparative figures for poems or dramatic texts are unlikely to be revealing. In prose analysis we can compare figures with (i) equivalent passages from other works or by other writers, or (ii) general statistical norms for prose writing produced by other researchers.
3　Just counting up the totals for, say, the incidence of adjectives, or Direct Speech, in a text is not very helpful unless the text(s) we are comparing it with are very similar in length. By and large, it is better to calculate percentages or averages, which can then be compared with percentages or averages for other texts.
4　If we are creating averages or percentages, we have to answer the question 'averages or percentages of what?'. Often we will want to use percentages in relation to the

total number of words in the text(s) we are examining. But this will not always be the case. It is usually best to create percentages in relation to the nearest relevant superordinate category. So if we are comparing adjective frequencies we could do it as a percentage of the total number of words. For speech presentation categories we might want to compare the total number of words in a category with the words used for other categories or the total number of words for the passage(s) involved. On the other hand we might look at the number of clauses involved in the different kinds of speech presentation. Which superordinate category we choose will in part be determined by what we are trying to find out.

5 Averages or percentages for an entire passage may well conceal differences between one part of the passage and another, so it is important to examine how much internal variation from the average there is. A common measure–ment used by statisticians of this kind of variation is called 'standard deviation'.

6 Let us assume that we have compared two passages and find, say, that the average sentence–lengths for them are 28 words and 30 words. Although the second passage's average is higher than the first it is unlikely that we can base any findings on the difference. This is because a difference of two words over these sorts of totals is unlikely to be significant. Very big differences (e.g. averages of 12 and 28 words) are easily perceivable, of course, but there is a problem if you have figures which are between these two extremes. However, it is possible to determine whether such differences are attributable to random variation or not through what are usually called 'statistical significance' tests.

As this is an introductory book, I will keep the statistical work in the rest of this chapter very simple, merely using averages and percentages in relation to a set of norms for modern prose writing. But it should be remembered that more sophisticated forms of analysis are available, and would be expected for more advanced stylistics work in some areas.[4]

11.3 What language features should we examine to elucidate text style?

There are a number of areas already covered in this book for which we could examine a text or a corpus of an author's writing:

1 foregrounded features, including figures of speech, as described in Chapters 1, 2 and 4;
2 whether any patterns of style variation can be discerned (Chapter 3);
3 discoursal patterning of various kinds, like turn–taking or patterns of inferencing (Chapters 6 and 7);
4 patterns of viewpoint manipulation, including speech and thought presentation (Chapters 8 and 9).

I will assume that these areas are now well known to you and do not need reiteration. Instead, I will concentrate on aspects of language patterning in prose that are *not* covered by the above, and in effect on the narrative description of scenes and action. We will examine:

5 patterns of lexis (vocabulary);
6 patterns of grammatical organisation; and
7 patterns of textual organisation (how the units of textual organisation, from sentences to paragraphs and beyond, are arranged).

These areas, and questions related to them, are spelled out in a checksheet at the end of this chapter, which is derived from a more extensive checksheet in Chapter 3 of Leech and Short (1981), which presents comparative analyses of the beginnings of short stories by three well known writers. I will not compare the analysis below with those analyses, but instead will use a series of norms for modern prose as a comparator. Exercise 2, at the end of this chapter, will involve you in analysing one of the texts Leech and Short explore, and in comparing your findings with theirs.

In order to arrive at the analysis I present below, I have gone systematically through the questions on the checksheet at the end of this chapter. Of course, those questions do not *all* throw up interesting answers for *each passage* analysed. The checksheet, like the others in this book, is designed to be comprehensive enough to help with any passage. The description of the passage below concentrates on the areas of the checksheet which turn out to be interesting, along with any significant factors thrown up by an examination of the checksheets in the earlier chapters of this book.

11.4 Analysing style and meaning in a passage from The Great Gatsby

I will analyse a passage from *The Great Gatsby* where the I–narrator, Nick Carraway, is describing to us the series of large society parties which Jay Gatsby throws at his mansion in the hope that the young woman he is in love with, but who is now married to someone else, will come to one of them. Nick is a near neighbour, living in a small house from which he can observe the party at a distance. I have chosen this extract because there is almost no conversation in it (hence the style features will be univocal, as there is only one addresser, Nick), and because it is a description which is full of action and exhibits interesting internal textual contrasts:

Example 3

(1) At least once a fortnight a corps of caterers came down with several hundred feet of canvas and enough coloured lights to make a Christmas tree of Gatsby's enormous garden. (2) On buffet tables, garnished with glistening hors d'oeuvre, spiced baked hams crowded against salads of harlequin designs and pastry pigs and turkeys bewitched to a dark gold. (3) In the main hall a bar with a real brass rail was set up, and stocked with gins and liquors and with cordials so long forgotten that most of his female guests were too young to know one from another.

(4) By seven o'clock the orchestra has arrived, no thin five–piece affair, but a whole pitful of oboes and trombones and saxophones and viols and cornets and piccolos, and low and high drums. (5) The last swimmers have come in from the beach now and are dressing upstairs; the cars from New York are parked five deep in the drive, and already the halls and salons and verandas are gaudy with primary colours, and hair bobbed in strange new ways, and shawls beyond the dreams of Castile. (6) The bar is in full swing, and floating rounds of cocktails permeate the garden outside, until the air is alive with chatter and laughter, and casual innuendo and introductions forgotten on the spot, and enthusiastic meetings between women who never knew each other's names.

(7) The lights grow brighter as the earth lurches away from the sun, and now the orchestra is playing yellow cocktail music, and the opera of voices pitches a key higher. (8) Laughter is easier minute by minute, spilled with prodigality, tipped out at a cheerful word. (9) The groups change more swiftly, swell with new arrivals, dissolve and form in the same breath; already there are wanderers, confident girls who weave here and there among the stouter and more stable, become for a sharp, joyous moment the centre of a group and then, excited with triumph, glide on through the sea–change of faces and voices and colour under constantly changing light.

(10) Suddenly one of these gypsies, in trembling opal, seizes a cocktail out of the air, dumps it down for courage and, moving her hands like Frisco, dances out alone on the canvas platform. (11) A momentary hush; the orchestra leader varies his rhythm obligingly for her, and there is a burst of chatter as the erroneous news goes around that she is Gilda Gray's understudy from the Follies. (12) The party has begun.

(F. Scott Fitzgerald, The Great Gatsby, Ch. 3)

11.4.1 General remarks

This passage describes the preparations for, and prelude to, an extravagantly large and opulent high–society party which is representative of a fortnightly series of such lavish events. Most of the description appears to be from a viewpoint outside the party itself, appropriate to Nick's viewing position from his own house next door. Only external generalities are described. The first paragraph describes the food and drink. In the second and third paragraphs we see the arrival of the orchestra and guests, and the swirl of conversation and movement as the guests intermingle. The last paragraph suddenly moves to a more close–up perspective, focusing on the actions of a single girl, and ending on a climactic and summative note with the last sentence: *The party has begun*. In our analysis of the extract we will need to explain the linguistic basis for the impressions of opulence, lavishness and generality, as well as the progression in paragraphs 1–3 and the dramatic change in the last paragraph. In addition, we will need to explain the fact that Nick's description has an ironic quality pervading it. Despite being extremely lavish, it seems that the party is also a rather superficial experience. It is mere empty socialising.

11.4.2 Some statistics

One helpful way of giving a general characterisation of a piece of writing is to look at its grammatical characteristics in comparison with other texts. To do this we will compare the figures for this passage with an average, or norm, for a corpus of modern English writing produced by Ellegård (1978). The table below gives the Ellegård norm for sentence length and the major grammatical word classes, and compares them with *The Great Gatsby* passage in total and paragraph by paragraph:

	Average sentence length	Nouns	Main verbs	Adjectives	Ad-verbs
Ellegård norm	17.8	27.2%	12.1%	7.4%	5.3%
Whole text	33.9	28.5%	11.3%	10.3%	5.6%
Paragraph 1	32.3	28.9%	10.3%	12.3%	3.1%
Paragraph 2	49.3	30%	8.5%	11.5%	4.6%
Paragraph 3	36.3	27.5%	14.7%	10.1%	9.2%
Paragraph 4	24	26.4%	12.5%	5.6%	5.6%

The average sentence length for the passage (33.9 words) is approximately twice the Ellegård norm, indicating some complexity of style. By way of comparison, writers like John Steinbeck and D. H. Lawrence have sentence–length averages near the Ellegård norm.

The next thing to look for is how much variation there is when we look at individual paragraphs and sentences. There is quite a lot, and hence there is some style modulation within the passage. Paragraph 1, and each of its individual sentences, is close to the average. Paragraph 2, on the other hand, is more than a third above the norm for the passage as a whole, and its middle sentence (5), is 54 words long. Paragraph 3, although close to the average for the passage, has more dramatic variation from sentence to sentence. Sentence (8) is rather short (15 words), and (9) is the longest sentence of the extract (74 words). Paragraph 4's average is about a third below that for the passage, but if we look at its constituent sentences we find that the first two are about the average, while the last one is dramatically short (four words).

This very short sentence, coming at the end of the more complex description, is foregrounded through internal deviation (see 2.2.7). Appropriately, it is also rhetorically important. It has a climactic and summative effect: the moment everyone has been waiting for has finally arrived.[5]

The overall pattern for the major word classes is close to the Ellegård norm, but the proportion of adjectives is higher than the norm, presumably because this is a descriptive passage. The proportion of adjectives drops fairly dramatically in the last paragraph, suggesting less description there. The only other salient feature would appear to be the rather low proportion of main verbs in paragraph 2 and by far the highest proportion in 3, suggesting a description/action contrast between those parts of the text.

11.4.3 Lexis

Although there are also a number of quite common words, the lexis of the extract is fairly complex and rarefied. There is specialised vocabulary for the musical instruments and food in particular, and a number of words have foreign, and thus exotic connotations (*hors d'oeuvres, harlequin, Castile*). There is relatively little lexical repetition, and this suggests that a large number of different things are being referred to, as Fitzgerald gives the feeling of an exciting, ever-changing scene.

As there is not much repetition, those lexical items which are repeated will stand out. They relate to vision, drink, music and social interaction: *colour, bar, cordials, orchestra, chatter, laughter, group*. Most of the vocabulary at the beginning of the passage refers to concrete things: the food, the drink and the instruments of the orchestra, but later there are more abstract nouns, mainly describing social interaction. Many of the words in the passage have striking visual properties (*e.g. coloured lights, glistening, harlequin designs, dark gold, gaudy with primary colours, yellow cocktail music*) or associations of grandeur and the good life (*e.g.* the foreign words already mentioned and *orchestra, salons, cocktails*).

This party seems to be mainly peopled by women. It takes place at Gatsby's house, but Gatsby does not appear. The orchestra leader is the only male specifically referred to, and many nouns referring or alluding to people are not gender-specific (*cf. caterers, swimmers*). On the other hand, there are *female guests* in sentence (3), *women* in (6), *girls* in (9) and the extended description of the girl who dances out on the canvas

platform in (10) and (11). The references to hair–style and dress
in (5) also appear to be related to the female guests. Nick, the
narrator, is a young male, and so may be expected to notice
the opposite sex more than his own, and we also know that
Gatsby's purpose in throwing the parties is to attract a
particular woman.

Beside the marked opulence there are also a number of
words in the first two paragraphs which suggest the grand
scale in terms of quantity (*corps of caterers, several hundred feet of*
canvas, a whole *pitful of oboes* . . . , *cars* . . . *parked five deep*).

Our lexical description has so far concentrated almost
exclusively on the nouns and adjectives. If we now look at the
verbs, we find that the vast majority of main verbs are
dynamic, helping to give a sense of continual movement and
change to the passage: 69.6% of the main verbs are dynamic,
21.7% stative and 8.7% relate to cognition or perception. Not
only is movement on the agenda, but thought would appear
to be largely off it. Even what would normally be state
descriptions are portrayed in terms of movement. In the first
paragraph, for example, the hams are *crowded* against salads, and
the turkeys are *bewitched* to a dark gold. If we concentrate on
the dynamic verbs we find that an extremely high proportion
of them (68.8%) are intransitive. Because transitive verbs take
objects and intransitives do not, there is a tendency for
transitives to indicate purposeful, directed movement, whereas
intransitives appear more undirected. This gives rise to the
sense of purposeless action at the party, movement for the sake
of movement, a feature which becomes even more noticeable
if we look at the passage paragraph by paragraph. In the two
central paragraphs, which contain most of the description of
the general movement at the party, the proportion of
transitives within the set of dynamic verbs is only just over
25%. Ironically, for the description of the food the equivalent
figure is 50%, and for the last paragraph, which moves from
the general to describe the actions of the girl erroneously
named as Gilda Gray's understudy (and which we have already
noted as being contrastive in other ways), the figure is 42%.

Adverbs are usually the least represented of the major word
classes, and this passage is true to form, with the overall
average close to the norm. With such small totals, percentages
are less meaningful, and so I will give raw figures. The large
majority of the adverbs relate to three major semantic areas:
place (9), time (6) and manner (4). Given that there are so

many dynamic verbs the number of manner adverbs seems rather low, and is presumably related to the distanced viewpoint of the observer, who would not be able to make very fine discriminations in movement. There is also a sense in which we could combine the time and place adverbs. Together they represent changes of deictic focus, and so help to contribute to the feeling of constant change in the scene. This effect is even more marked when we note that, although only one sentence (the first in paragraph 4) begins with a focus–shifting adverb, when we take into account pre– positional phrases acting as adverbials inside clauses, we find that almost half of the sentences (including the first four), and three of the four paragraphs, begin with adverbials which switch time or place focus.

11.4.4   Grammar: sentence structure

All of the passage's sentences are statements, which corresponds with the its descriptive function. In spite of the comparatively high sentence–length average, the sentences are not particu-larly complex in the sense that we do not find many examples of clauses embedded inside other clauses. There is some sub-ordination, but it would appear that most of the complexity in the passage is occurring at phrase level.

To help show what is going on in terms of the grammatical structure of sentences in the text, I will first describe some basic sentence patterns which we can find in English, using some constructed examples:

Example 4
[1]   John loves Mary. (**simple sentence**)
[2]   John loves Mary and Mary loves John. (**coordination**)
[3]   John loves Mary; Mary loves John. (**parataxis**)
[4]   John loves Mary because Mary loves John.
       (**trailing structure**)
[5]   Because Mary loves John, John loves Mary.
       (**anticipatory structure**)
[6]   John, because Mary loves him, loves Mary.
       (**parenthetic structure**)

In [1], the simple sentence, there is only one clause. [2] effectively joins two simple sentences together with a coordin-ating conjunction ('and', 'or', 'but', 'so'), and the paratactic structure [3] juxtaposes the two main clauses together, with no linking conjunction at all.

Sentences [4]–[6] are all examples of **subordination**. A subordinate clause (*because Mary loves John*) is **embedded**, or **nested**, inside the main clause of which it is a part. In [4], with a trailing structure (see also Leech and Short 1981: 229–30, 238–9), the subordinate clause comes at the end of the main clause that it is nested in. In [5], with an anticipatory structure, it comes first (the embedded clause anticipates the rest of the sentence; see also Leech and Short 1981: 101–2). And in [6], with a parenthetic structure, it comes in the middle (the embedded clause could easily be placed in parentheses; see also Leech and Short 1981: 102).

The structures exemplified in sentences [2]–[4] are relatively easy to process when reading, as it is possible to understand the clauses in them 'one at a time'. Because of this the term 'trailing structure' can be used to refer to all three types. Structures like those in sentences [5] and [6], on the other hand, hold up the onset of one or more of the major constituents of the main clause. These sorts of structures, which are sometimes called **periodic** sentences, tend to be more difficult to process because to understand them properly we need to hold the anticipatory or parenthetical information in our heads until we get to the end of the main clause. As a consequence, these sorts of sentences are associated with style complexity and reading difficulty. The difficulty is not great in [5] and [6] because the sentences are short and only have two clauses, but if more anticipatory or parenthetic clauses were added, reading would become harder and harder. Consistent use of periodic sentence structures is often said to produce a **'tight style'**. We can see these two contrasting effects by comparing the structure of the part of the nursery rhyme 'This is the House that Jack Built' with an alternative way of structuring the same information:

Example 5
[1]   This is the dog that killed the cat that ate the rat.
[2]   This is the rat that the cat that the dog killed ate.

In [1] we start with the dog, and as a consequence get the following trailing construction involving the relative clauses post–modifying dog and cat:

This is the dog (that killed the cat (that ate the rat)).

There are two relative clauses, one embedded inside the other, and the most deeply embedded one comes at the end of the clause which it is embedded in. But in [2] we get a periodic structure:

This is the rat (that the cat (that the dog killed) ate).

This time the most deeply embedded relative clause comes in the middle of the other relative clause, producing a much more difficult reading experience.

The dominant pattern of clauses in *The Great Gatsby* passage would appear to be a series of main clauses coordinated together, or merely juxtaposed paratactically, along with the occasional subordinate clause. As a consequence, in spite of the length of some of the sentences, the passage is reasonably easy to read, because the predominant grammatical style is loose. Readers are thus likely to feel that Fitzgerald's style of writing is rather more demanding than that of Steinbeck or Lawrence, because his sentences are typically twice as long, but he will seem less complex and difficult than Virginia Woolf or Henry James. They typically produce a high proportion of anticipatory structures, whereas Fitzgerald makes consistent use of trailing structures.

This journey through the passage's sentence structure has shown us interesting things about Fitzgerald's general prose style, but, because what we have concentrated on is a pervasive aspect of the writing, it has told us less about textual meaning. However, if we look for unusual sentence structures and contrasts with the general pattern we can learn more about the meaning and effect of this particular passage. The last, summative, sentence is not only the shortest sentence by far. It is also the only simple sentence in the extract, making its contrastive effect greater. There is also an interesting effect in the penultimate sentence. Its first clause consists only of a noun phrase, *A momentary hush*. The semi–colon following the phrase indicates that it is intended to be construed as a clause, but there is no verb, the normal obligatory centre of clause structure. This startling effect is appropriate for, and hence to some extent *enacts*, the content expressed. An individual girl has stopped the rest of the party in its tracks, and this clause represents the hiatus and the moment of expectation before the orchestra leader changes the rhythm of the music to suit her dancing style, and everyone else takes her up as the topic of their mindless gossip. The party changes to conform to the girl's behaviour, and as a consequence integrates her into its pattern of mindless movement and variation.

11.4.5   Grammar: phrase structure

We have looked at how Fitzgerald constructs sentences with clausal building blocks. Now let us examine the phrases which constitute the building blocks of the clauses. We will begin with the verb phrases, as we have already discussed them to some extent when we looked at the effects associated with the stative/dynamic and transitive/intransitive patterns in the passage. In terms of aspect, the main verb phrases are mainly simple, or non–progressive[6] in type, and this feature of the text's structure, in alliance with the continual changes of focus mentioned earlier, helps to make the description appear to move quickly from one thing to the next rather than dwell on particular moments for a long time.

The other interesting feature of the verbs is the way in which the tense changes. The first paragraph, describing the *preparations* for the party, is in the past tense (*e.g. a corps of caterers came down*), and so integrates the party description with the default narrator tense for this particular novel (and for English novels in general). But at the beginning of the second paragraph, which describes the *prelude* to the party, as the guests arrive and get ready, the tense switches to the present perfect (*e.g. the orchestra has arrived*). In the middle of the second paragraph, when the guests begin to meet one another, there is another switch, to the present tense (*e.g. the bar is in full swing*). Hence, as we move through the preparatory stages to the socialising at the centre of the party we move from past to present, making us feel deictically that we are getting closer and closer to the action. The tense stays in the present until the very final, summation sentence, when it changes back to the present perfect. This is another way in which the final sentence of the passage is foregrounded.

Although the incidence of verbs in the passage is not high, 10% of the adjectives are participial adjectives (*e.g. changing light*), and in the last three paragraphs nearly 15% of the nouns (*e.g. chatter, laughter*) are also derived from verbs. This all helps to increase the feeling of continual movement and change in the description.

The most significant features relating to the noun phrases revolve around their occurrence in a series of long and distinctive 'and' coordinated list constructions (I have emboldened the coordinating conjunctions below):

> salads of harlequin designs **and** pastry pigs **and** turkeys bewitched to a dark gold (sentence 2)

> stocked with gins **and** liquors **and** with cordials so long forgotten that most of his female guests were too young to know one from another (sentence 3)

> a whole pitful of oboes **and** trombones **and** saxophones **and** viols **and** cornets **and** piccolos, **and** low **and** high drums (sentence 4)

> the halls **and** salons **and** verandas are gaudy with primary colours, **and** hair bobbed in strange new ways, **and** shawls beyond the dreams of Castile (sentence 5)

> chatter **and** laughter, **and** casual innuendo **and** introductions forgotten on the spot, **and** enthusiastic meetings between women who never knew each other's names (sentence 6)

> the sea–change of faces **and** voices **and** colour (sentence 9)

I will use the example from sentence (4) to show what is going on here, as it is the longest and, at the same time, one of the clearest examples. The head–word of the main noun phrase is *pitful*, and this head–word is post–modified by a long prepositional phrase beginning with *of* and consisting of a list of nouns coordinated together. The list is very long, with seven different kinds of instrument mentioned, one of which, the drum, is subdivided into two sub–types, high and low. The length of the list is itself very unusual, and increases the sense of copiousness in the description, and hence of the party's lavishness. But there are some other marked features too. Normally written lists in English (*e.g.* 'apples, pears and bananas') only separate the last two items by 'and'. The other items only have commas between them. But here, all of the items are separated by *and*. This has the effect of separating the items of the list further from one another than usual, a general effect which through inference we must make appropriate to the rest of the scene. My reaction is to feel that Nick watches the orchestra arrive not as one undifferentiated mass of players, but one instrument group at a time, thus helping to increase the grandeur of this representative party and his reaction to it and the other, similar, occasions.

You might like to compare my discussion of the list in sentence (4) with your impressions of the other lists with too many 'ands' above. Short (1986) contains a discussion of the meanings associated with various kinds of list construction, including this type.

All of the examples above exhibit list constructions with 'too many "ands" ', and so the feature becomes a pervasive aspect of the description. Moreover, the nouns which are listed together in this way are generic, plural, or both. This is another way in which the size and grandeur of the parties are emphasised. As the party progresses, the areas referred to in the lists change – from objects to people to insignificant social chatter – thus helping to establish the narrator's critical attitude, which pervades the description, even though it is not expressed directly. We have noticed in other areas of analysis that the last paragraph contrasts with the others. The same is true of the noun phrases. With the description of the young woman who dances alone on the canvas platform, we move from generic, pluralised description to individual reference. This change to the specific is the main reason for the series of contrasts which we have noted between the last paragraph and the others.

11.4.6   Cohesion and coherence

We have already noted that there is relatively little lexical repetition to link parts of the text together. Similarly, there is also little use of pronouns to create patterns of linked reference to one person or thing, and little use of **elegant variation** (where alternative expressions are used to refer to the same individual or thing). These infrequencies, which would be made clear by a complete statistical examination of the passage, are all connected with the effect of constant change and movement which we have noted on a number of occasions. And this area of linguistic organisation also produces another contrast between the last paragraph and the rest. The dancing girl is referred to both through elegant variation *and* pronominal reference (*confident girls . . . one of these gypsies . . . her*).

There are also no explicit cohesive links like *and*, *but*, or *therefore* to link sentences together. This adds to the effect of constant change. The paragraph–initial changes of time focus (*At least once a fortnight. . . By seven o'clock . . . Suddenly*) help to structure the various phases of the party which I have already referred to, but this does seem to be a description where most of the onus to find coherence in what is happening is on the reader.

11.4.7 'Poetic features'

Although this is a prose passage, it exhibits two features which we typically associate with poetry: alliteration and metaphor. These aspects of the text's structure help to highlight aspects of the description of the party which we have already mentioned. The first two sentences contain a number of alliterative patterns based on word–initial /k/ and /g/ which emphasise the copiousness and glamour of the party we have seen in other aspects of this analysis: *corps of caterers . . . Christmas tree of Gatsby's enormous garden . . . garnished with glistening hors d'oeuvres . . .'.*

Turning to the metaphors, the turkeys are *bewitched to a dark gold* instead, more mundanely, of being baked brown. Inanimate aspects of the party are often portrayed as being as alive as the guests through a pattern of animising metaphors (*spiced baked hams crowded against salads* (2), *floating rounds of cocktails permeate the garden . . . the air is alive* (6)), and the people are portrayed as groups which have a 'life' of their own (*The groups change . . . swell . . . dissolve and form . . .'* (9).

The playing of the orchestra is connected to the gaudy visual scene by a synaesthetic metaphor melding together sight and sound (*yellow cocktail music* (7)), and the interfusion of the music and the rest of the party is then continued with a set of metaphors, intertwined in one clause, portraying the meaningless talk of the partygoers as if it were music (*the opera of voices pitches a key higher* (7)). Finally, the young girl who emerges from anonymity and dances onto the platform at the end of the description is foregrounded through the reference to her dress, *in trembling opal* (10) which involves a com–bination of metonymy and metaphor. The dress cannot literally be made out of a precious stone; the reference to opal is metonymic of the dress's colour. In addition, neither opals nor dresses are normally capable of trembling. The metaphoric description cleverly links the glamour of the occasion, the dress shimmering as the girl dances, with the suggestion that she is nervous, and so trembling, as she moves out into the limelight.

11.4.8   Aspects of irony in the passage

There is no thought presentation in the scene as it would be inappropriate in the distanced description of a rather insignificant party. There is some reference to speech, but what individual characters say or what words they use to say it, is never revealed. We are merely told (see paragraphs 2 and 3) that speech occurred between unidentified people, perhaps with some kind of indication of the speech acts involved. Sentence (6) is the clearest representative of this trend. In the last paragraph we do get a kind of generalised indirect speech, when we are told that the news goes around that the dancing girl is Gilda Gray's understudy. But this Indirect Speech appears to be a summary of the common thread of a large number of conversations.

The speech presentation patterns indicate some of the ironic flavour of the passage. In novels we expect to be told what characters say, and the fact that we are given such imprecise and distanced representations of the speech helps us to infer that what is said is shallow. What speech 'content' that is reported is clearly ironic. The end of sentence (6) indicates the mismatch between socialite conversation and personal relations: *introductions forgotten on the spot and enthusiastic meetings between women who never knew each other's names*. We are also explicitly told in sentence (11) that the *news* about the dancing girl being Gilda Gray's understudy is false.

Although all the reference to people in this passage is in the third person, the fact that the description is by a first–person narrator is important in helping us to recognise the ironic character of the description. We can see this in the way that assumptions are embedded in the text. The erroneous news about the girl being *Gilda Gray's understudy from the Follies* is one example. The Follies was a place of light entertainment with dancing girls, and so the allusion which attracts everybody's interest is to a rather insignificant aspect of

American culture, and the reference to Gilda Gray suggests that she was someone famous, but as far as I know, this person is merely an invention of Fitzgerald's. Another example is the phrase *a bar with a real brass rail* in sentence (1), which interestingly 'engineers' the reader's assumptions. It appears designed to cancel a possible presupposition which otherwise would probably not have entered our heads, that the bar might have a *false* brass rail, thus introducing a discordant note into the description of the party. Similar things can be said of the orchestra being described as *no five piece affair*. Once we have noticed these ironic notes, other parts of the description can be construed in a similar light. The orchestra plays *yellow cocktail music*, a striking synaesthetic metaphor linking bright colour and trivial sound together. The alliterating *pastry pigs* can be seen as false as well as clever, and the *turkeys bewitched to a dark gold* can have associations of trickery as well as magic. The turkeys have presumably been roasted, and *bewitched* is a rather fanciful way of alluding to the cooking process. The phrase is thus lexically deviant, and *dark gold* is unusual as well, helping to foreground the note of falseness. In sentence (5) the shawls of the women are described as *beyond the dreams of Castile*, and this also seems rather odd, as concrete items of fashionable dress are being described in terms of abstractions out of all proportion to their importance.

The party described in this scene is large, opulent and superficially extremely attractive. But, as we have seen, Nick's description of it is also imbued with irony throughout. Although at first sight everything is captivating, the more we look, the more we discover that the lavishness hides under its veneer an emptiness which permeates the social whirl, leading us finally to feel pity rather than envy for the bright thought–less world of the socialites. This correlation between wealth and emptiness is emblematic of Gatsby, the lavish host who has everything except the woman he loves, and contrasts dramatically with the evocation of the dull and dismal world of the poor characters with which Gatsby and Nick also interact.

11.5 Concluding remarks

We began this chapter with a general discussion of style before embarking on a description of the text style of *The Great*

Gatsby passage. Our analysis has been quite detailed and hence long. You may feel that it has been exhausting as well as exhaustive, but it has needed to be detailed in order to capture the organisation and nuances of what is clearly a subtle and carefully engineered piece of writing. Indeed, there are even more aspects which I could have explored if there had been time. I have concentrated on the more salient features, and hope to have shown that the apparently straightforward process of reading and understanding a piece of writing is in fact complex and interesting. Looking at writing in this kind of detail helps to reveal important aspects which might otherwise have gone unnoticed, and it also provides detailed and interesting ways of testing out or supporting critical hypotheses about style and meaning which we may have arrived at through our initial reading.

Exercise 2

Analyse one or more of the following short story openings:

The first paragraph of Joseph Conrad's 'The Secret Sharer';
The first three paragraphs of 'Odour of Chrysanthemums' by D. H. Lawrence;
The first two paragraphs of Henry James's 'The Pupil'.

Discussion of exercises

Exercise 1
No 'answers' are possible here as I cannot know which extracts you will analyse.

Exercise 2
You can compare your findings for all three passages with Leech and Short (1981: Ch. 3). Nash (1982) also analyses the opening of 'Odour of Chrysanthemums'.

Notes

1. Hendricks (1976: Ch. 7) contains an interesting comparison of a passage by James Fenimore Cooper and a rewrite of it by Mark Twain.

2. The notion of 'mind style' is first discussed in Fowler (1977: 76 and 103–13), and is developed in Leech and Short (1981: Ch. 6) and Bockting (1994). Short (1994) is an introductory account.
3. See Hendricks (1976: Ch. 5)
4. See Butler (1985).
5. A similar contrastive effect involving a short, summative sentence is discussed in Leech and Short (1981: 85–6).
6. Aspect is discussed in most grammars of English, for example Leech, Deuchar and Hoogenraad (1982: 66–8) and Quirk and Greenbaum (1973: 40–58).

Further reading

There are analyses of three passages from the beginnings of short stories in Leech and Short (1981: Ch. 3). Fowler (1986: Chs 5, 6) and Toolan (1990: Chs 3–11) cover areas related to this chapter, and Halliday (1971) contains an advanced and influential discussion of passages from William Golding's *The Inheritors*. See note 2 for reading on mind style and world view. If you are interested in statistical techniques for linguistic analysis, Butler (1985) is an accessible introduction.

CHECKSHEET 10: STYLE FEATURES OF NARRATIVE DESCRIPTION

This checksheet (which is derived from the checklist in Leech and Short 1981: 75–82) covers three major areas: lexis, grammar, and textual cohesion and coherence. If it involves terms or areas of work you are not familiar with, please refer to the further reading at the end of Chapter 1. There is not space in this book to provide a comprehensive account of these areas in English.

A. Lexis

General

Examine the open class (lexical or meaning–carrying) words in the text.

(a) Is the vocabulary simple or complex (*i.e.* many or few syllables or morphemes in each word)? Is it descriptive or evaluative? Is it general or specific?

(b) Does the writer make greatest use of referential or denotative (central/core) meanings, or do you have to think about connotations or other emotive associations of the words?

(c) Are there idioms in the text (*i.e.* non–literal phrases, such as *under the weather*)? If so, are they associated with a particular register or dialect?

(d) Are there any unusual words – archaic, rare or specialised vocabulary?

(e) Do the words fall into groups which form noticeable semantic fields?

Examine the closed class words (*i.e.* grammatical words: pronouns, prepositions, conjunctions, determiners, auxiliaries, interjections). Do they play any significant role in the text?. Is there frequent or striking use of, for example, the first–person pronouns ('I', 'we'), negative words ('no', 'not', 'neither') or the definite or indefinite article ('the', 'a(n)')?

Specific

(a) NOUNS. Are they abstract or concrete? If abstract, do they refer to similar kinds of element, *e.g.* events, perceptions, processes, moral qualities, social qualities? Are there proper names or collective nouns?

(b) ADJECTIVES. Do they occur frequently? What kinds of attributes do they embody (physical, emotional, visual, colour, etc.)? Do they occur in comparative or superlative forms? Do they occur singly or in groups?

(c) VERBS. How frequently do they occur? Are they linking, transitive or intransitive? Are they stative (referring to states) or dynamic (referring to actions, events)? Do they refer to physical movement, psychological states or activities, perception, etc.? Are there more finite (complete–sense) verbs, or more participles (present or past)?

(d) ADVERBS. Do they occur frequently? What kinds of meaning do they have (*i.e.* do they describe manner, place, direction, frequency, degree etc.)? Do they occur in comparative or superlative forms?

B: Grammar

General

Are any general types of grammatical construction used to special effect, *e.g.* comparative or superlative constructions, parallelisms, listing, interjections or other speech–like phenomena?

Specific

(a) SENTENCES. Are they statements, questions, commands, etc. or are they like 'speech sentences', *e.g.* without a finite main verb? Are they simple, compound or complex? How long are they? Are there striking contrasts in sentence length or structure at any point in the text? If the sentences are long, is their length due to the embedding of clauses inside one another, coordination of clauses, long phrases acting as single clause elements (like subject or object), or other reasons?

(b) CLAUSES. What types of clauses are noticeably favoured (*e.g.* relative, adverbial, noun clauses etc.)? Is there anything special about the clauses, *e.g.* a frequent and unusual placement of adverbials, or 'fronting' of object or complement? Are there clauses with 'dummy subjects' (*i.e.* 'there', 'it')?

(c) PHRASES

  (i) NOUN PHRASES: are they simple or complex? If complex, is this due to the frequency of pre–modifiers (adjectives, noun–modifiers, etc.) or is it due to post–modification (prepositional phrases, relative clauses, complement clauses, etc.)?

  (ii) VERB PHRASES: what is the tense? present or past? Are there sections of apparent narration where the tense is other than the simple past tense (*e.g.* continuous past, present, perfect, or where modal auxiliaries such as 'can', 'must', 'should', etc. occur)?

  (iii) OTHER PHRASES: are there any remarkable features about other phrases (*i.e.* prepositional, adverbial, adjectival)?

C. Cohesion and coherence

(a) COHESION

  (i) Does the text contain logical or other links between sentences (*e.g. and, or, but, and so, then* etc.) or does it rely on implicit connections (*e.g.* juxtaposition, sequence)?

  (ii) Is there a lot of *cross–reference* by means of pronouns or ellipsis? Or is there 'elegant variation' – the use of different ways of describing the same thing/person (so as to avoid repetition or to give you an idea of whose view of the thing/person you are getting)?

  (iii) Are meaning connections made by means of lexical repetition or by the frequent use of words from the same semantic field?

(iv)   Are any of these factors of interest in the 'interaction' between the author/narrator and the reader?

(b)   COHERENCE

    (i)   Are there any portions of the text which are not overtly cohesive, where the reader has to supply coherence by inferencing work? If so, what effects are associated with this?

CHAPTER 12

Bringing it all together

12.1 Introduction

I now want to pick up a theme which has run through this book, namely that modes of analysis which work well for one literary genre also give us interesting insights into texts from the other genres. Although the three genres can be distinguished in general terms from one another through (i) reference to their different prototypical discourse structures (see 2.2.1, 6.2 and 9.2) and (ii) some prototypical language features (for example the fact that poetry is written in lines and typically has a high density of metaphor and other rhetorical figures), there are many texts which have mixed genre characteristics. We tend to think of prose as narrative, but it also contains a lot of the interactional discourse which we associate primarily with drama, and quite a lot of poems have interactive patterns too. Some plays, in spite of being composed of dialogue, consist largely of poetry, Elizabethan and Jacobean drama being obvious examples. It is to these 'mixed' genre texts which we will now turn. I will provide extended analyses of (i) a scene from a poetic drama, *Macbeth*, and (ii) an extract from a short story, Somerset Maugham's 'The Force of Circumstance', which consists almost entirely of character–character interaction.

One of the reasons for providing these extended analyses in addition to the one I have presented in Chapter 11 is to show how the various aspects of the stylistic approach can be brought together to explore different kinds of texts. Another reason is to help you, through demonstration, to do extended analytical work yourself. So before presenting my analyses I will first make some general points about stylistic analysis and how to go about it.

12.2 How to go about a stylistic analysis

12.2.1 Why bother?

A question my students often ask is 'Why bother to do stylistic analysis when you can just read literature and enjoy it?' A related question (sometimes almost an accusation) is 'Doesn't analysing literature spoil the wonder of it: once you've done stylistic analysis, how can you ever read literary texts for pleasure?'

Knowing how to analyse the language of literary texts certainly doesn't spoil them for me. On the contrary, the more I know about how a good piece of writing works the more I appreciate it, not less. I understand better how many complex things the writer has controlled and brought together to form a successful whole. The view that analysing literature inexorably spoils it is a romantic view which just does not hold up under scrutiny. We all know more about the meteorological conditions which generate beautiful sunsets than people from earlier centuries, but this knowledge does not stop the feeling of awe when we walk over the top of a hill and are confronted by an orange sun sliding slowly into a blazing sea.

I certainly don't find that knowing about the linguistic control of viewpoint, say, gets in my way of enjoying novels. I can be transported by a piece of writing as much as the next person. And through analysis I can also go on to understand and respond to pieces of good writing in a deeper way precisely because I appreciate in a more precise way how a particular writer has succeeded at something I know I could never manage.

Analytical understanding is one of the things which makes human beings special, and if you choose to *study* literature rather than just read it in your spare time, you commit yourself to rather more than curling up by a fire with a good book. Given that literature is written in language, once you decide to study literature, one of the things you also commit yourself to is the study of language in literary texts and how we interact with it (as well, of course, as other things, for example understanding the social conditions which helped to produce particular literary works). To study painting without learning in a detailed way about how different colours, tones or textures can be produced, or about how the human observer interacts cognitively with perspective or with foregrounding would seem quixotic. The same is true of the study of the language in literary texts. It is not enough to say 'language study is difficult work, so I won't bother'. If we set out to do something and achieving that goal involves hard work, the logic of the situation demands that we just get on and do it.

12.2.2 How do I set about doing a stylistic analysis?

Hopefully, the experience of reading this book and understanding the areas we have explored will help you to try out different forms of analysis for yourself. The checksheets have been designed to help in this aim. But it will be useful to make some more general matters clear.

It is important that you make a distinction between analy-sing the text and writing up an account of it. When you analyse, it is important to be systematic. An enduring problem in literary criticism is that critics sometimes come to partial conclusions by concentrating on some aspects of a text to the exclusion of others. One reason for the checksheets in this book is to help you collect *all* the evidence that is in the text. This will probably also mean that you will need to work through the text one linguistic level at a time, to make sure that you don't miss out on important matters.

Going carefully through the checksheets will mean you collect some data which will turn out not to be of real interpretative interest. Clearly it would be sensible, when you write up your analysis, only to present the findings which are significant, in the sense that they bear reasonably directly on your account of the text. This does *not* mean only presenting findings which support your interpretation. You will also need to take into account significant details or patterns which appear to work against your view. As a consequence, you may modify your interpretation, or admit finally that you can't successfully integrate interpretatively what you discover.

Part of what is involved here is the logic of argument. But you are also presenting your findings to another human being, who needs to be taken into account. One aspect of helping your reader is the order in which you present information. Some students tend to let the process by which they did their original analysis dominate the writing–up of their research, presenting their findings in the order that they happened to discover them, and delaying the presentation of their interpretation to the final section of their essay. But this way of going about things has considerable disadvantages.

First, readers usually cope better with complex analysis if they already know how, in general terms, they are meant to organise the detailed information they receive. The easiest way to do this is to begin an essay by summarising your findings or the interpretative position you wish to take, and then proceed to the more detailed analysis. Your readers will then know where you are trying to lead them, and so be able to assess more easily how, and how well, the analyses you present relate to the general case. Your presentation of your detailed analytical findings then become a way of fleshing out the detail of your interpretation as well as substantiating the view you are arguing for.

Secondly, once you have decided to begin with a general account of your interpretation, it makes good sense to order your stylistic information so that *the areas which bear most directly on that interpretation come first*, and areas more indirectly related come later. Generally, there is good sense in dealing with more meaningful levels of linguistic organisation, like lexis and pragmatics, early on in your essay, leaving areas less intrinsically meaning–related, like phonetic structure, to later. But the main organising factor should be putting first what happens to be most salient, even if on some occasions that does turn out to be phonetic or graphological structure.[1]

12.2.3 Isn't it less objective if my interpretation comes first and my analysis second?

The short answer is no. The idea that you can do your analysis in some mechanically objective way and have your interpretation pop out at the end of it in some automatic way does not hold up under examination. If you analyse a text you cannot help but read it, and if you read it you cannot help but understand it. You could get someone else to do the analysis and then work out some findings on the basis of that analysis, but the analysis done by the other person would itself be based on understanding (for example, you can't parse sentences accurately without understanding them), and it is difficult to see how you could draw conclusions from the analysis without having some initial understanding of the text.

Objectivity comes not from the order in which you do things, but in being systematic and careful in your argument, not overlooking unhelpful facts, and, in more general terms, constructing a clear and detailed relationship between your interpretative hypothesis on the one hand and your analysis on the other. Note also that 'objective' does not mean 'true for all time'. Physical scientists, who are often held up as paragons of objectivity, also change their minds over the interpretation of their data, particularly when new aspects, previously undiscovered or overlooked, are taken into account. So it is with stylistic analysis. No analysis is entirely objective in the sense that it is true for all time. The discovery of new forms of analysis will always throw up new findings; and as meaning is generated through the interaction between texts and their readers, they will always be open to reinterpretation.

In making our analyses as open, clear and well argued as we can make them, we put in place the foundations on which others will be able to build, sometimes leading to new and interesting interpretations which would have been difficult to establish without that initial work. There is nothing dis–honourable in turning out to be mistaken or only half–right, as long as the analysis you present is systematic, clear and well argued. This is what learning, and taking part in the co–operative enterprise of academic research, is all about.

12.3 Lady Macbeth tries to calm Macbeth

In the scene we are about to examine, Macbeth returns to his wife immediately after murdering King Duncan and his grooms. Not surprisingly, he is disturbed by the experience:

Example 1
Macb: I have done the deed. Didst thou not hear a noise?
Lady M: I heard the owl scream and the crickets cry.   (15)

Did not you speak?

Macb: When?

Lady M: Now.

Macb: As I descended?

Lady M: Ay.

Macb: Hark!

Who lies i' th' second chamber?

Lady M: Donalbain.

Macb: This is a sorry sight.   (20)

[*Looking on his hands.*]

Lady M: A foolish thought to say a sorry sight.

Macb: There's one did laugh in's sleep, and one

cried, 'Murder!'

That they did wake each other. I stood and

heard them;

But they did say their prayers, and address'd them

Again to sleep.

Lady M: There are two lodg'd together.   (25)

Macb: One cried 'God bless us', and 'Amen' the other,

As they had seen me with these hangman's hands.

List'ning their fear, I could not say 'Amen'

When they did say 'God bless us!'

Lady M: Consider it not so deeply.   (30)

Macb: But wherefore could not I pronounce 'Amen'?

I had most need of blessing, and 'Amen'

Stuck in my throat.

Lady M: These deeds must not be thought

After these ways: so, it will make us mad.

Macb: Methought I heard a voice cry 'Sleep no more;   (35)

Macbeth does murder sleep' – the innocent sleep,

Sleep that knits up the ravell'd sleave of care,

The death of each day's life, sore labour's bath,

Balm of hurt minds, great nature's second course,

Chief nourisher in life's feast.

Lady M: What do you mean? (40)

Macb: Still it cried 'Sleep no more' to all the house;

'Glamis hath murdered sleep; and therefore Cawdor

Shall sleep no more – Macbeth shall sleep no more'.

Lady M: Who was it that thus cried? Why, worthy Thane,

You do unbend your noble strength to think   (45)

So brainsickly of things. Go get some water

And wash this filthy witness from your hand.

Why did you bring these daggers from the place?

They must lie there. Go carry them, and smear

    The sleepy grooms with blood.

Macb: I'll go no more: (50)

    I am afraid to think what I have done;

    Look on't again I dare not.

Lady M: Infirm of purpose!

    Give me the daggers. The sleeping and the dead

    Are but as pictures; 'tis the eye of childhood

    That fears a painted devil. If he do bleed,   (55)

    I'll gild the faces of the grooms withal,

    For it must seem their guilt.

                [*Exit. Knocking within.*]

Macb: Whence is that knocking?

    How is't with me, when every noise appalls me?

    What hands are here? Ha! they pluck out mine eyes.

    Will all great Neptune's ocean wash this blood   (60)

    Clean from my hand? No; this my hand will rather

    The multitudinous seas incarnadine,

    Making the green one red.

            Re–enter LADY MACBETH.

Lady M: My hands are of your colour; but I shame

    To wear a heart so white. [*Knock*] I hear a

                   knocking   (65)

    At the south entry; retire we to our chamber.

    A little water clears us of this deed.

    How easy is it then! Your constancy

    Hath left you unattended. [*Knock*] Hark! more

                   knocking.

    Get on your nightgown, lest occasion call us   (70)

    And show us to be watchers. Be not lost

    So poorly in your thoughts.

Macb: To know my deed, 'twere best not know myself.

                    [*Knock.*]

    Wake Duncan with thy knocking! I would thou

                couldst! [*Exeunt.*]

(William Shakespeare, Macbeth, II, ii, 14–74)

I will examine the extract by grouping my comments together under a series of linguistic headings, bringing out my characterisation of the scene through the analysis as it proceeds.

12.3.1   Verse structure

As we would expect for Shakespearean drama, the two main protagonists of the play, who are nobles, speak in verse in contrast with the prose of less important characters. The famous porter's scene, which immediately follows this one, is in prose. Lady Macbeth has just been soliloquising in verse at the point when Macbeth appears. However, the first part of the interchange between them has elliptical questions and immediate responses that are so short that the normal poetic form more or less disappears. This helps to point up the drama and urgency of the moment.

12.3.2   Discoursal and pragmatic structure

There are only two characters present, and so they are bound to have roughly equal numbers of turns. Their turn size in the passage as a whole is also similar. Macbeth has an average of 21.3 words per turn, and Lady Macbeth 19. This indication of their rough equality in terms of power is reinforced by the fact that neither character interrupts the other. There is a change in the course of the extract, however. Lady Macbeth's utterances are at first short, but get longer towards the end, as she begins to exercise some measure of control over her disturbed husband.

Macbeth appears unable to cope with the realisation of what he has just done, and Lady Macbeth struggles throughout the scene to get him back under control and achieve what is necessary to disguise their involvement in the murder of Duncan and his grooms. Macbeth has stupidly brought with him the daggers that he has used to commit the murder, and they need to be returned to help create the illusion that the grooms murdered Duncan. Lady Macbeth also needs to get Macbeth into a state of mind in which he can successfully pretend to everyone else that the grooms murdered Duncan and that he then killed the grooms in anger at their heinous 'crime'. It is when we turn to topic control, speech acts and patterns of initiation and response that we begin to uncover how these things are made clear.

In line 20 Macbeth looks in horror at his hands, which we infer must still be covered in the blood of those he has murdered. Lady Macbeth tries to take his mind off the awfulness of his deed, but does not succeed. We then move into a pattern of discourse where Lady Macbeth tries to interact with her husband, asking questions and issuing commands to try to get him to react. But for some time Macbeth does not respond to her, continually skip–connecting to his own previous utterances instead. This helps us to infer that for much of the scene Macbeth is so bound up in his own thoughts that he hardly notices his wife's presence. Lines (31–9) are representative of this pattern. Macbeth worries about not having been able to say *Amen*, and so gain God's blessing in response to the servant's ironic cry of *God Bless us* in his sleep just before Macbeth murdered him. Lady Macbeth tells her husband that he should not think of such things, but he clearly does not have control over what thoughts come unbidden into his mind. Lady Macbeth tries hard to affect Macbeth: she responds to what he says and at the same time tries to change his behaviour. But Macbeth acts as if he has not even heard her, indicating the psychological salience of his realisation of what he has done.

If we examine Lady Macbeth's turns from *A foolish thought to say a sorry sight* (21) onwards we can observe a pattern where she moves from indirect speech acts to more and more overt attempts to control Macbeth. *A foolish thought to say a sorry sight* is an indirect command. Lady Macbeth tells Macbeth to stop saying, and thinking, what he does merely by stating a precondition for the command which we can thus infer that she intends. She moves to a direct command in line (30), and back to an indirect one, along with the reason for her command in (33–4). Indirectness is clearly not forceful enough to have the desired effect, and the topic of her commands also means that she is acceding to Macbeth's topics and so trying to control the uncontrollable, his thoughts. In (40) she asks a question about the meaning of what Macbeth says, which in essence has the same difficulties as her previous strategy, and, as with her previous attempts, it is not at all obvious that Macbeth even notices what she has said.

It is not until her speech in lines (44–50) that Lady Macbeth begins to get somewhere. This is her first speech of more than two lines. As before she asks a question about what Macbeth has said, and tells him not to think in the way that he does. But she then attempts to change his mind–set by trying to get him to perform the physical actions which need to be done in the immediate future (take the daggers back, smear the grooms with blood and wash his own hands). Performing the actions would also move his attention away from his own preoccupations. In fact, Macbeth does not do what she says, but he does respond to her at last: a considerable step forward for Lady Macbeth in her attempt to gain control over the situation.

Lady Macbeth does not manage to get Macbeth back to normal in this scene. He directly refuses to take the daggers back to Duncan's bed–chamber, and is still worrying over what he has done when she leads him to their bed–chamber to wash his hands at the end of the scene. But at least he is now taking notice of her, and of external events like the knocking at the door; and he does apparently perform some of the actions she orders him to. Given that there is no specific indication that he does not obey her, we must assume that he does put on his nightgown when she tells him to. And more importantly, Lady Macbeth does manage to get Macbeth to give her the daggers and set up the murder scene in a way which will disguise Macbeth's guilt.

When Lady Macbeth exits briefly at line (57) to replace the daggers, Macbeth is left on his own. The soliloquy he then engages in is highly interactive in structure. He continually asks himself questions, both about external events and his own situation and state of mind. Sometimes he answers his own questions and sometimes not. This interactive quality, and the exclamatory utterance he uses, indicate how much his mind is still disturbed in spite of his wife's interventions. When Lady Macbeth returns, she suggests that everything is now sat–isfactorily arranged. But although Macbeth's two–line speech which ends the scene is less discoursally disturbed than his soliloquy, and takes account of externals in that he reacts to the noise of someone knocking at the door, it is still essentially an introspective examination of his state of mind. He is still self–obsessed.

12.3.3 Point of view and speech presentation

If we examine Macbeth's speeches, we can see his obsessive preoccupation with his murder of Duncan in terms of viewpoint relations. In *This is a sorry sight* (20) Macbeth uses the proximal deictic *this* to refer to the state of his hands. Lady Macbeth and the audience can infer what he means by this because his hands are covered in blood. But there is no real attempt on Macbeth's part to take account of his wife and make things clear for her, presumably because he is already taken over entirely by the enormity of what he has done. Similarly, in line (22) *There's one did laugh in's sleep and one cried 'Murder!'*, the two referents for *one* are not made clear by Macbeth. For the audience these ambiguous features of Macbeth's speech will help to enact the disjointedness and uncertainty of the scene and Macbeth's disturbed state.

Another indication of the dramatic effect that his memory of the murder has on him is that Macbeth reports what the grooms said in their sleep, and also the mysterious voice that cried *Sleep no more; Macbeth does murder sleep,* in the fullest and most dramatic form of speech presentation, Direct Speech. Indeed, when he reports the utterance of the disembodied voice (which appears to be his conscience talking), the re-mainder of the utterance is a long series of noun phrases, all of which are in apposition to the quoted word *sleep* in spite of the fact that they occur outside the speech report. Macbeth's memories of the murder have so taken him over that they are inextricably interfused for him with the present moment.

12.3.4   Repetition, parallelism and metaphor

Most of Macbeth's speeches enact his remembrance of the murder, although he does not describe his murderous acts themselves, presumably because he cannot face up to them. Instead, he uses the vague and euphemistic word *deed* to refer to his killing of Duncan. He does repeat *murder*, but all three uses are in reports of what he has heard, and so are not conscious admissions of guilt on his part. One of these instances is a one–word quotation of what one of the sleeping grooms said (22). The other two, are metaphorical (*Macbeth does murder sleep* (45), *Glamis hath murdered sleep* (52)) and the product of the disembodied voice which Macbeth says he heard. The word *Sleep*, which is often, metaphorically and euphemistically, associated with death in our culture,[2] occurs eight times in Macbeth's speeches, an average of once every 34 words. There is one explicit parallel between sleep and death (*Sleep . . . The death of each day's life* (36–7)), but, interestingly, this parallel is disrupted when the disembodied voice suggests that Macbeth has murdered sleep. This metaphor plays instead on an alternative conceptual link between innocence and the ability to go to sleep. Lack of sleep is specifically related to guilt, and Macbeth repeats *murder sleep* twice and *sleep no more* four times. The other obvious patterns of repetition in Macbeth's speeches are also connected with his guilt feelings. We have already noted that he could not say *Amen* when one of the grooms said *God bless us*. In this short scene he repeats the phrase *God bless us* twice, and *Amen* four times. These words are all associated with God's forgiveness, and we can thus infer that the reason that Macbeth could not say *Amen*, and thus take part in the blessing unconsciously offered by the groom, was because of the strength of his feeling of guilt. Macbeth has not just murdered some men, although that might be thought bad enough. He has murdered his kinsman and his king. The Elizabethans assumed that the King was God's representative on earth (hence the phrase 'the divine right of Kings'). Killing the King thus implies possible eternal damnation for Macbeth, and so the issue of forgiveness is bound to be uppermost in his mind.

Macbeth's high repetition rate in semantic areas connected with death and guilt helps us to see how strongly his deeply troubled mind is fixed on what he has done. This is even more noticeable when we see that in the appositional structure mentioned above, there are extra references to sleep through elegant variation:

'. . . Macbeth does murder sleep' – the innocent sleep,
Sleep that knits up the ravell'd sleave of care,
The death of each day's life, sore labour's bath,
Balm of hurt minds, great nature's second course,
Chief nourisher in life's feast.

In addition to the appositions involving the word *sleep* itself, there are five more references to sleep through elegant variation.

The speech in which Macbeth declares that he has murdered innocent sleep, which I have re–quoted above, is full of metaphor as well as repeated reference, and the other metaphors he produces are also connected with the theme of guilt. In line (27) he says the grooms acted *As they had seen me with these hangman's hands*. But he has *stabbed* Duncan and the grooms, not hanged them. The hangman reference with its near deictic *these*, is thus more likely to be a psychologically induced allusion to his possible future execution for his heinous crime.

Lady Macbeth's utterances are, by and large, literal and unpoetic, thus forming a contrast with Macbeth's highly figurative speech. Interestingly though, the speech where she finally persuades Macbeth to take notice of her is also rich in figurative expressions:

> . . . Why, worthy Thane,
> You do unbend your noble strength to think
> So brainsickly of things. Go get some water
> And wash this filthy witness from your hand.

The word *brainsickly* is probably an original coinage of Shakespeare, thus making it strongly foregrounded for his audience. According to the *Oxford English Dictionary*, the compound adjective 'brain–sick' can be found in writings before Shakespeare, but *Macbeth* is the first quoted source of the adverb form. In addition, to bend strength is metaphorical, as the verb 'bend' would normally take an object which is both concrete and malleable. Shakespeare also negates the verb (*You do unbend your noble strength*). This suggests, rather unusually, that Macbeth's strength when he was murdering Duncan was already bent. One possible explanation for this is that the murder is being metaphorically related to using a bow and arrow. To fire the arrow, and hence kill, you have to bend the bow. If Macbeth unbends his strength, then, he is no longer in the right psychological frame for killing, or, by extension to carry on with the rest of the plan which he and his wife have agreed. Lady Macbeth's reflexive structure also implies that Macbeth has changed himself wilfully rather than that the change in him has been determined by outside circumstances.

The phrase *this filthy witness* is also metaphorical. It characterises the blood on Macbeth's hands as dirty and as an indication of his guilt at a possible future trial. This phrase in turn connects with Macbeth's earlier *these hangman's hands*. Thus Lady Macbeth's success in getting Macbeth to take notice of what she is saying here is not just related to her changed strategy, which we saw above, for ordering Macbeth to do things; it is also connected with her use of considerably more colourful and emotive language – language which will command Macbeth's attention and which, at the same time, indicates the strength of her own emotional involvement.

Macbeth's anguished introspective soliloquy which take place while Lady Macbeth is replacing the daggers is also, not surprisingly, full of metaphor. His own hands appear to him to take on a life of their own, being the subject of a dynamic verb which has himself as object: *Ha! they pluck out mine eyes*. The final part of this speech is very well known:

> . . . this my hand will rather
> The multitudinous seas incarnadine,
> Making the green one red.

The archaic verb 'to incarnadine' meant to make something red, but the *Oxford English Dictionary* tells us that from *Macbeth* onwards it took on specific connotations related to blood. These lines also contain an interesting example of style variation, where the same thing is first described in 'high style', Latinate terms, and then in a much more down to earth, or low, style. Adamson (1989) describes the effect of this style variation as follows:

> . . . Macbeth describes the bloodiness of his crime twice over; but whereas his initial formulation in H [high style] describes the magnitude of the act, the second, translating the same image into simple perceptual terms drawn from L [low style], seems rather to emphasize its unnaturalness.[3]

12.4 Doris begins to realise that she does not really know the man she has married

My final analysis will be of a conversation from a short story by Somerset Maugham. Guy, an Englishman, was born in Sembulu, part of Malaya, and works for the Sultan, as his father did before him. On leave in England he meets Doris, asks her to marry him after a month's acquaintance, and takes her back with him to Sembulu. Doris is at first very happy in her new life, but in this scene she begins to realise that her new husband is the father of a child through a relation with a native Malay woman (in fact they have three children). At the end of the story Doris decides to return to England, and Guy re–installs the Malay woman and their three children back in the bungalow, where they lived before her arrival. At the beginning of this extract Doris's servant–boy suddenly goes towards the door:

Example 2

(1) 'What is it?' she asked.

(2) '*Tuan* just coming.'

(3) He went out to take Guy's hat from him. (4) His quick ears had caught the footsteps before they were audible to her. (5) Guy did not as usual come up the steps immediately; he paused, and Doris at once surmised that the boy had gone down to meet him in order to tell him of the morning's incident. (6) She shrugged her shoulders. (7) The boy evidently wanted to get his story in first. (8) But she was astonished when Guy came in. (9) His face was ashy.

(10) 'Guy what on earth's the matter?'

(11) He flushed a sudden hot red.

(12) 'Nothing. (13) Why?'

(14) She was so taken aback that she let him pass into his room without a word of what she had meant to speak of at once. (15) It took him longer than usual to have his bath and change his clothes and luncheon was served when he came in.

(16) 'Guy,' she said, as they sat down, 'that woman we saw the other day was here again this morning.'

(17) 'So I've heard,' he answered.

(18) 'The boys were treating her brutally. (19) I had to stop them. (20) You must really speak to them about it.'

(21) Though the Malay understood every word she said, he made no sign that he heard. (22) He handed her the toast.

(23) 'She's been told not to come here. (24) I gave instructions that if she showed herself again she was to be turned out.'

(25) 'Were they obliged to be so rough?'

(26) 'She refused to go. (27) I don't think they were any rougher than they could help.'

(28) 'It was horrible to see a woman treated like that. (29) She had a baby in her arms.'

(30) 'Hardly a baby. (31) It's three years old.'

(32) 'How d'you know?'

(33) 'I know all about her. (34) She hasn't the least right to come here pestering everybody.'

(35) 'What does she want?'

(36) 'She wants to do exactly what she did. (37) She wants to make a disturbance.'

(38) For a little while Doris did not speak. (39) She was surprised at her husband's tone. (40) He spoke tersely. (41) He spoke as though all this were no concern of hers. (42) She thought him a little unkind. (43) He was nervous and irritable.

(W. Somerset Maugham, 'The Force of Circumstance')

Just before this passage begins Doris has seen the house–boy mistreat a woman with a baby who had apparently come to the house. Doris had reprimanded him, and this explains her surmise in sentences (5)–(7) that the Malay boy wanted to get to Guy first to give his side of the story before she could talk to Guy. In the rest of the passage Doris questions Guy about the incident. A woman who wants to see good in everything, she is puzzled, and somewhat upset, by the incident and her husband's reaction to it. But has not yet grasped the significance of what she has seen. Expecting some development in the plot, by the end of this passage the reader will suspect strongly that Guy has had a sexual relationship with the Malay woman, and is likely to see Doris, who has led a sheltered life in England, as rather naïve. Her eventual decision to return to England is a consequence of the fact that she cannot come to terms with the situation, rather than a moral decision in favour of the Malay woman and her children.

12.4.1 Style

The average sentence length in this passage is an exceptionally short 6.2 words. This low average is in part a consequence of the to and fro of the conversation between the characters, but if we examine the narrative sentences not involved in speech presentation, the average is still only 11.1 words per sentence, nearly half the Ellegård norm referred to in Chapter 11. With sentences as brief as this, there is little room for complexity in sentence, clause or phrase structure.

On the evidence of this story, Maugham's prose style is very simple and straight–forward. The vocabulary is also concrete and down–to–earth, helping to give a low–key air to the passage. In spite of the fact that important issues are beginning to be aired here, there is none of the high emotion, anguish and metaphorical density which we saw in the passage from

Macbeth. We could interpret this overall difference in style (i) as a consequence of the fact that the newly married couple still do not really know one another very well, (ii) as a function of the reservedness of the English ('not in front of the servants'), or (iii) as a result of a combination of these factors.

12.4.2   Discourse structure

Doris and Guy both have seven turns in their interaction. Doris has an average of 10.1 words per turn and Guy 11.9, indicating little difference in power. Neither character inter-rupts the other, in spite of the tension of the scene, adding to the reserved atmosphere.

However, it is clear that Doris consistently initiates in the conversational exchanges and Guy responds, indicating his defensive position. The only time he initiates is in sentence (13), *Why?*, a question which she does not answer because she is so taken aback. He does not wait for an answer, but goes straight to his room, suggesting that he would prefer not to be taking part in the conversation at all.

Most of the time Doris asks Guy questions about what happened in the incident with the Malay woman, but sentence (20) is an indirect command uttered with some force through the modal verb and attitudinal adverb of *must really*. Sentences (28–9), are ambiguous. They could be statements, but could also be interpreted as accusations because they indicate an attitude of disapproval on Doris's part. Throughout, Doris controls the topic and Guy acquiesces. For a woman who has so far been very happy in her new life, this discoursal pattern marks a considerable contrast with her previous attitude.

12.4.3   Speech and thought presentation and viewpoint

The conversation is presented consistently in Direct Speech, and with minimal use of reporting clauses. The reporting clauses which do occur have neutral, unemotional verbs (*asked, answered*) and no adjectives or adverbs to indicate high emotion. This helps us to feel that we are perceiving the upset between husband and wife without any narratorial intervention, and that although the issue between Doris and Guy is serious it is treated in a very 'civilised' way.

Guy and Doris 'speak' in a variety close to written English. There is some minimal suggestion of the characteristics of spoken English through elliptical sentence constructions (*e.g. Nothing.* and *Hardly a baby.*), and spelling contractions (*I've, d'you*) but no indication of dialect features or normal non–fluency. The speech of the Malay boy, on the other hand, is dialectally marked. It contains a Malay word *tuan,* which is italicised to show that it is not English, and the absence of an auxiliary verb also suggests a non–native speaker of English.

In spite of the apparently objective and unemotional character of the Direct Speech, the sentences of narration indicate that the scene is being presented to us from Doris's point of view, and to some extent we see inside her mind. On the other hand, we get no indication of Guy's perspective, except through what he says. This will mean, other things being equal, that we are likely to sympathise with Doris.

The narration of Guy's arrival (3)–(9) is from Doris's viewpoint. The verb of sentence (3) indicates movement on the part of the servant away from Doris as deictic centre. Sentence (4) is ambiguous: it could be a fact told to us by the narrator or a Free Indirect representation of what Doris realises. The movement verb *come* and the iterative adverbial *as usual* of (5) are both appropriate for Doris's viewpoint, and the second part of the sentence is her Indirect Thought. After the description of Doris's external action in (6) we are presented with her Free Indirect Thought in (7). Sentence (8) gives us internal evidence of her state of mind.

Sentence (14) informs us about Doris's state of mind as well as action, and (15) is a summary of Guy's actions from Doris's viewpoint. Sentence (21) is ambiguous. It could be the narrator's statement about what the Malay boy knew or alternatively a Free Indirect representation of Doris's interpretation of what happens. Sentences (38)–(43) are also from Doris's viewpoint, and indeed the last four sentences of the extract would appear to be a Free Indirect representation of her thoughts.

Doris is the only protagonist whose thoughts are presented, and the fact that most of her thoughts are presented in the Free Indirect mode indicates that the narrator is sharing her attitudinal position. Given also that she is clearly being treated unreasonably (though perhaps not as unreasonably as the

Malay woman with whom she sympathises and whose position she has unknowingly usurped), there is a very marked indication of sympathy relations in the passage.

12.4.4 Pragmatics: conversational maxims

I have left until last the examination of the pragmatic relations between the utterances of the characters as they reveal most clearly Guy's defensive attitude to his wife's questioning. It is this defensiveness which suggests that he has something to hide, and that Doris's view of him as *a little unkind* is not critical enough. The easiest way to show this aspect of our intuitive understanding of the text is through Grice's theory of inference *via* conversational maxims outlined in 8.4.1. Guy consistently breaks the conversational maxims as he tries to hide the true situation from Doris. He lies once, and is 'economical with the truth' throughout.

It is clear from the way in which the servant rushes out to meet Guy and the ashy expression on Guy's face when he comes into the house that he is unhappy. So he breaks the maxims of quantity and quality when he answers *Nothing* to Doris's first question. From the preceding narrative information we know that he is lying, or in Grice's terms, breaking rather than flouting the quality maxim, which in turn prompts us to infer a reason for his uncooperative conversational behaviour. It is this, in conjunction with the fact that the Malay woman has a baby, that leads us to believe that Guy has probably had sexual relations with her.

In her next turn, Doris states that the woman has visited the house again, behaviour which clearly needs explanation. But instead of providing that explanation Guy again breaks the maxim of quantity by stating what Doris already knows. In his next two turns he does provide relevant information, explaining that he had given orders for her to be removed. But he breaks the quantity and relation maxims by not explaining *why* he gave the orders.

In (29) Doris refers to the *baby* the woman was carrying, and in his response Guy cancels her presupposition concerning babyhood by stating the child's age, which suggests that he has more detailed knowledge of the family than he would normally be expected to have. In this case, then, he gives *more* information than one would expect, which leads us to infer that he has accidentally given the game away. Doris picks up on this in her next question *How d'you know?* (32), and Guy then breaks the maxims of quantity and relation by saying that he knows *all about her*, thus avoiding a specific answer to the questions. The same is true of his response to Doris's final question.

Guy's conversational behaviour is fairly consistent. He avoids giving relevant information whenever he can. This pattern suggests to us that he has something to hide, and given that he is under stress, when he accidentally shows that he knows more about the Malay woman and her child than we would expect, we will infer that he has given instructions to keep them away from the house because he does not want his new wife to find out about his relationship with them.

We thus have different 'conversational' behaviour at different level's of the story's discourse structure. At the character level Guy is breaking maxims unostentatiously in order to hide the truth from Doris. His conversational strategy is not entirely successful as Doris realises something is not right, even if she cannot yet arrive at a full understanding of her husband's behaviour. Higher up the story's discourse structure, where there is no obvious need to maintain a distinction between narrator and narratee on the one hand and writer and reader on the other, we have enough information to deduce that Maugham is telling us that Guy is the father of the Malay woman's child. The fact that Doris has apparently not quite realised this yet reinforces the view, indicated elsewhere, that we are also intended to view her as the innocent and naive victim of events. This in turn helps to promote reader sympathy for her, and provide a plausible motivation for her eventual decision to return to England and effectively end the marriage.

12.5 Concluding remarks

In the two analyses of the extracts from *Macbeth* and 'The Force of Circumstance' I have employed to some degree almost all the forms of analysis outlined in this book. As I have said throughout, it should not be forgotten that techniques of analysis which work particularly well on literary texts from one genre will also be helpful to some degree in exploring texts from other genres, literary or non–literary. My account of the extracts, although fairly detailed, has not been exhaustive by any means. But it should have helped to demonstrate the processes we are involved in when we read (or listen) and understand with such apparent ease. Because our processes of understanding are so deeply inculcated they seem almost instinctive. It often appears that to understand a text is merely to look at it, much as we would look through a transparent window onto the world outside. But this apparently transparent process turns out to be both complex and interesting. And looking in on the way in which we interact with the language of literary texts helps us to learn not just about those interesting writings but, just as importantly, about ourselves.

Notes

1. For advice on how to go about the stylistic analysis of a poem, see Short (1993).
2. For a discussion of the 'death is sleep' metaphor, see Lakoff and Turner (1989: 18–19).
3. These lines are difficult for the unwary to parse and therefore act successfully. In the first clause *The multitudinous seas* is object to the verb *incarnadine*, and, in the second, *the green* is object to *Making*, with *one red* as its complement. *The green* is thus a general noun phrase referring back to *multitudinous seas*, all of which are green, and all of which become red as a consequence of Macbeth trying to wash the blood from his hand. This would seem to fit well with Macbeth's general attitude in the scene. However, it is possible to arrive at a parsing of the last clause, which is more usual in modern English, whereby *the green one* is object to *Making* and *red* is the complement. But this analysis induces the rather odd semantic consequence where one green sea, out of a set not all of which are green, is made red, an oddity which is also difficult to integrate into our overall interpretation of the scene. Actors beware!

APPENDIX

A list of English phonemes

The list of English phonemes below is based on Knowles (1987: 221-2).

Vowels

iː	reed	/riːd/	ə	the	/ðə/
i	rid	/rid/	ə	about	/əbaut/
e	red	/red/	ə	sofa	/soufə/
a	bad	/bad/	ei	raise	/reiz/
aː	shah	/ʃaː/	ou	rose	/rouz/
o	cod	/kod/	ai	rise	/raiz/
oː	law	/loː/	au	rouse	/rauz/
u	could	/kud/	oi	toy	/toi/
uː	mood	/muːd/	iə	beer	/biə/
ʌ	bud	/bʌd/	eə	there	/ðeə/
əː	bird	/bəːd/	uə	lure	/luə/

Consonants

p	pop	/pop/	s	sauce	/soːs/
b	bob	/bob/	z	zoos	/zuːz/
t	tight	/tait/	ʃ	sheep	/ʃiːp/
d	dead	/ded/	ʒ	leisure	/leʒə/
k	cake	/keik/	h	hat	/hat/
g	gag	/gag/	m	mime	/maim/
tʃ	church	/tʃəːtʃ/	n	noon	/nuːn/
dʒ	judge	/dʒʌdʒ/	ŋ	singing	/siŋiŋ/

f	fife	/faif/	l	lull	/lʌl/
v	van	/van/	r	rain	/rein/
θ	thirty	/θəːti/	j	yacht	/jot/
ð	then	/ðen/	w	will	/wil/

References

Abercrombie, D. (1965) A phonetician's view of verse structure. In *Studies in Phonetics and Linguistics*. London: Oxford University Press, 16–25.

Abercrombie, D. (1971) Some functions of silent stress. In A. J. Aitken, A. McIntosh and H. Pálsson (eds) *Edinburgh Studies in English and Scots*. London: Longman, 147–56.

Adamson, S. (1989) With double tongue: Diglossia, stylistics and the teaching of English. In M. Short (ed.) *Reading, Analysing and Teaching Literature*. London: Longman, 204–40.

Bateson, F. W. (1971) Literature and linguistics: Reply by F. W. Bateson. In R. Fowler *The Languages of Literature: Some Linguistic Contributions to Criticism*. London: Routledge & Kegan Paul, 54–64.

Bennison, N. (1993) Discourse analysis, pragmatics and the dramatic 'character': Tom Stoppard's *Professional Foul*. *Language and Literature*, 2, 2: 79–99.

Birch, D. (1991) *The Language of Drama*. London: Macmillan.

Bockting, I. (1994) Mind style as an interdisciplinary approach to characterisation in Faulkner. *Language and Literature*, 3, 3: 157–74.

Booth, W. (1961) *The Rhetoric of Fiction*. Chicago: Chicago University Press.

Brown, G. and G. Yule (1983) *Discourse Analysis*. Cambridge: Cambridge University Press.

Brown, P. and S. Levinson (1978) Universals in language usage: politeness phenomena. In E. N. Goody (ed.) *Questions and Politeness: Strategies in Social Interaction.* Cambridge: Cambridge University Press, 56–289.

Brown, P. and S. Levinson (1987) *Politeness.* Cambridge: Cambridge University Press.

Burton, D. (1979) Making conversation: On conversational style, stylistics and Pinter. *Language and Style*, 12, 3 :188–200.

Burton, D. (1980) *Dialogue and Discourse: A Sociolinguistic Approach to Modern Drama Dialogue and Naturally Occurring Conversation.* London: Routledge & Kegan Paul.

Burton, D. (1982) Conversation pieces. In R. Carter and D. Burton *Literary Text and Language Study.* London: Edward Arnold, 86–115.

Burton–Roberts, N. (1986) *Analysing Sentences.* London: Longman.

Butler, C. (1985) *Statistics in Linguistics.* Oxford: Blackwell.

Calvo, C. (1992) Pronouns of address and social negotiation in *As You Like It. Language and Literature*, 1, 1: 5–27.

Carter, R. and P. Simpson (1989) (eds) *Language, Discourse and Literature: An Introductory Reader in Discourse Stylistics.* London: Unwin Hyman.

Cluysenaar, A. (1976) *Introduction to Literary Stylistics.* London: Batsford.

Cook, G. (1992) *The Discourse of Advertising.* London: Routledge.

Cook, G. (1994) *Discourse and Literature.* Oxford: Oxford University Press.

Cooper, M. (1981) Implicature, convention and *The Taming of the Shrew. Poetics*, 10: 1–14

Crystal, D. (1984a) *A Dictionary of Linguistics and Phonetics.* Oxford: Blackwell.

Crystal, D. (1984b) *Who Cares About English Usage?* Harmondsworth: Penguin.

Crystal, D. and D. Davy (1969) *Investigating English Style.* London: Longman.

Crystal, D. and D. Davy (1975) *Advanced Conversational English.* London: Longman.

Coulthard, M. (1977) *An Introduction to Discourse Analysis.*
London: Longman.

Culpeper, J. (1994) *Language and Characterisation with Special
Reference to Shakespeare's Plays.* Unpublished Ph.D. thesis,
Lancaster University.

Cureton. R. D. (1992) *Rhythmic Phrasing in English Verse.*
London: Longman.

Downes, W. (1988) King Lear's question to his daughters. In
W. van Peer (ed.) *The Taming of the Text.* London:
Routledge, 225–57.

Elam, K. (1980) *The Semiotics of Theatre and Drama.* London:
Routledge.

Ellegård, A. (1978) *The Syntactic Structure of English Texts: A
Computer–based Study of Four Kinds of Text in the Brown
University Corpus.* Gothenburg Studies in English, 43.
Gothenburg: Gothenburg University Press.

Epstein, E. L. (1978) *Language and Style.* London: Methuen.

Fludernik, M. (1993) *The Fictions of Language and the Languages
of Fiction.* London: Routledge.

Fowler, R. (1966a) (ed.) *Essays on Style and Language: Linguistic
and Critical Approaches to Literary Style.* London: Routledge
& Kegan Paul.

Fowler, R. (1966b) 'Prose Rhythm' and Metre. In R. Fowler
(ed.) *Essays on Style and Language: Linguistic and Critical
Approaches to Literary Style.* London: Routledge & Kegan
Paul, 82–99.

Fowler, R. (1971a) *The Languages of Literature: Some Linguistic
Contributions to Criticism.* London: Routledge & Kegan
Paul.

Fowler, R. (1971b) Three blank verse textures. In R. Fowler
*The Languages of Literature: Some Linguistic Contributions to
Criticism.* London: Routledge & Kegan Paul, 184–99.

Fowler, R. (ed.) (1973) *A Dictionary of Modern Critical Terms.*
London: Longman.

Fowler, R. (1977) *Linguistics and the Novel.* London: Methuen.

Fowler, R. (1986) *Linguistic Criticism.* Oxford: Oxford
University Press.

Freeborn, D., P. French and D. Langford (1986) *Varieties of
English: An Introduction to the Study of Language.* London:
Macmillan.

Fromkin, V. and R. Rodman (1988) *Introduction to Language* (4th edition). New York: Holt Rinehart.

Gibson, W. (1970) Style and stylistics: A model T style machine. In D. C. Freeman (ed.) *Linguistics and Literary Style*. New York: Holt, Rinehart and Winston, 143–64.

Graddol, D., J. Cheshire and J. Swann (1987) *Describing Language*. Milton Keynes, Open University Press.

Greenfield, S. B. (1967) Grammar and meaning in poetry. *PMLA*, 82: 377–87.

Grice, H. P. (1975) Logic and conversation. In P. Cole and J. Morgan (eds) *Syntax and Semantics, III: Speech Acts*. New York: Academic Press, 41–58.

Halliday, M. A. K. (1971) Linguistic function and literary style: an enquiry into William Golding's *The Inheritors*. In S. Chatman (ed.) *Literary Style: A Symposium*. Oxford: Oxford University Press, 330–65.

Haynes, J. (1989) Metre and discourse. In Carter and Simpson (1989), 235–56.

Hendricks, W. O. (1976) *Grammars of Style and Styles of Grammar*. Amsterdam: North–Holland.

Herman, D. (1993) Towards a pragmatics of represented discourse: Narrative, speech and context in Woolf's *Between the Acts*. *Poetics*, 21: 377–409.

Herman, V. (1991) Dramatic dialogue and the systematics of turn–taking. *Semiotica*, 83: 97–121.

Hurford, J. R. (1994) *Grammar: A Student's Guide*. Cambridge: Cambridge University Press.

Hurford, J. R. and B. Heasley (1983) *Semantics: A Coursebook*. Cambridge: Cambridge University Press.

Hurst, M. (1987) Speech Acts in Ivy Compton–Burnett's *A Family and a Fortune*. *Language and Style*, 20, 4: 342–58.

Jackson, H. (1988) *Words and Their Meaning*. London: Longman.

Jackson, H. (1990) *Grammar and Meaning: A Semantic Approach to English Grammar*. London: Longman.

Knowles, G. (1987) *Patterns of Spoken English*. London: Longman.

Lakoff, G. and M. Johnson (1980) *Metaphors We Live By*. Chicago: University of Chicago Press.

Lakoff, G. and M. Turner (1989) *More Than Cool Reason: A Field Guide to Poetic Metaphor*. Chicago: University of Chicago Press.

Leavis, F. R. (1952) *The Common Pursuit*. London: Chatto and Windus.

Leech G. N. (1966a) *English in Advertising: A Linguistic Study of Advertising in Great Britain*. London: Longman.

Leech, G. N. (1966b) Linguistics and the figures of rhetoric. In R. Fowler (ed.) *Essays on Style and Language: Linguistic and Critical Approaches to Literary Style*. London: Routledge & Kegan Paul, 135–56.

Leech, G. N. (1969) *A Linguistic Guide to English Poetry*. London: Longman.

Leech, G. N. (1970) 'This Bread I Break' – language and interpretation. In D. C. Freeman (ed.) *Linguistics and Literary Style*. New York: Holt, Rinehart and Winston, 119–28.

Leech, G. N. (1974) *Semantics*. Harmondsworth: Penguin.

Leech, G. N. (1983) *Principles of Pragmatics*. London: Longman.

Leech, G. N. (1986) Music in metre: 'sprung rhythm' in Victorian and Georgian poetry. In T. D'Haen (ed.) *Linguistics and the Study of Literature*. Amsterdam: Rodopi, 112–27.

Leech, G. N. (1989) *An A–Z of English Grammar and Usage*. London: Edward Arnold.

Leech, G. N. (1992) Pragmatic principles in Shaw's *You Never Can Tell*. In M. Toolan (ed.) *Language, Text and Context: Essays in Stylistics*. London: Routledge, 259–78.

Leech, G. N., M. Deuchar and R. Hoogenraad (1982) *English Grammar for Today*. London: Macmillan.

Leech, G. N. and M. Short (1981) *Style in Fiction*. London: Longman.

Levin, S. R. (1965) Internal and external deviation in poetry. *Word*, 21: 225–39.

Lowe, V. (1994) 'Unsafe convictions': unhappy confessions in *The Crucible*. *Language and Literature* 3, 3: 175–95.

Lyons, J. (1981) *Language, Meaning and Context*. London: Fontana.

Mason, M. (1982) Deixis: a point of entry into *Little Dorritt*. In R. Carter (ed.) *Language and Literature: An Introductory Reader in Stylistics*. London: George Allen & Unwin, 29–38

McHale, B. (1978) Free indirect discourse: a survey of recent accounts. *Poetics and Theory of Literature*, 3: 235–87.

Minsky, M. L. (1975) A framework for representing knowledge. In P. Winston (ed.) *The Psychology of Computer Vision*. New York: McGraw–Hill, 211–27.

Myers, G. (1990) *Writing Biology: Texts in the Social Construction of Science*. Madison: Wisconsin University Press.

Myers, G. (1994) *Words in Ads*. London: Edward Arnold.

Nash, W. (1982) On a passage from Lawrence's 'Odour of Chrysanthemums'. In R. Carter (ed.) *Language and Literature: An Introductory Reader in Stylistics*. London: George Allen & Unwin, 101–20.

Nash, W. (1986) Sound and the pattern of poetic meaning. In T. D'Haen (ed.) *Linguistics and the Study of Literature*. Amsterdam: Rodopi, 128–51.

Nash, W. (1989) Changing the Guard at Elsinore. In R. Carter and P. Simpson (eds) *Language, Discourse and Literature: An Introductory Reader in Discourse Stylistics*. London: Unwin Hyman, 23–42.

O'Donnell, W. R. and L. Todd (1980) *Variety in Contemporary English*. London: George Allen & Unwin.

van Peer, W. (1986) *Stylistics and Psychology: Investigations of Foregrounding*. London: Croom Helm.

van Peer, W. (1993) Typographic foregrounding. *Language and Literature*, 2, 1: 49–61.

Quirk, R. and S. Greenbaum (1973) *A University Grammar of English*. London: Longman.

Quirk, R., S. Greenbaum, G. N. Leech and J. Svartvik (1985) *A Comprehensive Grammar of the English Language*. London: Longman.

Riffaterre, M. (1965) Describing poetic structures: two approaches to Baudelaire's 'Les Chats'. *Yale French Studies*, 36/7, 200–42.

Rodger, A. (1982) 'O Where Are You Going': a suggested experiment in classroom stylistics. In R. Carter (ed.) *Language and Literature: An Introductory Reader in Stylistics*. London: George Allen & Unwin, 123–162.

Sasaki, T. (1994) Towards a systematic description of narrative 'point of view': an examination of Chatman's theory with an analysis of 'The Blind Man' by D. H. Lawrence. *Language and Literature* 3, 2, 125–38.

Schank, R. and R. Abelson (1977) *Scripts, Plans, Goals and Understanding: An Enquiry into Human Knowledge Structures.* Hillsdale, New Jersey: Lawrence Erlbaum Associates.

Short, M. (1982a). Prelude I to a literary linguistic stylistics. In R. Carter (ed.) *Language and Literature: An Introductory Reader in Stylistics.* London: George Allen & Unwin, 55–64.

Short, M. (1982b). Stylistics and the teaching of literature: with an example from James Joyce's *Portrait of the Artist as a Young Man.* In R. Carter (ed.) *Language and Literature: An Introductory Reader in Stylistics.* London: George Allen & Unwin, 179–92.

Short, M. (1986) Literature and language teaching and the nature of language. In T. D'Haen (ed.) *Linguistic Contributions to the Study of Literature.* Amsterdam: Rodopi, 152–86.

Short, M. (1988) Speech presentation, the novel and the press. In W. van Peer (ed.) *The Taming of the Text.* New York: Routledge, 61–81

Short, M. (1989) Discourse analysis and the analysis of drama. In R. Carter and P. Simpson (1989) (eds) *Language, Discourse and Literature: An Introductory Reader in Discourse Stylistics.* London: Unwin Hyman, 139–68.

Short, M. (1990) Literature and Language. In M. Coyle, P. Garside. M. Kelsall and J. Peck (eds) *Encyclopedia of Literature and Criticism.* London: Routledge, 1082–97.

Short, M. (1993) To analyse a poem stylistically: 'To Paint a Water Lily' by Ted Hughes. In P. Verdonk (ed.) *Twentieth–Century Poetry: From Text to Context.* London: Routledge, 7–20.

Short, M. (1994) Mind style. In R. Asher (ed.) *The Encyclopaedia of Language and Linguistics.* London: Pergamon, 2504–5.

Short, M. and C. Candlin (1988) Teaching study skills for English literature. In M. Short (ed.) *Reading, Analysing and Teaching Literature.* London: Longman, 178–203.

Short, M. and W. van Peer (1988) Accident: stylisticians evaluate. In M. Short (ed.) *Reading, Analysing and Teaching Literature*. London: Longman, 22–71.

Simpson, J. M. Y. (1979) *A First Course in Linguistics*. Edinburgh: Edinburgh University Press.

Simpson, P. (1989a) Phatic Communication and Fictional Dialogue. In Carter and Simpson (1989), 43–56.

Simpson, P. (1989b) Politeness Phenomena in Ionesco's *The Lesson*. In Carter and Simpson (1989), 171–93.

Simpson, P. (1993) *Language, Ideology and Point of View*. London: Routledge.

Sinclair, J. McH. (1966) Taking a Poem to Pieces. In R. Fowler (ed.) *Essays on Style and Language: Linguistic Approaches to Literary Style*. London: Routledge & Kegan Paul, 68–81.

Sinclair, J. McH. (1968) A Technique of Stylistic Description. *Language and Style* 1: 215–42.

Sinclair, J. McH. (1972) Lines about 'Lines'. In B. B. Kachru and H. F. W. Stahlke (eds) *Current Trends in Stylistics*. Alberta: Linguistic Research, 241–62.

Sperber, D. and D. Wilson (1986) *Relevance: Communication and Cognition*. Oxford: Blackwell.

Tannen, D. (1989) *Talking Voices: Repetition, Dialogue and Imagery in Conversational Discourse*. Cambridge: Cambridge University Press.

Thomas, J. (1994) *Meaning in Interaction: An Introduction to Pragmatics*. London: Longman.

Toolan, M. J. (1988) *Narrative: A Critical Linguistic Introduction*. London: Routledge.

Toolan, M. J. (1990) *The Stylistics of Fiction: A Literary–Linguistic Approach*. London: Routledge.

Traugott, E. C. and M. L. Pratt (1980) *Linguistics for Students of Literature*. New York: Harcourt, Brace, Jovanovich.

Trengove, G. (1989). 'Vers de Société': Towards some society. In M. Short (ed.) *Reading, Analysing and Teaching Literature*. London: Longman, 146–60.

Verdonk, P. (1988) The language of poetry: The application of literary stylistic theory in university teaching. In M. Short (ed.) *Reading, Analysing and Teaching Literature*. London: Longman, 241–66.

Verdonk, P. (1993) *Twentieth–Century Poetry: From Text to Context.* London: Routledge.

Wales, K. (1983) 'Thou' and 'you' in Early Modern English: Brown and Gilman re–appraised. *Studia Linguistica*, 37: 283–302.

Wales, K. (1989) *A Dictionary of Stylistics.* London: Longman.

Wardhaugh, R. (1986) *How Conversation Works.* Oxford: Blackwell.

Widdowson, H. G. (1974) Stylistics. In J. P. B. Allen and S. P. Corder (eds) *The Edinburgh Course in Applied Linguistics Volume III: Techniques in Applied Linguistics.* Oxford, OUP, 202–31.

Index

of, 293–4, 295–325
passim
speech acts, 195–204, 206,
219, 250–1, 362
checksheet, 219–20
felicity conditions, 199,
220, 247
hybrid, 202, 203–4
indirect, 210, 220, 248–9,
250–1, 362
narrator's representation
of, 293, 296, 298,
305–25 *passim*
speech features, 75
speech presentation,
288–325, 333, 334, 347,
363–4, 370–2
checksheet, 324–5
continuum, 289, 291–310
passim
speech realism, 173–86
checksheet, 194
speech situation,
anterior 290–1
posterior, 290–1
reported, 290–1
reporting, 290–1
Spencer, Edmund,
The Faerie Queene 132,
134–5
Sperber, D., 244–5
standard deviation, 333
Stanislawski, K., 181
statistical significance tests,
333
statistics, 331–3, 337–8
Steinbeck, John, 337, 342
stereotype, 75
Sterne, Lawrence,
Tristram Shandy, 57–8
Stoppard, Tom,
Professional Foul, 219,
252

stream of consciousness
writing, 316–19, 325
stressed syllable, 109, 130,
140, 151–2, 163
stress–timing, 151
structure, 5, 7–9, 13–15, 23,
26, 28–31, 37, 52, 61,
63–70, 72, 77, 83, 90,
93–4, 96, 104, 106,
115–16, 122–4
discoursal, 361–3
pragmatic, 361–3
style, 27, 48, 68–9, 326–53
authorial, 27, 326–33,
369–70
fingerprinting, 329–30
checksheet, 350–3
conversational, 48
group, 329
loose, 157, 166
modulation, 337
poetic, 48, 156
text, 27, 326, 330–1, 334,
349
tight, 156, 166, 341
variation, 80–105, 334,
337, 367
checksheet, 105
stylistic analysis, 2, 5–6, 9,
10, 16, 27, 33–4, 72,
106, 146, 355–8
stylistic features, 17, 18, 25
stylistics, 1–10, 16–27, 28,
32, 33, 34, 72, 106, 124
sub–discourse, 41
subordination, 22, 81, 341
sub–text, 181
Svartvik, J., 33
Swann, J., 33
synonymy, 66, 115
quasi–, 66, 67
syntax, 43, 134, 143, 155,
160